The Rise

Bradley Campbell • Jason Manning

The Rise of Victimhood Culture

Microaggressions, Safe Spaces, and the New Culture Wars

palgrave
macmillan

Bradley Campbell
California State University
Los Angeles, CA, USA

Jason Manning
Sociology and Anthropology
West Virginia University
Morgantown, WV, USA

ISBN 978-3-319-70328-2   ISBN 978-3-319-70329-9   (eBook)
https://doi.org/10.1007/978-3-319-70329-9

Library of Congress Control Number: 2017962098

This Palgrave Macmillan imprint is published by Springer Nature
The registered company is Springer International Publishing AG
The registered company address is: Gewerbestrasse 11, 6330 Cham, Switzerland

For Brian and Erin
—Bradley Campbell
For George and Barbara Bowden
—Jason Manning

ACKNOWLEDGMENTS

Our work on this topic began with two articles in the journal *Comparative Sociology*: "Microaggression and Moral Cultures," published in 2014 in volume 13, issue number 6, and "Campus Culture Wars and the Sociology of Morality," published in 2016 in volume 15, issue number 2. We thank *Comparative Sociology*'s editor, David Weakliem, for accepting those, and we thank the journal's publisher, Brill, for permission to use them here. Much of the material from those two articles appears in Chaps. 1, 2, and 8, and much smaller portions appear in some of the other chapters.

Our initial article on microaggression appeared at a time when people were just beginning to hear of the term. Even many longtime academics we knew had never heard of it. Likewise with trigger warnings, safe spaces, and many of the other things we talk about here—they were pretty much unknown outside of activist circles. We wrote that these things were important, that they were signs of an emerging victimhood culture, but we did not realize just how fast things would move. Within a year universities were putting out lists of microaggressions, and victimhood eruptions were occurring at campuses across the country. At the same time others began writing about the subject, such as Greg Lukianoff and Jonathan Haidt, who in the fall of 2015 wrote about microaggressions, trigger warnings, and safe spaces in their superb *Atlantic* article "The Coddling of the American Mind." We had previously found both authors inspirational—Lukianoff for his work defending free speech with the Foundation for Individual Rights in Education (FIRE) and Haidt for his work on the social psychology of morality—and we are very grateful to both of them for encouraging us in our own work on the subject of campus conflict.

The attention that "Microaggression and Moral Cultures" ended up receiving was entirely due to Haidt's discussion of our article on his blog and elsewhere, and without that this book would not have come to be.

The book would not have come to be without Alexis Nelson from Palgrave Macmillan, either. We appreciate her enthusiasm for the project and her many helpful suggestions for improving it. Before the book was complete Alexis left Palgrave Macmillan to attend law school at Duke University, and we wish her well there. We also thank Kyra Saniewski, who became our editorial contact after Alexis departed and who patiently answered our questions about manuscript preparation.

Those who disapprove of victimhood culture, or who at least are troubled by some of its more extreme manifestations, will see a lot of the behavior we describe here as misconduct. We tend to view it that way, too, but as the product of universities we are aware of how much good they still do, too, and we want to thank the academics who have shaped our thinking and shaped this book. We are both graduates of the University of Virginia's doctoral program in sociology, and it would be hard to exaggerate how much the faculty there influenced us. James Hunter's work on culture wars led us to notice and to think more about contemporary conflict and changing culture. Courses and conversations with Rae Lesser Blumberg, Stephan Fuchs, Paul Kingston, Krishan Kumar, Murray Milner, and Jeffrey K. Olick instilled an interest in history and culture, an appreciation of general theory, and a critical orientation toward the field of sociology. We have also been influenced and encouraged by Mark Cooney of the University of Georgia and Roberta Senechal de la Roche of Washington and Lee University.

Donald Black, who supervised our dissertations and completely reoriented our sociological thinking, has influenced us more than anyone else. He introduced us to our subject matter—moral conflict—and to a theoretical strategy for explaining it, and his influence can be seen on every page of this book. In Chap. 7 we quote Thomas Jefferson, founder of the University of Virginia, who wrote that the new university was "based on the illimitable freedom of the human mind, for here we are not afraid to follow truth wherever it may lead." It is hard to imagine that anyone else at Mr. Jefferson's university exhibits this ideal more than Donald Black. He has spent his whole life rebelling against constraints that others in the field sought to impose. He has done what others said could not be done—first developing a purely sociological theory of law, then of multiple other forms of social control, and then of morality itself. He has pursued the truth in his work and in his life, and we are grateful for all the help he has given us and for the example of scholarly life that he has provided.

Finally, Bradley Campbell thanks his mother, who along with his late father introduced him to the values of dignity that continue to guide his life and to shape his thinking about moral conflict. He dedicates this book to his brother and sister, Brian and Erin, with whom he had so many of his earliest clashes of right and wrong. He is grateful for their love and admires their integrity. Jason Manning thanks Corey Colyer for his advice and insightful comments on chapter drafts, Jeff Giosi for his infectiously positive attitude toward challenges, and Kirsten Song for her constant understanding and encouragement. He dedicates the book to his beloved grandparents, George and Barbara Bowden, who have long inspired him by leading lives of dignity, humility, industry, and charity.

PROLOGUE: AFTER THE ELECTION

Going into Election Day, the outcome of the 2016 US presidential race seemed to be a foregone conclusion. All major polls showed that Democratic candidate Hillary Clinton had a substantial lead over Republican candidate Donald Trump. Respected pollster Nate Silver put the odds of a Trump victory at less than 30 percent. Most mainstream politicians, journalists, and academics expected a resounding defeat for Trump, as did many people in the urban areas where Clinton carried large majorities of the electorate. Even Trump expected a loss.

As votes were tallied that evening the outlook rapidly changed. Trump began winning states he had been projected to lose. The "blue wall" of reliably Democratic states in America's deindustrialized Rust Belt voted Republican for the first time in decades. By early the next day, it was clear Trump had won.

The reaction was swift and severe. Protesters poured into the streets of cities throughout the country, many chanting, "Not my President!" Thousands participated in marches and rallies, some of which lasted for days on end. In Los Angeles as many as 8000 protesters marched on City Hall, where they burned Trump in effigy. Protesters in Boston called for his immediate impeachment (Eversley et al. 2016a). In several cities—including Chicago, Portland, and Washington, DC—protesters blocked traffic on freeways and city streets. The protests sometimes grew violent as angry mobs destroyed property or attacked bystanders. Protesters in Oakland, California set fires and got into shoving matches with police, while rioters in Portland, Oregon damaged cars and threw objects at police officers (Shoichet et al. 2016; Eversly et al. 2016a, b). A cell phone video showed a Chicago man beaten by three men as onlookers screamed at him for being a Trump voter (Caruso 2016; Randall 2016).

Students were particularly active in all this. Thousands of middle and high school students—in Los Angeles, Washington, DC, and elsewhere—staged walkouts, leaving their classes in protest (Massimo 2016; Stein and Helm 2016; Resmovits 2016; Rocha 2016). Protesters at American University burned US flags (Eversley et al. 2016a). Graduate students at Harvard University reacted to their "existential" despair by starting a "resistance school" (Harrington 2017).[1] Administrators and faculty also took action. The presidents of several institutions—Harvard University, Johns Hopkins University, Stanford University, and more—made formal announcements of support for students and faculty upset over the election results. "We must stand together," wrote the president of Vanderbilt University, while the president of the University of Michigan comforted students and also notified them of a vigil planned for that evening. "Partisan, inflammatory statements unfortunately seem to be part of modern campaign rhetoric, but they cause real wounds," read a message from Northwestern University's administration to its students, which went on to direct students to such resources as the Campus Multicultural Center (Eversley et al. 2016a). The president of Harvard announced open office hours during which concerned students could visit. The Office of Multicultural Studies at the University of Tennessee invited students to "join us for a moment of reflection and gathering in solidarity," noting that "counseling staff will be available" (Dickerson and Saul 2016). The president of the University of Vermont offered "time for tea and reflections, meditations and structured discussion" (Eversley et al. 2016a). In addition to offering counseling, several universities cancelled classes and postponed exams. Some institutions of higher learning even took steps reminiscent of the way parents soothe small children: "The University of Kansas offered therapy dogs for comfort, Cornell set up a 'cry-in' where staff handed out cocoa, and the University of Michigan had a play area with coloring books" (Nolan 2017).

Such reactions were, to many, at least as shocking as the result of the election itself. True, there was nothing mysterious about this election being more controversial than others, given Trump's unusual qualities as

[1] At the first class in this school, a lecturer from the university's Kennedy School of Government gave a talk on such topics as "anticolonialism, white privilege, intersectionality, and 'allyship.'" He ended his talk by telling students to "stay woke" (Harrington 2017).

a candidate. A businessman with no prior political experience, he was best known to many as the host of a reality television show. His romantic affairs, business failures, and other personal dramas had long been fodder for tabloid news and television comedians. He had been accused of fraudulent business practices, endorsed implausible conspiracy theories, and appeared more dishonest than most politicians.[2] By the standards of contemporary US politics, his positions and rhetoric were extreme. He advocated trade protectionism and seemed willing to sour international relations to achieve it. He called for a border wall between the United States and Mexico and made harsh generalizations about illegal Mexican immigrants. His "law and order" talk was fairly conventional, but it alarmed many in light of recent controversies about police brutality. Perhaps most extreme was his proposed response to Islamic terrorist attacks: He called for a temporary ban on the immigration of Muslims and expressed openness to the idea of a national registry to track Muslim citizens (*Wikipedia* 2017). Such positions would have been controversial enough on their own. Adding fuel to the fire was Trump's unusual interpersonal style. Speaking in a loose, improvisational manner, he tended to be bombastic and aggressive, frequently boasting about himself and insulting his rivals and critics. He was, by many people's standards, coarse and vulgar. In short, there were many reasons to expect much of the country to be greatly upset by his victory.

Still, the scale and intensity of the reaction to his election left many taken aback. And some of the claims made by protesters and other concerned citizens seemed bizarre and unrealistic. A number of people seemed convinced that Americans had knowingly elected a white supremacist ideologue who ran on a campaign of hatred toward Hispanics, blacks, women, Jews, gays, and transgender persons. His campaign did not merely benefit from the kind of cognitive biases that might lead many citizens to fear terrorism more than heart disease, or to focus on losing jobs to foreign workers over losing them to automation. Rather, his 62 million voters were primarily fueled by outright hatred of all kinds of American minorities. America had elected another Adolf Hitler, and his victory meant persecution for everyone who was not a straight white male.

---

[2] These conspiracy theories included the claim that president Barack Obama was not born in the United States and was thus ineligible to be president of the United States. He also intimated that rival Republican candidate Ted Cruz's father was involved in the assassination of John F. Kennedy.

True, Trump's positions on immigration and terrorism were especially appealing to racial ideologues, who were vocal supporters. But the picture painted by protesters is otherwise hard to square with reality (Alexander 2016). One of Trump's campaign stops was at a black church in Detroit, Michigan, where he told the congregation that black churches inspired "a sense of charity and unity that binds us all together" and spoke of the need for a "civil rights agenda for our time" (quoted in Goldmacher 2016). "African-Americans citizens have sacrificed so much for this nation," Trump said at a speech in Charlotte, North Carolina. "From the pews and the picket lines they have lifted up the conscience of our country in the long march for Civil Rights" (quoted in Hains 2016). In his speech at the Republican national convention, he claimed he would "work to ensure that all of our kids are treated equally, and protected equally" and seek to make life better "for young Americans in Baltimore, Chicago, Detroit [and] Ferguson" (*Politico* 2016). After returning from a meeting with the president of Mexico, he said the two had discussed "the great contributions of Mexican-American citizens to our two countries" and "my love for the people of Mexico" (*Washington Examiner* 2016). He claimed that illegal immigration was a concern in part because it lowered the wages of American workers, "especially African-American and Hispanic workers," and he spoke of the need to ensure upward mobility for previous generations of legal immigrants who had "enriched" the country (*Washington Examiner* 2016). Such statements may be no more than the empty rhetoric common in politics, but they hardly suggest an openly racist campaign. It seems many minority voters would agree: Post-election polls showed Trump won about one in three Hispanic voters and may have actually outperformed previous Republican candidates among blacks and Hispanics (Enten 2016; Ramakrishan 2016).[3]

Still, protesters, pundits, and media sources declared Trump was "running on pure white supremacy" and was "an openly white supremacist nominee" (quoted in Alexander 2016). One commentator claimed that "Trump's followers are breathtakingly racist and overwhelmingly motivated by white supremacy" (Rosario 2016). A writer at *Slate* declared,

---

[3] Again, we are not arguing there were no white supremacists or white nationalists among Trump's voters. Nor do we dispute that many overtly bigoted people found his rhetoric congenial to their worldviews and so gave him unusually strong and vocal support. We suspect that both Trump's supporters on the far right and his opponents on the left were prone to similar exaggerations, one projecting their hopes and the other their fears.

"There's no such thing as a good Trump voter" (Bouie 2016). A headline at the *Atlanta Black Star* proclaimed, "Trump's rise proves that America is in denial about the depths of hatred in this country" (Love 2016). Writing of the "racist panic" that led to Donald Trump's electoral victory, an author at *Salon* says, "The mask of white civility hides the face of a monster" (Masciotra 2016). One headline at *Vox* read, "Donald Trump's win tells people of color they aren't welcome in America," while another claimed, "Trump's win is a reminder of the incredible, unbeatable power of racism" (Lopez 2016; Desmond-Harris 2016a). A Brooklyn woman quoted in another *Vox* story claims her five-year-old son asked her if the election meant "all the black and brown people have to leave and we're going to become slaves" (Desmond-Harris 2016b).

Even stranger was the notion that Trump had campaigned against rights for gays, lesbians, and other sexual minorities. At an event in Colorado, Trump walked around stage displaying the rainbow flag, a symbol of lesbian, gay, bisexual, and transgender (LGBT) pride. He criticized a North Carolina law banning schools and public buildings from letting transgender people use the bathroom of the gender they identified with instead of the one corresponding to their biological sex (Ford 2016). At the Republican Convention where Trump received his nomination, gay entrepreneur Peter Thiel gave a speech endorsing Trump and stating that he was proud to be both gay and Republican. When Trump himself took the stage, he promised to do everything in his power "to protect our LGBTQ citizens from the violence and oppression" of Islamic radicals, such as the Islamic State (ISIS) supporter who had recently massacred 49 people at a gay night club in Orlando (Politico Staff 2016).[4]

Despite this, a psychology professor at the University of Tennessee told reporters, "Our lesbian, gay, bisexual and transgender students are deeply concerned about Trump.... After enduring months of homophobic and

---

[4] Reporters also drew attention to anti-Semites who supported Trump, and some accused him of encouraging or engaging in anti-Semitism himself (Mahler 2016; Perry 2016). The latter seems the least plausible accusation of all. Trump's daughter is Jewish, having converted when she married his Jewish son-in-law. Both played an important role in his campaign and continue to be influential in his administration. Trump also once led New York's Israel Day parade, an Israeli poll picked him as the candidate most likely to represent the Jewish state's interests, and during his career he has won several awards from Jewish organizations (Alexander 2016; Carlstrom 2016; Freelander 2016). A wave of anti-Semitic bomb threats allegedly inspired by his campaign turned out to be the work of a black left-wing reporter and a Jewish Israeli youth (Federman 2017; *Intercept* 2017).

transphobic rhetoric during the campaign, many of us—sexual minorities and gender nonconforming individuals—are asking ourselves, What happens next?" (quoted in Dickerson and Saul 2016). Some of our personal acquaintances shared this view. "I'm really worried gay people will lose all their rights," a concerned friend said to one of us over the phone. Someone else posted on Facebook that anyone who voted for Trump was endorsing hatred toward her and other LGBTs and should no longer claim to be her friend. University administrators were, again, active in supporting these concerns. The University of California, Berkeley announced the creation of "healing spaces" for "women who identify as lesbian, gay, bisexual, or transgender" who felt threatened or persecuted by the election (Eversley et al. 2016a). The president of Amherst College spoke of the "virulent forms of racism, misogyny, homophobia" being celebrated around the country, while the Amherst student newspaper condemned a professor of political science for supporting a homophobic and misogynist candidate (Hartcollis 2016). A story even began circulating on social media claiming that up to nine transgender persons, mostly children, had committed or attempted suicide due to Trump's election.[5]

Many expressed fears about their physical safety, seemingly believing a government-approved pogrom was about to erupt. One protester, a high school student, said that people around her were worried about "violence against them because of their sexual and ethnic identities" (Resmovits 2016). Another young protester told reporters, "Trump makes us fear for our lives" (Resmovits 2016). And a transgender protester in Chicago, who had begun exploring options for emigrating to another country, said, "I am terrified for my life" (Eversley et al. 2016a).

These fears seem premised on the idea that the president-elect not only despised all racial and sexual minorities, but that he would now wield dictatorial power, acting without legal constraint and judicial or legislative oversight. Such a view was encouraged by those who described his election victory as a transition from democracy to fascism. A headline at *Newsweek* reported the claim that "Trump's victory is one for fascists" (Gidda 2016). An op-ed at *The Washington Post* claimed, "This is how fascism comes to America" (Kagan 2016). The newspaper itself changed its motto to the ominous warning "Democracy Dies in Darkness." A headline at *The Nation* approvingly described the black-masked members of

---

[5] The fact-checking website Snopes.com currently classifies this claim as "unproven" (Lacapria 2016).

the militant organization Antifa as willing to "fight Trump's fascism in the streets" (Lennard 2017). And a blogger at *The Huffington Post* proclaimed that "America committed suicide," as its citizens "chose fascism over a democratic republic" (Beyer 2016).

The impression of a coming purge was bolstered by the reports of hate crimes against racial and religious minorities that dominated headlines in the weeks following the election (Dickerson 2016; Besant 2016). Curiously, however, many of these were not what they seemed (Hayward 2016). A Florida woman found her car burned at her home, along with a note full of anti-black racial slurs directed at her children that included the words "Trump" and "KKK." The perpetrator, it later turned out, was the children's own father, a black man who had also faked his own kidnapping (Spargo 2016). Similarly, a black man was arrested in Philadelphia for spray painting "Trump rules" and "black bitch" on his ex-girlfriend's car (Shaw 2016).

As with the protests, students played an active role in these false alarms (Dickerson and Saul 2016). A black student at Bowling Green State University claimed that she had been assaulted by three white men wearing Trump campaign paraphernalia who threw rocks at her and called her racial slurs. After finding evidence she was never at the time and place of the alleged attack, police concluded she falsified the report due to anger at members of her own family who supported Trump (Burnett 2016). A bisexual student at Chicago's North Park University made headlines after claiming she received hateful notes and emails from Trump supporters that contained homophobic slurs; the university president later announced she had authored the notes herself and was no longer enrolled in the school (Ray 2016). At Elon University faculty and staff were outraged that someone had written "Bye Bye Latinos" on a whiteboard. But after the administration vowed to track down the offender, a Latino student admitted to having written the statement "as a joke" (Anderson 2016). A Muslim student in New York City made headlines after claiming she was harassed on the subway by three men who yelled anti-Islamic insults at her, yelled "Donald Trump," and tried to remove her hijab. After reviewing subway security footage, police concluded that the assault never took place, and she admitted to making up the incident (Politi 2016; Moore and Cohen 2016). Similar hate crimes reported by Muslim students at the University of Michigan and Lafayette University also turned out to be hoaxes (WXYZ 2016; Felten 2017). Despite the inaccuracy of these stories, they supported the narrative that the country was under the rule of a racist, sexist, homophobic dictator and his violent mobs.[6] Danger and oppression were everywhere.

Many on the political and cultural right, even those who had opposed Trump, took a very different view. To them, the degree of outrage was itself outrageous. Some complained of the destructiveness of the protesters, which led the author of a letter to *The American Conservative* to write, "I did not vote for that piece of shit Donald Trump, but this is the kind of shit that almost makes me wish I had" (quoted in Dreher 2016b). Others described the reactions as infantile, as when former New York City Mayor Rudy Giuliani referred to protesters as "a bunch of spoiled cry-babies" (Eversly et al. 2016b). University students in particular became a target for derision. A Republican lawmaker in Iowa, who accused protesters of throwing "temper tantrums," introduced a bill called "Suck it up, Buttercup," which would levy fines against state schools that offered "cry rooms" and other election-specific counseling services (David 2016; Hoover 2016).

Remarkably, there were many who advanced a narrative in which Trump's supporters, rather than being violent oppressors, were actually the oppressed underdogs. Rather than an act of dominance over women and minorities, Trump's election represented an act of rebellion against political and cultural elites. The elites, these commentators claimed, were not only indifferent to working-class and rural communities, but openly hostile to them. Educated professionals in America's coastal urban centers were said to look down upon those living in what they dismissively term "flyover country," believing them to be little more than ignorant, racist buffoons (see, e.g., Dayen 2016; Dreher 2016a). Knowledge of this disdain supposedly fueled resentment among these masses. Conservative columnist Rod Dreher writes that Trump supporters "know that the academic elites despise them and their culture" (quoted in Soave 2016). They were said to be especially sick of a body of elite-enforced speech codes called "political correctness." "It is a grind and so draining to be so politically correct every day in our personal and professional lives," wrote one Trump supporter to *The Atlantic* (Friedersdorf 2015). "The thing that really attracted me to Trump was his stance against political correctness," said another (Darcy 2017). Trump was seen as standing up against political

---

[6] That so many prominent reports were false, does not mean there was not an actual rise in hate crimes, or that some prominently reported crimes were not real and possibly connected to Trump's election.

correctness and the dominance of coastal elites. In this narrative, it was the elites—particularly leftist and progressive elites—who were the real bullies, and working class whites who were the real victims. Trump, for all his flaws, was their champion—or, perhaps, their weapon.

This then was the strange reality visible in the days and months following America's 58th presidential election. Protests and counseling, exaggerated claims and false reports, outrage about outrage, and people on all sides claiming to be the victimized underdog fighting against a superior power. Surely many observers were puzzled and confused.

What on earth is going on?

REFERENCES

Alexander, Scott. 2016. You're Still Crying Wolf. *Slate Star Codex*, November 16. http://slatestarcodex.com/2016/11/16/you-are-still-crying-wolf/.

Anderson, Bryan. 2016. Note Reading 'Bye Bye Latinos Hasta La Vista' Found in Kivette Hall. *Elon News Network*, November 11. http://www.elonnewsnetwork.com/article/2016/11/note-found-whiteboard-kivette-bye-bye-latinos.

Besant, Alexander. 2016. U.S. Protesters March Against Trump Presidency for Fifth Day. *Reuters*, November 13. http://www.reuters.com/article/us-usa-election-protests-saturday-idUSKBN1370D2.

Beyer, Dana. 2016. America Commits Suicide. *The Huffington Post*, November 9. http://www.huffingtonpost.com/dana-beyer/america-commits-suicide_b_12879586.html.

Bouie, Jamelle. 2016. There's No Such Thing as a Good Trump Voter. *Slate*, November 16. http://www.slate.com/articles/news_and_politics/politics/2016/11/there_is_no_such_thing_as_a_good_trump_voter.html.

Burnett, Bridgett. 2016. BG Police Say Student Lied About Politically Driven Attack. *ABC13*, November 17. http://www.13abc.com/content/news/BG-police-say-student-lied-about-politically-driven-attack-401814426.html.

Carlstrom, Gregg. 2016. Why Israel Loves Donald Trump. *Politico*, March 20. http://www.politico.com/magazine/story/2016/03/donald-trump-israel-2016-netanyahu-213748.

Caruso, Justin. 2016. Here's a List of Completely Substantiated (and Underreported) Attacks on Trump Supporters. *The Daily Caller*, November 17. http://dailycaller.com/2016/11/17/heres-a-list-of-completely-substantiated-and-underreported-attacks-on-trump-supporters/.

Darcy, Oliver. 2017. The Untold Story of Baked Alaska, a Rapper Turned BuzzFeed Personality Turned Alt-Right Troll. *Business Insider*, May 1. http://www.businessinsider.com/who-is-baked-alaska-milo-mike-cernovich-alt-right-trump-2017-4.

David, John. 2016. Iowa Lawmaker Tells Trump Protesters to "Suck It Up, Buttercup. *WQAD*, November 15. http://wqad.com/2016/11/14/iowa-lawmaker-tells-trump-protesters-to-suck-it-up-buttercup/.

Dayen, David. 2016. The 'Deplorables' Got the Last Laugh. *The New Republic*, November 9. https://newrepublic.com/article/138615/deplorables-got-last-laugh.

Desmond-Harris, Jenée. 2016a. Trump's Win Is a Reminder of the Incredible, Unbeatable Power of Racism. *Vox*, November 9. https://www.vox.com/policy-and-politics/2016/11/9/13571676/trump-win-racism-power.

Desmond-Harris, Jenée. 2016b. 'All the Black and Brown People Have to Leave': Trump's Scary Impact on How Kids Think. *Vox*, November 9. https://www.vox.com/identities/2016/10/20/13319366/donald-trump-racism-bigotry-children-bullying-muslim-mexican-black-immigrant.

Dickerson, Caitlin. 2016. Postelection Harassment, Case by Case. *New York Times*, November 23. https://www.nytimes.com/2016/11/23/us/post-trump-how-people-explain-bias-based-attacks.html.

Dickerson, Caitlin, and Stephanie Saul. 2016. Campuses Confront Hostile Acts Against Minorities After Donald Trump's Election. *New York Times*, November 10. https://www.nytimes.com/2016/11/11/us/police-investigate-attacks-on-muslim-students-at-universities.html.

Dreher, Rod. 2016a. Trump: Tribune of Poor White People. *The American Conservative*, July 22. http://www.theamericanconservative.com/dreher/trump-us-politics-poor-whites/.

Dreher, Rod. 2016b. Leftists Make a Post-election Trump Voter. *The American Conservative*, November 11. http://www.theamericanconservative.com/dreher/leftists-make-a-post-election-trump-voter/.

Enten, Harry. 2016. Trump Probably Did Better with Latino Voters than Romney Did. *FiveThirtyEight*, November 18. https://fivethirtyeight.com/features/trump-probably-did-better-with-latino-voters-than-romney-did/.

Eversley, Melanie, Aamer Madhani, and Natalie DiBlasio. 2016a. Thousands Across the USA Protest Trump Victory. *USA Today*, November 9. https://www.usatoday.com/story/news/2016/11/09/anti-trump-protests-erupt-new-york-chicago/93570584/.

Eversley, Melanie, Aamer Madhani, and Rick Jervis. 2016b. Anti-Trump Protests, Some Violent, Erupt for 3rd Night Nationwide. *USA Today*, November 11. https://www.usatoday.com/story/news/nation/2016/11/11/anti-trump-protesters-pepper-sprayed-demonstrations-erupt-across-us/93633154/.

Federman, Josef. 2017. Israel Arrests Hacker Linked to Threats on US Jewish Centers. *Associated Press News*, March 24. https://apnews.com/a6a67fb7613 04e3cae7497faa32dcdc9?utm_campaign=SocialFlow&utm_source=Twitter&utm_medium=AP.

Felten, Eric. 2017. Untruth and Consequences: The Great Hate-Crime Hysteria. *The Weekly Standard*, January 13. http://www.weeklystandard.com/untruth-and-consequences/article/2006276.

Ford, Zack. 2016. Trump Blasts North Carolina Law, Says Caitlyn Jenner Should Pee Where She Wants. *Think Progress*, April 21. https://thinkprogress.org/trump-blasts-north-carolina-law-says-caitlyn-jenner-should-pee-where-she-wants-143de1e6e81e.

Freelander, David. 2016. How Donald Trump Got Tapped to Lead New York's Israel Day Parade. *New York Magazine*, May 15. http://nymag.com/daily/intelligencer/2016/05/how-trump-got-tapped-to-lead-nycs-israel-parade.html.

Friedersdorf, Conner. 2015. What Do Donald Trump Voters Actually Want? *The Atlantic*, August 17. https://www.theatlantic.com/politics/archive/2015/08/donald-trump-voters/401408/.

Gidda, Mirren. 2016. British Historian Simon Schama Says Donald Trump's Victory Is One for Fascists. *Newsweek*, November 9. http://www.newsweek.com/2016-us-election-donald-trump-simon-schama-fascism-hitler-518838.

Goldmacher, Shane. 2016. Trump Flashes Humility in First Ever Black Church Visit. *Politico*, September 3. http://www.politico.com/story/2016/09/donald-trump-detroit-african-american-church-227712.

Hains, Tim. 2016. Trump Proposes 'New Deal for Black America' in Charlotte. *Real Clear Politics*, October 26. https://www.realclearpolitics.com/video/2016/10/26/trump_proposes_new_deal_for_black_america_in_charlotte.html.

Harrington, Elizabeth. 2017. Harvard Grad Students Faced 'Existential' Crisis of Sadness, Despair After Election. *The Washington Free Beacon*, April 7. http://freebeacon.com/culture/harvard-grad-students-faced-existential-crisis-sadness-despair-election/.

Hartcollis, Amenoma. 2016. On Campus, Trump Fans Say They Need 'Safe Spaces'. *New York Times*, December 8. https://www.nytimes.com/2016/12/08/us/politics/political-divide-on-campuses-hardens-after-trumps-victory.html.

Hayward, John. 2016. Faked News: Your Guide to 22 Post-election Hate Hoaxes. *Breitbart*, December 30. http://www.breitbart.com/big-government/2016/12/30/faked-news-your-guide-to-22-post-election-hate-hoaxes/.

Hoover, Amanda. 2016. Iowa Bill Named 'Suck It Up, Buttercup' Seeks to Stop Student Coddling. *The Christian Science Monitor*, November 16. https://www.csmonitor.com/USA/2016/1116/Iowa-bill-named-Suck-it-up-Buttercup-seeks-to-stop-student-coddling.

Intercept. 2017. Statement on the Arrest of Former Intercept Reporter Juan Thompson. March 3. https://theintercept.com/2017/03/03/statement-on-the-arrest-of-former-intercept-reporter-juan-thompson/.

Kagan, Robert. 2016. This Is How Fascism Comes to America. *Washington Post*, May 18. https://www.washingtonpost.com/opinions/this-is-how-fascism-comes-to-america/2016/05/17/c4e32c58-1c47-11e6-8c7b-6931e66333e7_story.html?utm_term=.aa0e66aa1658.

LaCapria, Kim. 2016. Transgender Parenting Groups Report Eight Suicides After 2016 Election. *Snopes.* http://www.snopes.com/transgender-suicides-after-2016-election/.

Lennard, Natasha. 2017. Anti-fascists Will Fight Trump's Fascism in the Streets. *The Nation*, January 19. https://www.thenation.com/article/anti-fascist-activists-are-fighting-the-alt-right-in-the-streets/.

Lopez, German. 2016. Donald Trump's Win Tells People of Color They Aren't Welcome in America. *Vox*, November 9. https://www.vox.com/identities/2016/11/9/13570922/trump-election-2016-racism.

Love, David. 2016. Not Just a 'Southern' Thing: Trump's Rise Proves That America Is in Denial About the Depths of Hatred in This Country. *The Atlanta Black Star*,March2.http://atlantablackstar.com/2016/03/02/not-just-a-southern-thing-trumps-rise-proves-that-america-is-in-denial-about-the-depths-of-hatred-in-this-country/.

Mahler, Jonathan. 2016. Anti-Semitic Posts, Many from Trump Supporters, Surge on Twitter. *New York Times*, October 19. https://www.nytimes.com/2016/10/19/us/politics/anti-semitism-trump-supporters-twitter.html.

Masciotra, David. 2016. White Flight from Reality: Inside the Racist Panic that Fueled Donald Trump's Victory. *Salon*, November 12. http://www.salon.com/2016/11/12/white-flight-from-reality-inside-the-racist-panic-that-fueled-donald-trumps-victory/.

Massimo, Rick. 2016. Hundreds of MD. Students Leave Class to Protest Trump. *WTOP*, November 15. http://wtop.com/montgomery-county/2016/11/montgomery-co-students-walk-in-protest-of-election/slide/1/.

Moore, Tina, and Shawn Cohen. 2016. Teen Made Up Story About Anti-Muslim Attack on Subway. *The New York Post*, December 14. http://nypost.com/2016/12/14/teen-made-up-story-about-anti-muslim-attack-on-subway/.

Nolan, Larissa. 2017. Free Speech Under Threat on Our College Campuses. *The Irish Times*, April 20. http://www.irishtimes.com/news/education/free-speech-under-threat-on-our-college-campuses-1.3045149.

Perry, Tod. 2016. Senator Al Franken Accuses the Trump Campaign of Anti-Semitism. *Good*, November 7. https://www.good.is/articles/donald-trumps-anti-semitic-ad.

Politi, Daniel. 2016. NYPD Says Story About Muslim Teenager Being Verbally Assaulted on Subway Is a Hoax. *Slate*, December 4. http://www.slate.com/blogs/the_slatest/2016/12/04/subway_riders_in_new_york_stand_by_as_three_men_verbally_assault_muslim.html.

Politico. 2016. Full Text: Donald Trump 2016 RNC Draft Speech Transcript. July 21. http://www.politico.com/story/2016/07/full-transcript-donald-trump-nomination-acceptance-speech-at-rnc-225974.

Ramakrishan, Karthick. 2016. Trump Got More Votes from People of Color than Romney Did. Here's the Data. *Washington Post*, November 11. https://www.washingtonpost.com/news/monkey-cage/wp/2016/11/11/trump-got-more-votes-from-people-of-color-than-romney-did-heres-the-data/?utm_term=.c74d07b3102d.

Randall, Amber. 2016. Black Guys Assault White Man While Shouting Anti-Trump Slogans. *The Daily Caller*, November 10. http://dailycaller.com/2016/11/10/hillary-supporters-assault-white-trump-supporter-video/.

Ray, Richard. 2016. Hateful 'Trump' Notes Allegedly Aimed at Student Were Fabricated, University Says. *NBC Chicago*, November 26. http://www.nbcchicago.com/news/local/north-park-fabricated-notes-402556366.html?_osource=SocialFlowTwt_CHBrand.

Resmovits, Joy. 2016. Students Head Back to School After Hours-Long Anti-Trump Protest. *Los Angeles Times*, November 14. http://www.latimes.com/local/california/la-live-major-anti-trump-protest-students-head-back-to-school-after-1479159291-htmlstory.html.

Rocha, Veronica. 2016. L.A. Teachers Union Says It Supports Mass Student Protest. *The Los Angeles Times*, November 14. http://www.latimes.com/local/california/la-live-major-anti-trump-protest-l-a-teachers-union-says-it-supports-1479153578-htmlstory.html.

Rosario, Justin. 2016. The 'Liberal Media' Is Already Whitewashing the Racism of Trump's Supporters. *The Daily Banter*, October 17. https://thedailybanter.com/2016/10/media-whitewahsing-trump-racism/.

Shaw, Julie. 2016. Man Charged with 'pro-Trump' Vandalism in S. Philly Was a Victim's Ex. *Philly.com*, December 2. http://www.philly.com/philly/blogs/real-time/Man-charged-with-pro-Trump-vandalism-in-S-Philly-was-1-victims-ex.html.

Shoichet, Catherine E., Amanda Jackson, and Rolando Zenteno. 2016. What Do Anti-Trump Protesters Want? Here Are 5 Key Demands. *CNN*, November 15. http://www.cnn.com/2016/11/11/politics/trump-protests-key-demands/index.html.

Soave, Robby. 2016. How Political Correctness Caused College Students to Cheer for Trump. *Reason*, February 23. http://reason.com/blog/2016/02/23/how-political-correctness-caused-college.

Spargo, Chris. 2016. Florida Man Faked a Pro-Trump KKK Hate Crime, Set His Ex's Car on Fire, and Then Staged His Own Kidnapping in Ransom Note Covered with His Blood. *The Daily Mail*, December 26. http://www.daily-mail.co.uk/news/article-4029134/Florida-man-faked-pro-Trump-hate-crime-set-ex-s-car-fire-staged-kidnapping-ransom-note-covered-blood-said-taken-member-KKK.html.

Stein, Perr, and Joe Helm. 2016. D.C. Students Walk Out of Class to Protest Trump. *Washington Post*, November 15. https://www.washingtonpost.com/local/education/dc-students-plan-to-march-on-trump-hotel-protest-election-outcome/2016/11/15/f4238db6-ab24-11e6-977a-1030f822fc35_story.html?utm_term=.a2ed29a385a0.

Washington Examiner. 2016. FULL TEXT: Donald Trump's Immigration Speech. August 31. http://www.washingtonexaminer.com/full-text-donald-trumps-immigration-speech/article/2600729.

Wikipedia. 2017. Donald Trump Presidential Campaign, 2016. https://en.wikipedia.org/wiki/Donald_Trump_presidential_campaign,_2016.

WXYZ. 2016. U-M Student Made Up Story About Man Threatening to Burn Hijab, Police Say. *WXYZ.com,* December 21. http://www.wxyz.com/news/u-m-student-made-up-story-about-man-threatening-to-set-her-hijab-on-fire-police.

CONTENTS

CHAPTER 1

Microaggression and the Culture of Victimhood

In March of 2013 Oberlin College canceled classes after a student reported seeing someone on campus wearing Ku Klux Klan regalia. Our initial thoughts were that there was unlikely to be a KKK chapter at Oberlin College, a private liberal arts school with a reputation for progressive activism. Indeed, the apparent Klansman later turned out to be a woman wrapped in a blanket (Dicken 2013). The sighting occurred after racist, anti-Semitic, and otherwise offensive messages had been posted on campus during the previous few weeks. These were also not what they seemed, as the culprits were not racists, but two progressive students attempting to get a reaction from the community (Ross 2013).

Reading about this from a distance, we found it puzzling that the Oberlin College community was so ready to believe that virulent racists lurked among them. Then we came across something even more remarkable: the Oberlin Microaggressions website, which invited submissions from those who "hear racist, heterosexist/homophobic, anti-Semitic, classist, ableist, sexist/cissexist speech." The aim of the site was to "demonstrate that these are not simply isolated incidents, but rather part of structural inequalities" (Oberlin Microaggressions 2017). Again some students seemed to think Oberlin, of all places, was a hotbed of bigotry and oppression. But they did not just concern themselves with overt displays of racism, or even with imagined Klan conspiracies. These students wanted to

© The Author(s) 2018
B. Campbell, J. Manning, *The Rise of Victimhood Culture*,
https://doi.org/10.1007/978-3-319-70329-9_1

1

document microaggressions—tiny offenses, possibly unintentional ones—as if to strain out every gnat of bigotry on campus. One of the documented microaggressions was a man asking his sexual partner to wear nothing but a bindi, the red dot that decorates the forehead of Hindu women. "Exoticizing women of color is not flattering," explained the complainant. Another student objected to someone's annoyance over hearing the phrase "in solidarity," saying, "If you're tired of talking, *take action.*" One complaint dealt with a professor at the gym telling someone she was glad she and her husband both had blue eyes so her children would have blue eyes, something the poster described as "casual racism." And a Hispanic student called attention to a white soccer teammate referring to the game with the Spanish word *futbol.* "Keep my heritage language out of your mouth," wrote the poster, who vowed to never play soccer with whites again (Anonymous 2013a, b, c, d).

The term *microaggression* has become popular only recently, and this was the first we had heard of it. As sociologists of morality we were immediately intrigued. We thought of Emile Durkheim, the nineteenth-century French sociologist, who famously asked his readers to imagine what would happen in a "society of saints." The answer is that there would still be sinners because "faults which appear venial to the layman" would there create scandal (Durkheim 1982:100). And it did seem that people were most concerned about rooting out racism and bigotry in the very places where there was the least of it. These so-called microaggressions, many of which outsiders would see as no more than venial faults, were causing great scandal in our universities. We set out to understand why. This book is the result of that endeavor to contextualize and explain microaggression complaints and related phenomena.

The seventeenth-century biologist Jan Swammerdam once said, "Here I bring you proof of God's providence in the anatomy of a louse" (quoted in Weber 1958:142). In this spirit we focus in these first two chapters on microaggression complaints. Though they might seem small and insignificant, they have broad implications, revealing much about the patterning of moral conflict and the nature of ongoing moral change in contemporary societies.

MICROAGGRESSION AND ITS DISCONTENTS

Even as campus activists and many others have embraced the concept of microaggression, much of the broader public has fiercely resisted it. The opposition arises because microaggression complaints violate many long-standing social norms, such as those encouraging people to have thick skin, brush off slights, and charitably interpret the intentions of others. The proponents of the concept, though, believe microaggressions cause severe distress to members of marginalized groups, and that the consequences are too great to be ignored. Each side has radically different moral assumptions, and the debates between them involve a clash of moral cultures.

The Microaggression Program

On one side are the microaggression complainants and others who see value in the concept. These are the supporters of what can be called the "microaggression program," which refers to "the combination of [microaggression] theory and [its] on-campus applications" (Haidt 2017:176). Harvard education and psychiatry professor Chester Pierce coined the term microaggression in the 1970s, but counseling psychologist and diversity training specialist Derald Wing Sue is probably more responsible for the success of the microaggression program than anyone else. Sue, who has been called the godfather of the concept of microaggression (Schwartz 2016), defines microaggressions as "the brief and common-place daily verbal, behavioral, and environmental indignities, whether intentional or unintentional, that communicate hostile, derogatory, or negative racial, gender, and sexual orientation, and religious slights and insults to the target person or group" (Sue 2010:5). Sue says that he and an African American colleague were microaggression victims because a white flight attendant asked them to change seats in order to redistribute the weight on a small, mostly empty airplane. While acknowledging that "balancing the weight on the plane seemed reasonable," he suggests that he and his colleague were singled out because of their race—that the flight attendant should have asked a pair of white passengers to move instead. He describes his reaction after complying with the request: "I could feel my blood pressure rising, heart beating faster, and face flush with anger" (quoted in Sue et al. 2007:275). He describes himself as unable to contain his anger. When he confronted the flight attendant, she denied having any racial motives, and as Sue tells it, "Attempts to explain my perceptions and feelings only generated greater defensiveness from her" (Sue et al. 2007:275). Sue does not claim the flight attendant was lying. In fact Sue and his colleagues say the power of microaggressions "lies in their invisibility to the perpetrator" (Sue et al. 2007:275). "In some respects," they go on to say, "people of color may find an overt and obvious racist act easier to handle than microaggressions that seem vague or disguised" (Sue et al. 2007:277).

From the overt and obvious, then, to the vague or disguised, microaggressions are wide ranging. Writer Samhita Mukhopadhyay tells of being the target of a racial insult by a classmate in the second grade ("Ew, it's the smelly Indian girl") and also of having a teacher who had trouble pronouncing her name on the first day of ninth grade. She considers both the insult and the mistake to be microaggressions, and the accumulation of such experiences, she says, "played a big role in how I have experienced being South Asian in the United States" (Mukhopadhyay 2015). Here are some other actions that have been identified as microaggressions:

- Saying "You are a credit to your race" or "You are so articulate" to an African American (Sue et al. 2008:331).
- Telling an Asian American that he or she speaks English well (Sue et al. 2008:331).
- Suggesting an African American student take "less challenging courses in African American studies" rather than majoring in biology (Runyowa 2015).
- Clutching one's purse when an African American walks onto an elevator (Nadal et al. 2013:190).
- Staring at lesbians or gays expressing affection in public (Boysen 2012:123).
- Saying "All lives matter" (Phillips 2014).
- Using the phrase "you guys" to address a group of men and women (Saul 2016).
- Correcting a student's use of "Indigenous" in a paper by changing it from upper to lowercase (Flaherty 2013).
- Complimenting a woman's shoes (Shimshock 2016).

A number of websites like the one at Oberlin have been dedicated to documenting such conduct at various educational institutions, including Brown University, Carleton College, Columbia University, Dartmouth

College, Harvard University, St. Olaf College, Swarthmore College, and Willamette University in the United States, as well as McGill University in Canada, the University of Oxford in the United Kingdom, and the University of Sydney in Australia.[1] At *The Microaggressions Project*, a blog founded by two Columbia University students, a female professor in her 30s reports being told by a stranger that she looks too young to be a professor, and the white mother of a black child tells of being asked, "Is she yours?" (Anonymous 2015a, b). On the site *Carleton Microaggressions*, a black female student tells of a friend who asked her during sports practice if she could play with her braids (Anonymous 2015c). And at *St.Olaf Microaggressions*, a poster complains about a friend describing a movie character's recovery from mental illness as becoming "normal": "Are individuals with mental illness not normal all of a sudden?" (Anonymous 2013e).

We have now seen many examples of microaggressions, but readers unfamiliar with the concept might still be wondering what exactly they are. Some are things probably everyone reading sees as offensive or at least awkward, but others certainly are not. What is wrong with correcting a student's writing, complimenting someone's shoes, or using the word *futbol*?

But remember that microaggressions can be unintentional, even invisible to their perpetrators. They can be almost anything, since almost anything might be said to communicate various kinds of slights and insults. *Microaggression* is not our concept—we are describing others' use of the term—and it is not a worthwhile social scientific concept precisely because it does not refer to any clearly defined behavior (compare Lilienfeld 2017). If it did, it would make sense to ask whether any of the alleged microaggressions mentioned above were really microaggressions. It would also be possible for people to sincerely but wrongly claim to have experienced a microaggression or to wrongly accuse others of microaggressing. In that case Derald Wing Sue's perception might be wrong and the flight attendant might be innocent. But Sue and others define the term in a way that no defense is possible. The flight attendant said she had no ill intent, but

---

[1] The websites for Harvard, Oxford, and Sydney feature individuals posting photos of themselves holding written messages, most of which address offensive things the poster has heard from others—such as one Australian poster whose sign reads "'You're not like the other aboriginals'" followed by "But you ARE like the other RACISTS!" (*I Too Am Sydney* 2014).

no intent is required. Nothing determines whether the behavior—asking two passengers to move—is a microaggression other than Sue's reaction. Sociologically, a microaggression is not a kind of statement someone makes or a kind of behavior someone engages in; it is a label that someone else attaches to a statement or behavior. The labeling of something as a microaggression is thus a moralistic behavior, an act of defining right and wrong, and we want to make sociological sense of it.

Critics of the Microaggression Program

We also want to make sense of the moral reactions to the labeling. Sue's flight attendant was angry about being accused of a racial microaggression. Others might likewise be angry about personal accusations, or they might object to the microaggression program more generally, for a number of reasons. One reason is that from the perspective of the critics, many of the statements and behaviors being labeled microaggressions are actually completely unobjectionable. Some of these, they say, are just ordinary political views someone disagrees with. In 2014, for example, the University of California system, drawing from the work of Sue and his colleagues, created a document for faculty training that listed 52 possible microaggressions. Among these were saying "America is a melting pot" and "I believe the most qualified person should get the job" (University of California 2014). Law professor Eugene Volokh (2015) says statements like these are simply "ideas that the UC wants to exclude from university classrooms," and he proclaims, "Well, I'm happy to say that I'm just going to keep on microaggressing."

Other alleged microaggressions, the critics say, might just be well meant statements or behaviors misinterpreted by the complainants. Sue's experience with the flight attendant would fall into this category for some. Psychologist Kenneth Thomas concludes that Sue's characterization of the incident "may speak more about Sue's personal need to feel special or privileged than about any prejudice on the part of the flight attendant." "Many people who fly regularly," he points out, "have been asked at one time or another to change their seats" (Thomas 2008:274). Psychologist Rafael Harris (2008) discusses the incident, too, and he wonders whether Sue's perception and that of his colleague should be enough to conclude that the flight attendant's behavior was discriminatory. He also wonders whether someone with Sue's celebrity status in the field "can be questioned or otherwise held accountable." "Once on the pedestal," he asks, "is everything uttered supposed to be accepted as a fact?" (Harris 2008:276).

What the critics are objecting to is that someone's interpretation of another person's action matters more than the intentions of the actor. Some of the statements included in the UC document might be criticized on these grounds as well. It is a microaggression, according to the document, to say "Where are you from?" or "Where were you born" to an Asian American or Latino American, "Why are you so quiet?" to an Asian, Latino, or Native American, or "Why do you have to be so loud/animated?" to an African American. Note that what is required of people is not that they treat minorities or women as they would anyone else. "Why are you so quiet" might be asked of any quiet person of whatever race or ethnicity, but asking it of an Asian, Latino, or Native American is a microaggression, according to the document, because it conveys "the notion that the values and communication styles of the dominant/White culture are ideal/'normal'" (University of California 2014). Whether the person asking the question actually means this or is even aware of any such cultural differences between the "dominant/White culture" and others seems to have no bearing on whether the question is a microaggression. Similarly, "Where are you from?" is a staple of small talk anywhere people do not know one another well, but it becomes a microaggression when asked of an Asian American or Latino American, according to the UC document, because it conveys the message "You are not a true American."

That this question might be asked of anyone was illustrated recently during a panel discussion on microaggressions at the University of California, Irvine. Members of the panel had already discussed various examples of microaggressions when the moderator, radio talk show host Larry Mantle, invited questions from the audience. After calling on the first questioner, Mantle asked, "Where are you from?" The audience laughed, and though Mantle did not realize why at first, the questioner explained: "People are laughing because of the question. I don't need to take offense at that because I'm part of the privileged majority who don't constantly have to put up with questions of where I'm from" (quoted in Barbash 2015). But she had been asked just that. The question is commonplace.

Even when the question is in fact an attempt to find out someone's ethnic or national background, many people would still see it as unobjectionable. Kenneth Thomas asks why, given the high levels of immigration in the United States, it would be "unusual for any American, native born of foreign born, to ask questions regarding whether some individuals are native born or foreign born." "Because the United States is a nation of immigrants," he says, "many Americans, White and non-White, have been asked occasionally about their ethnicity. It is, in fact, a matter of pride for many Americans to say their heritage is Irish, Italian, Polish, Vietnamese, or whatever" (Thomas 2008:274). Sociologist Frank Furedi, noting that he has always been fascinated by people's origins, tells of asking cab drivers with unusual surnames where they are from, and columnist David Harsanyi tells of asking the question upon meeting a couple whose accent he could not place (Furedi 2015; Harsanyi 2015). Each goes on to critique the microaggression framework. Furedi points out that for the microaggression complainant, "neither the content of the words nor the intention behind them is important," and he urges readers to ignore such complaints. "We all should be free to decide the meanings of our words," he concludes. Harsanyi says of his own question that he was "merely curious about people who were originally 'from' some other place," and after discussing the concept of microaggressions, says "the whole thing is basically a macroassault on your intelligence."

Critics of microaggression complaints might also object to the very idea of focusing so much on minor offenses. Those who mock the concept with humor often call attention to this. In a letter to the *Los Angeles Times*, for example, reader Jim Tanksley (2015) suggested moving "to the next step: ridding the world (or at least colleges) of nanoaggression." Other critics argue that various negative consequences are likely to result from this kind of focus. Sociologist and communitarian Amitai Etzioni suggests that we instead "focus on acts of aggression that are far from micro." Much of what microaggressions complainants call attention to, he says, are "the standard noise, the normal sounds of human rambling," and "we should not take umbrage at every negative note or adjective that is employed." Doing so will poison interactions between groups, when "what we need is more contact and fewer grounds for mutual accusations and sense of being victimized" (Etzioni 2014).

If calling attention to microaggressions increases racial and ethnic conflict, it would seem to be working against the goals of the activists calling for it. And it certainly is working against their goals if it harms members of the groups said to be the microaggression victims, as campus free speech advocate Greg Lukianoff and social psychologist Jonathan Haidt (2015) claim it is likely to do. They say that the concept of microaggressions and the attention given to them encourage many of what cognitive behavioral therapists have identified as the cognitive distortions that cause depression and anxiety. Cognitive behavioral therapists treat patients by teaching them to identify and correct these cognitive distortions—things like magnification (exaggerating something's importance), mind reading (assuming without evidence that others have negative thoughts about you), and labeling (assigning people "global negative traits"). There are others, but it is clear the idea of microaggressions encourages each of these three distortions—the opposite tactic of the therapists. Magnifying small offenses, mind reading by identifying subconscious thoughts even the offenders are unaware of, and labeling others as aggressors are all integral to the microaggression program but possibly harmful to mental health.

Elsewhere Haidt argues that magnifying small offenses goes against much of the traditional advice from philosophy and religion as well. He points to statements from the Buddha—"It is easy to see the faults of others, but difficult to see one's own faults"—and Jesus—"Why do you see the speck in your neighbor's eye, but do not notice the log in your own eye?"—that caution against obsessing over the minor faults of others. Microaggression complainants seem to reject such ideas completely: "Microaggression training is ... instruction in how to detect ever-smaller specks in your neighbor's eye" (Haidt 2017:176). Like Etzioni, Haidt suggests this will increase intergroup conflict. He says that if we want to decrease such conflict, if we want to "teach students to give each other the benefit of the doubt" and "cultivate generosity of spirit," we should "teach ancient wisdom instead of microaggression theory" (2017:177).

One final issue in the microaggression debate stems from the fact that most slights and insults, whether real or imagined, are never labeled microaggressions. Recognizing only some of them as such privileges some victims over others. Opponents of affirmative action might be as offended as its supporters upon hearing someone disagree with them, but it is "I believe the most qualified person should get the job" and not "I believe employers should make ethnic diversity a goal in hiring decisions" that the University of California (2014) calls a microaggression. Likewise the examples suggest that only women or various minorities, such as blacks, Asians, Latinos, and lesbian, gay, bisexual, and transgender (LGBT) persons, can be victims of microaggression, though it is surely possible for men to experience slights based on their sex or for whites to experience slights based on their ethnicity. Even some minority groups, such as Mormons or evangelical Christians, are notably absent from the lists of possible victims.

Returning to Derald Wing Sue's example, he was clearly angry, but so was the flight attendant. If we are simply talking about perceived insults, why is the flight attendant's behavior a microaggression but Sue's behavior toward her is not? Surely suddenly having to deal with angry passengers berating her and accusing her of racism might have been as unpleasant an experience for the flight attendant as being asked to change seats to redistribute the weight on the plane was for the two professors. It also likely would not have happened if she were not white. And the perceived slights and snubs of day-to-day life are unpleasant even when they clearly have nothing to do with one's group identities. According to those promoting the concept, though, these are not microaggressions. "There was a white, male elementary school teacher doing a workshop," Sue says, "talking about microaggression he experienced as a white male elementary teacher. That's a misapplication of the concept" (quoted in Hampson 2016). Whether an act is a microaggression depends not only on how it is perceived, but also on who perceives themselves as being wronged by whom.

Many of the critics have noted this. "Deciding who is eligible to complain about microaggressions," according to blogger and journalist Megan McArdle, "is itself an act by which the majority imposes its will" (McArdle 2015). And the linguist and political commentator John McWhorter says that the way those calling attention to racial microaggressions tend to employ the concept "seems fixed so that whites can't do anything right." He says this creates "endless conflict, under an idea that basically being white is, in itself, a microaggression." He sees this as a kind of "bullying disguised as progressive thought" (McWhorter 2014).

McWhorter is not the only one to suggest microaggression complaints are a form of bullying. Even some supporters of the microaggression program, including Derald Wing Sue himself, agree that some of those using the concept have used it punitively. Sue says he intended to educate those engaging in microaggressions, not punish or shame them (Zamudio-Suarez 2016). One of Sue's collaborators, psychologist Christina Capodilupo, says the point of her work was not to shut down conversations, but to "ask people to be flexible in their thinking and to be open-minded to the concept that we don't all walk through the world in the same shoes" (quoted in Zamudio-Suarez 2016).

Critics like McWhorter see the bullying behavior more closely tied to the concept itself. The recent term *crybully*, an amalgam of *crybaby* and *bully*, points to the bullying potential of claims of victimhood. Roger

Kimball, a longtime critic of the campus left, says crybullies are "a new academic phenomenon, at once tender and vicious," that arises from rhetoric about microaggressions (Kimball 2015). The English writer Julie Burchill describes crybullies as "a hideous hybrid of victim and victor, weeper and walloper." She says the crybully "always explains to the point of demanding that one agree with them and always complains to the point of insisting that one is persecuting them" (Burchill 2015). Lukianoff and Haidt's (2015) concept of *vindictive protectiveness* is similar in that it points not only to the protectiveness of the microaggression program, as it seeks to shield people "from words and ideas that make some uncomfortable," but also to the vindictiveness, as it "seeks to punish anyone who interferes with that aim, even accidentally."

Microaggression and Moral Polarization

The two sides of the debate over microaggressions seem to share little common ground. One side argues that microaggressions are "the new face of racism," that they "lead to macroaggressions," or that they harm "student performance, mental health, and worker productivity" (Watanabe and Song 2015). For the other side the whole concept is misguided and perhaps worthy of ridicule. They may see it as "the unwisest idea on campus" (Haidt 2017), as an "assault on everyday life" (Furedi 2015), as "pure nonsense" (Thomas 2008:274), or as "madness" (Kabbany 2015). Our argument is that the microaggression program is controversial because its approach to morality is relatively new to the modern West and is by no means universally shared. Microaggression complaints arise from a culture of victimhood in which individuals and groups display a high sensitivity to slight, have a tendency to handle conflicts through complaints to authorities and other third parties, and seek to cultivate an image of being victims who deserve assistance. This new moral culture, we shall see, differs sharply from other moral cultures—such as cultures of honor, where people are sensitive to slight but handle their conflicts aggressively, and cultures of dignity, where people ignore slights and insults. The current debate about microaggressions arises from a clash between dignity culture and the newer culture of victimhood. The debate is polarized because the moral assumptions of each side are so different.

MICROAGGRESSION AND MORAL CHANGE

Conflicts and ways of handling them vary immensely. We are not all aggrieved by the same things, and we do not handle our grievances in the same way. Within just about any society, sometimes people handle grievances by appealing to third parties, sometimes they negotiate with the offender, sometimes they use violence against the offender, and so forth. But sometimes we can observe patterns of moral life that distinguish a society or segment of society from others. We might then refer to a prevailing pattern of morality as a *moral culture*. For example, social scientists have long recognized a distinction between societies and other groups with a *culture of honor* and those with a *culture of dignity* (Ayers 1984:Chapter 1; Berger 1970; Cooney 1998:Chapter 5; Nisbett and Cohen 1996; Leung and Cohen 2011).[2] The moral evolution of modern Western society can be understood in part as a transition between these two cultures.[3]

A Culture of Honor

Honor is a kind of status attached to physical bravery and the unwillingness to be dominated by anyone. Honor in this sense is a status that depends on the evaluations of others, and members of honor societies are often expected to display their bravery by engaging in violent retaliation against those who offend them (Black 2011:71–73; Cooney 1998:108–109; Leung and Cohen 2011; Nisbett and Cohen 1996).[4] Those who engage

---

[2] It can be misleading to talk about moral cultures if it leads us to gloss over the moral variation within a society, but otherwise it can be a useful simplification. And the prevailing moral ideas often draw in even those who would rather reject them.

[3] For practical reasons we focus here on Western societies and their major moral cultures. Scholars such as Angela Leung and Dov Cohen (2011) argue that east Asian societies typically share a moral framework—a *culture of face*—that is distinct from the moral cultures we discuss here.

[4] Of course the term "honor" is used to refer to other things, such as honesty and integrity (McKay 2016). These meanings will probably be more familiar to most Western readers—for example, some universities have "honor codes" that forbid cheating on exams. But these connotations of honor are a vestige of an earlier time when the same word that was used to refer to bravery and willingness to fight was extended to other virtues. Also note that even within honor cultures, honor might mean different things to men and women. Female honor was usually tied to sexual modesty rather than bravery. But since it was a man's duty to violently defend the honor of female kin, and their dishonor would lead to his own, female virtue was still connected to physical bravery (Nye 1993; Vandello and Cohen 2003).

in such violence often say that the opinions of others left them with no choice at all. For example, after an exchange of insults between two men in nineteenth-century Greece led to a knife fight, legal officials asked the victorious fighter, Theodoros, why he cut the other man's face. Theodoros said that "no man would call his wife and daughters whores and get away with it. His reputation would not allow it" (Gallant 2000:359). Certain kinds of insults might require violence by the one insulted, as in that case, but it is also true that someone who has insulted another might have to accept a challenge to fight. Alexander Hamilton, killed in a duel by US Vice President Aaron Burr in 1804, wrote a letter before the duel explaining why he believed he had to accept Burr's challenge. Like Theodoros, he referred to the necessity of protecting his reputation, writing that "the ability to be in [the] future useful ... would probably be inseparable from a conformity with public prejudice in this particular" (quoted in Seitz 1929:100–101).

In honor cultures, it is one's *reputation* that makes one honorable or not, and one must respond aggressively to insults, aggressions, and challenges or else lose honor. Not to fight back is itself a kind of moral failing, such that "in honor cultures, people are shunned or criticized not for exacting vengeance but for failing to do so" (Cooney 1998:110). Honorable people must guard their reputations, so they are highly sensitive to insult, often responding aggressively to what might seem to outsiders to be minor slights (Cohen et al. 1996; Cooney 1998:115–119; Leung and Cohen 2011). It might seem that knowing people would respond this way would lead to people to avoid offending others, to walk on eggshells, but this would be a sign of cowardice. Insulting others when such insults might invite violence helps establish one's reputation for bravery, so honorable people are often verbally aggressive and quick to insult others. The result is a high frequency of violent conflict as participants in the culture aggressively compete for respect (Leung and Cohen 2011; e.g., see Anderson 1999:Chapter 2).

Cultures of honor tend to arise in places where legal authority is weak or nonexistent and where a reputation for toughness is perhaps the only effective deterrent against predation or attack (Cooney 1998:122; Leung and Cohen 2011:510; Nisbett and Cohen 1996:Chapter 1). Because of their belief in the value of personal bravery and capability, people socialized into a culture of honor often shun reliance on law or any other authority even when it is available, refusing to lower their standing by depending on another to handle their affairs (Cooney 1998:122–129;

Woldoff and Weiss 2010). But historically, as state authority has expanded and reliance on the law has increased, honor culture has given way to something else: a culture of dignity.

A Culture of Dignity

Honor has not disappeared. It is still prevalent throughout the Arab world, and enclaves of honor exist in the United States, the United Kingdom, and other Western nations, including among street gangs and other groups of poor young men. Still, the prevailing culture in the modern West is one whose moral code is nearly the exact opposite of that of an honor culture. Rather than honor, a status based primarily on public opinion, people are said to have dignity, a kind of inherent worth that cannot be alienated by others (Berger 1970; Leung and Cohen 2011; Rosen 2012). Dignity exists independently of what others think, so a culture of dignity is one in which public reputation is less important. Insults might provoke offense, but they no longer have the same impact as a way of establishing or destroying a reputation for bravery. People from dignity culture are less touchy (Cohen et al. 1996). It is even commendable to have thick skin that allows one to shrug off slights and insults, and in a dignity-based society parents might teach children some version of "sticks and stones may break my bones, but words will never hurt me"—an idea that would be alien in a culture of honor (Leung and Cohen 2011:509). People are to avoid insulting others, too, whether intentionally or not, and in general an ethic of self-restraint prevails (Elias 1982:230–286; see, e.g., Vidich and Bensman 1958:38–39, 45–46).[5]

When intolerable conflicts do arise, dignity cultures prescribe direct but non-violent actions, such as negotiated compromise geared toward solving the problem (Aslani et al. 2011). Failing this, or if the offense is sufficiently severe, people are to go to the police or appeal to the courts—it would be wrong for them to take the law into their own hands. For offenses like theft, assault, or breach of contract, people in a dignity culture use law without shame. But in keeping with their ethic of restraint

---

[5] While everyone has inherent dignity, conduct might be more or less dignified. To act in a dignified manner is to exercise self-control and display a quiet assurance in one's own worth, neither abasing oneself nor aggressively pursuing recognition (Meyer 1989). One may also fail to recognize others' dignity by treating them badly—though in dignity culture, this is considered immoral and undignified (Rosen 2012).

and toleration, it is not necessarily their first resort, and they might condemn many uses of the authorities as frivolous. People are criticized for being too litigious or otherwise quarrelsome, and even legal officials might reprimand litigants for not having solved their dispute without law (see, e.g., Greenhouse et al. 1994). Sometimes people might even be expected to tolerate serious but accidental personal injuries. In "Sander County," Illinois, for example, legal scholar David M. Engel (1984) found that personal injury litigation was rare and that longtime residents stigmatized those few who did use courts to try to get compensation in such cases. The ideal in dignity cultures is to use the courts as quickly, quietly, and rarely as possible.

The growth of law, order, and commerce in the modern world facilitated the rise of the culture of dignity, which largely supplanted the culture of honor among the middle and upper classes of the West. The culture of dignity existed in perhaps its purest form among respectable people in the homogeneous towns of mid-twentieth century America, where the presence of a stable and powerful legal system discouraged the aggressiveness and hostility toward settlement seen in honor cultures, while social closeness—ties of culture and intimacy—encouraged an ethic of toleration or peaceful confrontation. Social relations in late-twentieth-century suburbs were often similar, though without the ties of intimacy, and here a variant of dignity culture prevailed, an avoidance culture where toleration was also common but negotiation less so (Baumgartner 1988). But the rise of microaggression complaints suggests a new direction in the evolution of moral culture.

A Culture of Victimhood

The ideals of dignity are no longer settled morality. The microaggression program rejects one of dignity culture's main injunctions—to ignore insults and slights—and instead encourages at least some people to take notice of them and take action against them. The idea is that such offenses do cause harm, just like violence. Law professor Catharine Wells says, "The time has come to recognize the harm that microaggressions cause to women and people of color. There is an old saying about sticks and stones and words that never hurt, but these words are hurtful" (2013:337). She sees the physical pain and injury from "sticks and stones" as equivalent to the emotional hurt said to result from microaggressions.

In rejecting dignity culture's distinction between violent offenses and merely verbal ones, victimhood culture resembles honor culture. Honorable people are sensitive to insult, so they might understand how microaggressions could be severe offenses demanding a serious response. But honor cultures value unilateral aggression and disparage appeals for help. Public complaints that advertise or even exaggerate one's own victimization and need for sympathy would be anathema to a person of honor, tantamount to showing that one had no honor at all.[6] Complaints about microaggressions combine the sensitivity to slight that we see in honor cultures with the willingness to appeal to authorities and other third parties that we see in dignity cultures. And victimhood culture differs from both honor and dignity cultures in highlighting rather than downplaying the complainants' victimhood.

BEYOND MICROAGGRESSION

The microaggression program has had enormous success. Some of the microaggression websites are now inactive, but students on Twitter and in other forums continue making microaggression complaints. And the concept has been taken up and institutionalized by university administrators, professors, and student governments. The University of Wisconsin-Stevens Point uses a document for faculty training very similar to the University of California's, and Purdue University uses something similar in a business class (Hookstead 2015). Suffolk University has announced a mandatory microaggression training program for faculty (Jaschik 2016). Freshmen at Clark University and the University of Wisconsin-Madison get microaggression training (Melchior 2016a; Saul 2016). Even an engineering class at Iowa State teaches it (Beaman 2016). The student government at Ithaca College has called for the school to create an electronic microaggression

---

[6] Members of honor cultures might call attention to offenses against themselves, but only as a way of pressuring the offender to agree to a violent confrontation. In the antebellum American South, for instance, aggrieved parties might take out advertisements in newspapers calling attention to insults. One such advertisement read, "Sir—I am informed you applied to me on the day of the election the epithet 'puppy.' If so, I shall expect that satisfaction which is due from one gentleman to another for such an indignity" (quoted in Williams 1980:22–23). Again, touchiness goes hand in hand with verbal aggression in such settings, so honorable Southerners might also use newspapers to insult others. In 1809, for instance, the Savannah *Republican* printed this: "I hold Francis H. Welman a Liar, Coward, and Poltroon. John Moorhead" (quoted in Williams 1980:22).

reporting system, students at Occidental College have asked for a system for reporting microaggressions committed by professors, and students at Emory University have asked for student evaluation forms to include questions about whether the professor has committed microaggressions (Popp 2015; Soave 2015a, b).

Outside of universities, some corporations have begun training people to avoid microaggressions (Fisher 2015). And the concept has spread beyond the United States. In 2012, for example, an American-Japanese columnist complained in *The Japan Times* that native Japanese frequently subject him to such microaggressions as being surprised by his ability to use chopsticks or speak fluent Japanese (Arudou 2012).[7]

The microaggression program is just one manifestation of victimhood culture, though. The same sensitivity to slight that has led to its success has given rise to new jargon for describing more specific kinds of verbal oppression. For instance, the term *sweat shaming*, pointing out a woman's sweatiness, and many other variants were recently added to the more familiar *slut shaming* and *body shaming* (Moyer 2015a; Peters 2013). Another new kind of offense is *cultural appropriation*. At the University of Ottawa, concerns about the appropriation of Indian culture led to the cancellation of a yoga class for the disabled (Moyer 2015b). And after complaints from students, Clemson University apologized for the "Maximum Mexican" event held by the school's cafeteria, at which the staff wore sombreros and served Mexican food (Hasson 2015).

Remember that in a victimhood culture, along with the sensitivity to slight goes a tendency to handle conflicts through appeals to third parties. Sometimes appeals to third parties may simply be a matter of seeking support and validation from one's social media network and other distant sympathizers, but for campus activists the focus is often on compelling authoritative action from administrators. At the University of Missouri, the president and chancellor both resigned in the face of student protests

---

[7] As the concept has spread, the kinds of controversies discussed earlier follow. The article produced in the *Japan Times* led to a flood of responses from Americans, Europeans, and Australians who have lived in Japan. Many of these agreed with the author that such microaggressions were a major problem, but others viewed his complaint as a form of offensive behavior in its own right. One disapproving commenter stated that he would "never let [such microaggressions] get to me" (Von Jettmar 2012), while another explains that "when Japanese compliment my chopstick use, I tell them thank you, and then politely let them know that some non-Japanese might not take it as a compliment.... I'd say this is much more effective than ... bitterly complaining ... to other non-Japanese" (Ben 2012).

accusing them of not taking sufficient action when African American students reported being the targets of racial slurs (Gaude 2015; Severn 2015). Among the protesters' demands were that the president "acknowledge his white male privilege," and as a result of the uproar, campus police now urge students to call them in cases where someone uses racial slurs (S. Nelson 2015b; Severn 2015). For the protesters, failing to take drastic action in response to verbal offenses made campus officials oppressors in their own right, and the students appealed to still higher authorities and public opinion at large to pressure the authorities out of their jobs. Notably, one protester resorted to a hunger strike, a method of winning attention and sympathy by victimizing oneself. And win attention and sympathy it did, as the conflict drew the attention of the governor of Missouri and sparked protests at colleges across the United States (Hartocollis and Bidgood 2015). It may have even inspired a student at Claremont McKenna College in California to threaten a hunger strike when offended by an email written by the school's dean, who quickly offered her resignation when accused of verbally victimizing the school's Latina population (Margolis 2015).

Professors Erika and Nicholas Christakis of Yale University became the targets of protests when students accused them of creating an unsafe space for questioning whether the university should be involved in regulating potentially offensive Halloween costumes. The protesters were unsatisfied when Nicholas Christakis responded by offering an apology in which he said he had "disappointed" the students who took offense when he attempted to engage them in dialogue about the issue (Stanley-Becker 2015; Worland 2015). Eventually the Christakises resigned their positions as the headmasters of one of Yale's residential colleges, and Erika Christakis left Yale entirely.

The targets of such complaints often apologize in some manner, as Nicholas Christakis did; others fully capitulate and may even endorse further regulation from above. One University of Chicago student who was sanctioned for wearing a culturally insensitive Halloween costume, for example, stated that he agreed the university should do more to regulate what costumes students wear (Coyne 2015).

The Christakises' comments about the debates over Halloween costumes were narrowly focused and fairly nuanced. Others have been more sweeping in their criticisms of various manifestations of victimhood culture and have likewise elicited strong reactions from campus activists. When individualist feminist Wendy McElroy appeared at Brown University to debate the merits of the term *rape culture*, some students set up a *safe space* for people who needed to escape from or recuperate from McElroy's arguments. This was a room with "cookies, coloring books, bubbles, Play-Doh, calming music, pillows, blankets and a video of frolicking puppies, as well as students and staff members trained to deal with trauma" (Shulevitz 2015). Student Emma Hall tells of attending part of the talk but retreating to the safe space after "feeling bombarded by a lot of viewpoints that really go against my dearly and closely held beliefs" (quoted in Shulevitz 2015).

Activists have tried to prevent other speakers from appearing on campuses at all, or when failing to prevent the speakers from coming, they have disrupted their talks. DePaul University banned conservative Ben Shapiro from speaking on campus, or even from stepping foot on the campus. When he showed up planning to attend the panel talk he was originally supposed to participate in, security guards threatened to have him arrested (Zanotti 2016). Previously, at California State University, Los Angeles, a conservative student group invited Shapiro to give a talk entitled "When Diversity Becomes a Problem." Three days prior to the event, the university president cancelled it, but reversed his decision after Shapiro announced he would come to the public university anyway. The event, in which Shapiro criticized the microaggression program, the Black Lives Matter movement, and other leftist projects, went on, but protesters outside the venue blocked the doors to prevent people from entering or leaving and activated a fire alarm during the talk. At the end of the talk police escorted Shapiro through a secret exit to protect him from the crowd gathered outside (Melchior 2016b).

Right-wing provocateur Milo Yiannopoulos inspires similar reactions. Like Shapiro, he has been banned from speaking at DePaul University, but at an earlier event there, prior to the ban, students rushed the stage and took away his microphone, and one student punched him in the face (Chasmar 2016). At the University of Massachusetts, where Yiannopoulos spoke on a panel with Christina Hoff Sommers and Steven Crowder, who are also critics of various manifestations of victimhood culture, protesters tried to disrupt the event by screaming things like "Hate speech is not welcome here!" and "Fuck you! Fuck you!" (Fricke and Gockowski 2016).[8]

---

[8] As with the microaggression program, critics of these other manifestations of victimhood culture describe the activists as overly sensitive, bullying, and the like, and sometimes this

We see in these examples that whether to take offense at something, and what to do about it, is in part an expression of moral culture, and the rise of a new moral culture alters patterns of conflict. It shapes social life even beyond that, since moral ideas orient our entire lives (Nisbett and Cohen 1996:Chapter 5). In an honor culture, for example, they affect people's leisure and self-presentation. Ever concerned with appearing brave and strong, the honorable often gamble, drink heavily, and openly boast about their exploits (Cooney 1998:Chapter 5). In dignity cultures, on the other hand, socialization tends to be aimed at teaching restraint, and people look down on reckless behavior and abhor boasting in most contexts (Elias 1982:230–286; Pinker 2011:59–116). The emerging victimhood culture appears to share dignity's disdain for risk, but it condones calling attention to oneself as long as one is calling attention to one's own hardships—to weaknesses rather than strengths and to exploitation rather than exploits. For example, students writing personal statements as part of their applications for colleges and graduate schools often write not of their academic achievements but instead—with the encouragement of the universities—about overcoming adversity such as a parent's job loss or having to shop at thrift stores (Lieber 2014).[9] And in a setting where people increasingly eschew toleration and publicly air complaints to compel official action, personal discomfort looms large in official policy. Consider recent calls for *trigger warnings* in college classes or on course syllabuses to forewarn students that they are about to be exposed to topics that might cause them distress, such as when a guide for faculty at Oberlin College (later withdrawn after faculty complaints) suggested that the novel *Things Fall Apart*, which takes place in colonial Nigeria, could "trigger students who have experienced racism, colonialism, religious persecution, violence, suicide, and more" (quoted in Medina 2014). Similarly, at Rutgers University an article in the student newspaper suggested that an

---

takes the form of mockery. After the University of Massachusetts event, a video of one of the student protesters was posted online, and the student became known as Trigglypuff, a combination of *trigger* (student activists often say they are triggered by the events they are protesting) and Jigglypuff, the name of a Pokemon character (Dillon 2016).

[9] Gender studies scholar Hugo Schwyzer (2006), in an essay critical of this phenomenon, complains that "too many of my students insist on writing essays that I can only describe as 'narratives of suffering.'" As he puts it, possibly exaggerating in describing the logic of the students' letters, "If your parents are immigrants, mention it. If one of your parents drinks, or is in prison, don't hide it—wallow in it! If you moved around a lot, if you grew up surrounded by drugs or violence—share, share, share!" (Schwyzer 2006).

appropriate trigger warning for *The Great Gatsby* would notify students that it depicted suicide, domestic abuse, and graphic violence (Wythe 2014; see also Jarvie 2014).

WHY CALL IT VICTIMHOOD CULTURE?

Clearly moral change is afoot, as campus activists and others reject long held norms about when to take offense, how to deal with offenders, and how to present themselves. We have called this new moral culture a culture of victimhood, but we know that many people—especially those who are advocates of microaggression complaints, trigger warnings, and the like—will object to our terminology. After publishing a piece in *The Atlantic* about our earlier work, journalist Conor Friedersdorf wrote several follow-up pieces discussing readers' reactions (2015a, b, c, d). One of these gave voice to the critics of our concept of victimhood culture, most of whom took umbrage at the term itself and its juxtaposition to honor and dignity. One reader calls our concept "tenuous and capricious" and says it "is itself a microaggression," actually "closer to a real aggression" because "it seeks to diminish our voices to ones without 'honor' and 'dignity.'"[10] Another says that we "have chosen very positive words in 'dignity' and 'honor' as well as a rather charged, potentially negative one in 'victimhood.'" Still another says, "'Honor' is a good thing. 'Dignity' is a good thing. 'Victimhood' is not" (quoted in Friedersdorf 2015d).

These criticisms and others like them (e.g., Mukhopadhyay 2015) suggest confusion about our use of the term victimhood. Remember that victimhood culture shares with honor culture the imperative to react strongly to certain kinds of minor offenses, and with dignity culture an approval of appeals to authorities. The differences in each moral culture

[10] Having one's work on microaggression called a microaggression was surreal—much too pat and predictable—but we had experienced a similar reproach before. After our initial article on microaggression appeared in the journal *Comparative Sociology* in December 2014, Jonathan Shieber, a Senior Editor at the online magazine *TechCrunch* asked us to write an op-ed piece based on the article. We wrote a piece we called "Microaggressions and the Moralistic Internet," and on May 1, 2015, Shieber called it a "fascinating topic" and thanked us for submitting it. On May 11 he told us it would run it within the next two weeks, and then we heard nothing from him until June 17, when in response to our inquiry he said they "had to ultimately pull it, because of some concerns about microaggression and bullying that arose from some of our staff" (Shieber 2015). Neither Shieber nor anyone else from *TechCrunch* ever told us what those concerns were, but it sounds as if the staff members found our analysis morally offensive in some way.

arise along with an orientation toward a particular type of moral status. Like honor and dignity, victimhood is a kind of moral status, and it is the status most distinctive of the emerging moral framework we are discussing here. But whether victims are accorded moral status is independent of the question of whether doing so is good or bad. Our terminology is intended to help us describe what is going on, not to praise or condemn it. We believe *victimhood culture* accomplishes this.

Moral Status and Victimhood

When we think of differences in social status, inequalities of wealth or authority come readily to mind. The rich are higher in status than the poor, and bosses are higher in status than their subordinates. Perhaps it is less obvious that morality engenders a form of inequality. It does so in part because people adhere to moral codes to different degrees, and others punish or reward them accordingly. Engaging in deviant acts lowers one's moral status, as does being punished, fairly or not, for such behavior. Conversely, engaging in praiseworthy acts or being rewarded for doing so raises one's moral status (Black 1976:111–112; Cooney 2009:110–111). Whether and to what extent various kinds of conduct are deviant or praiseworthy varies, though, so we can identify different types of moral status.

Honor, or physical bravery, is a virtue almost everywhere. But it has an exaggerated importance in honor cultures. It is in honor cultures that it becomes much easier to be labeled a coward, and more fateful. People might thus ignore competing virtues—such as peacefulness, prudence, and charity—as they violently defend their honor. It is not necessarily that honorable people do not value these things. They may even have some conception of dignity—the inherent worth of all persons. But these values and beliefs might not be enough to prevent them from worrying about their public reputation or violently attacking those who threaten it.

As with honor, various kinds of moral status normally increase or decrease as a result of deviant or praiseworthy behavior. Sometimes, though, being the victim of an offense might elevate one's status regardless of whether one has done anything praiseworthy. It is easy to see how this could come to be. Holding the victim of an offense in higher regard can be a way of reversing the harmful effects of the offense, and even a way of punishing the offender, since one is rewarding the person the offender wanted to harm or punish. This is victimhood, a kind of moral status based on suffering and neediness. And if victimhood is a virtue, privilege is a vice.

It has the same relationship to victimhood that cowardice does to honor, and admonitions to "check your privilege" are analogous to the shaming of cowards that we see in honor cultures.

Victimhood exists in a variety of contexts, but like honor and dignity it plays a greater role in some than in others. Those enmeshed in a culture of victimhood might also value dignity and perhaps even elements of honor, but to a greater degree than elsewhere they emphasize the moral worth of victims and their allies, while condemning the vice of privilege and the evil of oppression.

The moral status of victims varies substantially across settings. In honor cultures being harmed or oppressed can be a source of shame. To outsiders the degree to which victims attract condemnation rather than sympathy might be shocking. In some honor settings a rape victim might be executed by her own kin because public knowledge of her victimization has so damaged the family's honor (e.g., Hall 2015, see also Cooney 2014a, b). Now picture the opposite extreme: a setting where there is a high level of deference to and concern for those who have been hurt, oppressed, or in any way disadvantaged. Surely any offense against them would seem especially odious, as would any failure to fully take their side. If we came to view certain ethnicities and other groups of people as especially vulnerable, we might condemn any banter that might make them uncomfortable as a kind of *microaggression*. We would worry that exposure to any reminders of their oppression would *trigger* their trauma. We certainly would not minimize their victimhood or contest their definition of the situation by telling them to develop thick skin, to ignore slights, and to interpret others' actions in the best possible light. We might instead demand that authorities do something to protect them from all these threats and remedy their situation, perhaps by creating *safe spaces*. And those who see themselves as oppressed might agree, urging others to be conscious of their *privilege* and circumspect in their words.

Of course this describes the environment of college campuses today. This is the pattern of moral life—hunger strikes over racial slurs, protesters demanding a university president admit his privilege, calls for safe spaces and trigger warnings to protect minorities and victims of traumatic experiences—that we call victimhood culture. Calling it this highlights our concept of victimhood as moral status, just as the terms *honor culture* and *dignity culture* highlight the role of the moral statuses that distinguish those cultures. It does not imply anything about the motives or psychology of those who claim to have been hurt by others. To say that being recognized as a victim raises one's moral status does not imply that any particular victim is cynically taking advantage of this fact. It does not imply that any particular victim sought out or enjoys whatever status victimhood conveys. It does not imply that this status outweighs other disadvantages they might have. And it does not imply that anyone's grievances are illegitimate or that those who point out their marginality are being dishonest. Many who advertise their disadvantage or neediness are factually correct about their situation, but it is still of sociological interest that they would advertise it in this fashion, when in other settings they might hide such things or at least not emphasize them. Whatever terminology we use, we can ask why the moral life of today's college campuses differs from what is found elsewhere.

The Cultural Contradictions of Victimhood

Any term for the constellation of moral ideals and behaviors we describe is going to be a kind of shorthand to help move the discussion along. *Honor* and *dignity* are not perfect terms either. But even if we called victimhood culture something else, our terminology would still attract criticism, we believe, since the adherents of victimhood culture are especially likely to take offense at descriptions of their moral activity. One reason for this is simply that a key feature of this culture is the tendency to become aggrieved about minor matters, and taking offense at the terminology used to identify the culture is consistent with that. Another reason is that there is an inherent tension—a cultural contradiction—in vilifying the privileged and valorizing the oppressed.

Supporting one side in a conflict—judging it as virtuous and throwing your weight behind the cause—elevates that side's status. The contradiction is that support goes to those said to lack privilege, but the ability to attract support is itself a kind of privilege. It is perhaps then quite difficult— a source of what psychologists call cognitive dissonance—to openly acknowledge this: that a reduction in oppression, however limited in context and extent, comes from being recognized as oppressed. If this is the case, it is not really the term *victimhood culture* that people are objecting to, but the very idea of victimhood as a kind of status—the idea that anyone might find it advantageous to gain recognition as a victim or member of a disadvantaged group.

It is likewise difficult to admit that privilege can ever be a liability. Earlier we discussed Lukianoff and Haidt's concept of vindictive protectiveness, which involves the tendency to punish offenders in the name of guarding the feelings of those thought to be weak and disadvantaged. They say this "creates a culture in which everyone must think twice before they speak up, lest they face charges of insensitivity, aggression, or worse" (Lukianoff and Haidt 2015). The term crybully points to the same thing. But the advocates of this type of morality seldom acknowledge they are harming, much less bullying, anyone. Not everyone can be recognized as a victim, though, and designating one group as protected implicitly designates others as unprotected. While some advocates justify this inequality as serving the purpose of counterbalancing other systemic inequities, such as the continuing effects of historic oppression, it seems that others have difficulty recognizing that the distinction creates any inequality at all.

That it does so is an inevitable consequence of the culture, but it is such a challenge to the culture's core ideals that victimhood adherents have developed a specialized vocabulary defining offenses in a way that prevents speaking of members of dominant groups as victims. They might define *racism* so that blacks *by definition* cannot ever be racists or whites victims of racism (Neff 2015), *sexism* so that women cannot be sexist or men victims of sexism (Davoran 2015), and even *censorship* so that "the oppressed by definition cannot censor their oppressor" (Dean-Johnson et al. 2015). That these terms have different meanings outside these circles illustrates another reason for the objections to our terminology.

The Unconventionality of Victimhood Culture

Victimhood culture is new. Its moral ideals sometimes attract hostility even on the campuses where it is most influential, and they attract even more elsewhere. Particularly when the debate moves outside of the academy, proponents of this culture encounter resistance, including resistance from those who might be sympathetic to the activists' concerns but reluctant to abandon free speech or other ideals of dignity culture. And it is not just political conservatives, but also many moderates, libertarians, and liberals who take issue with various manifestations of victimhood culture (e.g., Bailey 2015; Chait 2015; Etzioni 2014; McArdle 2015). Former US President Barack Obama, known as a political liberal, has criticized the silencing of conservative speakers on campuses and has said he does not agree that "when you become students at colleges, [you] have to be coddled and protected from different points of view" (quoted in L. Nelson 2015a). Likewise former New York mayor Michael Bloomberg, in a commencement address at the University of Michigan, criticized the concepts of microaggressions, trigger warnings, and safe spaces. Safe spaces, he said, "create the false impression that we can insulate ourselves from those who hold different views." And "a microaggression," he said, "is exactly that: micro" (quoted in Richardson 2016).

Social movements often face the problem of winning allies and responding to critics, and the more unconventional the movement's ideology and tactics, the greater the difficulty in forming broad coalitions of support. A radical political movement might find that disruptive protest tactics increase its legitimacy among core supporters but alienate more moderate allies (Elsbach and Sutton 1992; see also Snow 1979). Extreme positions might alienate more moderate allies, too, so activists thus have an incentive to emphasize commonalities with mainstream culture when they address outsiders.[11] Their opponents, on the other hand, have an incentive to paint them as extreme and unconventional. Given such pressures and practices, any analysis that draws attention to a moral culture's distinctiveness and draws contrasts between that culture and the mainstream is likely to be taken as a smear campaign. Any accurate description of this moral milieu is bound to offend.

*   *   *

As sociologists of morality, we aim to discuss the conflicts we examine as clearly as we can. When we talk about the rise of a new moral culture, we mean that a cluster of traits has become frequent and prominent enough

---

[11] Sometimes this leads to the use of what philosopher Nicholas Shackel (2005) has called *motte and bailey doctrines*. A motte and bailey castle consists of the courtyard, or bailey, the desirable land where people spend their time, and the motte, a mound in the center with a stone castle on top. When under attack, people may retreat to the motte and lose the bailey, but always return to the bailey when it is safe. In the same way people may hold doctrines that are difficult to defend when challenged (*bailey* doctrines), so rather than attempt to defend them, they retreat and talk only about their less controversial ideas (*motte* doctrines), returning to the more exciting ideas when the challenge is over (Shackel 2005; see also Alexander 2014). Thus on campus, activists might busy themselves arguing outright against free speech and academic freedom as impediments to protecting the disadvantaged from verbal harm (e.g., Dean-Johnson et al. 2015; Korn 2014), while elsewhere their supporters claim no one is talking about limiting free speech or academic freedom.

that we think it ought to be distinguished from the others. In the contemporary United States, elements of honor survive, mainly among the poor, such as among urban street gangs (Anderson 1999; Leovy 2015). And dignity is still dominant, which is why in the debates over microaggression complaints, trigger warnings, and safe spaces, the opponents still have the upper hand. But moral life is changing, and we want to know why.

REFERENCES

Alexander, Scott. 2014. All in All, Another Brick in the Motte. *Slate Star Codex* (blog), November 3. http://slatestarcodex.com/2014/11/03/all-in-all-another-brick-in-the-motte/.

Anderson, Elijah. 1999. *Code of the Street: Decency, Violence, and the Moral Life of the Inner City.* New York: W. W. Norton.

Anonymous. 2013a. Futbol, and White People. *Oberlin Microaggressions,* September 19. http://obiemicroaggressions.tumblr.com/post/61719471286/futbol-and-white-people.

———. 2013b. Orientalism at Oberlin. *Oberlin Microaggressions,* February 24. http://obiemicroaggressions.tumblr.com/post/43892417626/orientalism-at-oberlin.

———. 2013c. Post at *Oberlin Microaggressions,* February 14. http://obiemicroaggressions.tumblr.com/post/43075452014/i-was-working-in-the-gym-last-week-and-a-group-of#notes.

———. 2013d. When We Get Tired of Talking. *Oberlin Microaggressions,* March 3. http://obiemicroaggressions.tumblr.com/post/44474914886/when-we-get-tired-of-talking.

———. 2013e. Crazy. *St. Olaf Microaggressions,* April 30. http://stolafmicroaggressions-blog.tumblr.com/post/49311592959/crazy.

———. 2015a. Post at *The Microaggressions Project.* http://www.microaggressions.com/post/77492511515/strangerwhat-do-you-do-meim-a.

———. 2015b. Post at *The Microaggressions Project.* http://www.microaggressions.com/post/105185109377/is-she-yours.

———. 2015c. Racial Microaggressions Can Come from Close Friends. *Carleton Microaggressions,* February 11. http://carlmicroaggressions.tumblr.com/post/110754036160/racial-microaggressions-can-come-from-close.

Arudou, Debito. 2012. Yes, I Can Use Chopsticks: The Everyday 'Microaggressions' that Grind Us Down. *The Japan Times,* May 1. http://www.japantimes.co.jp/community/2012/05/01/issues/yes-i-can-use-chopsticks-the-everyday-microaggressions-that-grind-us-down/#.WIbv3hiZN-U.

Aslani, Soroush, Jimena Ramirez-Martin, Jeanne Brett, Catherine Tinsley, Wendi Adair, and Laurie Weingart. 2011. Implications of Honor and Dignity Culture for Negotiations: A Comparative Study of Middle Easterners and Americans. Paper presented at the 24th Annual International Association of Conflict Management Conference.

Ayers, Edward L. 1984. *Vengeance and Justice: Crime and Punishment in the 19th-Century American South.* New York: Oxford University Press.

Bailey, Ronald. 2015. Victimhood Culture in America: Beyond Honor and Dignity. *Reason*, September 11. https://reason.com/blog/2015/09/11/victimhood-culture-in-america-beyond-dig.

Barbash, Fred. 2015. The War on 'Microaggressions': Has It Created a 'Victimhood Culture' on Campuses? *Washington Post*, October 28. https://www.washingtonpost.com/news/morning-mix/wp/2015/10/28/the-war-over-words-literally-on-some-american-campuses-where-asking-where-are-you-from-is-a-microaggression/.

Baumgartner, M.P. 1988. *The Moral Order of a Suburb.* New York: Oxford University Press.

Beaman, Jeremy. 2016. Iowa State Defends Lesson on Microaggressions in Software Engineering Class: 'Entirely Appropriate.' *The College Fix*, October 13. http://www.thecollegefix.com/post/29440/.

Ben. 2012. Divisive, Hateful Rabble-Rousing [Letter to the editor]. *The Japan Times*, May 22. http://www.japantimes.co.jp/community/2012/05/22/voices/the-elephant-in-the-foreigners-room-now-has-a-name-microaggression/#.WIbxgRiZN-U.

Berger, Peter L. 1970. On the Obsolescence of the Concept of Honor. *European Journal of Sociology* 11: 339–347.

Black, Donald. 1976. *The Behavior of Law.* San Diego: Academic Press.

———. 2011. *Moral Time.* New York: Oxford University Press.

Boysen, Guy A. 2012. Teacher and Student Perceptions of Microaggressions in Classrooms. *College Teaching* 60 (3): 122–129.

Burchill, Julie. 2015. Meet the Cry-Bully: A Hideous Hybrid of Victim and Victor. *The Spectator*, April 21. http://blogs.spectator.co.uk/2015/04/meet-the-cry-bully-a-hideous-hybrid-of-victim-and-victor/.

Chait, Jonathan. 2015. Not a Very P.C. Thing to Say: How the Language Police Are Perverting Liberalism. *New York Magazine*, January 27. http://nymag.com/daily/intelligencer/2015/01/not-a-very-pc-thing-to-say.html.

Chasmar, Jessica. 2016. Milo Yiannopoulos Banned from DePaul University for Creating 'Hostile Environment' During May Speech. *Washington Times*, July 7. http://www.washingtontimes.com/news/2016/jul/7/milo-yiannopoulos-banned-from-depaul-university-fo/.

Cohen, Dov, Richard E. Nisbett, Brian F. Bowdle, and Norbert Schwarz. 1996. Insult, Aggression, and the Southern Culture of Honor: An 'Experimental Ethnography'. *Journal of Personality and Social Psychology* 70 (5): 945–996.

Cooney, Mark. 1998. *Warriors and Peacemakers: How Third Parties Shape Violence.* New York: New York University Press.

———. 2009. *Is Killing Wrong?: A Study in Pure Sociology.* Charlottesville: University of Virginia Press.

———. 2014a. Family Honour and Social Time. *The Sociological Review* 62 (S2): 87–106.

———. 2014b. Death by Family: Honor Violence as Punishment. *Punishment & Society* 16 (4): 406–427.

Coyne, Jeremy A. 2015. Halloween-Costume Fracas Spreads to My University. *Why Evolution is True* (blog). https://whyevolutionistrue.wordpress.com/ 2015/11/18/halloween-costume-fracas-spreads-to-my-university/.

Davoran, Erin. 2015. Guest Column: Women Can't Be Sexist. *The Post.* http:// www.thepostathens.com/opinion/guest-column-women-can-t-be-sexist/ article_5c378728-cb5b-11e4-a44d-27a1b52d655c.html?mode=jqm.

Dean-Johnson, Liam, Aidan Dunbar, Anastasiya Gorodilova, Nico Sedivy, and Madison Shiver. 2015. Dean-Jonson '16, Dunbar '16, Gorodilova '16, Sedivy '17, Shiver '17: On Whiteness, Free Speech and Missing the Point. *The Brown Daily Herald,* October 19. http://www.browndailyherald.com/2015/10/19/ dean-johnson-16-dunbar-16-gorodilova-16-sedivy-17-shiver-17-on-whiten-ess-free-speech-and-missing-the-point/.

Dicken, Brad. 2013. Report of KKK Cancels Oberlin College Classes, Sparks Solidarity Events. *The Chronicle,* March 5. http://www.chroniclet.com/ news/2013/03/05/Report-of-KKK-cancels-Oberlin-College-classes-sparks-solidarity-events.html.

Dillon, Kassy. 2016. The Fempire Strikes Back: Anti-Milo 'Triggering' Activist Targeted Student Journalist. *Heat Street,* May 12. http://heatst.com/culture-wars/fempire-strikes-back-anti-milo-triggering-sjw-targeted-student-journalist/.

Durkheim, Emile. 1982. *The Rules of the Sociological Method and Selected Texts on Sociology and Its Method.* New York: Free Press.

Elias, Norbert. 1982. *The Civilizing Process,* Volume II, *Power and Civility.* Trans. Edmund Jephcott. New York: Pantheon Books.

Elsbach, Kimberly D., and Robert I. Sutton. 1992. Acquiring Institutional Legitimacy Through Illegitimate Actions: A Marriage of Institutional and Impression Management Theories. *Academy of Management Journal* 35 (4): 699–738.

Engel, David M. 1984. The Oven Bird's Song: Insiders, Outsiders, and Personal Injuries in an American Community. *Law and Society Review* 18 (4): 551–582.

Etzioni, Amitai. 2014. Don't Sweat the Microaggressions. *The Atlantic*, April 8. http://www.theatlantic.com/politics/archive/2014/04/dont-sweat-the-microaggressions/360278/.

Fisher, Anne. 2015. How Microaggressions Can Wreck Your Business. *Fortune*, November 19. http://fortune.com/2015/11/19/microaggressions-talent-business/.

Flaherty, Colleen. 2013. In-Class Sit-In. *Inside Higher Ed*, November 25. https://www.insidehighered.com/news/2013/11/25/ucla-grad-students-stage-sit-during-class-protest-what-they-see-racially-hostile.

Fricke, Peter, and Anthony Gockowski. 2016. UMass Amherst Students Throw Temper Tantrum at Free Speech Event. *Campus Reform*, April 26. http://www.campusreform.org/?ID=7528.

Friedersdorf, Conor. 2015a. The Rise of Victimhood Culture. *The Atlantic*, September 11. http://www.theatlantic.com/politics/archive/2015/09/the-rise-of-victimhood-culture/404794/.

———. 2015b. Why Critics of the 'Microaggressions' Framework Are Skeptical. *The Atlantic*, September 14. http://www.theatlantic.com/politics/archive/2015/09/why-critics-of-the-microaggressions-framework-are-skeptical/405106/.

———. 2015c. Readers Lament the Rise of Victimhood Culture. *The Atlantic*, September 18. http://www.theatlantic.com/politics/archive/2015/09/readers-lament-the-rise-of-victimhood-culture/405784/.

———. 2015d. Is 'Victimhood Culture' a Fair Description? *The Atlantic*, September 19. http://www.theatlantic.com/politics/archive/2015/09/the-problems-with-the-term-victimhood-culture/406057/.

Furedi, Frank. 2015. Microaggression Theory: An Assault on Everyday Life. *Spiked*, November 23. http://www.spiked-online.com/newsite/article/microaggression-theory-an-assault-on-everyday-life/17658#.WH5XNbHMx-U.

Gallant, Thomas W. 2000. Honor, Masculinity, and Ritual Knife Fighting in Nineteenth-Century Greece. *The American Historical Review* 105 (2): 359–382.

Gaude, Eddie S., Jr. 2015. What Happened in Missouri Puts the Nation on Notice. *Time*, November 10. http://time.com/4106572/missouri-more-student-protests/.

Greenhouse, Carol J., Barbara Yngvesson, and David M. Engel. 1994. *Law and Community in Three American Towns*. Ithaca: Cornell University Press.

Haidt, Jonathan. 2017. The Unwisest Idea on Campus: Commentary on Lilienfeld. *Perspectives on Psychological Science* 12 (1): 176–177.

Hall, Allan. 2015. 'I'm Too Young to Die': Chilling Last Words of Gang Rape Victim 'Butchered by Her Own Family in Honour Killing.' *Mirror*, October 7. http://www.mirror.co.uk/news/world-news/im-young-die-chilling-last-6589673.

Hampson, Sarah. 2016. Derald Wing Sue on Microaggression, the Implicit Racism Minorities Endure. *The Globe and Mail*, July 8. http://www.theglobeandmail. com/life/relationships/derald-wing-sue-on-microaggressions-racism/ article30821500/.

Harris, Rafael S., Jr. 2008. Racial Microaggression? How Do You Know? *American Psychologist* 63: 275–276.

Harsanyi, David. 2015. 'Where Are You from?' and Other Unspeakable Acts of Bigotry. *The Federalist*, July 2. http://thefederalist.com/2015/07/02/ where-are-you-from-and-other-unspeakable-acts-of-bigotry/.

Hartocollis, Anemona, and Jess Bidgood. 2015. Racial Discrimination Protests Ignite at Colleges Across the US. *The New York Times*, November 11. http:// www.nytimes.com/2015/11/12/us/racial-discrimination-protests-ignite-at-colleges-across-the-us.html?_r=1.

Hasson, Peter. 2015. Updated: Clemson University Apologizes for Serving Mexican Food. *Campus Reform*, October 9. http://www.campusreform. org/?ID=6873.

Hookstead, David. 2015. Wisconsin University Dubs 'America Is a Melting Pot' a Racial Microaggression. *The College Fix*, June 30. http://www.thecollegefix. com/post/23135/.

I Too Am Sydney (Tumbler site). 2014. http://itooamsydney.tumblr.com/page/3.

Jarvie, Jennie. 2014. Trigger Happy. *The New Republic*, March 3. https://newre-public.com/article/116842/trigger-warnings-have-spread-blogs-college-classes-thats-bad.

Jaschik, Scott. 2016. Mandatory Microaggression Training. *Inside Higher Education*, November 2. https://www.insidehighered.com/news/2016/11/02/suffolk-responding-controversy-over-treatment-latina-student-require-microaggression.

Kabbany, Jennifer. 2015. Do Not Miss This Epic Foray into Microaggression Madness. *The College Fix*, September 25. http://www.thecollegefix.com/ post/24370/.

Kimball, Roger. 2015. The Rise of the College Crybullies. *Wall Street Journal*, November 13. http://www.wsj.com/articles/the-rise-of-the-college-crybullies-1447458587.

Korn, Sandra Y.L. 2014. The Doctrine of Academic Freedom. *The Harvard Crimson*, February 18. http://www.thecrimson.com/column/the-red-line/ article/2014/2/18/academic-freedom-justice/?page=single#.

Leovy, Jill. 2015. *Ghettoside: A True Story of Murder in America*. New York: Spiegel & Grau.

Leung, Angela K.Y., and Dov Cohen. 2011. Within- and Between-Culture Variation: Individual Differences and the Cultural Logics of Honor, Face, and Dignity Cultures. *Journal of Personality and Social Psychology* 100 (3): 507–526.

Lieber, Ron. 2014. Four Stand-Out College Essays About Money. *The New York Times*, May 9. https://www.nytimes.com/2014/05/10/your-money/four-stand-out-college-essays-about-money.html.

Lilienfeld, Scott O. 2017. Microaggressions: Strong Claims, Inadequate Evidence. *Perspectives on Psychological Science* 12 (1): 138–169.

Lukianoff, Greg, and Jonathan Haidt. 2015. The Coddling of the American Mind. *The Atlantic*, September. http://www.theatlantic.com/magazine/archive/2015/09/the-coddling-of-the-american-mind/399356/.

Margolis, Jacob. 2015. Claremont McKenna College Update: Dean Resigns After Protests. *89.3 KPPC*, November 12. http://www.scpr.org/news/2015/11/12/55617/claremont-mckenna-college-dean-resigns-after-stude/.

McArdle, Megan. 2015. How Grown-Ups Deal with Microaggressions. *Bloomberg View*, September 11. http://www.bloombergview.com/articles/2015-09-11/how-grown-ups-deal-with-microaggressions-.

McKay, Brett H. 2016. *What Is Honor?: And How to Revive It*, Kindle Edition. Jenks: Semper Virilis Publishing. Jenks: Oklahoma.

McWhorter, John. 2014. 'Microaggression' Is the New Racism on Campus. *Time*, March 21. http://time.com/32618/microaggression-is-the-new-racism-on-campus/.

Medina, Jennifer. 2014. Warning: The Literary Canon Could Make Students Squirm. *The New York Times*, May 17. http://www.nytimes.com/2014/05/18/us/warning-the-literary-canon-could-make-students-squirm.html.

Melchior, Jillian Kay. 2016a. New at University of Wisconsin-Madison This Fall: Microaggression Training for Freshmen. *Heat Street*, June 21. https://heatst.com/culture-wars/new-at-university-of-wisconson-madison-this-fall-microaggression-training-for-freshman/.

———. 2016b. Ben Shapiro Threatened by Violent Mob, Called Nazi, at Cal State Diversity Speech. *Heat Street*, July 31. http://heatst.com/culture-wars/exclusive-ben-shapiro-threatened-by-violent-vitriolic-mob-called-a-nazi-at-his-cal-state-la-speech-on-diversity/.

Meyer, Michael J. 1989. Dignity, Rights, and Self-Control. *Ethics* 99 (3): 520–534.

Moyer, Justin Wm. 2015a. 'Sweat Shaming': A Woman's Workout Humiliation. *Washington Post*, October 1. http://www.washingtonpost.com/news/morning-mix/wp/2015/10/01/sweat-shaming-a-womans-workout-humiliation/.

———. 2015b. University Yoga Class Cancelled Because of 'Oppression, Cultural Genocide.' *Washington Post*, November 23. https://www.washingtonpost.com/news/morning-mix/wp/2015/11/23/university-yoga-class-canceled-because-of-oppression-cultural-genocide/?utm_term=.bed283538fb1.

Mukhopadhyay, Samhita. 2015. Stop Complaining About Victimhood Culture. *Al Jazeera America*, October 8. http://america.aljazeera.com/opinions/2015/10/stop-complaining-about-victimhood-culture.html.

Nadal, Kevin L., Julie Sriken, Kristin C. Davidoff, Yinglee Wong, and Kathryn McLean. 2013. Microaggressions Within Families: Experiences of Multiracial People. *Family Relations* 62 (1): 190–201.

Neff, Blake. 2015. University Officer: Minority Women Can't Be Racist. *The Daily Caller*, May 12. http://dailycaller.com/2015/05/12/university-diversity-officer-minority-women-cant-be-racist/.

Nelson, Libby. 2015a. Obama on Liberal College Students Who Want to Be 'Coddled': 'That's Not the Way We Learn.' *Vox*, September 14. http://www.vox.com/2015/9/14/9326965/obama-political-correctness.

Nelson, Steven. 2015b. Missouri Police Solicit Reports on 'Hurtful' Speech, Startling Scholars. *US News and World Report*, November 11. http://www.usnews.com/news/articles/2015/11/11/missouri-police-solicit-reports-on-hurtful-speech-startling-scholars.

Nisbett, Richard E., and Dov Cohen. 1996. *Culture of Honor: The Psychology of Violence in the South*. Boulder: Westview Press.

Nye, Robert A. 1993. *Codes of Honor in Modern France*. New York: Oxford University Press.

Oberlin Microaggressions (blog). 2017. http://obiemicroaggressions.tumblr.com.

Peters, Mark. 2013. Shame on Everyone. *Slate*, October 20. http://www.slate.com/articles/life/the_good_word/2013/10/stop_calling_all_criticism_shaming.html.

Phillips, Adam. 2014. #BlackLivesMatter: Why We Need to Stop Replying All Lives Matter. *Sojourners*, December 4. https://sojo.net/articles/blacklivesmatter-why-we-need-stop-replying-all-lives-matter.

Pinker, Steven. 2011. *The Better Angels of Our Nature: Why Violence Has Declined*. New York: Viking.

Popp, Evan. 2015. IC SGA Passes Bill to Create System to Report Microaggressions. *The Ithacan*, March 18. http://theithacan.org/news/ic-sga-passes-bill-to-create-system-to-report-microaggressions/.

Richardson, Bradford. 2016. Michael Bloomberg Booed at University of Michigan for Ripping into 'Safe Spaces.' *Washington Times*, May 2. http://www.washingtontimes.com/news/2016/may/2/michael-bloomberg-booed-university-michigan-rippin/.

Rosen, Michael. 2012. *Dignity: Its History and Meaning*. Cambridge: Harvard University Press.

Ross, Chuck. 2013. Meet the Privileged Obama-Supporting White Kids Who Perpetrated Cruel Oberlin Race Hoax. *The Daily Caller*, August 22. http://dailycaller.com/2013/08/22/meet-the-privileged-obama-supporting-white-kids-who-perpetrated-cruel-oberlin-race-hoax/.

Runyowa, Simba. 2015. Microaggressions Matter. *The Atlantic*, September 18. http://www.theatlantic.com/politics/archive/2015/09/microaggressions-matter/406090/.

Saul, Stephanie. 2016. Campuses Cautiously Train Freshman Against Subtle Insults. *New York Times*, September 6. https://www.nytimes.com/2016/09/07/us/campuses-cautiously-train-freshmen-against-subtle-insults.html?_r=1.

Schwartz, Howard S. 2016. Microaggressions and the 'Pristine Self.' *National Association of Scholars* website, February 24. https://www.nas.org/articles/microaggressions_and_the_pristine_self.

Schwyzer, Hugo. 2006. 'Narratives of Suffering Overcome': Admissions Essays and a Lamentable Trend. *History News Network*, November 27. http://m.hnn.us/blog/32280.

Seitz, Don C. 1929. *Famous American Duels*. New York: Thomas Y. Crowell Company.

Severn, Ruth. 2015. Departments State Support for Student Group, Group Calls for Wolfe's Resignation. *Missourian*, October 21. http://www.columbiamissourian.com/news/higher_education/departments-state-support-for-student-group-group-calls-for-wolfe/article_c46ec73e-7849-11e5-9edf-cf7d6918f57f.html.

Shackel, Nicholas. 2005. The Vacuity of Postmodernist Methodology. *Metaphilosophy* 36: 295–320.

Shieber, Jonathan. 2015. Email Messages to Authors, May 1, May 11, and June 17.

Shimshock, Rob. 2016. UNC Claims Christmas Vacations, Golf Outings Are Microaggressions. *Campus Reform*, June 24. http://www.campusreform.org/?ID=7751.

Shulevitz, Judith. 2015. In College and Hiding from Scary Ideas. *New York Times*, March 21. https://www.nytimes.com/2015/03/22/opinion/sunday/judith-shulevitz-hiding-from-scary-ideas.html?_r=0.

Snow, David A. 1979. A Dramaturgical Analysis of Movement Accommodation: Building Idiosyncrasy Credit as a Movement Mobilization Strategy. *Symbolic Interaction* 2: 23–24.

Soave, Robby. 2015a. Exclusive: Occidental Professors Voting to Give Power to Students to Report Them for Microaggression. *Reason*, November 23. https://reason.com/blog/2015/11/23/exclusive-occidental-faculty-voting-to-g.

———. 2015b. Emory Students Want Professors Evaluated on Number of Microaggressions They Commit. *Reason*, December 14. http://reason.com/blog/2015/12/14/emory-students-want-professors-evaluated.

Stanley-Becker, Isaac. 2015. Hundreds March at Yale in Solidarity with Minority Students. *The Washington Post*, November 9. https://www.washingtonpost.com/news/grade-point/wp/2015/11/09/hundreds-march-at-yale-in-solidarity-with-minority-students/.

Sue, Derald Wing. 2010. *Microaggressions in Everyday Life: Race, Gender, and Sexual Orientation*. Hoboken: Wiley and Sons.

Sue, Derald Wing, Christina M. Capodilupo, Gina C. Torino, Jennifer M. Bucceri, Aisha M.B. Holder, Kevin L. Nadal, and Marta Esquilin. 2007. Racial Microaggressions in Everyday Life: Implications for Clinical Practice. *American Psychologist* 62(4): 271–286.

Sue, Derald Wing, Kevin L. Nadal, Christina M. Capodilupo, Annie I. Lin, Gina C. Torino, and David P. Rivera. 2008. Racial Microaggressions Against Black Americans: Implications for Counseling. *Journal of Counseling and Development* 86: 330–338.

Tanksley, Jim. 2015. Letter to the Editor. *Los Angeles Times*, November 15. http://www.latimes.com/opinion/readersreact/la-le-1115-sunday-microaggression--20151115-story.html.

Thomas, Kenneth R. 2008. Macrononsense in Multiculturalism. *American Psychologist* 63: 274–275.

University of California. 2014. Tool: Recognizing Microaggressions and the Messages They Send. *Diversity in the Classroom, UCLA Diversity and Faculty Development.* http://academicaffairs.ucsc.edu/events/documents/Microaggressions_Examples_Arial_2014_11_12.pdf.

Vandello, Joseph A., and Dov Cohen. 2003. Male Honor and Female Fidelity: Implicit Cultural Scripts that Perpetuate Domestic Violence. *Journal of Personality and Social Psychology* 84 (5): 997–1010.

Vidich, Arthur J., and Joseph Bensman. 1958. *Small Town in Mass Society: Class, Power, and Religion in a Rural Community.* Garden City: Anchor Books.

Volokh, Eugene. 2015. UC Teaching Faculty Members Not to Criticize Race-Based Affirmative Action, Call America 'Melting Pot,' and More. *Washington Post*, June 16. https://www.washingtonpost.com/news/volokh-conspiracy/wp/2015/06/16/uc-teaching-faculty-members-not-to-criticize-race-based-affirmative-action-call-america-melting-pot-and-more/?utm_term=.5987eb7290d1.

Von Jettmar, Dieter F.A. 2012. Take 'Aggressors' Along a Tangent [Letter to the editor]. *The Japan Times*, May 22. http://www.japantimes.co.jp/community/2012/05/22/voices/the-elephant-in-the-foreigners-room-now-has-a-name-microaggression/#.WIbxgRiZN-U.

Watanabe, Teresa, and Jason Song. 2015. College Students Confront Subtler Forms of Bias: Slights and Snubs. *Los Angeles Times*, November 12. http://www.latimes.com/local/education/la-me-college-microaggression-20151112-story.html.

Weber, Max. 1958. Science as a Vocation. In *From Max Weber: Essays in Sociology*, ed. H.H. Gerth and C. Wright Mills, 129–156. New York: Oxford University Press.

Wells, Catharine. 2013. Microaggressions in the Context of Academic Communities. *Seattle Journal for Social Justice* 12 (2): 319–348.

Williams, Jack K. 1980. *Dueling in the Old South: Vignettes of Social History.* College Station: Texas A&M University Press.

Woldoff, Rachael A., and Karen G. Weiss. 2010. 'Stop Snitchin': Exploring Definitions of the Snitch and Implications for Urban Black Communities. *Journal of Criminal Justice and Popular Culture* 17 (1): 184–223.

Worland, Justin. 2015. Why Free Speech Fight Is Causing Protests at Yale. *Time*, November 10. http://time.com/4106265/yale-students-protest/.

Wythe, Philip. 2014. Trigger Warnings Needed in Classroom. *The Daily Targum*, February 18. http://www.dailytargum.com/article/2014/02/trigger-warnings-needed-in-classroom.

Zamudio-Suarez. 2016. What Happens When Your Research Is Featured on 'Fox & Friends.' *Chronicle of Higher Education*, June 29. http://www.chronicle.com/article/What-Happens-When-Your/236949.

Zanotti, Emily. 2016. DePaul Threatens to Arrest Ben Shapiro for Stepping Foot on Campus. *Heat Street*, November 16. http://heatst.com/culture-wars/watch-depaul-threatens-to-arrest-ben-shapiro-for-stepping-foot-on-campus/.

CHAPTER 2

Microaggression and the Structure of Victimhood

In 1804 US Vice President Aaron Burr challenged former Treasury Secretary Alexander Hamilton to a duel. Burr had long-standing grievances against his political opponent Hamilton, and the final straw was the evidence that Hamilton had privately expressed a "despicable opinion" of Burr. In an exchange of letters Burr questioned Hamilton about the statement and reminded him of the "necessity of rigid adherence to the laws of honour" (Seitz 1929:83). Hamilton neither denied nor apologized for the harsh words, so Burr issued the challenge. Hamilton was reluctant, writing that his "moral and religious principles" were "strongly opposed to the practice of dueling" (quoted in Seitz 1929:98). But he also thought that if he failed to live up to the code of honor, he would greatly damage himself and his family, and ultimately his fear of public disapproval led him to agree to a duel with pistols. The duel took place on the morning of June 27, and Hamilton was mortally wounded.

The reaction to the duel was not what either man was expecting. Burr, the man acting to preserve his honor, was vilified as a murderer. A public outcry against dueling emerged, and new legislation was passed to curtail it. Though both men participated in the duel to defend their public reputation, in the end the duel was treated as a crime rather than a test of virtue.

The incident shows how different moral systems clash and how changes in moral culture can catch people unaware. We see similar cases today, as people striving to act in ways that would seem virtuous according to the norms of dignity culture are vilified in a culture of victimhood. Consider again a case mentioned in Chap. 1—that of the controversial email from

© The Author(s) 2018
B. Campbell, J. Manning, *The Rise of Victimhood Culture*,
https://doi.org/10.1007/978-3-319-70329-9_2

former Yale headmaster Erika Christakis. In the email, written in response to the administration's guidelines for avoiding offensive Halloween costumes, Christakis stated that she did not want to "trivialize" concerns, but that she endorsed the freedom of college students to choose their own costumes without official supervision, suggesting that they are mature enough to "talk to each other" and handle offensive behavior through "self-censure" and "social norming" (Christakis 2015). Had we been privy to this email before it was sent out, we might have imagined Professor Christakis being celebrated by students for defending their autonomy and maturity. Instead she was vilified, and her communication sparked public demonstrations and calls for officials to dismiss both her and her husband from their posts.

These kinds of conflicts illustrate the different moral cultures we outlined in the previous chapter. The clash between dignity and victimhood engenders moral confusion on campuses today, just as clashes of honor and dignity have in other settings. Whenever contradictory moral ideals exist alongside one another, people may be unsure how to act, not confident of whether others will praise or condemn them. One person's standard provokes another's grievance, and unintentional offenses abound. Those whose morality is rooted in the ideals of dignity thus see microaggression complainants and others who highlight their victimhood as thin-skinned, uncharitable, and perhaps delusional, while those who draw from the newer morality of victimhood see their critics as insensitive, privileged, and perhaps bigoted.

But while our framework gives us a way of making sense of these debates, it does not explain why moral cultures differ in the first place. Why do people condemn what they condemn and praise what they praise? Why do they handle their conflicts in some ways but not others? Why do moral cultures differ, and why do they change over time?

Moral cultures are not simply free-floating ideas occurring at random. They are the product of social conditions. In this chapter we identify the social context that gives rise to microaggression complaints and to victimhood culture more broadly. In doing so we draw from sociologist Donald Black's theories of conflict.

The Sociology of Conflict

Conflict occurs whenever anyone has a grievance against someone else (Black 1998:xiii). It exists whenever someone treats someone else's conduct as wrong—rude, immoral, evil, inappropriate, insane, criminal, negligent, or otherwise objectionable. Conflict in this sense occurs all the time, in all human relationships. People complain that their spouse is not attentive enough, that their roommates do not do their share of the cleaning, that an acquaintance says mean things, or that the clerk at the store gave them a dirty look. They might condemn violence, theft, lying, insults, blasphemy, greed, laziness, failure to pay back debts, and many other things. And they might react to these grievances in many different ways. In Black's terminology, these reactions are called *social control*. Social control can range from mild reactions, like rolling your eyes to express displeasure at an irritating statement, to responses that are much more dramatic and severe, like executing a criminal or assassinating a political leader. It can take the form of giving someone the cold shoulder or reporting a crime to the police, yelling at an adversary or calmly negotiating some solution to the problem. These are all ways of handling conflict, all instances of social control (Black 1976, 1998).

Conflict and social control are extremely diverse. People have grievances over a variety of things, and they handle these grievances in a variety of ways. Furthermore, conflict and social control vary enormously across different social settings. One society might treat heresy as a serious crime and punish anyone who expresses the wrong religious ideas, while another society enshrines freedom of religion and punishes anyone who would try to suppress heresy. In one society it might be common to handle a murder by starting a blood feud against the killer's family, while in another society murder is a matter for the police and courts. And even within the same society, conflict and social control vary across social classes, subcultures, and relationships.

Black's theories of conflict and social control help us explain all of this. The fundamental insight of these theories is that the nature of conflict depends on its *social structure*—that is, with the social characteristics and relationships between everyone involved in the conflict (Black 1995). People who are intimate with one another, like spouses, tend to fight about different things than strangers do, and they tend to handle their conflicts in different ways. People tend to express grievances toward those of higher status—such as their employers—differently than they express them toward those of lower status—such as their employees. High-status people like the wealthy and educated also handle conflicts among themselves differently than do low-status people, such as poor minorities. And social control between people from the same cultural background is often different from social control between people with different religions or ethnicities.

The key to explaining conflict and social control is to specify the exact nature of these differences. For example, in Black's early work on *law*, or governmental social control, he claims that conflicts between strangers are more likely to be handled with law, and with a greater degree of law, than conflicts between people who are close to one another (Black 1976:Chapter 2, 1989:11–13). Thus, someone assaulted by a stranger is more likely to call the police than someone assaulted by an acquaintance, and homicides between strangers get punished more severely than homicides between acquaintances. By specifying which social factors encourage which kinds of conflict and social control, we can make sense of variation across place and time. Social settings with lots of intimacy—small villages, tight-knit neighborhoods, and so forth—will have much of the kind of social control that is common among intimates and little of what is common among strangers. For instance, according to Black's theory of law, we should not expect to see much reliance on lawsuits and police in such settings; instead we should see people handling conflicts in a more private fashion. Following this logic, understanding the influence of social conditions on conflict can help us explain why different times and places develop different moral cultures.

What social conditions produce a moral culture filled with microaggression complaints and related forms of behavior? In other words, what accounts for the rise of victimhood culture? To answer this we need to start by identifying the ways microaggression complaints are similar to and different from other ways of handling conflict. First of all, they involve the public airing of grievances—complaining to outsiders. In this way microaggression complaints belong to a larger class of conflict tactics in which people who have grievances appeal to third parties. Second, microaggression complaints are attempts to demonstrate a pattern of injustice, and in this way they belong to a class of tactics by which people persuade reluctant third parties that their cause is just and they badly need help. And third, microaggression complaints are complaints about the domination and oppression of cultural minorities. Each of these three features of microaggression complaints occurs under particular social conditions, and identifying those conditions gets us a long way toward explaining victimhood culture. Let us address them one by one, then, starting with a look at the conditions leading to appeals to third parties.

CONFLICT AND THIRD PARTIES

We can usually divide a conflict into two major sides: the aggrieved (the one who takes offense at someone's behavior) and the offender (the one whose behavior has offended someone). Third parties are all others who might enter the conflict, whether they just passively witness, try to make peace, or wind up taking sides.

Much of the social control that occurs in day-to-day life involves only the aggrieved and the offender.[1] Microaggression complaints are usually different, however. When people post accounts of microaggressions on websites, or when they report them to campus administrators, they are publicly airing their grievances to people who might otherwise be unaware of them. In doing so they recruit other people to join the conflict. And they sometimes do so with the stated purpose of compelling further action—motivating either the general public or the authorities to take action against wrongdoing. Like gossipers, protesters, litigants, and so many others, they seek to attract the attention, sympathy, or intervention of third parties.

Gossip, Protest, and Complaint to Authority

Of the many ways people bring their grievances to the attention of others, perhaps the most common is to complain privately to family, friends, co-workers, and acquaintances. This is *gossip*—"evaluative talk about a person who is not present" (Eder and Enke 1991:494; compare Black 1995:855, n. 129; Hannerz 1967:36; Merry 1984:275). While we may not usually think of gossip as a way of handling conflict, it is surely one of the most common ways of expressing grievances in everyday life. Gossip is ubiquitous, and as anthropologist Max Gluckman points out, "for a large part of each day, most of us are engaged in gossip" (Gluckman 1963:308). The people we gossip about are often unaware of our complaints, but the complaints still qualify as a form of social control in the sense we use that term here. Gossipers may even conduct a kind of trial in absentia (Black 1995:855, n.129). And like a real trial gossip might lead to further sanctions, as when gossipers decide to avoid and exclude someone.

Most gossip occurs in intimate settings between people who are personally acquainted (Merry 1984; Black 1995:855, n.129; see, e.g., Vidich and

---

[1] Those who deem someone's conduct deviant or offensive might deal with it in a number of ways without involving others. They could use direct aggression, verbally berating or physically assaulting the offender. They could exercise covert avoidance, quietly cutting off relations with the offender without any confrontation or complaint. Or they could treat the problem as a disruption to their relationship and seek only to restore harmony without passing judgment. There are many ways to handle conflict without having a third party actively involved. Oftentimes other people will never even know that the conflict took place (Black 1998:Chapter 5).

Bensman 1958:45–46).[2] But not all complaints to third parties are as private as gossip; sometimes people broadcast their grievances to a wide audience. Often such complaints are not merely grievances about one individual offending another, but the shared grievances of some social group, such as a political faction, workers' union, or ethnic group. In such cases people might seek the attention and sympathy of third parties through various forms of protest, such as rallies, strikes, and marches. These actions not only express grievances directly to the adversary, but also communicate information to third parties (Gibbs 1989:332, n. 4; Reiss 2007:2–3).[3]

Another kind of third party involvement occurs when people bring their complaints to authorities. Small children, for example, often bring their complaints to adults. One sociological study of a day care center found the majority of disputes between children ended with the intervention of a teacher, often in response to a direct request from the child (Baumgartner 1992:7). Adults might likewise turn to authorities. They might complain to a boss about an intolerable coworker, perhaps resulting in the offender being reprimanded, demoted, transferred, or fired. Or they might take their complaints before the state by filing lawsuits, calling the police, or otherwise mobilizing the legal system against their adversaries.[4]

Social Structure and Moral Dependency

What makes people more likely to take their grievances to third parties? And why do they express grievances in public or to authorities rather than keeping them confined to private gossip?

---

[2] Anthropologist Sally Engle Merry distinguishes private gossip from *scandal*—something that exists when "gossip is elevated to a public arena" (Merry 1984:275).

[3] Consider a description of the activities of New England Resistance, an American activist organization that campaigned against military conscription during the Vietnam War: "Demonstrations, draft card turn-ins, marches, and sanctuaries were public events which set participants (who in a sense became performers) apart from onlookers or media audiences. These events were not intended to be passively watched or consumed; they were partly staged for persuasive effect, to force people to take sides and thereby enlist them in the protest cause" (Thorne 1975:118).

[4] Such authorities might intervene as mediators, trying to bring about some peaceful and mutually agreeable resolution to the conflict. Police and court clerks, for instance, often handle disputes informally, attempting to pacify the disputants rather than making an arrest or arranging a formal hearing (Black 1980:Chapter 5; Greenhouse et al. 1994:55–90). Or they might respond authoritatively, subjecting offenders to punishment or forcing them to pay compensation for damages. However they ultimately end up handling the case, complaining to authorities—legal or otherwise—is a common response to conflict.

One major factor is the presence of authorities, such as legal authorities. The importance of authorities is not simply a matter of people being unable to complain to them if they do not exist. Social settings with strong and stable authority systems actively discourage competing forms of social control. This can be seen most clearly in the historical development of law.

Not all societies have had governments capable of policing misconduct. For most of human history people lived in small bands of hunter-gatherers which, to judge from anthropological studies of hunter-gatherer groups that survive in modern times, had no official or permanent leaders of any kind (Boehm 1999; Lenski et al. 1995:Chapter 5). If by law we mean governmental social control, these societies were lawless (Black 1976:Chapter 7). State governments with full-time leaders and a hierarchy of officials emerged only with the development of intensive agriculture 10,000 years ago. States have since spread around the globe, with the last large stateless populations (the peoples of the New Guinea Highlands) falling under government authority in the twentieth century. But even in areas that have long had governments, the state's ability to enforce law has grown over time. Most premodern states lacked anything resembling the massive bureaucracy of the modern state or its extensive legal system. And without modern technology for communication and travel, states were less able to penetrate the lives of their subjects, to learn about wrongdoing, pursue offenders, or enforce regulations (Elias 1982). Law is a matter of degree, and earlier societies had less of it. Even strong states like Imperial Rome had comparatively little law at the local level, particularly in areas distant from the centers of power. Weak or fragmented governments, like the feudal system in medieval Europe, had much less (Elias 1982).

When law is weak or absent, how do people handle wrongdoing? How do they respond to theft, assault, and other offenses? In times and places where people cannot count on the legal system to protect their persons and property, they often rely on violent aggression to defend themselves and punish offenders. Students of law and social control refer to this kind of aggression as *self-help* because the aggrieved parties take matters into their own hands rather than relying on a legal system (Black 1998:74).[5] One of the most dramatic manifestations of self-help is vengeance killing, which may spark a cycle of retaliatory killings in the form of a blood feud—two different kinship groups exchanging killings over time, a life for a life

[5] This usage goes back to before the term was closely associated with books on self-improvement.

(Black 2004). Stateless societies have a great deal of vengeance and other kinds of self-help, and thus high rates of violence.[6]

When societies develop state governments, or have state governments imposed on them through conquest or colonization, one of the first things the state does is to suppress violent self-help among it subjects. First to go are the more extreme forms of self-help such as feuding and raiding between different families or local communities (Cooney 1998: Chapter 3, 2009:7–10; Pinker 2011:31–36). This can happen relatively suddenly, as when Australian authorities used the threat of legal punishment to quickly suppress vengeance killing among New Guinea tribesmen (Cooney 1998:52–54; Diamond 2013:Chapter 4). But it can also unfold over time, as states grow larger, stronger, and are able to assume more control over their subjects. Thus, violence in Europe steadily declined as the loose patchwork of warring feudal lords gave way to centralized monarchies and eventually modern bureaucratic states (Cooney 1998:Chapter 3; Elias 1982; Pinker 2011:Chapters 2–3). The growth of law led to a decline in violence.

But the state does not stop at deterring vengeance and feuding. In medieval England, as in other locations, the growing state began by out-lawing private vengeance, using the threat of punishment to compel aggrieved individuals or families to handle offenses—including homicide—through peaceful negotiation and compensation. The offense was still a private matter, however, with the state's role being only to discourage vengeance and ratify private justice. Gradually the state moved beyond this passive role, increasingly claiming that it alone had the right to handle any conflicts severe enough to merit punishment or compensation. It was the state that ultimately decided the right and wrong of the case and levied the appropriate sanctions (Cooney 2009:8–9).

Thus, the state increasingly dominated the handling of conflict and discouraged private justice.

Law tends to supplant other mechanisms of social control—not just extremely violent ones like vengeance killings, but also peaceful means such as negotiated compromise and informal mediation (Black 1976:107). Alternatives to law—good, bad, or ugly—flourish where law is weak or

[6]For example, detailed studies of hunter-gatherer groups, stateless farming societies in New Guinea and the Amazon, and the remains found at prehistorical archeological sites all indicate that stateless societies have drastically higher rates of violent killing than state societies (Cooney 1998:Chapter 3; Diamond 2013:Chapters 2–4; Pinker 2011:Chapter 2).

absent, and they decline where law is strong and readily available. The growth of law can lead people to increasingly depend on law alone, reducing their willingness or ability to solve conflicts through other means. This can produce a condition that Black calls *legal overdependency* (Black 1989:77).

The highest degrees of legal overdependency occur in totalitarian societies, such as Nazi Germany or the Soviet Union. In these settings law is omnipresent, and "the rank and file members of society … can and do use the state freely for the settlement of private disputes" (Gross 1984:67). For instance, the Soviet state encouraged its citizens to denounce one another, and it was common for citizens to write letters denouncing others for alleged disloyalty, origin in a stigmatized social class, or personal misconduct (Gross 1982, 1984; Fitzpatrick 1996). The state was "very responsive to denunciations," and thus "always vulnerable to manipulation by denunciation writers with personal agendas" (Fitzpatrick 1996:853). All manner of personal grievances might lead people to denounce their fellows: "For example, the wife of a biologist denounced a powerful communist in the same profession as 'a vulgarian who pulls the wool over people's eyes, a pitiful scientific pigmy, a plagiarist and compiler'" while "the agitprop files in Moscow contain many letters from leading actors, actresses, and opera singers denouncing the theater directors who had insulted them and failed to give them appropriate roles" (Fitzpatrick 1996:854). Another major source of denunciations were quarrels between neighbors forced to live cheek to jowl in communal apartments (Fitzpatrick 1996:856). One man served an eight-year sentence due to a complaint about "counterrevolutionary agitation" that apparently arose because his communal neighbors were jealous of the size of his family's room (Fitzpatrick 1996:856). Throughout Soviet society, "accusations, denunciations, and personal animosities could lead to arrest at any moment" (quoted in Gross 1982:374).

The power of denunciation—potentially resulting in arrest, imprisonment, torture, or execution—gives it a self-reinforcing quality. Even if citizens would rather not denounce their adversaries, they must face the possibility that trying to handle the conflict in another way might well provoke their adversaries into denouncing them. Thus, "to bring a grievance to anyone but a government official can be dangerous.… Hence, the choice is often between bringing an official complaint and doing nothing at all" (Black 1989:79).

While such extremes are limited to totalitarian dictatorships, lesser degrees of legal dependency can occur in democratic societies. People might be less likely to try to prevent or break up fights because they view this as a job for the police, not ordinary citizens. Or they might increasingly turn to lawsuits as a way of handling conflicts not previously considered the domain of law, such as the unusual case of a young US man suing his parents for "parental malpractice" (Friedman 1985:21–22; see also Christie 1977; Lieberman 1981).

Resorting to police and courts is only a special case of relying on a third party to handle the conflict (Black and Baumgartner 1983). As noted above people bring their complaints to other kinds of authorities, such as children complaining to parents or employees reporting misconduct to their supervisor (Baumgartner 1984; Black 1998:85–88). All these behaviors share a major social condition: The people involved in the dispute have access to a higher-status third party. The third party might be someone only slightly higher in status, such as people in a tribal village bringing their dispute before a respected elder, or the third party might have the power and authority of the state. And just as law can discourage people from handling conflicts on their own, so too can other kinds of authorities. Whether these authorities actively suppress other ways of handling conflict or merely provide an easy and appealing alternative, their presence can lead to a kind of moral dependency.

We can observe this on college and university campuses, where administrators often handle conflicts among students and faculty. Educational institutions not only police such academic misconduct as cheating and plagiarism, but also increasingly enact codes forbidding interpersonal offenses, such as Fordham University's ban on using email to insult another person, or New York University's prohibition of mocking others (Lukianoff 2014:41). When two students at Dartmouth College were insulted by a third student who "verbally harassed them by speaking gibberish that was perceived to be mock Chinese," they reacted not by confronting the offender but instead by reporting the incident to the College's Office of Pluralism and Leadership, leading both the school's Department of Safety and Security and its Bias Incident Response Team to launch an investigation into the identity of the offender (Owens 2013). In other social settings the same offense might have met with a direct response, whether a complaint to the offender, a retaliatory insult, or physical violence. But in a setting where a powerful organization metes out justice, the aggrieved relied on complaint rather than action.

In sum, the presence of people of higher social status—especially those such as legal officials or private administrators who are part of an organizational hierarchy—is conducive to reliance on third parties. But remember that relying on third parties can involve more than complaining to authorities. People might also bring their grievances to the attention of the general public. This can be a powerful sanction in and of itself, possibly shaming an offender, but it can also be a tool for motivating the authorities to intervene. Politicians and campus administrators might be reluctant to act unless public opinion demands it.[7] The core of much modern activism seems to be to draw attention to grievances and so convince either the public or authorities to remedy the situation.

CAMPAIGNING FOR SUPPORT

The first major feature of microaggression complaints is that they involve appeals to third parties, and we have looked at the context of such appeals. But why do the complainants portray the offenses the way they do? Why do they use the term *aggression* to refer to remarks or behaviors that might otherwise be described as merely rude, awkward, or ignorant? The term has the connotation of intentional attack, something generally viewed as more severe than the often inadvertent slights condemned as microaggressions. Calling them aggressions is a way of pointing out that they are part of a pattern of systematic oppression. But why do microaggression complainants conceptualize and present the offenses this way, as part of a pattern rather than as isolated offenses? It is a way of campaigning for support. Remember that the second major feature of microaggression complaints is that they are attempts to convince third parties that the offenses are actually severe enough to concern them. But why do they need convincing?

The Logic of Microaggression Campaigns

As the *micro* in *microaggression* implies, the slights and insults are acts that many would consider to be only minor offenses and that others might not deem offensive at all. Thus those who started the first websites dedicated to documenting microaggressions stated that their aim was to call attention to numerous offenses in order to demonstrate the existence of a larger pattern of inequality. The concept of microaggression gained currency as part of a movement seeking to make the case that, collectively, these offenses were more severe than any individual incident. Those who publicize microaggressions hope to draw support for a moral crusade by showing that the injustices are more severe than observers might realize—that people

---

[7] For instance, the US federal government avoided forcefully intervening on behalf of Southern blacks until activists succeeded in convincing non-Southern whites that black civil rights was a major public concern (Santoro 2008).

complaining about microaggressions are not, as some critics charge, merely being oversensitive, given that, as one microaggression website puts it, the "slow accumulation" of such offenses "during a childhood and over a lifetime is in part what defines a marginalized experience" (*Microaggressions Project* 2014). In this view the offenses in question contribute to the marginalization of entire groups of people. Either side in a conflict might create a reality tailored to portraying its adversary in the worst possible light, and itself in the best, with the aim of convincing others to take sides. Thus the movement to document microaggressions resembles other campaigns to convince reluctant third parties to take sides and take action, from the propaganda of political parties to the evidence presented in courts of law (Feeley 1979:168–74; Cooney 1994; Pizzi 1999:194–97).

But while disputants often amass and shape evidence to convince others of the righteousness of their cause, it is not inevitable. Those who seek the assistance of third parties to handle a conflict do not always go to the trouble of building a case. In many tribal and village societies, aggrieved individuals can count on the nearly automatic support of their close kin in any conflict (Black 1998:128–131; Cooney 1998:79). For example, among the !Kung, a hunting and gathering people in Africa's Kalahari desert, fights between individuals quickly escalate into camp-wide brawls as people rush to intervene on behalf of their closest relatives (Lee 1979:372). In other societies solidary clusters of male kin are so willing to offer strong support that even a minor conflict between families easily escalates into a blood feud (Cooney 1998:67–89; Senechal de la Roche 2001; Thoden van Velzen and van Wetering 1960). People in these settings might have to inform their allies of the conflict, if it is not already known, but they have little or no need of widely publicizing their grievances or building a case by accumulating a list of offensive acts and identifying many separate victims. The conditions that undermine such quick action increase the likelihood that aggrieved individuals will accumulate, shape, and create evidence to bolster their case. To understand why such campaigns occur, then, and why they succeed or fail, we need to understand the social conditions that encourage or hamper partisanship.

The Structural Logic of Partisanship

Partisanship is taking sides in a conflict, and like any other conflict behavior we can explain it with the social features of the conflict. Black's theory of partisanship identifies two conditions that make support from third parties more likely. First, third parties are more likely to act as partisans when they are socially closer to one side of the conflict than to the other, as they take the side of the socially closer disputant (Black 1998:126). They may be relationally closer to, or more intimate with, one side, or they may be culturally closer, meaning they share social characteristics such as religion, ethnicity, or language. All else equal, any social tie or social similarity a third party shares with one disputant but not the other increases the chance of partisanship. For example, among the Arusha of Tanzania, people are "readily able to determine their allegiance, or their exclusion from allegiance, in a situation of conflict and dispute" based on membership in patrilineal kin groups and genealogical segments within those groups (Gulliver 1963:118, quoted in Black 1998:128). The Bedouins of Arabia express this sociological law of partisanship in the proverb "myself against my brother, my brother and I against my cousin, my cousin, my brother, and I against the stranger" (Murphy and Kasdan 1959:20).

Tribal and traditional societies are typically organized around kinship, and kinship groups often have a level of intimacy and solidarity difficult for people in more individualistic societies to imagine, leading to extremes of partisanship when kin are wronged by outsiders. As Jared Diamond observes, it can be difficult for modern people to understand how these dense networks of lifelong ties affect the handling of conflict: "To us Westerners, it seems absurd that the damaging of a garden of a member of one clan by a pig belonging to a member of another clan could trigger a war between the two clans; to New Guinea Highlanders, that outcome is unsurprising" (Diamond 2013:90). The quasi-religious intensity of kinship ties helps explain why conflicts between people from groups with no common connection are prone to escalate into collective violence (Cooney 1998:79; Senechal de la Roche 2001). Members of modern street gangs also tend to have unusually close bonds and uphold partisanship toward fellow gang members against outsiders as a "sacred duty" (Decker and Van Winkle 1996:180, quoted in Cooney 1998:79). But note that the strongest partisanship requires a combination of closeness and distance. When third parties are equally close to or distant from both sides, they tend toward neutrality (Black 1998, see also Cooney 1998:Chapter 4).[8]

---

[8] Cultural closeness and distance predict partisanship as well. We can see the influence of culture on partisanship in cases where people express preference for members of their own racial or ethnic group against outsiders, even when both disputants are strangers. Consider the famous case of former football star O.J. Simpson, a black man accused of

Second, third parties are more likely to act as partisans when one side of a conflict is higher in status than the other, as they take the side of the higher-status disputant (Black 1998:126). Social elites throughout history have been able to count on the support of their subordinates: "In ancient Rome, upper-class men ... could rally a 'gang' of followers to resist their legal opponents and enemies. In medieval England, where servants were widespread (even among wealthier peasants), masters had similar advantages" (Black 1998:127, citations omitted). In modern societies those with wealth and fame also attract more support in their conflicts, including people willing to testify on their behalf in court (Cooney 2009:92). A poor and disreputable person, such as a street-level drug dealer or homeless vagrant, is unlikely to attract such spontaneous help, especially when facing wealthy and powerful opponents.

This is not to say that no one ever expresses greater sympathy toward or tries to help the weaker party in a conflict. The entire basis of claims of victimhood is to generate exactly this kind of sympathy. But such sympathy for the underdog is likely only under particular conditions, and the more general pattern is for low-status people to attract less support against high-status people than vice versa. Someone who lacks wealth and education, who has a bad reputation or criminal record, and who belongs to a cultural minority will find it extremely hard if not impossible to attract strong and uncompromising support against an adversary who is very wealthy and educated, reputable, and part of the cultural majority.

The Structure of Campaigns

We propose that active campaigns to convince third parties to give their support are most likely to arise under conditions conducive to slow and weak partisanship. In other words, efforts to produce and shape evidence

---

killing two white victims. During his criminal trial for murder, nine of 12 jurors were black, and the jury found him not guilty. But in a later civil trial for wrongful death, 11 of the 12 jurors were white and none were black, and Simpson was found liable for the deaths. According to Black, "The crucial difference in the two Simpson trials was the cultural location of the juries. The largely African-American jury favored the African-American, and the largely white jury favored the whites.... Public opinion polls at the time of the criminal trial also showed the same pattern of partisanship: About 90 percent of African-Americans said Simpson was not guilty, while about 70 percent of white Americans said he was guilty" (Black 2002:123). Experiments with simulated juries likewise find a pattern of racial favoritism (Ugwuegbu 1979).

operate most frequently and effectively where third parties might be willing to take a side but are not certain to do so.

Campaigns will tend to be aimed at those who are not so close to the aggrieved or distant from the adversary that their support is automatic, but also not so distant from the aggrieved and close to the adversary that it is unthinkable. Campaigns will be most frequent in social settings where many third parties occupy a neutral zone and usually either do not get involved at all or else just express a weak preference for one side or the other. Again, quick, strong, certain partisanship occurs most frequently in settings where people are divided up into groups that are internally solidary but mutually alien—like feuding clans in tribal societies. The opposite condition—social atomization, where people act as autonomous individuals with little involvement in stable and solidary groups—leads to a decline in strong partisanship (Senechal de la Roche 2001).

Social atomization is typically greater in present-day industrial societies than in past societies. Large, dense populations and a market economy require constant dealings with non-kin. Wealth and technology result in high levels of geographic and social mobility. Formal schooling displaces parental socialization, and insurance companies and state welfare agencies reduce the need to rely on family in hard times. The breakdown of strong communal bonds began long ago in the West, and in modern America and elsewhere this social atomization has continued throughout the twentieth century. In his book *Bowling Alone*, political scientist Robert Putnam documents the decline of a variety of voluntary organizations that were once a part of the fabric of American communities, including religious congregations, social clubs, fraternal organizations like the Masons or Elks, and parent–teacher associations (Putnam 2000). Even bowling leagues have seen their memberships plummet, and as the title of Putnam's book hints, it is not because fewer people bowl; it is because they are less likely to do so as part of an enduring and formally organized group.[9]

[9] This leads to less partisanship in day-to-day conflicts. Consider the description from M.P. Baumgartner's study of conflict in middle class suburb: "When tensions erupt, individuals are generally left to their own devices. Extended family members, who might otherwise be expected to lend assistance, are usually living some distance away and are, in any case, caught up in their own networks and concerns…. Friends, neighbors, and other associates are near at hand but are rarely intimate enough to be relied upon. Even advice is difficult to obtain from those who know little or nothing about a problem, and many people are reluctant to give it under any circumstances (believing it preferable not to get involved in other's conflicts at all)" (Baumgartner 1988:97, quoted in Black 1998:131).

The decline of dense networks of strong, enduring, and overlapping bonds has two major results. The first is to render an increasing amount of conflict private.[10] Marital arguments, family quarrels, and tensions between friends and neighbors increasingly occur behind closed doors and without the involvement of anyone else at all.[11] The second is that when people do seek the support of third parties, they are less likely to rely on a core group of die-hard supporters and more likely to find themselves campaigning to attract the attention and sympathy of distant acquaintances and total strangers.

Consider also the role of social status. Here too we expect to see campaigns for support flourishing when the conditions are conducive to weak or hesitant partisanship rather than automatic support or automatic opposition. Thus campaigns for support should be more likely when a person or group has grievances against someone of higher status, but not when the status differences between the two are at their most extreme. Microaggression complaints have just that kind of structure. They are typically complaints on behalf of cultural minorities or other social groups that have lower aggregate status, such as lower levels of wealth, education, and authority. Many are concerned with discrimination by white Americans against black Americans, who as a group were historically dominated by whites and who continue to have drastically lower levels of aggregate wealth and education (see, e.g., Conley 1999). Microaggression complaints also commonly have to do with slights against gays and lesbians, who have often been treated as deviant or disreputable. But note that while microaggression complaints tend to be upward—minority against

---

[10] Even violent conflicts are less likely to involve partisans: Twentieth century homicides were less likely to involve multiple offenders than the homicides of previous centuries (Cooney 2003:1385). In modernizing societies, such as the United States and France during the nineteenth century, there is also a strong rural-urban gradient: Urban settings, with their more fluid and mobile populations, produce fewer homicides with multiple offenders than did rural settings, where traditional tight-knit communities prevailed (Cooney 2003:1384).

[11] Note that the decline of third party involvement affects the nature of social control that occurs between disputants. For example, people may be more inclined to pursue grievances forcefully or aggressively when they have strong supporters in their corner, providing assistance or at least assuring them that they are right and encouraging them to seek justice. A decline in third party involvement thus contributes to what M.P. Baumgartner refers to as "moral minimalism"—a tendency to tolerate offenses or handle them in nonconfrontational ways (Baumgartner 1988:10). On the other hand, since third parties can also act as mediators or peacemakers, their absence can increase the severity of conflict in situations that are otherwise conducive to aggression and violence (Cooney 1998; Phillips and Cooney 2005).

majority, stigmatized against socially accepted—neither the complaints nor the campaigns to publicize them come from the lowest reaches of society. The concept of microaggression did not first proliferate among the chronically poor, such as among the unemployed coal miners of Eastern Kentucky or among the impoverished African Americans of Baltimore or New Orleans. It first proliferated among college and university students, a relatively affluent, educated, and respectable population. And the microaggression program seems to have developed most quickly at elite institutions, such as private liberal arts colleges and Ivy League universities. A minority student at Oberlin College or Harvard University may indeed be from a lower-status background than the average Oberlin or Harvard student, but compared to the US population as a whole, or even to students at other colleges and universities, students at elite educational institutions are not particularly lowly.

The socially down and out are unlikely to campaign for public support, just as they are unlikely to receive it. To what potentially sympathetic public could a slave turn to for support against an unusually brutal master? Slaves in the antebellum South might run away, or they might express grievances in various covert ways, but they did not post lists of accumulated grievances in the local newspaper.[12] Campaigns for support emerge not where the structure of partisanship favors only strong allies or strong enemies, but somewhere in between, where third parties offer only weak or potential support.

Intervention by authorities often has this kind of weakly partisan structure, so those who rely on it often find themselves having to make a case for partisanship. Those who take their cases before the law are generally taking their case before strangers, representatives of a powerful organization that might have little interest in the conflicts of distant subordinates, let alone a

---

[12] Other members of the master's social class would have viewed any complaint as an offense in itself, as would almost all Southern whites. Other slaves might well have sympathized, but historically most of them were not willing to engage in strong partisanship against the powerful—compared to the day-to-day outrages that slaves suffered, open rebellions were quite rare. For their part, plantation owners would not have engaged in activism or consciousness-raising to convince their peers to help them put down rebellions or punish runaways. Attempts to campaign for support against the institution of slavery did eventually take place in the form of the books, pamphlets, and speeches of abolitionists. But note that these campaigns took place in the North, targeting an audience who were strangers to and culturally distinct from Southern whites. As with the civil rights movement a century later, abolitionists succeeded not by convincing the hostile, but by convincing the neutral.

preference for one side or the other. In places where law is far less omnipresent than it is in totalitarian societies, even gaining a hearing might be difficult. Indeed, studies of legal behavior in modern American towns and cities reveal that people who seek legal intervention are often frustrated by the unwillingness of legal officials to define their grievances as serious matters (Merry 1990; Greenhouse et al. (1994:55–90). Legal officials view many of the conflicts that ordinary people bring before them as "garbage cases" to be handled in a perfunctory manner by the lowest-ranking officials of the court, such as the clerks (Yngvesson 1989).

When authorities do intervene in the conflict, they start off taking a neutral role. If they are acting as mediators, they stay neutral throughout the conflict and never render a judgment at all. Mediation tends to flourish where authorities are relatively close to the disputants and relatively similar in status. An example would be two disputants from a small tribal village taking their case before a respected village elder. The elder in such a case is likely to handle the conflict in a way that seeks compromise and social repair and relies more on persuasion than authority (Black and Baumgartner 1983; Black 1998:146). More distant third parties and third parties who have relatively greater status tend to be more decisive, eventually rendering a judgment (Black 1998:145–149). Again, modern courts of law are an example: Defendants are either guilty or not guilty, while plaintiffs either win compensation or have their claims denied. While the court is initially neutral and willing to hear arguments from both sides, court cases ultimately produce a clear winner and a clear loser.[13] Here the authorities have a high degree of status and are socially distant from both disputants. They are inclined toward nonintervention and indifference, but if they can be convinced that wrongdoing has occurred, and that the wrongdoing was serious enough to merit an official response, they intervene forcefully on behalf of the victim. The presence of such authorities not only deters aggrieved individuals from engaging in violence, theft, and other crimes, but also encourages the use of tactics geared toward attracting attention and winning support.[14]

[13] Thus, Black argues that modern legal settlement is effectively "slow partisanship" (Black 1998:139).

[14] Since the type of authority most likely to generate campaigns for support is one that can be convinced to intervene, but whose intervention is not automatic, the closest and most distant authorities should both be less likely to produce them. The omnipresent totalitarian state is quick to respond to any accusation of disloyalty, so such accusations are often enough to mobilize the state against an enemy even without any evidence or argument. Conversely, people at the fringes of legal protection—such as peasants living on the frontier of a weak premodern state—are unlikely to attract the attention of socially distant and high-status authorities and unlikely to campaign for it.

These campaigns for support can take many forms besides the public documenting of offenses, and people in weakly partisan structures may sometimes go to much greater lengths to convince people to help them. For example, in many patriarchal societies—such as rural China and Iran, Afghanistan, or the tribal societies of the New Guinea Highlands—various factors mitigate the willingness of a woman's kin to intervene on her behalf during marital disputes. Her social subordination to her husband, military alliances between her husband and his male in-laws, or a lack of physical proximity to the marital homestead might all reduce their willingness or ability to provide support (Baumgartner 1993). They will still do so if the conflict becomes severe enough, but this may require drastic action on her part—for example, attempting or committing suicide. Following her suicide, the relatives who were hesitant to help her before now treat her husband as a murderer, demanding compensation or perhaps taking vengeance.[15] Thus in many of these severely patriarchal societies, local women recognize that self-destructive measures may be the only way to rouse potential supporters who are otherwise slow to react (Berndt 1962:180–192; Brown 1986; Counts 1980, 1987; Johnson 1981; Liu 2002; Manning 2012, 2015).

Modern political protesters, campaigning against a powerful adversary on behalf of a less powerful collectivity, might likewise turn to self-destructive extremes to convince others to support their cause. Most instances in which activists publicly burn themselves to death are aimed explicitly at attracting the support of third parties (Biggs 2005). For example, one study of the suicide notes left by Korean activists between 1970 and 2004 found that they burned themselves "in order to inspire movement activism among half-hearted activists and apathetic bystanders" (Kim 2008:573). Thus one activist wrote, "I beg the activists of all persuasions ... Do not let my death and all the deaths of my predecessors be in vain" (quoted in Kim 2008:567). When Buddhist monk Thich Quang Duc committed self-immolation in 1963 to protest the Vietnamese government's oppression of Buddhists, the act was clearly aimed at convincing third parties to side against Vietnam's president Diem: Quang Duc's

---

[15] For example, among the Aguaruna Jívaro, a tribal people of Peru, women "often find their relatives reluctant to defend them from abusive husbands" but "the very kinsmen who may be unwilling to intervene on a woman's behalf when she is alive are galvanized into action when she kills herself" (Brown 1986:320). And in one case in the New Guinea Highlands, when a woman killed herself due to her husband's abuse, her relatives hacked the abusive husband to death with axes (Counts 1987:199).

fellow monks ensured that Western journalists would be present at the event, and as he prepared to light the fire, they distributed leaflets written in English that explained the nature of their cause. They thus hoped to sway opinion in the United States so that the US government would withdraw its support of the oppressive regime—and they succeeded, leaving Diem bereft of US support and vulnerable to a coup (LePoer 1989:61–64; Biggs 2005).

Partisanship and Conflict Severity

If social structure predicts who will take sides in a conflict, why is it possible for campaigns for support to have an effect? Why are tactics such as documenting a list of offenses—or, for that matter, lighting oneself on fire—ever effective? Not every grievance is equally serious. We all intuitively understand that some offenses are worse than others. This is why the legal system typically punishes murder more severely than simple assault, rape more severely than unwanted touching, and so forth. It is clear that how people respond to a conflict depends not just on their social relationships, but also on the nature of the offense itself. Generally speaking, more serious types of offense merit greater intervention. Third parties such as legal officials take them more seriously, are more likely to intervene, and are more likely to side against the offender.

This might be obvious enough, but what is not obvious is what makes one offense more serious than another. This is especially so when we recognize that people might take offense to nearly any conduct at all, and that people in different social settings differ in what they consider to be the most serious sorts of wrongs. But Black's recent theory of conflict tells us that all conflicts erupt in response to social change. After all, a conflict is an event, and each event is caused by previous events—action and reaction, stimulus and response (Black 2011:5–8). Viewed sociologically these events are fundamentally changes in the structure of social relationships. It could be a change in the level of inequality between people or groups (Black 2011:59–95). Maybe someone falls below others in status, losing a job or other source of wealth, and blames them for the loss. Or perhaps someone rises above others, getting a promotion or windfall, and so inspires complaints of undeserved success. It could be a change in intimacy (Black 2011:21–54). Maybe a relationship loses intimacy, as when someone ends a romantic relationship and attracts accusations of heartlessness and betrayal from a jilted lover. Or maybe someone increases intimacy with another, causing complaints of being too clingy and intrusive. It could also be a change in culture (Black 2011:101–135). Maybe someone produces a new idea that is branded as heresy or enforces conformity and is lambasted for conservatism.

In all these cases the greater and faster the change in inequality, intimacy, or culture, the more serious the conflict (Black 2011:6–7). Peeping Toms and rapists are both offensive because they increase their closeness to an unwilling victim. But in rape the increase is much greater, with the rapist invading not just the victim's privacy but also the victim's body—so rape is generally more deviant than unwanted looking. Concerning partisanship, this means the victims of rape receive more support than the victims of Peeping Toms. Third parties are more likely to act as partisans when the offense underlying a conflict is more serious—when it involves a greater social change.

Viewed in this light, the thing about insults and slights that makes them offensive is that they lower the social standing of the recipient (Black 2011:71). To insult people is to engage in an act of dominance, and to insult them publicly might mean lowering their respectability in the eyes of onlookers. But the loss of status that comes from verbal insults is much smaller than, say, being robbed of one's life savings, permanently handicapped by violent assault, or enslaved and forced into a life of servitude. The insult is offensive, but in most settings it is a minor offense compared to other acts that have greater impact on someone's wealth, health, reputation, or autonomy. The conflict is less severe and is less likely to attract the attention and intervention of third parties. Black notes, however, that social changes can be cumulative, and the severity of the conflict might reflect the additive effect of many smaller incidents (Black 2011:6–7). He illustrates this idea by analogy to the effect of cigarette smoke on lung cancer. Each puff of cigarette smoke does not immediately result in cancer, but the more one smokes, the more likely cancer becomes. Likewise, even if a single theft or insult is not treated as a serious offense, a pattern of repeated offenses might be taken very seriously indeed.[16]

---

[16] Historian and sociologist Roberta Senechal de la Roche argues that repeat offending is one of the most important predictors of when lynch mobs will attack a member of their own community. Tight-knit communities are usually much more tolerant of insiders than outsiders, but recidivism is serious enough to merit violence: "While his fellows might ignore, excuse, or mildly rebuke a wrongful act of two, repeat offenses may eventually achieve for the recidivist what one anthropologist calls the 'status of the finally intolerable'" (Senechal de la Roche 2001, citing Llewellyn and Hoebel 1941).

The upshot of all this is that an aggrieved party can, by accumulating and documenting a variety of grievances, make third parties aware of a larger degree of loss. This magnifies the apparent severity of the conflict and thus increases the likelihood that third parties will intervene. Other tactics, like protest suicide, magnify the actual severity of the conflict by inflicting greater damage on the aggrieved. Both strategies have a similar logic: The greater the loss, the more severe the conflict, and the more likely third parties will intervene against the offender.

If the severity of the offense depends on its social impact—the degree to which it alters people's relationships and social standing—then offenses that impact many people are, all else equal, more severe than those that impact only one or a few. After all, if a million people suffer a loss in status, it is a greater change than if only one person does. This helps explain why conflicts over culture tend to be treated as more severe and to attract partisan support on one or both sides (Black 2011:108, 121). Cultural characteristics are shared with others, so any offense against an ethnicity, language, or religion—blasphemy, ridicule, discrimination, ethnic cleansing, or genocide—is an offense against all who identify with that ethnicity, speak that language, or practice that religion. Offending an entire social group is treated as more severe than an offense against an individual, and is likely to lead third parties—particularly fellow members of the victim's group—to intervene.

Offenses that involve slighting someone because of membership in a particular social group—a particular race, ethnicity, religion, gender, or sexual identity—are particularly likely to attract the attention and support of third parties. This includes websites, viral tweets, news stories, and other forms of public attention. And those who wish to bring more attention to their grievances or combat offensive behavior can effectively campaign for support by drawing attention to the collective nature of the offense.

DOMINATION AS DEVIANCE

Microaggression complaints are public complaints, and they occur as part of a campaign to convince third parties that microaggressions are serious, part of a pattern of offenses that needs to be addressed. We have examined the social conditions associated with these two features, and now let us examine those associated with the third notable feature of microaggression complaints: that the grievances focus on inequality and oppression—especially inequality and oppression based on cultural characteristics such as ethnicity or gender. Microaggressions are offensive to those aggrieved by them because they believe they perpetuate or increase the domination of some persons and groups by others.

Contemporary readers may take it for granted that the domination of one group by another, or for that matter any substantial kind of inter-group inequality, is an injustice to be condemned and remedied. But people might have grievances about many other matters. For instance, they might condemn others for vices such as drunkenness, sloth, and gluttony. They might criticize or punish people for illicit sexual acts such as sodomy, incest, or bestiality. And cross-culturally and historically, people might harshly judge and persecute religious, ethnic, and other cultural minorities merely for being different. Such grievances are largely absent from micro-aggression complaints, and those who promulgate microaggression complaints would surely view criticism of minorities as the very kind of oppression they seek to expose and eradicate. The phenomenon thus illustrates a particular type of morality that is especially concerned with equality and diversity and sees any act that perpetuates inequality or decreases diversity as a cause for serious moral condemnation.

Microaggression as Overstratification

We have discussed how changes in stratification, intimacy, and diversity cause conflict. Human conflicts are fundamentally conflicts about too much or too little inequality, too much or too little intimacy, too much or too little diversity. Microaggression complaints are largely about too much inequality. The behaviors documented in microaggression complaints are slights, insults, and attempts to disparage or dominate others. These are what Black calls *overstratification* offenses—acts that increase the level of social inequality in a relationship. Overstratification occurs whenever anyone rises above others in status, falls below others in status, or does something to dominate another person or group. Such incidents are often deemed offensive, but the seriousness of the offense varies across social settings. Black proposes that *overstratification conflict varies inversely with stratification* (Black 2011: 139). In other words, a morality that condemns inequality is most likely to arise precisely in settings that already have relatively high degrees of equality.

In rigid hierarchical settings or relationships, even subordinates might take dominance and subordination for granted. In some highly patriarchal societies, for example, women as well as men accept the right of a man to beat his wife for misbehavior (Counts 1980; Hindin 2003; Rani et al. 2004). The higher status of men is largely taken for granted, and even severe aggressions are not necessarily considered deviant. Similar patterns exist in societies with rigid class or caste systems, such as a division between nobles and commoners. Moral codes in such settings emphasize duty, loyalty, and knowing one's station (Leung and Cohen 2011; Rosen 2012:47–50). One medieval writer denounced "peasants who attempt to become squires," writing that "such rogues should be brought to justice and made to keep their class" (Tuchman 1978:442). Egalitarian hunter-gatherers, however, are quick to censure or ridicule anyone who claims any kind of status superiority, and they will ostracize anyone they deem aggressive or domineering (Boehm 1999).

In modern Western societies, egalitarian ethics have developed alongside actual political and economic equality. As women moved into the workforce in large numbers, became increasingly educated, made inroads into highly paid professions such as law and medicine, and became increasingly prominent in local, state, and national politics, sexism became increasingly deviant. Similarly the success of the US civil rights movement in dismantling the Southern racial caste system and the increased representation of African-Americans in professional and public life have been associated with the transformation of racism into a highly stigmatized behavior. The taboo has grown so strong that making racist statements, even in private, might jeopardize careers. For example, in 2013 popular television chef Paula Deen was sued for racial discrimination. Though the suit was dismissed, in part of her deposition Deen admitted to having used the word *nigger* in a private conversation decades earlier (in reference to being robbed at gunpoint by a black man). As a result of the admission, she was fired by the network that aired her show, lost numerous publishing and endorsement contracts, and had her product lines boycotted by several major retailers (Lynch 2013; see also Fenno et al. 2014).

Microaggression as Underdiversity

Settings with little diversity are likely to develop a morality that values cultural purity and is hostile to differences (Black 2011:144). In such settings, virtue means adhering to the accepted beliefs and rituals or family, neighbors, friends, and ancestors. This appears to be the case in the most homogeneous societies, such as tribal villages that have little contact with the outside world. People are so alike that deviation may hardly occur at all—for the most part people conform, and if deviant ideas occur to them at all, they are likely to self-censor. In societies that are larger and more complex, new ideas and practices are more likely to appear. But as long as these societies are highly homogeneous, these deviations quickly become the subject of rejection, ridicule, or far worse. In religiously homogeneous societies, heresy is a severe offense, possibly leading to torture and execution. Such was the case in medieval Christendom, and deviations from conventional religion continue to meet with severe punishment in some uniformly Muslim nations such as Saudi Arabia.

In contrast, settings that already have a great deal of diversity are less likely to treat differences as offensive, and more likely to positively value them. Indeed, the more diverse a setting, the more likely it is that people will develop a "live and let live" ethic that treats the rejection of diversity as itself a major offense. These offenses are what Black calls *underdiversity* conflicts (Black 2011:120–21). Large acts of underdiversity include things like genocide or political oppression, while smaller acts include ethnic jokes or insults. Microaggression complaints are concerned with the latter, as well as more subtle, perhaps inadvertent, cultural slights. They do not label all incidents of underdiversity as microaggression, though, but only those that increase stratification by lowering the status of those who are already disadvantaged—in other words, underdiversity combined with overstratification. They are concerned with offenses against minority or otherwise less powerful cultures, not offenses against historically dominant ethnic groups such as whites or historically dominant religious groups such as Christians. Still, the cultural nature of these offenses helps us further specify the context in which they are seen as offensive. Just as overstratification conflict varies inversely with stratification, *underdiversity conflict varies directly with diversity* (Black 2011:139). Attempts to increase stratification, we saw, are more deviant where stratification is at a minimum; likewise, attempts to decrease diversity are more deviant where diversity is at a maximum. In modern Western societies, an ethic of cultural tolerance—and often incompatibly, intolerance of intolerance—has developed in tandem with increasing diversity. Since microaggression offenses normally involve overstratification and underdiversity, intense concern about such offenses occurs at the intersection of the social conditions conducive to the seriousness of each. It is in egalitarian and diverse settings—such as at modern American universities—that equality and diversity are most valued, and it is in these settings that perceived offenses against these values are most deviant.[17]

THE SOCIAL STRUCTURE OF MICROAGGRESSION

In sum, microaggression complainants collect and publicize accounts of minor intercollective offenses, making the case that they are part of a larger pattern of injustice and that those who suffer them are socially marginalized and deserving of sympathy. The phenomenon is sociologically similar to other forms of social control that involve airing grievances to authorities or to the public as a whole, that actively manage social information in a campaign to convince others to intervene in some way, and that emphasize the dominance of the adversary and the victimization of the aggrieved. Insofar as these forms are sociologically similar, they should tend to arise under similar social conditions. These conditions include a social setting with cultural diversity and relatively high levels of equality, though with the presence of high-status third parties such as legal officials and organizational administrators. Furthermore, authorities and other third parties are in social locations—such as being distant from both disputants—that lead to a reluctance to get involved. They may intervene, but only after someone convinces them. Under these conditions individuals are likely to express grievances about oppression, and aggrieved individuals are likely to depend on the aid of third parties, to cast a wide net in their attempt to find supporters, and to campaign for support by emphasizing their own need against a bullying adversary. These conditions can be found to a greater or lesser extent in many social settings. But the recent popularity of the idea of microaggressions suggests that these conditions have increased in recent years, particularly in the social location inhabited by college and university students—a social group that is also prone to protest demonstrations and various campaigns to raise awareness of injustice.

Several social trends encourage the growth of these forms of social control, particularly in the United States. Since the rights movements of the 1960s and 1970s, racial, sexual, and other forms of intercollective inequality have declined, resulting in a more egalitarian society in which members are much

---

[17] The student population at US colleges and universities has diversified substantially over the past several decades. Between 1976 and 2008, the percent of all students who are white declined from 82 to 63 percent, while the percentages who are Asian, black, and Hispanic increased (National Center for Education Statistics 2010).

more sensitive to those inequalities that remain. The last few decades have seen the continued growth of legal and administrative authority, including growth in the size and scope of university administrations and in the salaries of top administrators and the creation of specialized agencies of social control, such as offices whose sole purpose is to increase social justice by combatting racial, ethnic, or other intercollective offenses (Lukianoff 2014:69–73). Social atomization has increased, undermining the tight-knit networks that once encouraged confrontational modes of social control and provided individuals with strong partisans, while at the same time modern technology has allowed for mass communication to a virtual sea of weak partisans.

This last trend has been especially dramatic during the past decade, with the result that aggrieved individuals can potentially appeal to millions of third parties. In our experience with media services such as Twitter and Facebook, we have noticed that many use these forums to publicly vent grievances and to solicit sympathetic responses not only from friends but also from distant acquaintances and total strangers. Sometimes grievances go viral as millions of sympathetic parties spread and endorse them. For instance, in reaction to the kidnapping and enslavement of hundreds of Nigerian girls by the Islamist militant group Boko Haram, numerous celebrities, politicians, and private individuals expressed their condemnation of the militants and support for their victims through a series of Twitter posts dubbed the "Bring Back Our Girls" campaign (Mackey 2014). Such Twitter campaigns—sometimes referred to as *hashtag activism*—are effectively episodes of mass gossip in which hundreds, thousands, or perhaps millions of third parties discuss deviant behavior and express support for one side against another. Like gossip in the small town or village, such public complaining may be the sole way of handling the conflict, or it might eventually lead to further action against the deviant, such as dismissal by supervisors or investigation by legal authorities. As social media becomes ever more ubiquitous, the ready availability of the court of public opinion may make public disclosure of offenses an increasingly likely course of action.[18]

[18] The creation of this massive audience of potential partisans is the culmination of a process that has altered the third party structure of conflicts throughout the past century. For example, the proliferation of print media in the twentieth century allowed those with grievances against the powerful, such as corporations or state agencies, to publicly disclose their wrongdoing in a phenomenon popularly known as *whistle-blowing* (e.g., Westin et al. 1981). The iconic photograph of Buddhist monk Thich Quang Duc' self-immolation in 1963 was seen by millions around the world, and the continued growth of media can help explain why self-immolation has become an increasingly common tactic of political protest (Biggs 2005).

PURITY AND TOLERANCE

Before closing this chapter, let us note one final feature of victimhood culture. We have discussed how microaggression complaints illustrate a morality that values diversity and is highly sensitive to intolerance of differences. But some manifestations of victimhood culture also display a kind of intolerance to difference and disagreement. The same progressive activists who campaign against microaggressions might also call for the banning of conservative speakers, for the forbidding of displays of support for certain political candidates, and for the creation of safe spaces where progressive ideas can go unchallenged by opposing views. They might also express extreme vitriol toward those holding views that are considered fairly moderate elsewhere in society. So in addition to the morality of tolerance, in which differences are celebrated, there also appears to be a morality of purity, in which differences are offensive.

The morality of tolerance and the morality of purity are opposites, and they arise from opposite conditions: Diversity breeds tolerance, and homogeneity breeds purity. How then is it possible for both to arise in the same setting? It is possible because there are multiple dimensions of diversity. A social setting might have a lot of racial diversity, but not religious diversity, a lot of political diversity, but no linguistic diversity, and so on. Because different dimensions of diversity can vary independently, a social setting might engender tolerance of one kind of diversity, such as ethnic diversity, and intolerance of another, such as political diversity.

This appears to be the situation on many campuses. Only 12 percent of US university faculty identify as politically conservative, and the proportion is even smaller in the social sciences and humanities, where many scholars openly identify as leftwing activists seeking to advance their political views through scholarship and teaching (Haidt et al. n.d.). Yet political and social conservatives are not a small minority in the larger society, and they are not a historically disadvantaged group that attracts sympathy and support in an egalitarian culture. Indeed, conservatives often oppose the preferred policies of campus activists and are openly critical of their views. The result is they are often treated not only as political adversaries, but as heretics who pollute the ideological purity of politically homogeneous environments. Microaggression complaints do not deal with slights against these ideological minorities, and the champions of victimhood culture on college campuses freely demonize the enemies in their midst. Yet even as they do so, they do so in terms of the framework of victimhood culture: Those who disagree are racist, misogynist, ableist, homophobic, Islamophobic, transphobic, and so forth. They are bullies who attack those who are disadvantaged and different. Blind to their power and privilege, they victimize entire classes of vulnerable and sympathetic people. Their offense is severe, and must be made known to all.

*   *   *

Microaggression complaints occur under a particular set of social conditions, and it is these conditions that explain victimhood culture. Each can be found to varying degrees in many other times and places, where they give rise to forms of conflict and social control that share some aspect of microaggression complaints. Yet it is historically rare for all these conditions to be present at the same time, in high degrees. It is thus rare to see social control that combines all aspects of microaggression complaints. Minorities throughout history might have resented slights by the majority, but publicly complaining about these was rarely feasible. We see extreme reliance on third parties in totalitarian states, but little concern with ethnic equality. We see fierce egalitarianism in hunter-gatherer societies, but no campaigns for support. Only in more recent times have conditions like equality, diversity, authority, and weak ties combined. One place these conditions are highly developed is at modern colleges and universities, where students from different social groups interact as social equals under the paternalistic authority of a rapidly growing bureaucracy—one that will come to their aid if only they cause enough of a stir. Uprooted from home and making their way through an environment of fluid and transient relationships, they have electronic access to many potential supporters who share their egalitarian ethic and will sympathize with an underdog. Sensitive to slight, they police even unintentional verbal offenses; concerned with the oppressed, they champion minorities and vilify the privileged; reliant on help, they publicly air lists of grievances. The university is the epicenter of victimhood culture. As such it is the epicenter of microaggression complaints, as well as trigger warnings, safe spaces, and hate crime hoaxes. We devote the next two chapters to discussing these other manifestations in more detail.

REFERENCES

Baumgartner, M.P. 1984. Social Control from Below. In *Toward a General Theory of Social Control. Volume 1: Fundamentals*, ed. Donald Black, 303–345. Orlando: Academic Press.

———. 1988. *The Moral Order of a Suburb*. New York: Oxford University Press.

———. 1992. War and Peace in Early Childhood. In *Virginia Review of Sociology, Volume 1: Law and Conflict Management*, ed. James Tucker, 1–38. Greenwich: JAI Press.

———. 1993. Violent Networks: The Origins and Management of Domestic Conflict. In *Aggression and Violence: Social Interactionist Perspectives*, ed. Richard B. Felson and James T. Tedeschi, 209–231. Washington, DC: American Psychological Association.

Berndt, Ronald M. 1962. *Excess and Restraint: Social Control Among a New Guinean Mountain People*. Chicago: The University of Chicago Press.

Biggs, Michael. 2005. Dying Without Killing: Self-Immolations, 1963–2002. In *Making Sense of Suicide Missions*, ed. Diego Gambetta, 173–208. Oxford: Oxford University Press.

Black, Donald. 1976. *The Behavior of Law*. San Diego: Academic Press.

———. 1980. *The Manners and Customs of the Police*. New York: Academic Press.

———. 1989. *Sociological Justice*. New York: Oxford University Press.

———. 1995. The Epistemology of Pure Sociology. *Law and Social Inquiry* 20 (3): 829–870.

———. 1998. *The Social Structure of Right and Wrong*. Rev ed. San Diego: Academic Press.

———. 2002. The Geometry of Law: An Interview with Donald Black. *International Journal of Sociology of Law* 32 (2): 101–129.

———. 2004. Violent Structures. In *Violence: From Theory to Research*, ed. Margaret A. Zahn, Henry H. Brownstein, and Shelly L. Jackson, 145–158. Newark: LexisNexis/Anderson Publishing.

———. 2011. *Moral Time*. New York: Oxford University Press.

Black, Donald, and M.P. Baumgartner. 1983. Toward a Theory of the Third Party. In *Empirical Theories About Courts*, ed. Keith O. Boyum and Lynn Mather, 84–114. New York: Longman.

Boehm, Christopher. 1999. *Hierarchy in the Forest: The Evolution of Egalitarian Behavior*. Cambridge: Harvard University Press.

Brown, Michael F. 1986. Power, Gender, and the Social Meaning of Aguaruna Suicide. *Man* 21 (2): 311–328.

Christakis, Erika. 2015. 'Dressing Yourselves,' Email to Silliman College (Yale) Students on Halloween Costumes. *Foundation for Individual Rights in Education (FIRE)*, October 30. https://www.thefire.org/email-from-erika-christakis-dressing-yourselves-email-to-silliman-college-yale-students-on-halloween-costumes/.

Christie, Nils. 1977. Conflicts as Property. *British Journal of Criminology* 17 (1): 1–15.

Conley, Dalton. 1999. *Being Black, Living in the Red: Race, Wealth, and Social Policy in America.* Berkeley: University of California Press.

Cooney, Mark. 1994. Evidence as Partisanship. *Law and Society Review* 28 (8): 833–855.

———. 1998. *Warriors and Peacemakers: How Third Parties Shape Violence.* New York: New York University Press.

———. 2003. The Privatization of Violence. *Criminology* 41 (4): 1377–1406.

———. 2009. *Is Killing Wrong?: A Study in Pure Sociology.* Charlottesville: University of Virginia Press.

Counts, Dorothy Ayers. 1980. Fighting Back Is Not the Way: Suicide and the Women of Kaliai. *American Ethnologist* 7 (2): 332–351.

———. 1987. Female Suicide and Wife Abuse in Cross-Cultural Perspective. *Suicide and Life-threatening Behavior* 17 (3): 194–204.

Decker, Scott H., and Barrik Van Winkle. 1996. *Life in the Gang: Family, Friends, and Violence.* Cambridge: Cambridge University Press.

Diamond, Jared. 2013. *The World Until Yesterday: What Can We Learn from Traditional Societies?* New York: Penguin Books.

Eder, Donna, and Janet Lynne Enke. 1991. The Structure of Gossip: Opportunities and Constraints on Collective Expression Among Adolescents. *American Sociological Review* 56: 494–508.

Elias, Norbert. [1939] 1982. *The Civilizing Process*, Volume II, *Power and Civility.* Trans. Edmund Jephcott. New York: Pantheon Books.

Feeley, Malcolm M. 1979. *The Process Is the Punishment: Handling Cases in a Lower Criminal Court.* New York: Russell Sage Foundation.

Fenno, Nathan, Kim Christensen, and James Rainey. 2014. Donald Sterling Built an Empire and an Image; Words Were His Undoing. *Los Angeles Times*, August 2. http://www.latimes.com/local/la-me-donald-sterling-20140803-story. html#page=1

Fitzpatrick, Sheila. 1996. Signals from Below: Soviet Letters of Denunciation of the 1930s. *The Journal of Modern History* 68 (4): 831–866.

Friedman, Lawrence M. 1985. *Total Justice.* New York: Russell Sage Foundation.

Gibbs, Jack A. 1989. Conceptualization of Terrorism. *American Sociological Review* 54 (3): 329–340.

Gluckman, Max. 1963. Gossip and Scandal. *Current Anthropology* 4 (3): 307–316.

Greenhouse, Carol J., Barbara Yngvesson, and David M. Engel. 1994. *Law and Community in Three American Towns.* Ithaca: Cornell University Press.

Gross, Jan T. 1982. A Note on the Nature of Soviet Totalitarianism. *Soviet Studies* 34 (3): 367–376.

———. 1984. Social Control Under Totalitarianism. In *Toward a General Theory of Social Control. Volume 2: Selected Problems,* ed. Donald Black, 59–77. Orlando: Academic Press.

Gulliver, P.H. 1963. *Social Control in an African Society: A Study of the Arusha, Agricultural Masai of Northern Tanganyika.* Boston: Boston University Press.

Haidt, Jonathan, Lee Jussim, and Chris Martin. n.d. The Problem. Heterodox Academy. http://heterodoxacademy.org/problems/.

Hannerz, Ulf. 1967. Gossip, Networks and Culture in a Black American Ghetto. *Ethnos* 32: 35–60.

Hindin, Michelle J. 2003. Understanding Women's Attitudes Towards Wife Beating in Zimbabwe. *Bulletin of the World Health Organization* 81 (7): 501–508.

Johnson, Patricia Lyons. 1981. When Dying Is Better Than Living: Female Suicide Among the Gainj of Papua New Guinea. *Ethnology* 20 (4): 325–334.

Kim, Hyojoung. 2008. Micromobilization and Suicide Protest in South Korea, 1970–2004. *Social Research* 75 (2): 543–578.

Lee, Richard B. 1979. *The !Kung San: Men, Women, and Work in a Foraging Society.* Cambridge: Cambridge University Press.

Lenski, Gerhard, Patrick Nolan, and Jean Lenski. 1995. *Human Societies: An Introduction to Macrosociology.* 7th ed. New York: McGraw-Hill.

LePoer, Barbara Leitch. 1989. *Vietnam: A Country Study,* ed. Richard J. Cima. Washington, DC: Federal Research Division.

Leung, Angela K.-Y., and Dov Cohen. 2011. Within- and Between-Culture Variation: Individual Differences and the Cultural Logics of Honor, Face, and Dignity Cultures. *Journal of Personality and Social Psychology* 100 (3): 507–526.

Lieberman, Jethro K. 1981. *The Litigious Society.* New York: Basic Books.

Llewellyn, K.N., and E.A. Hoebel. 1941. *The Cheyenne Way: Conflict and Case Law in Primitive Jurisprudence.* Norman: University of Oklahoma Press.

Liu, Meng. 2002. Rebellion and Revenge: The Meaning of Suicide of Women in Rural China. *International Journal of Social Welfare* 11 (4): 300–309.

Lukianoff, Greg. 2014. *Unlearning Liberty: Campus Censorship and the End of American Debate.* New York: Encounter Books.

Lynch, Rene. 2013. Paula Deen Lawsuit Dismissed, but Not Before It Destroyed Career. *Los Angeles Times,* August 23. http://www.latimes.com/food/dailydish/la-dd-paula-deen-lawsuit-dismissed-20130823-story.html.

Mackey, Robert. 2014. Can Hashtag Activism Save Kidnapped Nigerian Girls? *The New York Times New Blog,* May 7. http://thelede.blogs.nytimes.com/2014/0/07/can-hashtag-activism-save-kidnapped-nigerian-girls/.

Manning, Jason. 2012. Suicide as Social Control. *Sociological Forum* 27 (1): 207–227.

———. 2015. Aggressive Suicide. *International Journal of Law, Crime, and Justice* 43 (3): 326–341.

Merry, Sally Engle. 1984. Rethinking Gossip and Scandal. In *Toward a General Theory of Social Control. Volume 1: Fundamentals,* ed. Donald Black, 271–302. Orlando: Academic Press.

————. 1990. *Getting Justice and Getting Even: Legal Consciousness among Working-Class Americans.* Chicago: University of Chicago Press.

Microaggressions: Power, Privilege, and Everyday Life (blog). 2014. http://microaggressions.tumblr.com/about.

Murphy, Robert F., and Leonard Kasdan. 1959. The Structure of Parallel Cousin Marriage. *American Anthropologist* 61 (1): 17–29.

National Center for Education Statistics. 2010. *Status and Trends in the Education of Racial and Ethnic Minorities.* https://nces.ed.gov/pubs2010/2010015/indicator6_24.asp.

Owens, Eric. 2013. Dartmouth Student Who Spoke 'Mock Chinese' Remains on the Lam. *The Daily Caller*, February 7. http://dailycaller.com/2013/02/07/dartmouth-student-who-spoke-mock-chinese-remains-on-the-lam/.

Phillips, Scott, and Mark Cooney. 2005. Aiding Peace, Abetting Violence: Third Parties and the Management of Conflict. *American Sociological Review* 70 (2): 334–354.

Pinker, Steven. 2011. *The Better Angels of Our Nature: Why Violence Has Declined.* New York: Viking.

Pizzi, William T. 1999. *Trials Without Truth: Why Our System of Criminal Trials Has Become an Expensive Failure and What We Need to Do to Rebuild It.* New York: New York University Press.

Putnam, Robert D. 2000. *Bowling Alone: The Collapse and Revival of American Community.* New York: Simon and Schuster.

Rani, Manju, Sekhar Bonu, and Nafissatou Diop-Sidibe. 2004. An Empirical Investigation of Attitudes Towards Wife-Beating Among Men and Women in Seven Sub-Saharan African Countries. *African Journal of Reproductive Health* 8 (3): 116–136.

Reiss, Matthias. 2007. Introduction. In *The Street as Stage: Protest Marches and Public Rallies since the Nineteenth Century*, ed. Matthias Reiss, 1–21. London: Oxford University Press.

Rosen, Michael. 2012. *Dignity: Its History and Meaning.* Cambridge: Harvard University Press.

Santoro, Wayne A. 2008. The Civil Rights Movement and the Right to Vote: Black Protest, Segregationist Violence and the Audience. *Social Forces* 86 (4): 1391–1414.

Seitz, Don C. 1929. *Famous American Duels.* New York: Thomas Y. Crowell Company.

Senechal de la Roche, Roberta. 2001. Why Is Collective Violence Collective? *Sociological Theory* 19 (2): 126–144.

Thoden van Velzen, H.U.E., and W. van Wetering. 1960. Residence, Power Groups and Intra-Societal Aggression: An Enquiry into Conditions Leading to Peacefulness Within Non-stratified Societies. *International Archives of Ethnography* 49: 169–200.

Thorne, Barrie. 1975. Protest and the Problem of Credibility: Uses of Knowledge and Risk-Taking in the Draft Resistance Movement of the 1960's. *Social Problems* 23 (2): 111–123.

Tuchman, Barbara W. 1978. *A Distant Mirror: The Calamitous 14th Century.* New York: Balantine Books.

Ugwuegbu, Denis Chimaeze E. 1979. Racial and Evidential Factors in Juror Attribution of Legal Responsibility. *Journal of Experimental Social Psychology* 15 (2): 133–146.

Vidich, Arthur J., and Joseph Bensman. 1958. *Small Town in Mass Society: Class, Power, and Religion in a Rural Community.* Garden City: Anchor Books.

Westin, Alan F., Henry I. Kurtz, and Albert Robbins. 1981. *Whistle Blowing: Loyalty and Dissent in the Corporation.* New York: McGraw-Hill.

Yngvesson, Barbara. 1989. Inventing Law in Local Settings: Rethinking Popular Legal Culture. *The Yale Law Journal* 98 (8): 1694–1689.

CHAPTER 3

Trigger Warnings, Safe Spaces, and the Language of Victimhood

Those who compare honor and dignity cultures have long noted that there are many differences between them other than the way they encourage people to handle insults (see, e.g., Wyatt-Brown 1982; Leung and Cohen 2011; Ijzerman and Cohen 2011; Nisbett and Cohen 1996:Chapter 5). Consider what people do for fun. Where violence is a common way of handling conflict, it is a common source of recreation as well. Those who prize fighting skills often make sport of those same skills, with contests in wrestling, fencing, or marksmanship. The feudal lords of medieval Europe were fond of tournaments in which knights used their military skills to compete for prizes. Also popular were such violent pastimes as hunting, falconry, bear-baiting, and dog fighting. Swordsmanship, both for fun and as practice for dueling, remained popular among the English aristocracy well into the 1700s, and gangs of young gentlemen engaged in a popular recreation known as *scrowning* "in which [they] forcibly cleared taverns, broke windows and assaulted bystanders" including "attacking without provocation young men and women by cutting their faces and heads with swords and penknives" (Shoemaker 2001:199).

The honorable also gravitate toward other forms of competitive risk-taking. Aristocrats in seventeenth- and eighteenth-century England spent much of their time gambling for high stakes. Especially popular were elaborate card games, which allowed contestants to best their competitors through skill: "The true courtier never plays only to win money. If he gambles, it is to demonstrate a prowess superior to that of his adversary"

© The Author(s) 2018
B. Campbell, J. Manning, *The Rise of Victimhood Culture*,
https://doi.org/10.1007/978-3-319-70329-9_3

(quoted in Evans 2002:4). The planters of colonial Virginia would bet "on almost any proposition in which there was an element of chance," though they too preferred tests of skill such as card games and quarter-horse racing (Breen 1977:239). Throughout the antebellum South, plantation owners would play card games that lasted throughout the night, and "betting was almost a social obligation" (Wyatt-Brown 1982:343).

The rise of dignity culture in the eighteenth and nineteenth centuries involved moralizing social movements that condemned not just dueling, but also excessive gambling, drinking, and blood sports involving animals (Harrison 1967). Of course these pastimes did not disappear, but they did decline in popularity and social importance, especially among the middle and upper classes. Fighting and gambling were no longer necessary skills for a young member of the social elite. Contact sports that persisted evolved into safer, more regulated, and less violent forms (Dunning 1983).[1] Competitive risk-taking generally declined as society no longer placed the same degree of emphasis on fearlessness, allowing for prudence and safety to become more highly valued (Friedman 1994:Chapter 4; Furedi 2002:17–18, 2016:10–11).[2] In the United States the decline of honor was uneven, happening more quickly and thoroughly in the North than in the South (Nisbett and Cohen 1996). Even today the South has higher rates of accidental death than the North, and surveys reveal that people who endorse honor norms—something more common in the South—report engaging in more risky behavior (Barnes et al. 2012).

Moral culture also affects the way people comport and present themselves (Cohen and Leung 2009; Ijzerman and Cohen 2011). Among honorable people such as the Sarakastani shepherds of Greece, "the weak, the humble, the modest … are not virtuous" (Campbell 1965:152, see also Campbell 1964:317). The honorable therefore present themselves in bold

---

[1] Modern rugby, for example, is descended from a medieval game in which an unrestricted number of people, some on foot and some on horseback, played according to loosely defined rules, without a referee, using cudgels to batter fellow players (Dunning 1983:132–133).

[2] Legal scholar Lawrence Friedman (1994) argues that historical increases in safety and security have led to a greater expectation that life will be safe, such that modern people are less likely than their predecessors to tolerate accident and misfortune as normal parts of existence. While we emphasize the role of the legal system in providing security and suppressing violent conflict, Friedman points to other social trends—such as improvements in medical technology and food production—that could also contribute to a greater cultural expectation of safety.

and forceful fashion. They are prone to bragging about their exploits and engaging in conspicuous displays of their wealth and status. A prominent modern example is the boastful lyrics of rap songs. Rap, especially gangsta rap, is a genre rooted in poor black communities governed by an honorable "code of the street," and its lyrics often consist of performers bragging about their violence, wealth, drug use, sexual prowess, and contempt for the law (Anderson 1999; Armstrong 2001; Herd 2009).[3] People in dignity cultures would be apt to find this level of boastfulness distasteful, even if it were about behaviors otherwise consistent with their morality. And while the dignified also concern themselves with outward status symbols, such as fashionable clothing, most would not understand the degree to which the honorable are willing to risk impoverishment or even death for the sake of maintaining appearances.[4]

These and other differences are not surprising. For one thing moral cultures do not crop up at random, but are shaped by social conditions—conditions that have predictable effects on various aspects of life.[5] Additionally, the presence of different forms of conflict and social control has a direct effect on the incentives and constraints present in people's lives.

---

[3] English gentlemen in the sixteenth century also considered "sexual rapacity ... to be an essential characteristic of men of fashion" (Dabhoiwala 1996:206).

[4] In seventeenth-century England, where being honorable and being fashionable went hand in hand, many gentlemen turned to suicide after squandering their fortunes on gambling and other kinds of expensive living that were the outward mark of their social status (MacDonald and Murphy 1990:278–280). Urban ethnographer Elijah Anderson (1999) describes how fashionable shoes, clothing, and other status symbols are a crucial part of "campaigning for respect" in a poor black neighborhood in Philadelphia, such that young people spend their meager resources on acquiring these symbols and then flaunt them even though it makes them a target for predators. Honor is, as sociologist Mark Cooney observes, "the antithesis of middle-class rationality" (Cooney 1998:113). Dignity, on the other hand, is more consistent with the so-called Protestant ethic of systematic labor, frugality, and savings famously described by the early sociologist Max Weber (1958).

[5] Black proposes that all kinds of social behavior conform to underlying social conditions—or, in technical terms, *social life is isomorphic with its social field* (Black 1989:91, 2004:21; see also Campbell 2015:322). The result is that different types of behavior often exhibit similarities in form and style when they occur in the same social setting. For example, Black (1989:Chapter 4) argues that the conditions that lead people to handle conflict with extensive negotiations also promote extensive negotiation in other realms of life, such as in economic exchanges or arranging marriages between two family groups. Similarly, Campbell (2015) proposes that social structures conducive to extreme, coercive, one-sided moralism—as in genocide—are also conducive to extreme, coercive, one-sided economic transactions—as in the extensive looting and enslavement that often accompany genocide.

Someone who lives in a world riven by blood feuds faces a very different set of circumstances than someone who does not. Furthermore, as we noted in the first chapter, moral ideas orient our entire lives. They influence how we carry ourselves, how we treat others, and how we understand our world.

Victimhood culture is no different. As we have already argued, its effects go beyond reporting slights as microaggressions. It influences how people present themselves. For instance, just as the honorable are prone to boast of their wealth and power, people socialized into victimhood are prone to advertise their disadvantage and marginality. Thus, a letter of application to a graduate program might begin with a litany of reasons the candidate has always been "hated" for his minority status, while another tells of the applicant enduring sexual harassment "every" day of her life.[6] And some who might be taken for members of a majority group strive to be identified as minorities instead (e.g., Devaney 2016; Carroll 2017).[7] We have also noted that victimhood culture includes students beseeching campus administrators for other kinds of assistance and protection, most notably in the form of trigger warnings and safe spaces. In this chapter we consider these two manifestations of victimhood culture in more detail. As we shall see, both these practices mesh with victimhood culture's central moral concerns, and both illustrate how the rise of victimhood leads to another cultural change—a distinctive language that shapes how people describe and understand the world.

TRIGGER WARNINGS

Victimhood culture, as we define it, is marked by a low tolerance for slight. It produces a correspondingly low tolerance for all sorts of discomfort and difficulty, even if these are not considered offenses as such. Victimhood culture is also distinguished by a tendency to ask third parties for support in conflicts, and to do so in ways that advertise or exaggerate one's victimization. It likewise produces a tendency to ask third parties, especially

[6] These examples are based on personal observations.

[7] For example, the president of the American–Arab Anti-Discrimination Committee supports the recognition of Arabs as a distinct racial category on the US census, saying, "We want to be counted in the census as Arab Americans.... Right now, Arab Americans are defined as white" (Devaney 2016). Note that *white* is a category that includes multiple ethnic groups (Spaniards, Albanians, Germans, Irish, etc.), so the campaign is not simply a matter of ethnic pride, but of preferring to avoid a supposedly privileged racial category.

authorities, for help with a variety of problems, and a tendency to do so in ways that emphasize one's vulnerability. One result of these tendencies is the campaign to implement trigger warnings that protect people from coming into contact with words, images, or ideas that might cause them distress.

The concept of *trigger warning* is fairly new, having been coined on feminist blogs and online discussion forums before rapidly spreading across college campuses and beyond (Lukianoff and Haidt 2015). It refers to the effects of post-traumatic stress disorder (PTSD), a mental condition in which people who have been through extreme situations might later experience symptoms such as panic attacks and flashbacks in which they relive aspects of the traumatic event. A *trigger* is any experience that sparks these symptoms. For instance, one veteran of the Vietnam War has flash-backs to his wartime experiences triggered by helicopters flying over his house (Snyder 2014). It is difficult to predict or prevent the experiences that will trigger these episodes. One rape victim, for example, had panic attacks when seeing a fish butchered at a market, while another suffered vivid recollections of her rape while giving birth in a hospital (Snyder 2009:42–55, 211, citing Raine 2002:181–182; Francisco 1999:132). But the core idea behind trigger warnings is to inform those with PTSD if they are about to see or hear something likely to remind them of their trau-matic experience, such as a film depiction of rape. This then allows the trauma victim to avoid the trigger and the problems it might cause.

By 2014 student activists on many campuses were calling for trigger warnings regarding content in their courses. While some of them asked professors to voluntarily issue them as a matter of courtesy, others—in keeping with victimhood culture's reliance on authority—demanded the administration implement policies requiring them.

In March of that year the University of California, Santa Barbara's stu-dent government called for the administration to institute a policy requir-ing all course syllabi to have a warning about any class content that could trigger trauma symptoms, and to allow students to miss classes containing such material without harming their grade (Diamba 2014; Medina 2014). More recently, in 2017, student delegates in Oklahoma voted to petition the state government to pass a resolution requiring that professors "give written warning one day before a class will discuss rape, self-harm, and kidnapping, among other topics, and … that professors label classes that deal with such content" (Shimshock 2017).

Many of those who call for trigger warnings focus on graphic film portrayals of rape, warfare, and other violence, with the intention of protecting those who have endured such extreme ordeals. Others, however, have a broader conception of what constitutes a trauma trigger. Mere discussion of violence may qualify. In February 2014 a student at Rutgers University wrote a column calling for trigger warnings to be attached to the novels and stories commonly assigned in literature courses, such as F. Scott Fitzgerald's *The Great Gatsby* and Virginia Woolf's *Mrs. Dalloway*, the latter of which contains "a disturbing narrative that examines the suicidal inclinations and post-traumatic experiences of an English war veteran" (Wythe 2014). Discussions of inequality and intolerance may also be triggering. At Oberlin College, suggested guidelines for faculty stated that trigger warnings should extend to any material involving "racism, classism, sexism, heterosexism, cissexism, ableism, and other issues of privilege and oppression" (Jarvie 2014; Medina 2014). This could include, for example, Chinua Achebe's novel *Things Fall Apart*, set in nineteenth-century Nigeria and depicting life before and after the arrival of British invaders, which might trigger trauma related to racism and colonialism (Medina 2014). Students at Columbia University warned that Greek mythology could be triggering:

> "Ovid's 'Metamorphoses' … like so many texts in the Western canon … contains triggering and offensive material that marginalizes student identities in the classroom," wrote the four students, who are members of Columbia's Multicultural Affairs Advisory Board. "These texts, wrought with histories and narratives of exclusion and oppression, can be difficult to read and discuss as a survivor, a person of color, or a student from a low-income background." (Quoted in Miller 2015)

Depictions of the male body might trigger as well. In April 2014 a Wellesley student published an editorial in the *Huffington Post* calling for the removal of a life-like statue of a man in his underwear. She argued that the statue, entitled "Sleepwalker," was "potentially triggering" for victims of sexual assault (Mahmood 2014). Over 300 people signed a petition to remove the statue, which, according to the petition, was "a source of apprehension, fear, and triggering thoughts" and thus "a source of undue stress for many Wellesley College students" (Mahmood 2014). So too for paintings: A mural in a cafeteria at Pitzer College, depicting a handgun with flowers projecting from its barrel (a reference to anti-war protests of the 1960s), attracted criticism from a student senator who found it "emotionally triggering for very obvious reasons" (quoted in Glick 2016). In an email to the student body he wrote, "My Black Mental and Emotional Health Matters. I shouldn't be reminded every time I leave my dorm room of how easy my life can be taken away, or how many Black lives have been taken away because of police brutality" (quoted in Glick 2016). Even warnings of possible physical danger may themselves require a warning. At the University of Iowa an email sent out by the campus alert system was prefaced by the statement "Trigger Warning: This warning addresses a report of sexual misconduct" (quoted in McDonald 2016).

Harvard law professor Jeannie Suk Gerson argues that the increasingly expansive definition of what constitutes a trigger makes it difficult for her to teach about rape law:

> Student organizations representing women's interests now routinely advise students that they should not feel pressured to attend or participate in class sessions that focus on the law of sexual violence, and which might therefore be traumatic. These organizations also ask criminal-law teachers to warn their classes that the rape-law unit might "trigger" traumatic memories. Individual students often ask teachers not to include the law of rape on exams for fear that the material would cause them to perform less well. One teacher I know was recently asked by a student not to use the word "violate" in class—as in "Does this conduct violate the law?"—because the word was triggering. Some students have even suggested that rape law should not be taught because of its potential to cause distress. (Gerson 2014)

Trigger warnings are not limited to US campuses. Undergraduates studying law at Oxford University in the United Kingdom receive warnings about lectures addressing "potentially distressing" content such as sexual offenses (Scott 2016). Those studying English are warned before reading Robert Lowell's poem "Before the Union Dead," which contains a racial slur, and told they can leave the room or cover up the page (Manning and Wace 2016). Faculty at the University of Edinburgh, the London School of Economics, and elsewhere provide warnings for a range of subjects including "Christianity, popular culture, history, forensic science, photography, politics and law" (Bulman 2016, see also Grant and Harding 2017). And in 2017 Monash University became the first Australian institution to enact a policy regarding trigger warnings for its courses, asking faculty "to review course content looking for 'emotionally confronting material'" present in discussions of "sexual assault, violence, domestic abuse, child abuse, eating disorders, self-harm, suicide, pornography, abortion, kidnapping, hate speech, animal cruelty and animal deaths including abattoirs" (Palmer 2017).

Trigger warnings have also spread off campus. A Canadian government website "National Inquiry into Missing and Murdered Indigenous Women and Girls" features the following warning:

> This website deals with topics which may cause trauma to readers due to its troubling subject matter. The Government of Canada recognizes the need for safety measures to minimize the risks associated with traumatic subject matter. A national, toll-free crisis call line has been set up to provide support for anyone who requires assistance.... Please call ... if you or someone you know is triggered and needs help or support while reading the content on this website. (Government of Canada 2016)

Some now suggest trigger warnings for television shows and periodicals (Jarvie 2014). Of course movies and television programs have long come with advisories regarding sex, profanity, and graphic violence. The Motion Picture Association of America provides film ratings for this purpose, and television shows are sometimes prefaced with a warning that "viewer discretion is advised." But judging from their activities on campus, many advocates of trigger warnings have a much broader conception of what content is harmful to viewers and prefer measures that are more stringent than those already in use. For example, the recent Netflix series "13 Reasons Why"—which depicts sexual violence and suicide—featured a TV-MA rating indicating it was for mature audiences only and included a "content warning" before two of its episodes, but still received much backlash from those who found it potentially damaging to its audience and demanded additional precautions (Kelley 2017).[8]

---

[8] In some ways these complaints about the dangers of modern media resemble earlier moral panics about the threats of comic books, rock n' roll music, heavy metal music, and so on. Notably, though, these earlier campaigns focused to a greater extent on entertainment's influence on children and adolescents, whereas contemporary campaigns do not restrict themselves to concern with protecting the very young. Also notable is that adolescents and young adults appear likely to support and partake in campaigns for trigger warnings, and may be much less resistant than youth in previous generations were to such protection and regulation.

SAFE SPACES

In some ways the transition to victimhood culture is an intensification of the trends seen in the transition from honor to dignity. Recreational violence and risk-taking continue to decline, especially among young elites, and safety becomes increasingly important (Wilson 2002; Lukianoff and Haidt 2015). Sociologist Frank Furedi argues that for Western society as a whole safety has become a moral value, such that "the term 'safe' signals more than the absence of danger: It also conveys the connotation of a virtue. The adverb 'safe,' as in safe sex, safe drinking, safe eating, and safe space, signals responsibility" (Furedi 2017:10). If dignity culture makes safety a virtue, then victimhood culture practically deifies it. We see this in the spread of trigger warnings meant to protect the vulnerable from psychological damage. We also see it in the growing calls for campus safe spaces.

The meaning of *safe space* varies. The term originated in the women's rights movement, where it referred to forums where women's issues could be discussed, and was later adopted by LGBT activists to refer to a place where sexual minorities could be themselves without fear of judgment or discrimination (Paxson 2016). In some contexts, the term is a way of advertising that LGBT individuals are welcome and need not hide their sexuality. For instance, in the early 2000s, some faculty at the University of Virginia used rainbow-colored "safe space" stickers on their office doors to advertise their willingness to listen to students who wanted to talk about LGBT related issues. Similarly, the Counseling Center at Georgia's Columbus State University recently led a push to have offices and rooms marked as safe spaces where students could expect to be "heard, respected and accepted" (WVTM 2017). The goal of these safe spaces was to "provide an informal means of counseling by simply offering a quick stop for students to vent, ask questions, or get further resources and connections if needed" (WVTM 2017).

Increasingly, however, calls for safe spaces mean something quite different. When student leaders at Clemson University wrote a letter to a campus administrator demanding a safe space for LGBT students, they were not asking supportive faculty to advertise their willingness to help. Instead they were asking for a specially designated area for sexual minorities who "enter campus with the deck stacked against them" (quoted in Chumley 2017). Similarly, when a microaggression complaint against a dean led to a rash of protests at Claremont McKenna College, the college president agreed to the students' demands to create "a permanent safe space for students of color in the near future" (Glick 2015). American University likewise responded to a racial controversy by designating a lounge area as a "sanctuary for people of color" (quoted in Owens 2017; see also Fortin 2017). And in 2015 activists at Princeton occupied the office of the university's president and presented a number of demands, including "a dedicated space on campus for black students that is clearly marked" (Knapp 2015).

In these cases a safe space is not merely a place where members of a minority group are welcome, but an officially designated area in which they may be free from interaction with others unlike themselves. The idea is that interacting with the cultural majority causes stress for minorities, perhaps in the form of microaggressions or in feelings of anxiety and isolation that arise just from being different. Safe spaces protect minorities from such stress by providing a special area where they can be themselves without fear of judgment or social awkwardness, and where they can provide one another with mutual support in the face of the virulent prejudice believed to infect their campus.

These kinds of safe spaces thus involve a degree of racial, ethnic, or sexual segregation. During the 2015 microaggression protests at the Claremont colleges, a coffeehouse at Scripps College announced that for one night it would only allow "people of color" and their personal guests so that they might "decompress, discuss, grieve, plan, support each other, etc." (Glick 2015). While the Scripps College coffee house allowed white students invited by nonwhites, an art show at Pomona College forbade whites altogether. According to the event website, "This show's intent is to create a space that is pro-POC [people of color], pro-black, and anti-white supremacist.... While you may want to invite a white friend or ally, to make this a safe and comfortable space for other POC, we ask that you do not" (quoted in Glick 2015).

The logic of segregation can also extend to dining arrangements. Morton Schapiro, president of Northwestern University, defends the desire of a group of black students not to have white students join them in the cafeteria because "we all deserve safe spaces" and "those black students had every right to enjoy their lunches in peace" (Schapiro 2016). Demand for safe spaces has likewise led to a growing demand for segregated housing. Housing for blacks and other minorities is now institutionalized at Berkeley and MIT, while in the United Kingdom similar movements have led to LGBT-only housing at the Universities of

Birmingham, Central Lancashire, and York (Furedi 2017:83–84). Safe space segregation even occurs among university faculty: "In the U.K. the equality committee of the University and College Union has decided that its academic members who are white, male, straight, and have no disability cannot participate in all its conference discussions" because some of these are meant to be "unique 'safe spaces'" (Furedi 2017:83–84).

In addition to safe spaces defined by race, ethnicity, gender, and sexuality, there are safe spaces dedicated to the protection of other kinds of oppressed, marginalized, or otherwise victimized people. Trigger warnings might not suffice to protect victims of trauma, who require safe spaces in which potential triggers are completely absent. Given the expansive notion of what constitutes a trigger, this can in practice mean a space where they are shielded from all manner of words and images. Indeed, some consider ideas they disagree with to be threats to their safety. We have already mentioned the example of Brown University's debate between feminist Jessica Valenti and libertarian Wendy McElroy. One Brown senior, knowing that McElroy would likely criticize the description of college campuses as a rape culture, became concerned that McElroy's speech would be "damaging" to students because "it could serve to invalidate people's experiences" (Shulevitz 2015). The student and several fellow members of the campus Sexual Assault Task Force sprang into action. After a meeting with campus administrators, the university's president announced plans to stage a simultaneous competing event, while the student activists posted flyers advertising a safe space equipped with various soothing comforts (including blankets, coloring books, and a puppy) for anyone upset by the debate (Shulevitz 2015).

As demand for safe spaces grows, student activists have begun to argue that their entire college or university should be a safe space where students can exist without emotional discomfort. In the words of Smith College's Student Government Association, responding to the presence of a racial slur in a scholar's lecture about the historical use of racial slurs, "If Smith is unsafe for one student, it is unsafe for all students" (Shulevitz 2015). Given the range of words and ideas considered offensive, triggering, or otherwise harmful, maintaining this campus-wide safe space often entails banning or disinviting guest speakers. At Oxford University's Christ Church College in November 2014, student activists succeeded in convincing administrators to cancel a debate on "abortion culture." One student praised the decision, saying, "It clearly makes the most sense for the safety—both physical and mental—of the students who live and work in

Christ Church" (Calver 2014, quoted in Shulevitz 2015). At the University of London students from the school's Islamic Society opposing a talk by human rights campaigner Maryam Namazie claimed she had "violated their safe space" and that "the university should be a safe space for all our students" (Furedi 2017:82). In 2017, Oregon's Linfield College pulled funding for a talk by University of Toronto psychologist Jordan Peterson, who had attracted condemnation for his refusal to use gender-neutral pronouns. Prior to the cancellation Peterson had tweeted that he was going to Linfield to "violate" its "safe spaces"—seemingly a reference to his controversial opinions and those who take offense at them. A Linfield faculty dean noted this in her statement on the cancellation, saying that Jordan "intended to violate the safety of our community" (Piper 2017).

Other forms of political expression also threaten safety. At Emory University a group of about 50 students confronted the president after seeing "Trump 2016" written in chalk on campus grounds. According to these students the messages endorsing a presidential candidate made them feel intimidated. One remarked, "I'm supposed to feel comfortable and safe [here]" (quoted in Messing 2016). Not surprisingly, criticism of safe spaces is itself unsafe. At Ohio University in April 2016, college Republicans left a message on the campus graffiti wall (where students are allowed to paint messages) mocking the idea of trigger warnings and safe spaces: "Trigger Warning: There are no safe spaces in real life!" Another student responded on Twitter by calling for an immediate investigation into the "threat," and the campus police department held an open meeting with an LGBT student group whose own recent message on the wall had been painted over (Gockowski 2016). Even events that seemingly have no connection to politics or opinions of any kind still might be deemed threatening. For instance, at the University of Minnesota in 2014 a student group cancelled a planned event called "Hump Day"—in which students would be allowed to pet a camel—because some students saw it as both cruel to animals and insensitive to Middle Easterners, thus creating "an uncomfortable and possibly unsafe environment" (Lukianoff and Haidt 2015).

Maintaining the campus safe space can also require erasing reminders of historical injustice, so student activists campaign to remove statues and rename buildings commemorating historical figures whose actions are now seen as immoral (Furedi 2017:58–60). At Princeton student protesters demanded that the name of the former US President Woodrow Wilson be removed from all buildings and programs because Wilson believed in racial segregation (Sunstein 2017). In 2017, Yale changed the name of its

Calhoun College because its namesake, nineteenth-century statesman John C. Calhoun, supported slavery (Parker and Yared 2017). Harvard Law School opted to change its seal, which derived from the family crest of an eighteenth-century benefactor who owned slaves (Schramm 2017). A student group at Columbia demanded the administration remove a statue of Thomas Jefferson, author of the Declaration of Independence and third President of the United States, because Jefferson was a slave holder who fathered children with one of his slaves. According to a statement from the group, "venerating Thomas Jefferson validates rape, sexual violence, and racism on this campus" (Knighton 2017). Students at the University of Missouri likewise demanded the removal of a Jefferson statue, calling him a "racist rapist" (Rohrer 2015). A statue of Jefferson at William and Mary was covered with sticky notes reading, "Racism is a choice" and "How dare you glorify him?" (Holcomb 2015). Protesters at Bristol University in the United Kingdom wanted the school to change the name of Willis Memorial Hall, named for the school's first chancellor who, during his lifetime in the nineteenth century, had links with the slave trade (Nolan 2017). Students at Oxford and the University of Capetown mounted campaigns to remove statues of Cecil Rhodes, a nineteenth-century imperialist and founder of both the University of Capetown and Oxford's prestigious Rhodes Scholarship (Nolan 2017; Furedi 2017:59).

   In some cases, mere mental association with bad history is enough to disturb and trigger. In 2015 students at Pennsylvania's Lebanon Valley College demanded that Lynch Memorial Hall be renamed. This was not because of any objection to Clyde A. Lynch, the former president of the college for whom the building was named, but because the name reminded them of the practice of lynching (Marks 2017). That demand was not met, but in 2016 Harvard University changed the name of its *house masters* to *faculty deans* because students objected that the word *master* reminded them of the institution of slavery (Cunningham et al. 2016). Yale likewise changed the title of its residential college *masters* to *heads of college*. In his statement announcing the change, Yale's president noted that master derives from the Latin *magister*, "meaning 'chief, head, director, teacher,' and it appears in the titles of university degrees (master of arts, master of science, and others) and in many aspects of the larger culture (master craftsman, master builder)" but he still conceded to the demands of those who associated the term with slavery (Salovey 2016).

   As with microaggressions and trigger warnings, a concern with safe spaces has expanded beyond the university into other realms of life. Media outlet *Buzzfeed* announced in 2017 it would accept applications from high school students who "need access to a safe space from [their] prom" and want to attend an LGBT "queer prom" in Los Angeles (Stites 2017). In 2017, as part of Toronto's Centre for Social Innovation's "How to Be an Ally" series, a local spoken word artist ran workshops to help people create "brave safe spaces," defined as "an environment where a group or community can be authentic, honest and vulnerable about their experiences" in order to counteract threats to "tolerance and inclusion" (Ngabo 2017). Some musical acts now seek to make their concerts safe spaces. This includes punk acts that have eliminated moshing (a kind of violent dancing in which concertgoers shove and slam into one another). According to one performer, "we're trying to create a safer space, and, right now, I can't see a way to have moshing that's completely respectful of everyone there" (quoted in Ewens 2017). By rejecting "a very masculine type of aggression" such acts ensure that "minorities—women, trans people, people of colour, and so on—are able to feel free" (Ewens 2017).

The Harms of Safety

Trigger warnings and safe spaces are consistent with the logic and concerns of victimhood culture, as both individual loss and collective disadvantage are emphasized, advertised, and made a matter for official policy. The common denominator of both practices is the attempt to protect people, especially minorities, from harm or distress. Proponents of these practices assume that they succeed in doing so and so are beneficial for the people they are meant to help. Writing in the *Huffington Post*, journalist Linsday Holmes says that "trigger warnings are potentially lifesaving for people who have dealt with traumas like sexual assault, hate crimes or violence" (Holmes 2016). Brown University President Christina Paxson says that by employing trigger warnings and safe spaces, universities give students "the space to have the discussions that will make them better scholars and prepare them to best serve society" (2016).

Others raise the possibility that this protectiveness may be counterproductive. In Chap. 1 we mentioned Lukianoff and Haidt's (2015) argument that teaching students to recognize microaggressions goes against the principles of cognitive behavioral therapy, a technique known to be successful in helping patients deal with depression and anxiety. Such therapy is rooted in the idea that our own thought patterns are a major source of suffering, so learning to think differently is an effective way to alleviate it. For instance, we may make ourselves miserable through a tendency to read negative intentions into someone else's behavior and to assume, without reasonable evidence, that they dislike us. Learning to recognize and avoid such thinking removes a major source of negative emotions. Contrariwise, encouraging people to see others' words and actions as subtle gibes and evidence of bias can increase negative emotions, leading to greater anxiety and depression.

Lukianoff and Haidt (2015) also apply this argument to trigger warnings, safe spaces, and other attempts to protect students from harm or discomfort. Therapists teach patients to avoid *fortune-telling*—a tendency to anticipate bad outcomes, which carried to extremes can cause people to see danger and disaster looming at every turn. Frequent trigger warnings appear to contradict this therapeutic strategy by constantly reminding people that something they are about to read, see, or hear is potentially dangerous and harmful. Teaching young people that so many mundane things are threatening may very well increase their anxiety. Perhaps it can even become a kind of self-fulfilling prophecy, conditioning people to have strong aversive reactions they would not have had otherwise.

Therapists also teach patients to avoid *magnification*—emphasizing and exaggerating the significance of bad things in their lives—and *negative filtering*—tending to focus on the bad aspects of life rather than the good. Again, the culture of extreme protectiveness encourages the opposite. All manner of unpleasant things are magnified into threats to personal safety— not challenges to be overcome or hassles to be dealt with, but dangers from which only the powerful can protect. Moral crusades to eliminate these threats make them a constant focus of attention and topic of conversation.

Trigger warnings and safe spaces may even be counterproductive for the small proportion of students whose experiences and symptoms match the classical definition of PTSD. Lukianoff and Haidt (2015) argue that attempting to help such people by shielding them from anything that remotely reminds them of their traumatic experience is actually the opposite of how therapists try to return such patients to normality. Therapists try to help sufferers overcome uncontrollable fears of everyday situations through *exposure therapy*, gradually habituating the patient to their triggers until they no longer provoke the same extreme reactions. Lukianoff and Haidt say the classroom is likely to be a good environment for such exposure:

Students with PTSD should of course get treatment, but they should not try to avoid normal life, with its many opportunities for habituation. Classroom discussions are safe places to be exposed to incidental reminders of trauma (such as the word *violate*). A discussion of violence is unlikely to be followed by actual violence, so it is a good way to help students change the associations that are causing them discomfort. (Lukianoff and Haidt 2015)

The overall result of trigger warnings and safe spaces, then, may be to retard the healing of trauma victims, and to encourage fear, anxiety, and depression in the population as a whole.

As noted above, calls for trigger warnings and safe spaces might be using the terms in different ways or focusing on different things. Any discussion of their costs and benefits should therefore take account of exactly what kind of policies are under consideration. But a complete discussion of costs and benefits would at least consider the possibility that safe spaces and trigger warnings, especially in their most extreme forms, actually harm those they are meant to protect. A rational debate about this possibility would, however, require that the parties involved agree on how to define and measure harm. This may be easier said than done, as victimhood and dignity culture often use the concept quite differently.

THE LANGUAGE OF HARM

Perhaps the most notable feature of trigger warnings and safe spaces is that they demonstrate a marked tendency to describe various issues in a language of harm. The same goes for other complaints and demands made by student activists. For instance, when a group of Yale students demanded that white poets be dropped from the curriculum, they did not phrase this as a matter of preference ("We'd rather read non-white poets") or even as a matter of virtue ("Ethnic diversity is good") but as a matter of students being hurt. Thus, they argued that a "year spent around a seminar table where the literary contributions of women, people of color, and queer folk are absent actively harms all students, regardless of their identity" (quoted in Furedi 2017:29).

People in other cultures might describe their discomfort with a written description of violence as being squeamish or tenderhearted. They might describe bad memories as challenges to be overcome, not threats that require protection. They might say a depiction of racism made them sad or angry, but not that it impaired their mental health. They might say they disagree with someone else's views, but not that they are assaulted by them. They might describe daily problems in terms of difficulty rather than damage, and aversion to certain experiences as a matter of dislike rather than danger. Indeed, we see in trigger warnings and safe spaces many behaviors—silencing political opponents, preferentially associating with coethnics, criticizing ugly artwork, avoiding uncomfortable conversations—that appear elsewhere with different descriptions and justifications.

Here we have another facet of changing moral cultures: With the rise of new patterns of conflict and social control comes new moral language—new words, new meanings for old words, and different ways of describing the world. This is significant. One need not endorse more extreme claims about the degree to which language shapes thought to agree that it has an impact on the course of social life. Words and concepts affect what people talk about, what they pay attention to, how they understand problems, and how they try to solve them. Consider some of these linguistic differences and their effects on social life.

Moral Vocabulary

People often develop extensive and specialized vocabularies for those things that matter most to them. An urban dweller might describe a field full of animals as horses, but to the horse farmer they are appaloosas and palominos, mares, fillies, colts, and geldings. The moral concerns of a society are likewise reflected in its moral vocabulary. The Turkish language, for example, has several different words for describing various kinds and aspects of honor—individual male honor, family and female honor, honorable pride, sensitivity to honor, and so forth (Sev'er and Yurdakul 2001:972–973). Given the value they place on bravery, we might also expect honor cultures to have a rich vocabulary of derogatory terms for cowardice, such as the increasingly old-fashioned English terms *poltroon*, *pusillanimous*, *chicken-hearted*, *lily-livered*, and *yellow-bellied*.

Victimhood culture produces its own special vocabulary. In addition to the concept of microaggression, we now have a host of moral jargon to describe various kinds of slights and small acts of oppression. Subtypes of microaggression include the *microassault*, *microinsult*, and *microinvalidation*. *Mansplaining* is a new term for when a man explains something to a woman in a way she perceives as condescending; its kindred terms are *whitesplaining* (when a white person explains something to a nonwhite person) and *straightsplaining* (when a straight person explains something to a gay person). Then there are the various types of shaming. *Slut shaming* involves passing judgment on a woman's sexual immodesty or promiscuity, while *fat shaming* involves negative judgments of being overweight, and therefore belongs to the broader category of *body shaming*. These types of shaming are most commonly discussed, though others have been identified (see Roe 2015; Long 2017). *Cultural appropriation* is an offense that occurs when someone, usually a white Westerner, adopts elements of another culture—as when a white person wears a hairstyle popular among blacks or people who are not from India practice yoga. Assuming or implying that heterosexuality is normal—for instance, stating the expectation that an adolescent boy will soon show a romantic interest in girls— is the offense of *heteronormativity*. Making a similar assumption about gender—assuming an adolescent male even considers himself a boy in the first place—is the offense of *cisnormativity*, and perhaps also an act of *misgendering* that is indicative of *cissexism*, *transphobia*, and, if the offender is male, *toxic masculinity*. And any of these offenses may be among the various things that people find *triggering*.

There now exists an extensive lexicon of harm and oppression, so much so that some universities now post online glossaries of social justice terminology. There is, for example, a seven-page list of definitions compiled by University of Massachusetts, Lowell's Office of Multicultural Affairs, and a 17-page "Diversity and Social Justice Glossary" created by the Diversity Resource Center at the University of Washington, Tacoma (Diversity Resource Center 2015; Office of Multicultural Affairs n.d.). This new moral vocabulary can focus people's attention on things they would not otherwise discuss or worry about. As journalist Megan McArdle notes, microaggression was "an offense most of us didn't even know existed" that "suddenly we were all afraid of being accused of" (2015). Social justice activists surely see this as a benefit. Having words for all these harms can help make people more mindful of them and careful to avoid them. Likewise, eschewing a general term like *prejudice* in favor of a growing list of terms for specific kinds of prejudice—*ableism*, *cissexism*, *Islamophobia*, and the like—might make people who want to avoid bias aware of particular prejudices they had not previously been conscious of.[9]

---

[9] For instance, it is plausible that men are, on an average, more likely to assume the ignorance of a woman than of a fellow man, and thus mistakenly explain to her things she already

The new vocabulary can have other effects, though, including those that run counter to activists' aims. The new moral jargon introduces another kind of cultural difference between victimhood culture and outsiders. Though the terminology is steadily filtering beyond university campuses into the wider world, many ordinary people surely find it ridiculous, foreign, and perhaps incomprehensible. Critics of campus culture often treat the strange words as a source of humor, employing them ironically or stringing them together in a parody of campus activist speech. There may be many ordinary people who are alienated by the victimhood dialect who would be sympathetic if the issues were described in more familiar terms—as matters of being polite and avoiding rudeness, or accepting that people differ and "to each his own." But even when victimhood culture employs more familiar words, it often uses them in markedly different ways.

Changing Concepts

Safety is not a new concept, but the calls for campus wide safe spaces suggest it has acquired a different meaning. What constitutes safety is defined more narrowly, while threats to safety are defined much more broadly. This shift illustrates a larger trend in the evolution of language—a trend that is visible in various realms of society but most extreme in the settings where victimhood culture thrives. In recent decades, psychologist Nick Haslam argues, concepts that refer to "undesirable, harmful, or pathological aspects of human experience," such as abuse, bullying, and mental disorder, have expanded so that they now refer to a much wider variety of things (2016).[10]

One example of this is the concept of abuse. Once limited to physical violence and sexual abuse, it has since expanded to include emotional abuse and neglect. In this way a term that originally referred to harmful physical acts now also refers to harmful words as well as failure to engage in beneficial acts. The term has also become more ambiguous and prone to being stretched to cases that are less extreme: Some studies measure

well knows. Identifying and labeling this behavior could make men more likely to recognize and curb this behavior in their own lives.

[10] Haslam (2016) refers to this shift in meaning as "concept creep" and notes that it occurs in two forms: *Horizontal* creep occurs when a category expands to include different types of thing, and *vertical* creep occurs when a category that once referred to an extreme degree of something is expanded to include lesser degrees. Most of the examples we discuss involve both sorts of expansion.

abuse simply with the participants' subjective perception of having ever felt "unwanted or emotionally neglected" (Haslam 2016:3). The result is that a much greater range of behaviors can now be labeled as abusive.

The concept of violence has expanded in a similar fashion. Most still use the term to refer to physical force, such as punching, kicking, or stabbing. But many also apply the term to harsh language, social inequality, and whatever else they consider harmful. Agencies such as the World Health Organization and the US Center for Disease Control now define violence to include verbal abuse and psychological harm. Sociologists might refer to patterns of disadvantage as *structural violence*. Student activists often have an even more expansive conception. One Oxford student demanding the removal of Cecil Rhodes's statue explains, "There's a violence to having to walk past the statue every day on the way to lectures, there's a violence to having to sit with paintings of former slave holders whilst writing your exams" (quoted in Furedi 2017:59). When a student at Scripps College reported someone had written "Trump 2016" on her white board, the student government president condemned the slogan as "intentional violence" (Soave 2016). Even terms for specific and extreme kinds of violence get stretched in this way: When one Canadian artist displayed paintings influenced by a Native American style, activists accused her not just of cultural appropriation, but of "cultural genocide" (Nasser 2017).

Racism is another kind of harm with much broader meaning. The term once referred to overt bigotry—dislike and hostility based on race—but now covers implicit biases so subtle that the alleged racist might not even be aware of them. Beyond this, it can refer to anything that offends or discomforts members of another race, regardless of anyone's biases or intentions (Haslam 2016; McWhorter 2016). And there are those who argue that racism is an inherent property of all white people, as when one Oklahoma high school teacher told students, "To be white is to be racist, period" (Rosen 2016). Not surprisingly, given the expanding definitions of both racism and violence, there are also those such as Berkeley professor Michael Dumas who argue that "whiteness … is inherently violent" (Caruso 2017).

As the definition of what is harmful grows, there is a corresponding expansion of concepts related to victimization. More and more people are seen as vulnerable and in need of special protection from harms. Frank Furedi, searching for references to "vulnerable" university students in a database of English language newspapers, found none prior to 1986, less than 200 during the 1990s, over a 1000 between 2005 and 2010, and over 1400 from 2015 to 2016 (Furedi 2017:20). One source of vulnerability is mental illness, and the threshold for being diagnosed with depression, anxiety, and other conditions is much lower now than before (Horwitz 2002; Horwitz and Wakefield 2007; Haslam 2016). One result is alarming statistics, such as the British National Union of Students' 2015 claim that 78 percent of students experienced mental health problems (Furedi 2017:26, 44).[11] Not surprisingly, students at Johns Hopkins University drew on this category of vulnerability to object to the school's decision to cease concealing first semester grades from future employers and graduate schools, claiming that such a move would harm their mental health by leading to depression and anxiety (Furedi 2017:24).

Expanding definitions of harm and fragility are a core feature of the spread of trigger warnings. Ostensibly these warnings are meant to protect victims of trauma, and their proliferation involves a drastic expansion of what counts as a traumatic experience.

Originally a term that referred exclusively to physical injuries, by the late 1970s the concept also included the mental wounds associated with terrifying and horrifying experiences. At the time only extreme events were described as traumatic or traumatizing. The third edition of the American Psychiatric Association's Diagnostic and Statistical Manual (DSM), published in 1980, limits the concept to events "outside the range of usual human experience," focusing on life-threatening danger and specifically excluding such painful but common things as "simple bereavement, chronic illness, business losses, or marital conflict" (quoted in Haslam 2016:6). The concept soon grew to encompass a wider range of stresses. By the fourth edition of the DSM, published in 1994, it included indirect experiences, such as learning that a loved one had a life-threatening illness.[12] In recent years, some practitioners have argued for further

---

[11] Lukianoff and Haidt (2015) argue that the rising rates of mental health problems among students are not entirely a matter of increased recognition. As discussed above, the practices of victimhood culture can directly encourage symptoms of depression, anxiety, and other mental conditions. The increase in diagnosed mental and emotional problems may stem from a combination of broader definition of what constitutes a mental health issue, greater willingness of people to seek help from therapists, and an increase in the underlying symptoms.

[12] One study reported that using this version of the DSM, rather than the older one, led to a 22 percent increase in the number of traumatic events in their sample (Breslau and Kessler 2001, cited in Haslam 2016:6).

expansion to include "childbirth, sexual harassment, infidelity, and emotional losses such as abandonment by a spouse ... or a sudden move" (Haslam 2016:7). Colleges today certainly use the term in a broad sense. For example, "according to the Villanova University web page on coping with trauma, this condition 'occurs when a person experiences a very upsetting, negative event'" (Furedi 2017:44). The University of York's welfare web page defines trauma as "a stressful event in which the person feels threatened or out of control" (quoted in Furedi 2017:45).

With their calls for trigger warnings we see campus activists stretching the term even further to include things previously classified as merely unpleasant, annoying, or uncomfortable. Students at Seattle University, protesting that the liberal arts curriculum was too focused on classical Western material, casually inserted trauma into a list of more mundane complaints when they wrote of the "dissatisfaction, traumatization, and boredom" caused by learning Western history and philosophy (quoted in Furedi 2017:29). A student involved in the campaign to erase reminders of Cecil Rhodes at the University of Cape Town insists that the statue of Rhodes is "a source of pain and trauma to a lot of black students" (quoted in Furedi 2017:59). And just as some conceptualize racism as an inherent property of all white people, there are those who view trauma as a collective and hereditary condition shared by all members of an historically victimized group (Alexander 2004; Furedi 2017:55–57).

It is not difficult to see how victimhood culture leads to this sort of conceptual expansion. In a setting where people have high sensitivity to any kind of slight or inequality, they are apt to describe these things in the strongest terms possible. That can include lumping them together with things that are generally seen as far more serious. Describing a racial slur as an assault, for example, can simply be a way of expressing one's view that racial slurs are a very bad thing and should be treated more seriously, much as we already treat assault. Since it involves dependence on authority, victimhood culture also provides many incentives for people to classify their problems into categories that are deemed worthy of official action. If a government or university administration does not respond to claims of preference and interest, but does respond to claims of depression and trauma, it is only natural that many will be inclined to describe their problems in terms that advance their cause.

Understanding the logic of victimhood culture also helps make sense of another conceptual shift. While the main trend has been for concepts of harm and victimization to grow, there is at least one way in which they are now more restricted. The pattern here is that such concepts are defined in ways that make it impossible for members of a recognized victim group to ever engage in them, and impossible for members of a privileged group to ever be a victim of them. Thus, student activists, campus administrators, opinion journalists, and others might claim that whites are by definition incapable of experiencing racial discrimination, while conversely it is literally impossible for blacks and other minorities to ever be racist. When one student diversity officer at Goldsmiths' College was criticized for planning a "[Black and Minority Ethnic] Women and non-binary" only event at which "White Cis Men" were unwelcome, she responded by explaining "I, an ethnic minority woman, cannot be racist or sexist towards white men, because racism and sexism describe structures of privilege based on race and gender, and therefore women of color and minority genders cannot be racist or sexist, since we do not stand to benefit from such a system" (quoted in Neff 2015). Similarly, a student at Ohio University authored a column in the university newspaper arguing, "Women cannot be sexist; the same way people of color cannot be racist" (quoted in Schallhorn 2015). Off campus, Irish author and columnist Louise O'Neil explicitly rejects the dictionary definition of sexism and argues that "it is impossible for women to be sexist towards men" (O'Neil 2017). Students at Brown University even argue that whites cannot be subject to censorship at the behest of minorities, for "the oppressed by definition cannot censor their oppressor" (Dean-Johnson et al. 2015). Partisan definitions such as these are exactly what one might expect in a culture that valorizes victims and demonizes the privileged—moral concepts are now defined so that the latter can do no right and the former can do no wrong.

FAILURE TO COMMUNICATE

Language is another way in which dignity and victimhood culture differ. As such, it is another potential source of conflict and confusion between them. Campus activists might use strange terms that perplex an outsider, or use common terms in a way that strikes the outsider as completely incorrect. Are they intentionally lying? Are they crazy? Maybe they are so sheltered that they do not understand what real violence is.

Victimhood adherents, on the other hand, might be incensed to see critics minimize a problem by saying it was not *really* traumatizing, or not *really* violence. To them this might seem tantamount to saying it is not bad at all. How could anyone deny that this is violence? Are they just trying to justify it? Are their arguments just thinly veiled racism? Maybe they are completely blinded by their privilege.

Haidt (2012) shows that people of different political persuasions draw on different intuitive concepts—or *moral foundations*—when thinking about right and wrong. Liberals tend to emphasize the moral dimensions of care versus harm and fairness versus cheating. While conservatives also use these dimensions, they are equally likely to make judgments in terms of loyalty versus betrayal, authority versus submission, and sanctity versus degradation. One result, he argues, is that liberals are often unable to understand the moral judgments of conservatives, who are likely to employ moral bases that liberals rarely employ. A conservative might understand his or her position as balancing the value of loyalty or sanctity with the value of care, while a liberal might interpret the same position as simply lacking care or even wishing harm. The confusion can contribute to making political debates rancorous and unproductive. Even when the two might potentially agree that something is undesirable, or should be taken more seriously, or whatever, the differences in language might hamper persuasion and coordination. To a liberal the most damning facet of a married man bragging about his sexual escapades may be the misogyny they see in his treatment of women as sex objects; to a conservative it might be the breaking of marital vows, an act of disloyalty that degrades a sacred institution. The same words and images will not resonate equally well across the political spectrum.

Victimhood culture appears to take this emphasis on harm much further, and this can lead to even more severe misunderstandings—not just with conservatives, but also with mainstream liberals, blue-collar leftists, political moderates, civil libertarians, and others. It could even be that as victimhood culture's language of harm grows evermore extensive and specialized, those most enmeshed in it lose their ability to make or understand judgments—moral, aesthetic, or intellectual—in any other terms.[13] One reacts negatively to an ugly statue on campus—it must be a triggering threat. One finds a fictional character unlikable or unrelatable—it must be

---

[13] We have noted that the complaints and concerns of some activists might easily be described in terms other than harm. It even sometimes seems like some of their reactions, though described in the language of harm, derive from one of Haidt's (2012) other moral bases. The push to ban speakers with opposing views, for instance, could be understood as a concern for ideological purity, analogous to religious campaigns to cleanse their communities of heretics and unbelievers. Yet campus protesters appear to genuinely view it as a matter of safety.

a sexist stereotype. Some people are unpleasant or untrustworthy—they must be racist. Others are even worse—they must be openly white supremacist, misogynistic, and homophobic, perhaps even a literal Nazi. Not only is everything that is harmful and oppressive bad, but everything bad is harmful and oppressive. The result is that outsiders who might otherwise be convinced that someone or something is indeed undesirable find the connection to racism or trauma unconvincing and perhaps stop listening altogether.

THE HARMS OF HARM

Heavy reliance on the language of harm can have other consequences. Again some of these might be exactly what activists intend. Describing harms in the strongest possible terms may succeed in convincing people to take them more seriously. For instance, having emotional abuse classified as a kind of violence might well attract more attention to the problem and inspire more effort to stop it. But this sort of thing may also backfire. The association of meaning goes both ways, and using a term for something that people consider very severe to refer to things they do not take as seriously may eventually rob the term of its original connotation. The meaning of the word thus becomes diluted through overuse, and it therefore loses its rhetorical impact. *Racism*, for example, has a strong impact when it brings to mind hooded members of the Ku Klux Klan carrying out acts of physical violence. It has less force if the first image it calls to mind is a Mexican restaurant handing out sombreros. Yet at East Anglia University, when workers from a Mexican restaurant began doing just that, the student union deemed it racist and forced them to stop. Regarding the student union's decree, Frank Furedi argues that "the casual manner with which a publicity stunt was rebranded as racist indicates that the term is now used simply to convey disapproval" (2017:65). Certainly Furedi is not the only one who would come to that conclusion. While overt racism remains a strong taboo in the modern West, the term itself may be losing some of its currency. Some observers of the 2016 US presidential election suggest that candidate Donald Trump's ability to shrug off accusations of racism was partly due to their overuse—the labels applied to Trump were not much different from those applied to other recent Republican candidates, or to Republicans in general (e.g., Brennan 2016, McWhorter 2016). Perhaps for this reason, during the campaign and its aftermath critics escalated the rhetoric, using even more severe labels such as "openly white supremacist" and "Nazi." But if those terms are used too heavily, they too will lose their potency.

The dilution of these terms is not just a matter of a rhetorical weapon losing some of its effectiveness. It can also hamper the ability to combat various forms of prejudice and oppression. To those who still use the older, narrower definitions of violence, racism, and the like, the much broader applications must seem like lies or delusions. From their point of view, they are exposed to a continuous stream of false alarms. It stands to reason that this would make them less likely to pay attention in the case of a real alarm, perhaps surmising that it is just another overreaction. Along these lines, psychiatrist and blogger Scott Alexander argues that critics who accused Donald Trump of conducting an "openly racist" or "openly white supremacist" campaign might ultimately regret "crying wolf":

> What if, one day, there is a candidate who hates black people so much that he doesn't go on a campaign stop to a traditionally black church in Detroit, talk about all of the contributions black people have made to America, promise to fight for black people, and say that his campaign is about opposing racism in all its forms? What if there's a candidate who does something more like, say, go to a KKK meeting and say that black people are inferior and only whites are real Americans? We might want to use words like "openly racist" or "openly white supremacist" to describe him. And at that point, nobody will listen. (Alexander 2016)

Similarly, scholars Jonny Anomaly and Brian Boutwell (2016) argue that using extremely broad definitions of racism can actually provide a better environment for extreme racism to spread. Insofar as stigma and social disapproval deter people from engaging in deviant conduct, anything that reduces stigma and normalizes deviance should increase its frequency. It is therefore counterproductive to make racism or any other undesired behavior seem mainstream and perhaps even unavoidable. After all, how shameful can it be to be accused of racism when one is regularly told that all white people are racist by definition?

It is possible that these arguments are overstated and victimhood culture's escalating language of harm will not result in these sorts of counterproductive outcomes. And even if the critics are more or less correct, those who campaign against harm might see the benefits as worth the costs. Perhaps the cumulative benefit of preventing many small acts of bias is worth some growth in extreme bigotry at the margins; perhaps preventing one trauma victim from being triggered and committing suicide is worth inflicting greater anxiety on a thousand others. In any event there is reason to believe that such tradeoffs exist and that they will become more relevant to moral decision making as victimhood culture spreads.

*   *   *

Calls for trigger warnings and safe spaces are as much of an aspect of victimhood culture as are microaggression complaints. They too evince a strong tendency to emphasize victimization and to rely on third parties. Their success illustrates a tendency to defer to victims, to accept their definition of the situation, and to privilege their requests. And they are part and parcel of a language of victimhood that exaggerates harm and emphasizes vulnerability. Words and images are violence, disagreement is a threat, and some victimized groups need special protection from it all. Those who speak this language are not necessarily cynical: For good or for ill many participants in victimhood culture appear to actually view the world in these terms. But some are less honest, and a few of these go beyond emphasizing and exaggerating. As we shall see in the next chapter, there are those who manufacture victimhood out of thin air.

REFERENCES

Alexander, Jeffrey C. 2004. Toward a Theory of Cultural Trauma. In *Cultural Trauma and Collective Identity*, ed. Jeffrey C. Alexander, Ron Eyerman, Bernhard Giesen, Neil J. Smelser, and Peter Sztompka, 620–639. Berkeley: University of California Press.

Alexander, Scott. 2016. You're Still Crying Wolf. *Slate Star Codex* (blog), November 16. http://slatestarcodex.com/2016/11/16/you-are-still-crying-wolf/.

Anderson, Elijah. 1999. *Code of the Street: Decency, Violence, and the Moral Life of the Inner City*. New York: W. W. Norton.

Anomaly, Jonny, and Brian Boutwell. 2016. What Is a Racist? Why Moral Progress Hinges on Getting the Answer Right. *Quillette*, November 21. http://quillette.com/2016/11/21/what-is-a-racist-why-moral-progress-hinges-on-getting-the-answer-right/.

Armstrong, Edward G. 2001. Gangsta Misogyny: A Content Analysis of the Portrayals of Violence Against Women in Rap Music, 1987–1993. *Journal of Criminal Justice and Popular Culture* 8 (2): 96–126.

Barnes, Colin D., Ryan P. Brown, and Michael Tamborski. 2012. Living Dangerously: Culture of Honor, Risk-Taking, and the Nonrandomness of 'Accidental' Deaths. *Social Psychological and Personality Science* 3 (1): 100–107.

Black, Donald. 1989. *Sociological Justice*. New York: Oxford University Press.

———. 2004. The Geometry of Terrorism. *Sociological Theory* 22 (1): 14–25.

Breen, T.H. 1977. Horses and Gentlemen: The Cultural Significance of Gambling Among the Gentry of Virginia. *The William and Mary Quarterly* 34 (2): 293–257.

Brennan, Jason. 2016. Has 'Racist' Lost It's Sting? *Bleeding Heart Libertarians*, September 16. http://bleedingheartlibertarians.com/2016/09/racist-lost-sting/.

Breslau, N., and R.C. Kessler. 2001. The Stressor Criterion in DSM-IV Postraumatic Stress Disorder: An Empirical Investigation. *Biological Psychiatry* 50: 699–704.

Bulman, Mary. 2016. UK Universities Issue 'Trigger Warnings' to Warn Students of Potentially 'Upsetting' Material. *The Independent*, October 9. http://www.independent.co.uk/news/uk/home-news/trigger-warnings-universities-students-us-uk-a7353061.html.

Calver, Tom. 2014. Christ Church Refuses to Hold 'Abortion Culture' Debate. *Cherwell*, November 17. http://www.cherwell.org/2014/11/17/christ-church-refuses-to-hold-quotabortion-culturequot-debate/.

Campbell, John Kennedy. 1964. *Honour, Family and Patronage: A Study of Institutions and Moral Values in a Greek Mountain Community*. Oxford: Clarendon Press.

———. 1965. Honour and the Devil. In *Honour and Shame: The Values of Mediterranean Society*, ed. John G. Peristiany, 112–175. London: Weidenfeld and Nicolson.

Campbell, Bradley. 2015. Genocide as Predation. *International Journal of Law, Crime, and Justice* 43: 310–345.

Carroll, Rebecca. 2017. Black and Proud. Even if Strangers Can't Tell. *New York Times*, April 1. https://www.nytimes.com/2017/04/01/opinion/sunday/black-and-proud-even-if-strangers-cant-tell.html?_r=0.

Caruso, Justin. 2017. Prof Calls Diversity of Thought 'White Supremacist Bullshit'. *Campus Reform*, June 6. http://www.campusreform.org/?ID=9272.

Chumley, Cheryl K. 2017. Clemson College Kids Demand Safe Space for LGTBQ's. *The Washington Times*, May 1. http://www.washingtontimes.com/news/2017/may/1/clemson-college-kids-demand-safe-space-lgbtqs/.

Cohen, Dov, and Angela K.-Y. Leung. 2009. The Hard Embodiment of Culture. *European Journal of Social Psychology* 39 (7): 1278–1289.

Cooney, Mark. 1998. *Warriors and Peacemakers: How Third Parties Shape Violence*. New York: New York University Press.

Cunningham, Jalin P., Melissa C. Rodman, and Ignacio Sabate. 2016. Harvard House Masters Now Called 'Faculty Deans'. *The Harvard Crimson*, February 25. http://www.thecrimson.com/article/2016/2/25/house-master-new-name/.

Dabhoiwala, Faramerz. 1996. The Construction of Honour, Reputation and Status in Late Seventeenth- and Early Eighteenth-Century England. *Transactions of the Royal Historical Society* 6: 201–213.

Dean-Johnson, Liam, Aidan Dunbar, Anastasiya Gorodilova, Nico Sedivy, and Madison Shiver. 2015. Dean-Jonson '16, Dunbar '16, Gorodilova '16, Sedivy '17, Shiver '17: On Whiteness, Free Speech and Missing the Point. *The Brown Daily Herald*, October 19. http://www.browndailyherald.com/2015/10/19/dean-johnson-16-dunbar-16-gorodilova-16-sedivy-17-shiver-17-on-whiteness-free-speech-and-missing-the-point/.

Devaney, Tim. 2016. White House Proposes New Census Category for Arab Americans. *The Hill*, October 3. http://thehill.com/regulation/administration/299068-white-house-proposes-new-census-category-for-arab-americans.

Diamba, Jessy. 2014. A.S. Resolution Policy Aims to Protect Students from PTSD Triggers. *The Daily Nexus*, March 7. http://dailynexus.com/2014-03-07/a-s-resolution-policy-aims-to-protect-students-from-ptsd-triggers/.

Diversity Resource Center. 2015. Diversity and Social Justice Glossary. University of Washington, Tacoma. https://www.tacoma.uw.edu/sites/default/files/sections/Diversity/diversity_glossary.pdf.pdf.

Dunning, Eric. 1983. Social Bonding and Violence in Sports: A Theoretical-Empirical Analysis. In *Sports Violence*, ed. Jeffrey H. Goldstein, 129–146. New York: Springer.

Evans, James E. 2002. 'A Scene of Utmost Vanity': The Spectacle of Gambling in Late Stuart Culture. *Studies in Eighteenth-Century Culture* 31: 1–20.

Ewens, Hannah. 2017. Dance of Death: Are the Days of the Moshpit Numbered? *The Guardian*, May 5. https://www.theguardian.com/music/2017/may/05/dance-of-death-are-the-days-of-the-moshpit-numbered.

Fortin, Jacey. 2017. F.B.I. Helping American University Investigate Bananas Found Hanging from Nooses. *New York Times*, May 3. https://www.nytimes.com/2017/05/03/us/bananas-hang-from-black-nooses-and-a-campus-erupts-in-protest.html?_r=0.

Francisco, Patricia Weaver. 1999. *Telling: A Memoir of Rape and Recovery*. New York: Cliff Street Books.

Friedman, Lawrence M. 1994. *Total Justice*. New York: Russell Sage Foundation.

Furedi, Frank. 2002. *Culture of Fear: Risk Taking and the Morality of Low Expectations*. Rev ed. New York: Continuum.

———. 2017. *What's Happened to the University? A Sociological Exploration of Its Infantalization*. New York: Routledge.

Gerson, Jeannie Suk. 2014. The Trouble with Teaching Rape Law. *The New Yorker*. http://www.newyorker.com/news/news-desk/trouble-teaching-rape-law.

Glick, Steven. 2015. Safe Spaces Segregate the Claremont Colleges. *The Claremont Independent*, November 17. http://claremontindependent.com/safe-spaces-segregate-the-claremont-colleges/.

————. 2016. Student Senator: Picture of Gun Is a Threat to 'Black Mental and Emotional Health.' *The Claremont Independent*, April 19. http://claremontindependent.com/student-senator-picture-of-gun-is-a-threat-to-black-mental-and-emotional-health/.

Gockowski, Anthony. 2016. Ohio University Students Demand Police Investigation After Peers Mock Safe-Spaces. *Campus Reform*. https://www.campusreform. org/?ID=7494.

Government of Canada. 2016. *National Inquiry into Missing and Murdered Indigenous Women and Girls*. http://www.aadnc-aandc.gc.ca/eng/14486332 99414/1448633350146.

Grant, Graham, and Eleanor Harding. 2017. Bible Students Are Warned.... You May Find the Crucifixion Too Upsetting! *The Daily Mail*, January 5. http:// www.dailymail.co.uk/news/article-4089302/Bible-students-warned-crucifixion-upsetting-Critics-say-trigger-warnings-distressing-content-creating-generation-snowflake-students.html.

Haidt, Jonathan. 2012. *The Righteous Mind: Why Good People Are Divided by Politics and Religion*. New York: Pantheon Books.

Harrison, Brian. 1967. Religion and Recreation in Nineteenth-Century England. *Past & Present* 38: 98–125.

Haslam, Nick. 2016. Concept Creep: Psychology's Expanding Concepts of Harm and Pathology. *Psychological Inquiry* 27 (1): 1–17.

Herd, Denise. 2009. Changing Images of Violence in Rap Music Lyrics: 1979–1997. *Journal of Public Health Policy* 30 (4): 395–406.

Holcomb, Justin. 2015. Students Defile Thomas Jefferson's Statue at William and Mary. *Townhall*, November 25. https://townhall.com/tipsheet/justinholcomb/2015/11/25/william--mary-students-defile-thomas-jefferson-statue-n2085376.

Holmes, Linsday. 2016. A Quick Lesson on What Trigger Warnings Actually Do. *The Huffington Post*, February 6. http://www.huffingtonpost.com/entry/university-of-chicago-trigger-warning_us_57bf16d9e4b085c1ff28176d.

Horwitz, Allan V. 2002. *Creating Mental Illness*. Chicago/London: University of Chicago Press.

Horwitz, Alan V., and Jerome C. Wakefield. 2007. *The Loss of Sadness: How Psychiatry Transformed Normal Sorrow into Depressive Disorder*. Oxford: Oxford University Press.

Ijzerman, Hans, and Dov Cohen. 2011. Grounding Cultural Syndromes: Body Comportment and Values in Honor and Dignity Cultures. *European Journal of Social Psychology* 41: 456–467.

Jarvie, Jennie. 2014. Trigger Happy. *The New Republic*, March 3. https:// newrepublic.com/article/116842/trigger-warnings-have-spread-blogs-college-classes-thats-bad.

Kelley, Seth. 2017. Netflix Pledges to Add More Trigger Warnings to '13 Reasons Why.' *Variety*, March 7. http://variety.com/2017/digital/news/13-reasons-why-trigger-warnings-netflix-1202404969/.

Knapp, Krystal. 2015. Black Justice League at Princeton University Stages Sit-in, Demand's School Remove Woodrow Wilson's Name from Buildings. *Planet Princeton*, November 18. https://planetprinceton.com/2015/11/18/black-justice-from-buildings/#comment-8340.

Knighton, Tom. 2017. Columbia Students Say Thomas Jefferson Statue 'Validates Rape.' *PJ Media*, May 2. https://pjmedia.com/trending/2017/05/02/columbia-students-say-thomas-jefferson-statue-validates-rape/.

Leung, Angela K.Y., and Dov Cohen. 2011. Within- and Between-Culture Variation: Individual Differences and the Cultural Logics of Honor, Face, and Dignity Cultures. *Journal of Personality and Social Psychology* 100 (3): 507–526.

Long, Heather. 2017. 'No One Believes We Do This to Kids': Will Congress End School Lunch Shaming? *CNN Money*, May 15. http://money.cnn.com/2017/05/15/news/economy/school-lunch-shaming-congress-bill/index.html.

Lukianoff, Greg, and Jonathan Haidt. 2015. The Coddling of the American Mind. *The Atlantic*, September. http://www.theatlantic.com/magazine/archive/2015/09/the-coddling-of-the-american-mind/399356/.

MacDonald, Michael, and Terence R. Murphy. 1990. *Sleepless Souls: Suicide in Early Modern England*. Oxford: Clarendon Press.

Mahmood, Sarah. 2014. Why Wellesley Should Remove Lifelike Statue of a Man in His Underwear. *The Huffington Post*, February 6. http://www.huffington-post.com/sarah-mahmood/why-wellesley-should-remove-lifelike-statue-of-a-man-in-his-underwear_b_4732982.html.

Manning, Sanchez, and Charlotte Wace. 2016. Oxford Law Students Too 'Fragile' to Hear About Violent Crime: Undergraduates Given 'Trigger Warnings' Before Traumatic Material. *The Daily Mail*, May 7. http://www.dailymail.co.uk/news/article-3579086/Oxford-law-students-fragile-hear-violent-crime-Undergraduates-given-trigger-warnings-traumatic-material.html.

Marks, Jonathan. 2017. It's Not Just the Students. *Commentary*, August 10. https://www.commentarymagazine.com/culture-civilization/education/not-just-students-college/.

McArdle, Megan. 2015. How Grown-Ups Deal with Microaggressions. *Bloomberg View*, September 11. http://www.bloombergview.com/articles/2015-09-11/how-grown-ups-deal-with-microaggressions-.

McDonald, Matt. 2016. Isn't Sending Out Campus-Wide Alerts with Trigger Warnings in Them Slightly Counterproductive? *The Tab*. http://thetab.com/us/2016/02/17/why-are-campus-cops-sending-out-press-releases-with-trigger-warnings-in-them-1376.

McWhorter, John. 2016. The Idea that America 'Doesn't Talk About Racism' Is Absurd. *The Boston Globe*, November 13. http://www.bostonglobe.com/ideas/2016/11/13/the-recreational-use-racism/Tzxwl9Fg03ySKGYrCBv9SL/story.html?event=event25.

Medina, Jennifer. 2014. "Warning: The Literary Canon Could Make Students Squirm." *The New York Times*, May 17. http://www.nytimes.com/2014/05/18/us/warning-the-literary-canon-could-make-students-squirm.html

Messing, Phillip. 2016. Donald Trump Sparks Campus Trigger Warning. *The New York Post*, May 24. http://nypost.com/2016/03/24/college-kids-see-the-name-trump-and-start-crying/.

Miller, Michael E. 2015. Columbia Students Claim Greek Mythology Needs a Trigger Warning. *Washington Post*, May 14. https://www.washingtonpost.com/news/morning-mix/wp/2015/05/14/columbia-students-claim-greek-mythology-needs-a-trigger-warning/?utm_term=.f8bc16e6a3ea.

Nasser, Shanifa. 2017. Toronto Gallery Cancels Show After Concerns Artist 'Bastardizes' Indigenous Art. *CBC News*, April 28. http://www.cbc.ca/news/canada/toronto/toronto-gallery-indigenous-art-cancels-amandapl-1.4091529.

Neff, Blake. 2015. University Officer: Minority Women Can't Be Racist. *The Daily Caller*, May 12. http://dailycaller.com/2015/05/12/university-diversity-officer-minority-women-cant-be-racist/.

Nisbett, Richard E., and Dov Cohen. 1996. *Culture of Honor: The Psychology of Violence in the South*. Boulder: Westview Press.

Ngabo, Gilbert. 2017. Toronto Spoken Word Artist Creates Safe Space to Tackle Difficult Conversations. *Metro News*, May 20. http://www.metronews.ca/news/toronto/2017/05/10/creating-brave-safe-spaces.html.

Nolan, Larissa. 2017. Free Speech Under Threat on Our College Campuses. *The Irish Times*, April 18. http://www.irishtimes.com/news/education/free-speech-under-threat-on-our-college-campuses-1.3045149.

Office of Multicultural Affairs. n.d. *Diversity and Social Justice: A Glossary of Working Definitions*. Lowell: University of Massachusetts. https://www.uml.edu/docs/Glossary_tcm18-55041.pdf.

O'Neill, Louise. 2017. Louise O'Neill: It Is Impossible for Women to Be Sexist Towards Men. *The Irish Examiner*, January 21. http://www.irishexaminer.com/viewpoints/columnists/louise-oneill/louise-oneill-it-is-impossible-for-women-to-be-sexist-towards-men-440072.html.

Owens, Eric. 2017. Ritzy University Postpones Finals for 'Students of Color' Traumatized by Harambe Banana Nooses. *The Daily Caller*, May 8. http://dailycaller.com/2017/05/08/ritzy-university-postpones-finals-for-students-of-color-traumatized-by-harambe-banana-nooses/.

Palmer, Tim. 2017. Monash University Trigger Warning Policy Fires Up Free Speech Debate. *ABC.net*, March 28. http://www.abc.net.au/news/2017-03-28/monash-university-adopts-trigger-warning-policy/8390264.

Parker, Claire, and Leah S. Yared. 2017. Faust Says 'Fair Harvard' Change Is Warranted Reexamination. *The Harvard Crimson*, April 17. http://www. thecrimson.com/article/2017/4/17/faust-fair-harvard/.

Paxson, Christina. 2016. Brown University President: A Safe Space for Freedom of Expression. *Washington Post*, September 5. https://www.washingtonpost. com/opinions/brown-university-president-safe-spaces-dont-threaten-free-dom-of-expression-they-protect-it/2016/09/05/6201870e-736a-11e6-8149-b8d05321db62_story.html?utm_term=.a4b533ed7d9e.

Piper, Greg. 2017. College Disinvites Professor Who Won't Use Gender-Neutral Pronouns Because of 'Safe Space' Joke. *The College Fix*, April 20. https:// www.thecollegefix.com/post/32207/.

Raine, Barry. 2002. *Where the River Bends*. Princeton: Ontario Review Press.

Roe, Amy. 2015. Why I Was Sweat-Shamed as I Waited for My Coffee at Starbucks. *The Guardian*, September 30. https://www.theguardian.com/commentis-free/2015/sep/30/sweat-shamed-waited-for-my-coffee-at-starbucks.

Rohrer, Finlo. 2015. When Is It Right to Remove a Statue? *BBC News*, December 23. http://www.bbc.com/news/magazine-35161671.

Rosen, Ben. 2016. Discussing Race in the Classroom: 'Are All White People Racist'? *Christian Science Monitor*, October 19. http://www.csmonitor.com/USA/Education/2016/1019/Discussing-race-in-the-classroom-Are-all-white-people-racist.

Salovey, Peter. 2016. Decision on Residential College Names and 'Master' Title. Yale University Office of the President. http://president.yale.edu/speeches-writings/statements/decisions-residential-college-names-and-master-title.

Schallhorn, Kaitlyn. 2015. Female Student: Women Can't Be Sexist. *Campus Reform*, March 17. https://www.campusreform.org/?ID=6368.

Schapiro, Morton. 2016. I'm Northwestern's President. Here's Why Safe Spaces for Students Are Important. *Washington Post*, January 15. https://www.wash-ingtonpost.com/opinions/how-to-create-inclusive-campus-communities-first-create-safe-places/2016/01/15/069f3a66-bb94-11e5-829c-26ffb874a18d_story.html?utm_term=.f75edeb0eebe.

Schramm, Michael. 2017. Harvard Law Drops Controversial Seal. *USA Today*, March 17. http://college.usatoday.com/2016/03/17/harvard-law-drops-controversial-seal/.

Scott, Matthew. 2016. Trigger Warnings at Oxford Would Threaten Academic Freedom and Infantilise Our Future Judges. *The Telegraph*, May 11. http:// www.telegraph.co.uk/news/2016/05/11/trigger-warnings-at-oxford-would-threaten-academic-freedom-and-i/.

Sev'er, A., and G. Yurdakul. 2001. Culture of Honor, Culture of Change: A Feminist Analysis of Honor Killings in Rural Turkey. *Violence Against Women* 7 (9): 965–998.

Shimshock, Rob. 2017. Oklahoma Student Delegates Call on State Gov't to Mandate Trigger Warnings. *The Daily Caller*, March 29. http://dailycaller.com/2017/03/29/oklahoma-student-delegates-call-on-state-govt-to-mandate-trigger-warnings/.

Shoemaker, Robert. 2001. Male Honour and the Decline of Public Violence in Eighteenth-Century London. *Social History* 26 (2): 190–208.

Shulevitz, Judith. 2015. In College and Hiding from Scary Ideas. *The New York Times*, March 21. https://www.nytimes.com/2015/03/22/opinion/sunday/judith-shulevitz-hiding-from-scary-ideas.html?_r=0.

Snyder, Justin. 2009. *A Sociology of Trauma: Violence and Self Identity*, Doctoral Dissertation. Charlottesville: University of Virginia.

———. 2014. 'Blood, Guts, and Gore Galore:' Bodies, Moral Pollution, and Combat Trauma. *Symbolic Interaction* 37 (4): 524–540.

Soave, Robby. 2016. Scripps College Student Body President Says 'Trump 2016' Whiteboard Message Is 'Intentional Violence.' *Reason*, March 29. http://reason.com/blog/2016/03/29/scripps-college-student-body-president-s.

Stites, Sarah. 2017. BuzzFeed to Host L.A. Queer Prom as 'Safe Space' to Party. *Newsbusters*, April 28. http://www.newsbusters.org/blogs/culture/sarah-stites/2017/04/28/buzzfeed-host-la-queer-prom-safe-space-party.

Sunstein, Cass R. 2017. When Student Protesters Defeat Their Own Cause. *The Press of Atlantic City*, April 25. http://www.pressofatlanticcity.com/opinion/commentary/when-student-protesters-defeat-their-own-cause-by-cass-r/article_1b879ef1-4076-5290-a59b-2304c7fe9422.html.

Weber, Max. 1958. *The Protestant Ethic and the Spirit of Capitalism*. New York: Charles Scribner's Sons.

Wilson, Thomas C. 2002. The Paradox of Social Class and Sports Involvement: The Roles of Cultural and Economic Capital. *International Review for the Sociology of Sport* 37 (1): 5–16.

WVTM. 2017. Columbus State University Creates 'Safe Space' System for Students. http://www.wtvm.com/story/35323935/columbus-state-university-creates-safe-space-system-for-students.

Wyatt-Brown, Bertram. 1982. *Southern Honor: Ethics and Behavior in the Old South*. New York: Oxford University Press.

Wythe, Philip. 2014. Trigger Warnings Needed in Classroom. *The Daily Targum*, February 18. http://www.dailytargum.com/article/2014/.

CHAPTER 4

False Accusations, Moral Panics, and the Manufacture of Victimhood

Victimhood culture is a moral framework in which victimhood has greater moral status than it does elsewhere. We see in this in the intense concern with inadvertent slights against marginalized social groups—that is, microaggressions. We also see it in attempts to protect victims with trigger warnings and safe spaces, as well as in admonitions for people from high-status groups to confess their privilege as though it were a sin. But as we noted in Chap. 1, many critics of the concept of victimhood culture reject the idea that victimhood is a kind of status at all. One such critic, the feminist writer Samhita Mukhopadhyay, in an article called "Stop Complaining about 'Victimhood Culture,'" talks about the microaggressions she has experienced and then says, "The temporary power I might have felt from the 'gotcha' moment of pointing out a microaggression is not equivalent to the power that comes of being born into social or economic privilege" (2015).

We contend that the status arising from victimhood is much more than an emotional feeling produced by a "gotcha moment." And whether this kind of status is equivalent overall to some other kind of status is not the issue. Stratification in modern society can be situational, in that what confers privilege on a person in one situation might not in another (Collins 2000). The campus activists who deny the reality of victimhood status fail to account for their own success. As those activists mobilize on behalf of people they see as oppressed, university administrators implement many of

© The Author(s) 2018
B. Campbell, J. Manning, *The Rise of Victimhood Culture*,
https://doi.org/10.1007/978-3-319-70329-9_4

the policies they push for, and many others adopt their moral framework. People identified as victims thus receive recognition, support, and protection. In these settings victimhood becomes increasingly attractive. How could it be otherwise?

Even outside of campus victimhood culture, victimhood often results in some degree of moral status. As we shall see in Chap. 5, intercollective conflicts might lead to *competitive victimhood*, where groups argue over who has suffered more (see also Andrighetto et al. 2012; Black 1998:144–156). In other situations the adversaries in a conflict agree about the victim status of a third party and might each claim to have the victims' support. For example, sociologist Stephanie Chan found that in debates about US human rights policy toward China in the late twentieth and early twenty-first centuries, both sides viewed Chinese dissidents as having "moral authority" and argued about who accurately represented their position (Chan 2011:Chapter 4). Perhaps most remarkable is that some people falsely claim to have been the victim of a crime or other serious offenses.

If victimhood never conferred any benefits, why would any of this happen? Why would anyone falsely claim to be a victim if there were no advantage in doing so? That they do shows that victimhood is in fact a social resource—a form of status. Manufacturing a case of victimhood allows the aggrieved to elicit sympathy or even to mobilize third parties such as legal authorities against their enemies. Since a victimhood culture is one where this status is most valuable, we should expect it to be especially prone to false claims of victimization. In this chapter we examine such false claims, how they are used to win support for the apparent victim, and how they thrive under the conditions of victimhood culture.

THE LOGIC OF FALSE ACCUSATIONS

False accusations have the same core logic as microaggression complaints. Microaggression complainants seek to build a persuasive case by documenting a number of small offenses, arguing that even if each one is small, added together they become very serious. False accusers are also trying to get attention or support by magnifying the apparent severity of the conflict. The difference is that instead of doing this by documenting a pattern of small offenses, they convince third parties that a more serious offense has occurred. Not content merely to publicize the offenses of their adversaries, or even to exaggerate them, they make up offenses whole cloth.

There are different kinds of false accusations. In some cases, the accusers might genuinely believe what they say. People accused of witchcraft are innocent, but those who condemn them might genuinely believe that they are witches. In other cases, the accuser knows the accusation is false. Such cases can happen because the accuser and accused were embroiled in a conflict over something that third parties would not treat as a matter for intervention.[1] For example, legal officials might see little or no merit to the actual grievances in a squabble between ex-spouses, but a false accusation prods their intervention. In this way an aggrieved party might manipulate the law, using it essentially as a weapon against an adversary. Consider first the role of such false accusations in handling grievances against particular individuals.

Accusations Against Individuals

False allegations of child abuse are sometimes part of a deliberate strategy to win a divorce or custody dispute with an estranged or former spouse.[2] For example, one man reported his ex-wife, her boyfriend, and her mother and father for sexually abusing his child. Later he acknowledged that he made the reports to get more access to his daughter. In another case a woman accused her ex-husband of sexual abuse because he had accused her boyfriend of physical abuse (Faller and DeVoe 1995:20–21).

Sometimes rape accusations are similar. It is difficult to get good information on how often such cases occur, but in one study of rape complaints over a ten-year period in a small metropolitan area in the United States, 41 percent of the cases were false, and in about a quarter of these cases the accusation was a way of handling a grievance (Kanin 1994; see also Bryden and Lengnick 1997). The cases usually involved failed relationships. They

---

[1] Donald Black (2011:16) proposes that false accusations of all kinds—unintentional or intentional—result from social changes that are not themselves defined as wrong. For example, getting sick is not considered a crime or a sin, but it does alter status relationships, robbing people of their most fundamental resource: their health. And it is a social change that leads people to blame their illness on witchcraft. The false accusations we deal with in this chapter are similar, though in this case what is important is that the social change which sparks the conflict is something third parties do not see as deviant, or at least not as serious deviance.

[2] The findings are inconsistent, but most studies have found that false accusations are especially likely to arise in these situations (Benedek and Schetky 1985; Faller 1991; Faller and DeVoe 1995; Green 1986; Haskett et al. 1995; Trocmé and Bala 2005).

arose either out of disputes with boyfriends or former boyfriends or out of situations where men had spurned women. In one case, an 18-year-old woman had been having a sexual relationship with a boarder in her mother's house. When her mother found out, she ordered the man to leave. As he was packing, the woman went to tell him she would go with him, and he said, "Who the hell wants you?" She then went to the police to report he had raped her, though under questioning she admitted the charge was false. In another case, a 17-year-old girl reported being raped by a house parent in the group home where she lived, but she later said that she liked the man, and when he refused her advances, she reported the rape "to get even with him" (Kanin 1994:87). In some areas prostitutes are frequent sources of false rape claims. Prostitutes are more likely to be actual victims of forcible rape, but they may also make false claims against customers who do not pay. In one district, police report that many of the accused men are drug dealers who offer drugs in exchange for sex, but then refuse to hand over the drugs after the sexual encounter (Berger 1994).

The offenses here—romantic rejection and illicit debts—are deviant behaviors in the eyes of the accusers, but they are not crimes that the police will respond to. Rape is. False accusations can even convince legal officials or other third parties to change sides. Consider the case of Tracy West and Louis Gonzalez III, who had ended their brief relationship even before their son was born. They had been fighting in court over custody and visitation for the five-year-old's entire life. Louis had won visitation rights, but Tracy was infuriated over his continued involvement in their son's life. Shortly before one of their son's twice-monthly weekend visits to see his father, Tracy complained to Louis about the visits in an email, saying they caused great distress for her and her son and that Louis had proven incapable of being a good father (Goffard 2011a).

Tracy West did not want Louis Gonzalez involved in her life or her son's life. Yet on this point she had lost; the law was clearly against her. She was able to quickly turn things around and use the legal system against her adversary by falsely accusing him of rape. Shortly after the email exchange, Tracy told police that Louis came to her home, beat her, tied her up, burned her with matches, raped her with a wooden coat hanger, put a plastic bag over her head, and left her for dead. Her injuries—possibly self-inflicted—made her story especially convincing. Police immediately arrested Louis and held him in jail for nearly three months. Eventually he was released, mainly because his activities that day were so well documented (Goffard 2011a, b). But if things had gone differently, Tracy would have permanently removed Louis from their son's life. She would have won her dispute using a false accusation to mobilize a third party. Telling lies about one's adversaries can be a highly effective strategy, but also a risky one. Tracy West ended up losing primary custody of her son. Still, she escaped any kind of criminal punishment. Once prosecutors found evidence of Louis's innocence, they dropped the charges against him, and a judge provided him with a rare declaration of factual innocence. But prosecutors did not bring charges against his accuser for filing a false police report (Goffard 2011b).

Accusations Against Groups

Just as someone involved in an interpersonal conflict might falsely accuse an individual of wrongdoing, people involved in intercollective conflicts might falsely accuse adversaries such as enemy nations, political factions, or ethnic groups. With an audience of one's allies ready to believe good things about themselves and bad things about their adversaries, false accusations as well as other kinds of lies might even be more likely in intercollective conflicts.

People are especially prone to lie during wars. Warring states have no central authority to appeal to—just like stateless individuals, they rely on their own resources and care about defending their honor. Because of this state propaganda tends not to emphasize neediness and victimization. Rather, it is aimed at the state's own subjects, and it tends to emphasize strength and success so as to inspire respect, loyalty, and fear.[3] Efforts during war to exaggerate one's successes or deny one's failures are sometimes comical in their boldness. During World War II the Japanese would hide defeats and announce victories to captured enemy soldiers. Their attempts to convince them that Japan was winning went further, though, as they invented "stories of Allied losses and ridiculously implausible Japanese feats," such as on one occasion when they told a group of POWs

---

[3] For example, during World War II German propagandists saw their primary task as "spreading good news...and setting an example of indomitable confidence in final victory" (Bytwerk 2010:100). Thus "public media were understandably cautious in printing information on damage done by Allied bombing," and propagandists rushed to combat exaggerated (or sometimes accurate) accounts of casualties (Bytwerk 2010:108–109). Imperial Japan likewise maintained a policy that "the public was not to be informed of defeats or damage on the Japanese side. Only victories and damage imposed on the Allies were to be announced" (Sasaki 1999:178).

that Japan's military "had shot Abraham Lincoln and torpedoed Washington D.C." (Hillenbrand 2010:204–205).[4]

But propagandists also strive to portray enemies as evil and stoke popular hostility toward them. Thus atrocity stories are another staple of wartime propaganda. In war there are usually plenty of real atrocities to highlight, but exaggerations and false accusations still abound. Sociologist Randall Collins notes that as atrocity stories circulate, it becomes "difficult to distinguish between rumors and realities," and as conflicts escalate, "no one is interested in this distinction" (2012:3).

Even the perpetrators of one-sided mass violence such as genocide commonly falsely accuse those they are killing of atrocities and other crimes. Hitler blamed the Jews for the German defeat in World War I, and more generally for a worldwide conspiracy against Germans. The Hutu perpetrators of the 1994 Rwandan genocide accused the country's Tutsis of aiding the Tutsi rebel army that had invaded from Uganda. Sometimes they claimed Tutsis had been preparing for a genocide of Tutsis, as when they accused one Tutsi man of having 600 guns and a list of Hutus marked for death (Campbell 2015:14–15; 208). Likewise in 1992 Bosnia, where Muslims were the targets of genocide and ethnic cleansing by Serbs, Serbs claimed that Muslims had drawn up lists of Serb men to kill and women to put into harems (Campbell 2015:104). By accusing the targets of genocide of themselves preparing to carry out ethnic violence, the perpetrators could present the genocide as a kind of self-defense.

Nonviolent political conflicts also engender dishonesty. According to sociologist J. A. Barnes, "the political arena is second only to warfare as a domain where lies are expected, do in fact occur, and are to a substantial extent tolerated" (1994:30). The lies of politicians and activists are often mocked and condemned, but they do have defenders. Political philosopher Jason Brennan argues that the ignorance and irrationality of voters justifies lies by politicians to protect the common good. For example, if it is true that in 2008 candidate Barack Obama misled voters by promising protectionism in Ohio when he always intended to promote free trade, then according to Brennan, "Obama protected the world, my fellow

---

[4] More recently, Iraqi Information Minister Muhammed Saeed al-Sahhaf, nicknamed "Baghdad Bob" in the United States and "Comical Ali" in Britain, became famous for his many claims during the 2003 US invasion of Iraq that the Iraqi Army was prevailing and driving out the Americans.

citizens, my children, and me from culpably misinformed and foolish Ohio voters" (Brennan 2016:11).

Whether or not lying in politics is justified, it is certainly ubiquitous. Politicians and their spokespersons routinely engage in deceptive communication ("spin") and sometimes outright lying to put themselves in the best possible light and their opponents in the worst. Deception is common enough that news organizations that do fact checks of politicians' statements regularly identify falsehoods. The *Washington Post* rates the dishonesty of statements by awarding "Pinocchios," and in 2016 Donald Trump, Hillary Clinton, and Barack Obama each made at least one statement that was given four Pinocchios (Kessler 2016).

With so much dishonesty, it is little wonder that political activists and campaign workers tell lies of their own. And some of these lies are false claims of victimization. In 1994, for example, someone from the campaign of Donald Mintz, a Jewish man running to be mayor of New Orleans, created and distributed anti-Semitic flyers to attract sympathy for his campaign (Wilcox 1996:60–61). More recently, a volunteer for US presidential candidate John McCain's campaign in 2008 claimed to have been the victim of a politically motivated attack and robbery by a black supporter of the opposing candidate, Barack Obama. She said he cut a "B" into her face and said, "You are going to be a Barack supporter." It later became clear she had carved the "B" herself (Fuoco et al. 2008).

These are *hate crime hoaxes*. The logic is the same as the other false accusations we have discussed—a false claim of victimhood that attracts sympathy for the apparent victims and hostility toward their adversaries— but in these collective conflicts the adversaries are not individuals. Rather than falsely accuse a particular individual, an aggrieved party simply claims to have been the victim of a hate crime, an identity-based attack by an outsider.

HATE CRIME HOAXES

Cases like these also occur on college campuses, which seem to be a "breeding ground" (Pellegrini 2008:97) or "petri dish" (Zamichow and Silverstein 2004) for hate crime hoaxes (see also Gose 1999; Leo 2000; Parmar 2004; Sanders 1998; "When a Hate Crime Isn't a Hate Crime" 1998–1999; Wilcox 1996:31). For example, in 2011 University of Virginia law student Johnathan Perkins published a letter to the editor in the law school's student newspaper in which he described being the victim of mistreatment by two white police officers. Perkins, who is black, claimed the officers pulled him over as he was walking home to an apartment near campus, saying he "fit the description of someone we're looking for." They asked for his identification, laughed when he told them he was a law student, frisked and searched him, and then followed him home. "I hope that sharing this experience," he concluded, "will provide this community with some much needed awareness of the lives that many of their black classmates are forced to lead" (Perkins 2011). Later Perkins acknowledged that "the events in the article did not occur" and that he had made up the story "to bring attention to the topic of police misconduct" (quoted in Jaschik 2011).

Also in 2011, on "UW crushes," a Facebook page where students at the University of Wyoming could post anonymously about their romantic attractions, a post read, "I want to hatefuck Meg Lanker Simons so hard. That chick that runs her liberal mouth all the time and doesn't care who knows it. I think its [sic] hot and it makes me angry. One night with me and shes [sic] gonna be a good Republican bitch." Though written as if it came from a Republican man sexually attracted to Meghan Lanker-Simons but opposed to her politics, police say Lanker-Simons actually posted the comments herself (Owens 2013).

Both students seem to have been trying to bring awareness to what they saw as some more general pattern of cultural victimization. We see this clearly in other cases, as in 2004 when Claremont McKenna College visiting psychology professor Kerri Dunn, prior to giving a lecture on hate speech at an event on campus, slashed her own car's tires and painted ethnic slurs and a swastika on it to present herself as the victim of white male racists. Similarly, in 1998, Jennifer Prissel, a senior at St. Cloud University in Minnesota, said two men assaulted her, cut her face, and yelled anti-gay slurs at her. The alleged attack was on the same night as a memorial vigil for Matthew Shephard, a University of Wyoming student, murdered two weeks earlier in what many said was an anti-gay hate crime. Prissel soon acknowledged she had lied about the incident and had even slashed her own face. At Duke University in 1997, a black baby doll was hung in a noose from a tree outside the place where the Black Student Alliance was planning a protest over race relations at the university. Later two black students acknowledged doing it in order to make a political statement (Gose 1999; Parmar 2004:14; Pellegrini 2008:98–102).

Conservative students also make false claims of victimhood. In 2007 a Princeton University student who belonged to the Anscombe Society, a socially conservative campus group, scratched and bruised his own face before claiming two men in ski caps beat him because of his political views (Hu 2007). The logic is the same—presenting oneself as having been victimized because of one's group identity, in this case one's politics. Still, most hate crime hoaxes currently come from the campus left and usually involve tales of offenses against Muslims, blacks, gays, or others whom campus activists see as victims of oppression.

Fellow activists, as well as faculty, students, and administrators sympathetic to their concerns, tend immediately to accept these accusations and act upon them. At the University of Wyoming, after the Facebook post about Meghan Lanker-Simons, hundreds of students gathered to protest "rape culture." Following the apparent vandalizing of Kerri Dunn's car, not only were there protests, but the seven Claremont colleges also cancelled classes and held pro-diversity rallies. And before Jennifer Prissel acknowledged slashing her own face, St. Cloud University had raised $12,000 to fund a reward for information about her attackers (Pellegrini 2008:100–102). More recently at St. Olaf College in Minnesota, a black student reported receiving a note on her car that called her a racial slur as well as saying she had "spoken up too much." "You will change nothing," it went on. "Shut up or I will shut you up" (quoted in Rubbelke 2017). In response student activists, holding signs with messages such as "Fuck your white complacency," blocked entrances to the cafeteria and took over a common area. The administration cancelled classes for a day, but later announced that an investigation had revealed the note was "fabricated"— that the author had confessed and that the purpose was to "draw attention to the concerns about the campus climate." They did not reveal the identity of the author, but the student who reported finding it posted on Facebook that "it looks like something made its way back to me in the investigation" and "I will be reporting it as a hoax" (quoted in Rubbelke 2017).

Hate crime hoaxes are often effective because many third parties take such claims of victimhood at face value. They do so despite the fact that the hoaxes are often poorly done. Statements like "You will change nothing" or "that chick that runs her liberal mouth and doesn't care who knows it … I think it's hot" seem to accept the alleged victims' views of themselves, and even to flatter them, much more than one would expect if they were genuine.

Not only do hoaxes tend to be effective, but they also seem to carry relatively little risk for the hoaxer. Often those who were quick to believe the hoaxers are later reluctant to punish or condemn them after the hoax is exposed. After the 1997 Duke case, for example, where two black students hung a black baby doll from a noose, Duke's student newspaper published a letter from a student defending the hoaxers, saying "the idea behind the act...is being overlooked" (quoted in Gose 1999). More recently, after Yasmin Seweid of Baruch College was found to have fabricated a story about three Trump supporters assaulting her and tearing off her hijab, her sister expressed concern about "the mental state of young Muslim women who feel they have to lie so intensely to survive" (quoted in Huber 2016).

Hoaxers might be punished, but usually only when police have become involved. Kerri Dunn, the hate crime hoaxer at Claremont McKenna College, received a one-year prison sentence. And Meghan Lanker-Simons, the Wyoming hoaxer, was fined after pleading no contest to the charge of interfering with a police officer. Legal punishments such as these are rare, though, and university punishments rarer still. Johnathan Perkins, the University of Virginia student who acknowledged making up a story about mistreatment by the police, did face a hearing under the university's honor system, but was ultimately acquitted (Fitzgerald 2012).

False accusations thrive in an environment where people are ready to believe and act upon them while reluctant to punish them. The response incentivizes the behavior. What is puzzling, perhaps, is why people in certain environments respond this way. Why, for example, do some so quickly believe unsupported claims of victimhood? To put it another way, what is the social structure of credulity?

CREDULITY AND FALSE ACCUSATIONS

Credulity—a tendency to believe claims without proof—is not just a personality quirk. True, some individuals are generally more trusting than others. But in many situations whether or not people believe a claim is a sociological matter having little to do with personality. Credulity is often an aspect of partisanship. Rather than exhibiting blanket trust or skepticism across the board, people are trusting of one side of a conflict and are skeptical of the other. Recall from Chap. 2 that one factor associated with partisanship is social distance: People support those who are close to them and oppose those who are distant from them. In some settings partisanship is automatic, with fellow kinsmen or fellow gang members siding with one another against rivals no matter what. Since believing one side's accusations is an act of partisanship, we would expect this to be fairly automatic as well.

When social structures are conducive to extreme partisanship, we expect extreme credulity toward the claims of one's own side. This accounts for some of the credulity we see regarding hate crime hoaxes. It makes sense that campus activists are quick to believe the claims of their political allies—especially members of their own activist circles. But recall that hate crime hoaxes, like microaggression lists, are a tactic aimed at convincing reluctant third parties. The strongest partisans—such as fellow activists—can be mobilized without lying or otherwise campaigning for their support. They need no convincing to fight against patriarchy, or racism, or whatever the hoaxer intends to call attention to. The point is to convince the weaker supporters—uninvolved students, the administration, and the public. This raises the question of why socially distant parties, inclined to only weak or slow support, can also be easily convinced that the accusations are true.

The answer is that partisanship also depends on the status of the accuser and the accused. Moral status is especially important: People are inclined to believe the side they see as more virtuous and disbelieve the side they see as deviant. An accusation made by a highly respected person is taken more seriously, as is an accusation against someone who already has a bad reputation. In the context of victimhood culture, this means that accusations made by or on behalf of women, minorities, and other perceived victims are more credible, especially if the alleged victimizer belongs to a more privileged group. The greater the moral status of victims, the greater tendency to side with victims and to believe their stories. Those who initially believe a hoax further contribute to the victim status of the accuser and are likely to vilify those who question the accusation as contributing to the oppression of the victim. In this environment believing members of disadvantaged groups who claim victimhood carries little risk. Their victim status protects hoaxers from both scrutiny and consequences. The hoaxers themselves are treated gently, so certainly no one is faulted for believing them. Skepticism is more dangerous.

DUE PROCESS AND FALSE ACCUSATIONS

Whenever people fail to scrutinize accusations, they allow for this kind of conflict manipulation. But the moral culture is not the only thing that determines the scrutiny that accusations receive. It also matters what kinds of institutions and procedures are in place for examining claims of victimization. It is often the police who uncover hate crime hoaxes because a police investigation entails asking questions that others are not asking, trying to corroborate any claims, and looking for alternative explanations. Due process requirements shape the behavior of police and legal officials so that in response to any report of a crime, they must take certain steps and must not take others. Due process varies, though, both between and within legal systems, and along with it the ease of manipulating law.

In Chap. 2 we discussed legal overdependency in totalitarian societies such as Nazi Germany and the Soviet Union. Recall that citizens could easily mobilize the law by denouncing one another, and that other forms of social control withered away as people came to rely on this method of handling their private disputes. This was an extreme case of legal overdependency, and it is also an extreme case of the private manipulation of law. Historian Jan Gross (1984) has noted that there is a privatization of the state in totalitarian societies: "Everybody has immediate access to the apparatus of the state and uses it frequently against other members of society" (Gross 1984:67). Gross examined Soviet rule of southeastern Poland from 1939 to 1941, and found that people would denounce their neighbors to authorities in order to settle personal matters. The authorities encouraged them to bring accusations, and "whoever had a grudge against somebody else, an old feud, who had another as a grain of salt in his eye—he had a stage to show his skills, there was a cocked ear, willing to listen" (quoted in Gross 1984:67). Without due process, accusation meant conviction. False accusation was thus an easy and effective weapon.

Due process is an inherent part of the US legal system, but it varies, and in some contexts false accusations have more promise of success. This can occur because the nature of an offense requires legal officials to rely more on citizens' complaints. So many false crime reports involve accusations of rape and child abuse because with these crimes it is often difficult to distinguish genuine accusations from false ones. These offenses tend to occur in private, where they are hidden from legal officials and even other citizens besides the victims. In most genuine cases there is little evidence other than the victim's testimony, and the majority of these crimes go unreported or unpunished (Tjaden and Thoennes 2006). Yet the same feature that leads to vast underreporting and wrongful acquittals also opens up the opportunity for false reports and wrongful convictions. Furthermore, due process varies across parts of the US legal system, with some agencies having more or fewer safeguards for the accused. This is another reason that false reporting is easier in child abuse cases: Such cases are normally dealt with by family courts and child protection services, where the accused have fewer protections than they would have in the criminal justice system.

False accusations are most common when due process is absent or weak, where they have a better chance of success. This is another reason college campuses are an ideal environment for hate crime hoaxes. There third parties are ready to act without much scrutiny of the accuser, and institutional agencies exist specifically to take up their cause. For example, more than 200 colleges and universities have various kinds of "bias response teams" that might quickly mobilize in response to an apparent offense (FIRE 2017). At Vassar College, the "Bias Incident Response Team," part of the Campus Life and Diversity Office, was deployed in 2013 after someone spray-painted anti-black and anti-transgender slurs on campus, but the incident turned out to be a hoax perpetrated by a trans-gender student who was a member of the Bias Incident Response Team (Soave 2013). Even in the absence of these kinds of organizations, accusations typically get results. They might lead to cancelled classes, public rallies, curriculum changes, and new faculty positions. Campus victimhood culture is so conducive to accusations on behalf of victim groups that we should not be surprised if many turn out to be false.

FALSE ACCUSATIONS AND MORAL PANICS

In an atmosphere of moral fervor about certain kinds of offenses, it can be unpopular to withhold judgment or to resist responding. When emotions become heated and outrage prevails, people demand action, and the skepticism or procedural restraints that might prevent or delay action themselves come under attack. Accusations that might otherwise seem outlandish lead to punishment of the accused, and possibly of those who defend them. Sociologists Erich Goode and Nachman Ben-Yehuda describe what happens in this kind of atmosphere, which they and other sociologists call a *moral panic*:

> The behavior of some members of a society is thought to be so problematic to others, the evil they do, or are thought to do, is felt to be so wounding to the substance and fabric of the body social, that serious steps must be taken to control the behavior, punish the perpetrators, and repair the damage. The threat this evil presumably poses is felt to represent a crisis for that

society: something must be done about it, and that something must be done now.... The sentiment generated or stirred up by this threat can be referred to as a kind of fever; it can be characterized by heightened emotion, fear, dread, anxiety, hostility, and a strong feeling of righteousness. (1994:31)

A moral panic involves an intense reaction to a perceived threat, but the threat is, if not imaginary, at least not as great as imagined. The idea of a *panic* implies a belief "that a more sizeable number of individuals are engaged in the behavior in question than actually are, and [a belief that] the threat, danger, or damage ... caused by the behavior is far more substantial than" it really is (Goode and Ben-Yehuda 1994:36).[5] Those who are not caught up in the panic might find the levels of credulity and moralism hard to comprehend. Hardly anyone now believes that the people executed for witchcraft in Renaissance Europe or in colonial Massachusetts were really witches. Many people also look unfavorably at other moral panics of the past: the "Red Scare" over communist infiltration of the United States in the 1950s, the war on drugs in the 1980s, or the concern with Satanic child abuse in the 1980s and 1990s (deYoung 1998; Goode and Ben-Yehuda 1994; Pontikes et al. 2010; Victor 1998).

Witch hunts might be thought of as pure cases of moral panic, where the threat is wholly imaginary. Most moral panics are not like that. There really were communist infiltrators, many drugs really are dangerous, and children actually are abused. But the moral panics in those cases still involved an exaggeration of the threat, with many false accusations and sensational tales that were, if not false, not nearly as typical as they were believed to be.

Sociologist Jeffrey Victor identifies four factors associated with false accusations during moral panics. First, people have come to believe in a threat from new kinds of deviants. Second, newer and older agencies of social control are competing over jurisdictions. Third, the tests for detecting the new kind of deviance are defective—oversimplified and ambiguous.

---

[5] Sociologist Stanley Cohen, one of the first to use the term *moral panic*, gave this description of the phenomenon: "A condition, episode, person or group emerges to become defined as a threat to societal values and interests; its nature is presented in a stylized and stereotypical fashion by the mass media; the moral barricades are manned by editors, bishops, politicians and other right thinking people; socially accredited experts pronounce their diagnoses and solutions; ways of coping are evolved or (more often) resorted to; the condition then disappears, submerges or deteriorates and becomes more visible" (1972:9).

And fourth, the perceived threat resonates with a demonology, with ideas about evil (Victor 1998:549).

These factors match up well with our idea that hate crime accusations have more success where due process is weak and moral culture encourages credulity. The first and fourth factors—beliefs about deviance and evil—have to do with moral culture. Victimhood culture encourages concern with offenses against equality and diversity and belief in the nefariousness of privileged majorities. It thus encourages the acceptance of hate crime claims and facilitates moral panics over them. Victor's second and third factors—new agencies and inaccurate detection—have to do with institutions and procedures. New agencies of social control created specifically for dealing with a kind of deviance often have special prerogatives and are typically zealous in fulfilling their sole function. They are thus remarkably good at finding deviance, and faulty methods of detection ensure they will find it whether it actually exists or not. Witch finders, for example, proved their worth by identifying witches with methods guaranteed to produce false-positives. A popular method was torture, which inevitably leads to false confessions (Victor 1998:554). The Salem witch trials also relied on so-called spectral evidence, meaning that a witness's testimony that the accused appeared in the witness's dreams or visions as evidence of guilt. The new authorities' special status and faulty methods demolished due process and made accusation as good as proof.

Many today have difficulty understanding how the Puritans could execute people based on something like spectral evidence. Yet modern moral panics are more like witch hunts than one might suppose. During the moral panic over child abuse in the 1980s and 1990s, there were stories of secret groups of Satanists ritually torturing and abusing children. In high profile cases day care workers were accused of doing things like abusing children in underground tunnels, molesting them in hot air balloons, and raping them with magic wands (deYoung 1998; Victor 1998; Rabinowitz 2003). Some were convicted and given long prison sentences. This was possible because of the same kinds of factors that made the witch trials possible. There were the cultural factors—a belief in widespread child sexual abuse and Satanic activity and a resonance of these beliefs with several demonologies, including traditional Christian fear of the Devil. These ensured many would find the stories both alarming and plausible. There was also the erosion of due process as psychologists and other experts took on the role of witch finders by using faulty techniques to discover new cases (Victor 1998:550–556). This included interview techniques that encouraged children to make up stories. Convinced that the owners of Fells Acres Day School in Massachusetts had sexually abused their charges, pediatric nurse Susan Kelley interviewed the children, usually over and over, until they told of crimes. Journalist Dorothy Rabinowitz describes Kelley's technique:

> The rule of thumb guiding child interviews in these cases was a simple one: If children said they had been molested, they were telling the truth; those who denied they had been abused were not telling the truth and were described as 'not ready to disclose'.... Asked if something bad had happened they wanted to tell, children said repeatedly that nothing had happened.... Nurse Kelley promised rewards if the children talked about the bad things. She assured them that some of their friends had already told about the bad things and that they could help too if they would tell. The helping theme was central ... because telling would mean helping other children, the interviewers, and the child's parents, and it would give the child a chance to catch up with the other children, who, Susan Kelley informed them, had already helped everyone out by telling. (Rabinowitz 2003:29–30)

This was effective in eventually getting many of the children to accuse the owners, and the children's testimony sent them to prison. Interviews like this have little more value than spectral evidence. In other cases even spectral evidence of a sort—recovered memories from dreams or hypnosis—has led to accusations of abuse and punishment of the supposed offenders (Rabinowitz 2003:90; Victor 1998:554).

The outbreaks of fear, protest, and outrage on college campuses—such as the Oberlin Ku Klux Klan scare we described in Chap. 1—can be understood as moral panics.[6] Recall the response to Erika Christakis's email to the Yale residential college she led with her husband, Nicholas. When she questioned whether the university needed to regulate offensive Halloween costumes, students demanded the Christakises' resignation, and a screaming crowd confronted Nicholas. Around the same time a student claimed she was turned away from a fraternity party that was for "white girls only." It may or may not be true that she was told this, but it soon became clear that nonwhite students had attended the party, and a Yale investigation later found "no evidence of systematic discrimination" there (quoted in Miller 2015). Regardless of whether the claim was inaccurate or exaggerated,

---

[6] Note that whether or not they are moral panics depends on one's definition, and the existing literature often fails to define the concept clearly.

it added to the intensity of the conflict and fueled something like a localized moral panic. Journalist James Kirchick even compares the fracas to other prominent cases of moral panic, arguing that what happened at Yale "was a hysteria not dissimilar to the 1980s child-sex-abuse panic married to the inquisitorial paranoia of the Salem witch trial" (Kirchick 2016). Kirchick points out that one thing "lost in the massive news coverage about the Halloween costume brouhaha [at Yale] was any inquiry into whether there had even been incidents of Yalies donning racist costumes." The coverage missed the fact that "the administrators who sent out the reproachful email to which Christakis replied were not responding to an actual event (or events) in which a student (or students) had worn such costumes" (Kirchick 2016). The entire discussion, and the drastic response to Christakis's mild dissent, had to do with the mere possibility that someone might wear something offensive. Questioning the necessity of Halloween guidelines is like questioning the necessity of witch finders: It is heresy, and a sign that one is likely in league with the witches.[7]

CAMPUS RAPE HOAXES

Victimhood culture encourages hate crime hoaxes and moral panics about them. And once begun, the dynamics of moral panic can encourage further false accusations, or at least make it easier for them to succeed. Compared to many of the classic examples, these campus panics over the threat of racists, sexists, and homophobes tend to be small-scale. They mainly involve the most radical students and faculty, as well as the administrators seeking to placate them. But some false accusations are able to rouse more of the campus and to alarm the wider community. Rape accusations in particular seem suited to lead to more widespread moral panics, as happened in recent years at Duke University and at the University of Virginia.

The Duke University Rape Hoax

In March 2006 Crystal Gail Mangum accused three members of Duke University's lacrosse team of gang raping her at a lacrosse team party held

---

[7] "While the moral panic is raging," writes Megan McArdle, "ludicrous and improbable stories suddenly become convincing, and it's dangerous to question them, because why are you defending witches, are YOU a witch?" (2015).

at an off-campus residence. Mangum was a stripper who had come to the party to do a performance along with another stripper. She seemed intoxicated and was unable to perform for more than a few minutes, and some angry words were exchanged between the strippers and the partygoers. Mangum left with the other stripper, Kim Roberts, but when she later refused to leave Roberts's car, Roberts called the police, who took Mangum to a mental health and drug treatment facility. When Mangum, who is black, later accused the white players of rape, the national media quickly picked up the story and portrayed the incident as the ultimate hate crime. Explaining the media's response, Dan Okrent of the *New York Times* later said, "It was male over female. It was rich over poor. It was educated over uneducated. My God, all the things that we know happen in the world coming together in one place. And you know, journalists— they start to quiver with a thrill when something like this happens" (quoted in National Public Radio 2016).

Right away many students, professors, and others vilified the entire lacrosse team. Protesters gathered outside the house where the lacrosse party had been held, banging pots and pans and holding up signs that read "Castrate," "You can't rape and run," and "Sunday morning: time to confess" (Taylor and Johnson 2008:73). Catholic priest Joe Vetter condemned the team during a mass at Duke Cathedral, and when the father of one of the players told him afterward that the Catholic players needed his support Vetter replied, "Tell them to confess their sins first" (Taylor and Johnson 2008:75). Ruth Sheehan of the Raleigh-based *News & Observer* began a column with a message: "Members of the Duke men's lacrosse team: You know. We know you know…. And one of you needs to come forward and tell the police" (quoted in Taylor and Johnson 2008:76). Student activists posted wanted posters with the pictures of the lacrosse players, demanding that someone "come forward" (Taylor and Johnson 2008:104). Duke's president cancelled the rest of the lacrosse team's season and forced coach Mike Pressler to resign. And Duke's student newspaper ran an ad signed by 88 Duke faculty members thanking the protesters for "not waiting and for making yourselves heard" (quoted in Taylor and Johnson 2008:147). Individually, some of the signatories were even more hostile. English and African-American Studies Professor Houston A. Baker Jr., in a letter to the administration, called for "immediate dismissals" of the players and coaches. He called the players "white, violent, drunken men … veritably given license to rape, maraud, deploy hate speech" (quoted in Taylor and Johnson 2008:106). Another professor, political scientist Paula McClain, answered "no" when asked if she would "publicly urge due process" for the accused students (Taylor and Johnson 2008:338).

The case against the players began to collapse almost immediately, but Durham County District Attorney Mike Nifong pressed on. He had been appointed to fill out the term of his predecessor, and prosecuting this high-profile case was giving life to his political career, eventually leading him to be elected to a term of his own in the fall. To determine which players to prosecute, Nifong allowed the accuser to identify her three attackers from a lineup that included only lacrosse players. Normal procedures would have also included people unrelated to the case, but Nifong's method ensured that there would be no obviously wrong answers. And as he failed to find any DNA evidence, and as time stamped photos, receipts, and other evidence failed to line up with the accuser's changing stories, Nifong remained undeterred. Eventually he came under an ethics investigation by the State Bar for his conduct in the case, and he turned the case over to North Carolina Attorney General Roy Cooper. Cooper soon announced that the players were innocent and labeled Nifong a "rogue prosecutor" (Taylor and Johnson 2008:352). Nifong was later disbarred.

Here we see a false accusation succeeding, for a time, under conditions that resemble the moral panics we talked about earlier. The accusation that members of a privileged majority had raped a poor minority woman resonated with third parties geared toward combatting oppression and who believed that white student athletes regularly use their privilege to get away with such behavior. Supporters rushed to judgment and punishment, and at least one explicitly rejected the idea of due process. This particular case was prolonged by prosecutorial misconduct, but the reactions nonetheless show both the degree to which campus victimhood culture encourages immediate acceptance of accusations and the extent to which accusations of a serious crime like rape can generate outrage in the larger community.

The University of Virginia Rape Hoax

In November 2014 *Rolling Stone* published a story about a brutal gang rape at the University of Virginia. According to the article, Jackie, a first-year University of Virginia (UVA) student, was on a date with a member of the Phi Kappa Psi fraternity when he took her to a party at his fraternity house. Once there he brought her upstairs to a pitch-black bedroom, where eight other fraternity members awaited. One of the men quickly assaulted her and threw her onto a low glass table. She resisted, but someone punched her in the face. She heard the men laugh, and one of them said, "Grab its motherfucking leg." Seven of them then spent three hours raping her on top of the now-shattered glass table, while her date and another man looked on and encouraged them. When one of the men tried to get out of raping Jackie, the others asked, "Don't you want to be a brother?" "We all had to do it," they said, "so you do, too" (Erdely 2014). The article implied it was something they had done many times—a ritual required of all fraternity members.[8]

Author Sabrina Rubin Erdely portrayed the response to Jackie's rape as typical of universities and of the University of Virginia in particular, where students and administrators sought to cover up the problem and to protect fraternities. When Jackie went immediately to her three closest friends on campus, they debated the wisdom of reporting the rape while she "stood beside them, mute in her bloody dress." If they reported it, one of her friends said, "her reputation will be *shot* for the next four years" and "we'll never be allowed into any frat party again." The same female friend later asked, "Why didn't you have fun with it? A bunch of hot Phi Psi guys?" Jackie's two male friends worried that it would interfere with their plans to rush fraternities. Later on, as Jackie struggled academically due to depression, she met with a UVA dean and told her about the rape. The dean gave her options for pursuing the case, which Jackie declined to do, but as Erdely put it, the "administration took no action to warn the campus" about the allegation (Erdely 2014).

The article appeared on November 19, and a swift response followed. Late that night a small group of masked men and women threw bottles and bricks through the windows of the Phi Psi house and spray-painted, "Fuck boys," "Suspend us," and "UVA Center for Rape Studies" (Shapiro 2014). The next morning someone sent an anonymous letter claiming

---

[8] Accusations of evil rituals are a reoccurring pattern in social life and act to paint all members of a social group as equally complicit in wrongdoing. A common accusation against the Jews is that they consume the blood or flesh of murdered Gentiles—especially children—in their Passover rituals. This myth, known as *blood libel*, emerged in Europe in the Middle Ages and remains common in parts of the Muslim world today. Early Roman Christians were the target of a similar accusation, with pagan Romans believing that new Christian converts murdered a baby as part of their initiation into the church. Once Christianity became the official religion of the Empire, Christians likewise accused pagan cults of using child murder as part of their initiations (Dundes 1991; Perry and Schweitzer 2001).

responsibility for the vandalism and threatening to do more: "We will escalate and we will provoke until justice is achieved for the countless victims of rampant sexual violence at this University and around the nation" (quoted in Elliot 2014). Later about 1000 persons attended an on-campus rally called "Stand Up against Rape Culture" (Rourke and Moran 2014). That afternoon UVA's Phi Kappa Psi chapter suspended its activities (Phi Kappa Psi 2014). On November 22 UVA President Teresa Sullivan announced the temporary suspension of all of the university's fraternities and sororities (DeBonis and Shapiro 2014). That night a faculty-organized protest ended in front of the Phi Psi house, with protesters chanting, "What do we want? An end to rape. When do we want it? Now" (quoted in Seal 2014).

All this happened within just three days of the *Rolling Stone* article. Those who sprang into action did not seem to consider or care that any detail of the story might be exaggerated—that it was completely fabricated must have been unthinkable. If President Sullivan had any doubts about the story as she meted out collective punishment on the campus's fraternities and sororities, she did not express them. Nor did any of those who shouted, smashed windows, or painted graffiti. Nor did anyone prominent in the national media, until on November 24 journalist Richard Bradley published a blog post expressing doubts. Bradley asked his readers to consider the story, as he was, with the eyes of "a magazine editor who has seen fakes before" (Bradley 2014). He pointed out several things that raised alarms: that the story was coming from a single, unnamed source; that Erdely did not interview Jackie's friends despite giving extensive secondhand quotes from them; that she did not interview either of the alleged rapists whose identities were known to Jackie; that it seemed far-fetched that premeditated gang rape would be a regular fraternity ritual or that the attackers would continue having sex with their victim on top of broken glass; and so on.

This was not a line of thinking congenial to those caught up in the moral panic. Writer Anna Merlan called Bradley an "idiot" and referred to his post as a "giant ball of shit" (Merlan 2014). As more people asked questions and the story began to unravel, some feminists and anti-rape activists used the hashtags #IStandWithJackie and #IBelieveJackie to continue defending the accuser on Twitter. The National Alliance to End Sexual Violence tweeted, "We know institutions will bring their power to bear to obfuscate violence. That's why we stand with survivors. #IBelieveJackie" (quoted in Hess 2014). In *The Guardian* feminist writer

Jessica Valenti wrote, "The current frenzy to prove Jackie's story false ... will do incredible damage to all rape victims, but it is this one young woman who will suffer most" (Valenti 2014). And blogger Jeff Fecke tweeted, "I think it's pretty clear Jackie was assaulted, and that her memory of the trauma is inaccurate—which is far from uncommon" (quoted in Hess 2014).

But still the unraveling continued. Jackie had said she met the fraternity member who took her to the house while they both worked as lifeguards at the Aquatic and Fitness Center, but no member of Phi Psi at the time worked there as a lifeguard. There was no party at the Phi Psi house that night, either, and many other details did not fit. Once journalists interviewed the three friends Jackie had initially reported the rape to, something Erdely had not done, an account of what happened began to emerge. During the fall of 2012, her first semester at UVA, Jackie had a romantic interest in Ryan, one of the three friends said to have dissuaded Jackie from reporting the rape. Ryan was not interested, and Jackie soon informed him and their two friends that an upperclassman named Haven Monahan was interested in her. She would share text messages she had supposedly received from Haven Monahan, and the three friends, without ever meeting him in person, believed that they were exchanging messages with him as well. But Haven Monahan did not exist. The texts Jackie showed were sent from a website that allows one to send texts from fictitious phone numbers, and it appears she wrote them herself. This was apparently an attempt to interest Ryan by making him jealous, and by using the character of Haven to express her attraction to Ryan—one supposed message from Haven claimed he was jealous of Ryan because Jackie "said this kid is smart and funny and worth it" (Shapiro 2016). When this strategy failed Jackie informed her friends she was going on a date with Monahan. It was late on the night the date was to have taken place that she met with her friends and told them Monahan had taken her to his fraternity house and forced her to perform oral sex on five men. Jackie's academic problems later led to her telling a now altered story to a dean, and to getting involved in a support group for rape victims (French and Bryan 2016; Ganim and Sanchez 2014; Hartmann 2015; Neff 2016; Shapiro 2016).

The UVA case, like the Duke case, shows how a false report of rape can lead to a moral panic and to the vilification of an entire group—the lacrosse team at Duke, the Phi Psi fraternity at UVA. Both cases also show how, in a victimhood culture, believing certain claims of victimization is upheld as a kind of moral duty. The degree to which these accusations succeed, both on campus and off, have led some to suggest that these individual incidents are actually part of a larger moral panic about rape at American colleges and universities.

"RAPE CULTURE" AND MORAL PANIC

Feminist scholars and activists often point to what they say are manifestations of *rape culture*, as when someone recently complained via Twitter that a child's t-shirt with the slogan "Boys will be boys" was perpetuating rape culture. The complaint led Gonzaga University to stop selling the shirt. Gonzaga's Chair of Women's and Gender Studies, Ann Ciasullo, explained what she thought was wrong: "I think the problem with the phrase is that historically it's been used to justify bad behavior by boys—not just boys but also men—and some of that can be particularly bad behavior including rape" (quoted in Sokol 2017). The idea is that "Boys will be boys" promotes rape, and that it is not unusual in doing so (see, e.g., Weiss 2009). Dianne Herman says that our society's culture "can be characterized as a rape culture because the image of heterosexual intercourse is based on a rape model of sexuality" (1984:46). The "aggressive-passive, dominant-submissive, me-Tarzan-you-Jane nature of the relationship between the sexes in our culture," she says, makes it difficult to "differentiate rape from 'normal' heterosexual relations" (Herman 1984:45–46).

In this view rape culture is all-pervasive, a fundamental aspect of American or perhaps heterosexual American society. Others use the term to describe the norms of certain groups within the larger society, like college fraternities, or they see it as pervasive in particular settings, like college campuses. Gender scholars Ayres Boswell and Joan Spade describe rape culture as "a set of values and beliefs that provide an environment conducive to rape," and they believe their findings show that "a rape culture exists in some fraternities" (1996:133, 145). They compared fraternity houses on a campus that female students saw as having a high risk for rape with those they saw as having a low risk, and they found that at the high-risk houses the parties were more gender segregated, men treated women less respectfully, and the atmosphere was more sexually charged and less friendly. "The degradation of women as portrayed in rape culture was not found in all fraternities on this campus," they write. Instead, "some settings are more likely places for rape than are others" (Boswell and Spade 1996:143).

From a social scientific perspective, this second view is more promising. It allows the concept to be a shorthand for describing a cluster of quantitatively measurable traits. Doing this would allow us to talk about places that had more or less rape culture, and would help us understand differences between times and places with a high rate of rape and those with low rates of rape. *Rape culture* might be useful as a social scientific concept, but as such it is also subject to the scrutiny ordinarily applied to such concepts. We might argue over the best way to define the term, as well as over how to apply it to particular cases.

Yet many object to the idea that the concept's meaning, merits, and applications are up for debate. As described in Chap. 1, activists at Brown claimed a debate about the concept was a threat to their safety (Shulevitz 2015). Likewise, when Cal Poly San Luis Obispo's college Republicans hosted a presentation by libertarian activist Lauren Southern, who denies "there's a pervasive culture of rape and assault on college campuses," some students organized a "March against Rape Culture." "To allow someone like Lauren Southern to talk about rape culture and to deny rape culture, and make survivors here unsafe, it's disgusting," said Morgan Grace, a student affiliated with the Cal Poly Queer Student Union (Caris 2017). At Oberlin, when the campus Republican and Libertarian group brought in scholar Christina Hoff Sommers, dozens of students signed a letter calling her a "rape denialist ... who denies the prevalence of rape and denies the known causes of it" (Oberlin Community Members 2015). To many activists, any debate about rape culture is outside the bounds of normal academic discourse, a kind of "denial" that further victimizes rape victims. According to Rachel Venema, a professor of social work at Calvin College, "Denial of rape culture IS rape culture" (2017).

The idea of rape culture has become dogma even in the absence of a consensus on what it means or what it refers to. Is it American culture, or perhaps the culture of American colleges, or perhaps that of college fraternities? If the United States is a rape culture, then what about societies where some women receive no protection from rape at all? For example, among the Mehinaku Indians of Brazil, men would commonly "drag off" women to rape them, and as long as they raped unmarried women they were apparently never punished (Gregor 1990). What about rape during war or genocide? In Bosnia-Herzegovina during the early 1990s, Serbs raped between 20,000 and 50,000 Muslim women as a matter of deliberate policy (Campbell 2015:42). And which times and places are *not* rape cultures?

Though the concept is unclear, it has become popular, and people are sometimes vilified for questioning or criticizing it. This is because adopting the term demonstrates concern for rape victims. Recall that victimhood culture is one in which there is extreme sensitivity to what Donald Black (2011) calls overstratification and underdiversity—challenges to equality or offenses against cultural groups. Rape, overwhelmingly a crime committed by men against women, is especially offensive in this setting. Activists view it as another kind of exploitation of the powerless by the powerful. They also tend to view it as an intercollective conflict, a means by which one group suppresses or rejects another. Thus victimhood culture produces heightened concern with this crime. As discussed above, victimhood culture also privileges the accusations of the disadvantaged (women) against the advantaged (men), and it tends to uphold credulity toward claims of minority victimization as a moral duty.[9] We should not be surprised, then, that any term or concept that suggests the commonality of rape, and the complicity of large segments of the population in encouraging it, becomes popular. Believing that rape culture permeates a campus or the nation as a whole is a large-scale version of believing the accusations against the UVA fraternity members or the Duke lacrosse players: It is a way of siding with victims against oppressors, and failure to endorse the idea is seen as siding with oppressors against victims.

The concern with rape culture, especially on college campuses, has many of the hallmarks of a moral panic, and some have identified it as such. For example, Megan McArdle says we are "in the grip of a moral panic about campus rape" (2015), and journalist Emily Yoffe says this "moral panic is clouding our ability to rationally assess the problem" (2015). Christina Hoff Sommers says, "We are in the throes of one of those panics where paranoia, censorship, and false accusations flourish— and otherwise sensible people abandon their critical facilities" (2014). And historian KC Johnson and journalist Stuart Taylor Jr. say the current "atmosphere of moral panic ... shows no sign of abating" (2017:267).

[9] Commenting on the UVA rape hoax, activist Zerlina Maxwell says we should still "believe, as a matter of default, what an accuser says" (2014). Maxwell, like many others, sees credulity as a virtue, at least when it comes to rape accusations. The falsely accused are of less concern to her: though a falsely accused man "would have a rough period ... the cost of disbelieving women ... is far steeper. It signals that women don't matter and that they are disposable" (Maxwell 2014).

Recall that one feature of moral panics is an exaggeration of the threat. This does not necessarily mean the threat is non-existent, or that it is not a serious problem (Goode and Ben-Yehuda 1994:222–223). Hundreds of thousands of rapes occur in the United States every year, some proportion of them on college campuses (Tjaden and Thoennes 2006, see also National Research Council 2014). The Duke lacrosse and the UVA *Rolling Stone* cases were false accusations, but the Brock Turner case, the third most prominent campus rape story of recent years, was not. Turner, a Stanford swimmer, was digitally penetrating an unconscious woman when two students saw him and then chased him down and detained him when he ran away. The case shows how easily such an assault can occur and go unpunished—which would have likely happened here if the two students had not happened on the scene. Many would also take the fact that Turner was given a lenient sentence—six months in jail and registration as a sex offender—as a clear example of what they would call rape culture. Still, as Johnson and Taylor point out, even this case ran counter to aspects of the rape culture narrative (2017:11). The male students who saw the assault immediately intervened to stop Turner, the police arrested him, prosecutors tried him, and a jury convicted him. The public was outraged at the leniency of the sentence. "The national outcry," they say, "itself showed this case … to be highly atypical" (Johnson and Taylor 2017:11; see also Felson and Pare 2007; Paquette 2016).

In a moral panic, both false stories and true but atypical ones are treated as representative of the threat (Goode and Ben-Yehuda 1994; see, e.g., Weiss and Colyer 2010). There is also a tendency to exaggerate the scale of the threat, imagining that the number of drug addicts or communists is greater than it really is. Is this the case with rape on campus? Perhaps. Evidence suggests that rape is in fact more common among college students than among the general population, but no more common than among similarly aged people who are not attending college (Johnson and Taylor 2017:44; Sinozich and Langton 2014; Yoffe 2014). In other words, the elevated risk for college women has more to do with their being young than with their being on a campus, and focusing on campuses as a particularly dangerous environments might be misleading—and a distraction from more important risk factors (Felson and Cundiff 2014; Felson and Krohn 1990; see also Weiss 2013). We might also ask whether the rate of rape on college campuses has been increasing. Is the recent spike in concern following a spike in rape? Almost certainly not. Violent crime in the United States, including rape and sexual assault, has declined dramatically since the mid-1990s, and victimization surveys suggest it has declined on college campuses as well (Johnson and Taylor 2017:44; Yoffe 2014). The reporting of campus rape has gone up, but this is consistent with a growing attention to the issue (Johnson and Taylor 2017:49). Anti-rape activists could consider the increased reporting a victory, and to them this might justify their promulgating concern with rape culture. But if increased reporting is uncritically accepted as evidence of increased incidence, it contributes to exaggerated ideas about the threat of rape.

Moral panics usually inspire efforts to weaken due process protections for the accused. We see this in the push for universities to investigate and adjudicate rape allegations and punish offenders themselves, rather than leave this to the criminal justice system as they would for other crimes. In fact the Department of Education's Office for Civil Rights (OCR) has interpreted Title IX, a law forbidding sex discrimination in education, as requiring universities to do this. And a 2011 OCR directive, known as the "Dear Colleague letter," required them to lower the standard of proof in sexual assault cases to "preponderance of the evidence," meaning an accused student would be held responsible whenever it was just slightly more likely than not that the accusation was true. Prior to that many universities used the "clear and convincing evidence" standard, meaning the accusation needed to be much more likely to be true than not and that those deciding the outcome needed to have a firm conviction that it was true. This was still lower than the "beyond a reasonable doubt" standard used in criminal trials (Yoffe 2014).

Individual Title IX officers often go beyond this, further undermining protection for the accused. Cultural theorist Laura Kipnis, herself subject to a Title IX investigation over an essay she wrote criticizing such procedures, says the "utter capriciousness of the process" means that "an accusation itself pretty much suffices to constitute preponderance" (2017:37). For example, at the University of Cincinnati, a male student had a three-way sexual encounter with two female students in his dorm room. He said it was consensual, but they reported it to the police, saying that they were intoxicated and unable to give consent. The university pursued its own case even after the police dropped the investigation due to inconsistencies in the accusers' stories. A hearing panel found the accused student guilty, and he was expelled from the university. The panel had refused to examine evidence such as the accusers' text messages from that night or a surveillance video that showed the accused and the accusers going into the dorm. "The guilty finding seemed so preordained," write Johnson and Taylor, "that the university allowed one accuser to make a 'victim impact' statement before the panel had even reached its decision" (2017:90). Elsewhere a student's girlfriend accused him of a nonconsensual act of sexual intercourse, months after the event and after he had broken up with her. This panel did analyze the text and Facebook messages from the months following the alleged assault, but they decided that "if the woman had verbally assented, as he claimed, he would have mentioned that in the texts" (Kipnis 2017:163).

In cases like these, universities refuse to inform accused students of the details of the charges against them, refuse to allow them to ask questions of the accuser, refuse to look at evidence that might be exculpatory, and order them not to speak about the case to anyone. Such procedures, combined with a low standard of proof, mean an accusation is often enough to convict. Even provably false accusations might succeed, as at the University of North Dakota, where a panel found a student guilty of sexual assault a few months before police charged his accuser with filing a false police report (Sommers 2014). As in other moral panics, we see here new agents of social control—Title IX officers and other university bureaucrats—given special prerogatives and charged with punishing some class of deviants, who they locate using means that are likely to err on the side of false-positives.

We began this discussion by noting that the concern with campus rape goes far beyond the progressive student activists who are concerned with microaggressions and trigger warnings. If it is a moral panic, it is one that involves members of Congress, federal bureaucrats, university administrators, journalists, and many others. The concern is most intense on campuses in part because they are enclaves of victimhood culture. But unlike microaggressions, rape is something that almost everyone considers a severe offense. Indeed, it is felony, and even though some rapists are treated more leniently than most people would prefer, there are nonetheless many rapists serving lengthy prison sentences for their crime. Recall from the previous chapter that the seriousness of an offense depends on the extent to which it disrutps existing patterns of inequality, intimacy, and culture (Black 2011). Rape is a more severe act of domination than mere insult—it is a form of violent exploitation, using force to take away the victim's autonomy. It is a high degree of what Black calls *overstratification*. It is also a high degree of *overintimacy*—something that makes many view it as a particularly disgusting and stigmatizing form of violence (Black 2011:23–25). For these reasons, it is also an especially psychologically damaging form of violence. One does not need to be enmeshed in victim-hood culture to be appalled by rape, or to be concerned with its frequency among young people. But victimhood culture, with its hypersensitivity to inequality between groups and moral commitment to always support alleged victims, is likely to produce exaggerated beliefs and false accusations, and thus to fuel moral panic.

* * *

In the Prologue we described how in wake of the 2016 election, many highly publicized Trump-inspired hate crimes turned out to be false. A University of Michigan student said a man threatened to light her on fire if she did not remove her hijab. A student at the University of Louisiana at Lafayette said she was attacked by white men who stole her wallet and her hijab (Felten 2017). A North Park University student said she found a note with "Back to Hell," "#Trump," and homophobic slurs written on it. A University of Minnesota student said a white man assaulted her and told her to "go back to Asia" (Stoltzfoos 2016). None of these incidents happened, but they fit in with a media narrative of growing hate and oppression of minorities. They show a heightened concern with threats against equality and diversity, a tendency to portray political opponents as violent oppressors, and a resulting credulity toward claims of minority victimization. We also see patterns in the many more such stories that make the news despite a lack of much evidence for them, or in incidents that are framed as ethnic conflict but might be better explained with other factors, such as mental illness or interpersonal conflict.[10] Like rape, hate crimes really do exist. Some widely reported cases, such as the killing of a black man by a white supremacist in New York City in March 2017, are completely genuine (Byfield 2017). Some cases, such as the fatal shooting of an Indian immigrant in a Kansas bar in early 2017, may even be connected to the 2016 election (CBS News 2017; Suhr and Hanna 2017). But it remains the case that people are prone to believe certain kinds of

---

[10] For example, *The New York Times* series "This Week in Hate," created to document hate crimes since Trump's election, included a report of an anti-Muslim attack: "A man is accused of attacking a Muslim woman at a Manhattan Dunkin' Donuts on Sunday, throwing coffee in her face and putting her in a headlock.... He told the woman he 'hated Muslims' and was going to kill her" (*New York Times* Editorial Board 2016). Journalist Eric Felten (2017) notes that what the *Times* account leaves out is the fact that the attacker was a homeless man, likely someone struggling with a mental illness.

false accusations—and some are prone to make them—whenever they become intensely outraged toward some group of offenders or intensely concerned about some group of victims. Outrage and concern followed the unexpected election of Donald Trump, and hate crime hoaxes such as those we usually see only sporadically at universities proliferated and made headlines before they were debunked. Credulity and moral panic go hand in hand.

References

Andrighetto, Luca, Silvia Mari, Chaira Volpato, and Burim Behluli. 2012. Reducing Competitive Victimhood in Kosovo: The Role of Extended Contact and Common Ingroup Identity. *Political Psychology* 33 (4): 513–529.

Barnes, J.A. 1994. *A Pack of Lies: Towards a Sociology of Lying*. Melbourne: Cambridge University Press.

Benedek, Elissa P., and Diane H. Schetky. 1985. Allegations of Sexual Abuse in Child Custody and Visitation Disputes. In *Emerging Issues in Child Psychiatry and the Law*, ed. Elissa P. Benedek and Diane H. Schetky, 145–156. New York: Brunner/Mazel.

Berger, Leslie. 1994. Prostitutes Are Prime Victims in Leading Rape Area. *Los Angeles Times*, May 8. http://articles.latimes.com/1994-05-08/local/me-55157_1.

Black, Donald. 1998. *The Social Structure of Right and Wrong*. Rev ed. San Diego: Academic Press.

———. 2011. *Moral Time*. New York: Oxford University Press.

Boswell, A. Ayres, and Joan Z. Spade. 1996. Fraternities and Collegiate Rape Culture: Why Are Some Fraternities More Dangerous Places for Women? *Gender and Society* 10 (2): 133–147.

Bradley, Richard. 2014. Is the Rolling Stone Story True? *Shots in the Dark* (blog), November 14. http://www.richardbradley.net/shotsinthedark/2014/11/24/is-the-rolling-stone-story-true/.

Brennan, Jason. 2016. Murderers at the Ballot Box: When Philosophers May Lie to Bad Voters. In *Ethics in Politics: The Rights and Obligations of Individual Political Agents*, ed. Emily Crooksten, David Killoren, and Jonathan Trerise, 11–34. New York: Routledge.

Bryden, David P., and Sonja Lengnick. 1997. Rape in the Criminal Justice System. *The Journal of Criminal Law and Criminology* 87 (4): 1194–1384.

Byfield, Erica. 2017. White Supremacist in NYC Sword Killing Charged with Murder as Terrorism. *NBC New York*, March 27. http://www.nbcnewyork.com/news/local/White-Supremacist-NYC-Sword-Killing-Indicted-Murder-Terrorism-417219563.html.

Bytwerk, Randall L. 2010. Grassroots Propaganda in the Third Reich: The Reich Ring for National Sociologist Propaganda and Public Enlightenment. *German Studies Review* 33 (1): 93–118.

Campbell, Bradley. 2015. *The Geometry of Genocide*. Charlottesville: University of Virginia Press.

Caris, Keith. 2017. Cal Poly Protests Greet Controversial, Conservative Commentator. *KEYT*, May 25. http://www.keyt.com/news/local-news/cal-poly-protests-greet-controversial-conservative-commentator/517680245.

CBS News. 2017. Kansas Man Charged with Hate Crime in Fatal Shooting of Indian Engineer. June 9. https://www.cbsnews.com/news/adam-purinton-faces-hate-crime-charges-in-fatal-shooting-of-indian-engineer/.

Chan, Stephanie. 2011. *Moral Pressure: American Democracy and Chinese Human Rights*, Ph.D. Dissertation. San Diego: Department of Sociology, University of California.

Cohen, Stanley. 1972. *Folk Devils and Moral Panics: The Creation of the Mods and the Rockers*. Oxford: Basil Blackwell.

Collins, Randall. 2000. Situational Stratification: A Micro-Macro Theory of Inequality. *Sociological Theory* 18 (1): 17–43.

———. 2012. C-Escalation and D-Escalation: A Theory of the Time-Dynamics of Conflict. *American Sociological Review* 77 (1): 1–20.

DeBonis, Mike, and T. Rees Shapiro. 2014. U-Va. President Suspends Fraternities until Jan. 9 in Wake of Rape Allegations. *Washington Post*, November 22. https://www.washingtonpost.com/local/education/u-va-president-suspends-fraternities-until-jan-9-in-wake-of-rape-allegations/2014/11/22/023d3688-7272-11e4-8808-afaa1e3a33ef_story.html?utm_term=.dc42ea791b9e.

deYoung, Mary. 1998. Another Look at Moral Panics: The Case of Satanic Day Care Centers. *Deviant Behavior* 19: 257–278.

Dundes, Alan, ed. 1991. *The Blood Libel Legend: A Casebook in Anti-Semitic Folklore*. Madison: University of Wisconsin Press.

Elliot, Andrew. 2014. Students Claiming Responsibility for Phi Kappa Psi Vandalism Submit Anonymous Letter. *Cavalier Daily*, November 20. http://www.cavalierdaily.com/article/2014/11/letter-claiming-responsibility-for-phi-kappa-psi-vandalism-lists-anonymous-demands.

Erdely, Sabrina Rubin. 2014. A Rape on Campus: A Brutal Assault and Struggle for Justice at UVA. *Rolling Stone*, November 19. http://web.archive.org/web/20141119200349/http://www.rollingstone.com/culture/features/a-rape-on-campus-20141119.

Faller, Kathleen Coulborn. 1991. Possible Explanations for Child Sexual Abuse Allegations in Divorce. *American Journal of Orthopsychiatry* 61 (1): 86–91.

Faller, Kathleen Coulborn, and Ellen DeVoe. 1995. Allegations of Sexual Abuse in Divorce. *Journal of Child Sexual Abuse* 4 (4): 1–25.

Felson, Richard B., and Patrick R. Cundiff. 2014. Sexual Assault as a Crime Against Young People. *Archives of Sexual Behavior* 43 (2): 273–284.

Felson, Richard B., and Marvin Krohn. 1990. Motives for Rape. *Journal of Research in Crime and Delinquency* 27 (3): 222–242.

Felson, Richard B., and Paul-Philippe Pare. 2007. Does the Criminal Justice System Treat Domestic Violence and Sexual Assault Offenders Leniently? *Justice Quarterly* 24 (3): 435–459.

Felten, Eric. 2017. The Great Hate-Crime Hysteria. *The Weekly Standard*, January 17. http://www.weeklystandard.com/the-great-hate-crime-hysteria/article/2006338.

FIRE. 2017. Bias Response Team Report. Foundation for Individual Rights in Education (FIRE). https://www.thefire.org/first-amendment-library/special-collections/fire-guides/report-on-bias-reporting-systems-2017/.

Fitzgerald, Brendan. 2012. Johnathan Perkins Acquitted During Summer Honor Code Trial. *C-Ville*, January 11. http://www.c-ville.com/Johnathan_Perkins_acquitted_during_summer_Honor_Code_trial/#.WUC-eTOZOu4.

French, Laura, and Alix Bryan. 2016. Girl Who Cried UVa Rape Pretended to Be Her Rapist to Win a Boy, Lawyers Say. *WTVR*, December 8. http://wtvr.com/2016/02/08/jackie-uva-gang-rape-story-twist/.

Fuoco, Michael A., Jerome L. Sherman, and Sadie Gurman. 2008. McCain Volunteer Admits to Hoax. *Pittsburgh Post-Gazette*, October 25. http://www.post-gazette.com/neighborhoods/2008/10/25/McCain-volunteer-admits-to-hoax/stories/200810250133.

Ganim, Sara, and Ray Sanchez. 2014. Friends' Accounts Differ Significantly from Victim in UVA Rape Story. *CNN*, December 17. http://www.cnn.com/2014/12/16/us/uva-rape/.

Goffard, Christopher. 2011a. Could This Be Happening?: A Man's Nightmare Made Real. *Los Angeles Times*, June 26. http://articles.latimes.com/2011/jun/26/local/la-me-accused-20110626.

———. 2011b. In This Assault Case, the Puzzle Pieces Don't Fit. *Los Angeles Times*, June 27. http://articles.latimes.com/2011/jun/27/local/la-me-accused-20110628.

Goode, Erich, and Nachman Ben-Yehuda. 1994. *Moral Panics: The Social Construction of Deviance*. Malden: Blackwell Publishing.

Gose, Ben. 1999. Hate-Crime Hoaxes Unsettle Campuses. *Chronicle of Higher Education* 45 (18): A55–A56.

Green, Arthur H. 1986. True and False Allegations of Sexual Abuse in Child Custody Disputes. *Journal of the American Academy of Child Psychiatry* 25 (4): 449–456.

Gregor, Thomas. 1990. Male Dominance and Sexual Coercion. In *Cultural Psychology: Essays on Comparative Human Development*, ed. James W. Stigler,

Richard A. Shweder, and Gilbert Herdt, 477–495. New York: Cambridge University Press.

Gross, Jan T. 1984. Social Control Under Totalitarianism. In *Toward a General Theory of Social Control. Volume 2: Selected Problems*, ed. Donald Black, 59–77. Orlando: Academic Press.

Hartmann, Margaret. 2015. Everything We Know About the UVA Rape Case. *New York Magazine*, July 30. http://nymag.com/daily/intelligencer/2014/12/everything-we-know-uva-rape-case.html.

Haskett, Mary E., Kathleen Wayland, James S. Hutcheson, and Tiersa Tavana. 1995. Substantiation of Sexual Abuse Allegations: Factors Involved in the Decision-Making Process. *Journal of Child Sexual Abuse* 4 (2): 19–47.

Herman, Dianne F. 1984. The Rape Culture. In *Women: A Feminist Perspective*, ed. Jo Freeman, 45–53. Mountain View: Mayfield.

Hess, Amanda. 2014. Feminism Can Stand Without Jackie. *Slate*, December 11. http://www.slate.com/blogs/xx_factor/2014/12/11/_istandwithjackie_and_the_feminist_response_to_the_unraveling_of_rolling.html.

Hillenbrand, Laura. 2010. *Unbroken: A World War II Story of Survival, Resilience, and Redemption*. New York: Random House.

Hu, Winnie. 2007. Princeton Student Admits Faking Attack. *The New York Times*, December 18. http://www.nytimes.com/2007/12/18/nyregion/18hoax.html?_r=0.

Huber, David. 2016. 'Hate Crime' Hysteria: The Best of the Worst Post-election Pro-Trump 'Incidents' and Hoaxes. *The College Fix*, December 17. https://www.thecollegefix.com/post/30414/.

Jaschik, Scott. 2011. Truth Without Consequences? *Inside Higher Ed*, May 9. http://www.insidehighered.com/news/2011/05/09/false_claim_of_police_harassment_is_debated_at_university_of_virginia.

Johnson, K.C., and Stuart Taylor Jr. 2017. *The Campus Rape Frenzy: The Attack on Due Process at America's Universities*. New York: Encounter Books.

Kanin, Eugene J. 1994. False Rape Allegations. *Archives of Sexual Behavior* 23 (1): 81–92.

Kessler, Glenn. 2016. The Biggest Pinocchios of 2016. *Washington Post*, December 16. https://www.washingtonpost.com/news/fact-checker/wp/2016/12/16/the-biggest-pinocchios-of-2016/?utm_term=.d36d53cb4049.

Kipnis, Laura. 2017. *Unwanted Advances: Sexual Paranoia Comes to Campus*. New York: HarperCollins.

Kirchick, James. 2016. The New Yorker vs. Free Speech. *Commentary*, March 16. https://www.commentarymagazine.com/articles/new-yorker-vs-free-speech/.

Leo, John. 2000. Faking the Hate. *U.S. News and World Report*, June 5. http://www.usnews.com/usnews/opinion/articles/000605/archive_034129.htm.

Maxwell, Zerlina. 2014. No Matter What Jackie Said, We Should Generally Believe Rape Claims. *Washington Post*, December 6. https://www.washingtonpost. com/posteverything/wp/2014/12/06/no-matter-what-jackie-said-we-should-automatically-believe-rape-claims/?utm_term=.6718e9419093.

McArdle, Megan. 2015. Moral Panics Won't End Campus Rape. *Bloomberg View*, January 28. https://www.bloomberg.com/view/articles/2015-01-28/moral-panics-won-t-end-campus-rape.

Merlan, Anna. 2014. 'Is the UVA Rape Story a Gigantic Hoax?' Asks Idiot. *Jezebel*, December 1. https://jezebel.com/is-the-uva-rape-story-a-gigantic-hoax-asks-idiot-1665233387.

Miller, Michael E. 2015. Yale Investigation Finds 'No Evidence' of Racism at Frat Party Alleged to Have Been for 'White Girls Only.' *Washington Post*, December 11. https://www.washingtonpost.com/news/morning-mix/wp/2015/12/11/yale-investigation-finds-no-evidence-of-racism-at-frat-party-alleged-to-have-been-for-white-girls-only/?utm_term=.6a5ea0356738.

Mukhopadhyay, Samhita. 2015. Stop Complaining About Victimhood Culture. *Al Jazeera America*, October 8. http://america.aljazeera.com/opinions/2015/10/stop-complaining-about-victimhood-culture.html.

National Public Radio. 2016. 'Fantastic Lies' Lays Out 2006 Duke Lacrosse Case. March 10. http://www.npr.org/2016/03/10/469897698/fantastic-lies-lays-out-2006-duke-lacrosse-rape-case.

National Research Council. 2014. *Estimating the Incidence of Rape and Sexual Assault*. Panel on Measuring Rape and Sexual Assault in Bureau of Justice Statistics Household Surveys, C. Kruttschnitt, W.D. Kalsbeek, and C.C. House, Editors. Committee on National Statistics, Division of Behavioral and Social Sciences and Education. Washington, DC: The National Academies Press.

Neff, Blake. 2016. You Can Finally Read UVA Jackie's Bizarre Catfishing Texts. *The Daily Caller*, February 10. http://dailycaller.com/2016/02/10/you-can-finally-read-uva-jackies-bizarre-catfishing-texts/.

Oberlin Community Members. 2015. In Response to Sommers' Talk: A Love Letter to Ourselves. *The Oberlin Review*, April 18. https://oberlinreview. org/8032/opinions/in-response-to-sommers-talk-a-love-letter-to-ourselves/.

Owens, Eric. 2013. Police Say 28-Year-Old Undergrad Threatened Herself with Rape in Facebook Hoax. *The Daily Caller*, May 1. http://dailycaller. com/2013/05/01/police-say-28-year-old-undergrad-threatened-herself-with-rape-in-facebook-hoax/.

Paquette, Danielle. 2016. What Makes the Stanford Sex Offender's Six Month Sentence so Unusual. *The Washington Post*, June 16. https://www.washingtonpost.com/news/wonk/wp/2016/06/06/what-makes-the-stanford-sex-offenders-six-month-jail-sentence-so-unusual/?utm_term=.a8de76cb4be9.

Parmar, Neil. 2004. Crying Wolf. *Psychology Today* 37 (4): 13–14.

Pellegrini, Laura A. 2008. *An Argument for the Criminal Hoax*, Ph.D. Dissertation. Los Angeles: Department of Political Science, University of Southern California.
Perkins, Johnathan. 2011. Letter to the Editor. *Virginia Law Weekly* 63(26). http://www.lawweekly.org/?module=displaystory&story_id=3368&edition_id=180&format=html.
Perry, Marvin, and Frederick M. Schweitzer. 2001. *Myth and Hate from Antiquity to the Present*. New York: Palgrave Macmillan.
Phi Kappa Psi. 2014. Statement from Phi Kappa Psi. *Cavalier Daily*, November 20. http://www.cavalierdaily.com/article/2014/11/letter-statement-from-phi-kappa-psi.
Pontikes, Elizabeth, Giacoma Negro, and Hayagreeva Rao. 2010. Stained Red: A Study of Stigman by Association to Blacklisted Artists During the 'Red Scare' in Hollywood, 1945 to 1960. *American Sociological Review* 75 (3): 456–478.
Rabinowitz, Dorothy. 2003. *No Crueler Tyrannies: Accusation, False Witness, and Other Terrors of Our Times*. New York: Free Press.
Rourke, Sara, and Victoria Moran. 2014. Community Confronts Sexual Assault on Grounds. *Cavalier Daily*, November 21. http://www.cavalierdaily.com/article/2014/11/community-confronts-sexual-assault.
Rubbelke, Nathan. 2017. 'Student Coup' at St. Olaf College: Students Block Buildings, Classes Shut Down over Racial Unrest. *The Daily Caller*, May 1. https://www.thecollegefix.com/post/32392/.
Sanders, Jon. 1998. Hoax Crimes. *National Review*, September 14, pp. 38–40.
Sasaki, Mako. 1999. Who Became Kamikaze Pilots, and How Did They Feel Towards Their Suicide Mission? *Concord Review* 7 (1): 175–209.
Seal, Dean. 2014. Hundreds Protest at UVa; Students Says Memorial to Victims Vandalized. *The Daily Progress*, November 23. http://www.dailyprogress.com/news/local/hundreds-protest-at-uva-student-says-memorial-to-victims-vandalized/article_81bc9d24-7379-11e4-a91e-f70a4bc5767c.html.
Shapiro, Jeffrey Scott. 2014. Unpunished Vandalism Rampage Inspired by Rolling Stone's Rape Story. *Washington Times*, December 21. http://www.washingtontontimes.com/news/2014/dec/21/rolling-stone-university-of-virginia-rape-story-sp/#ixzz3Ml3pWRHc%20.
Shapiro, T. Rees. 2016. 'Catfishing' over Love Interest Might Have Spurred U-Va. Gang Rape Debacle. *Washington Post*, January 8. https://www.washingtonpost.com/news/grade-point/wp/2016/01/08/catfishing-over-love-interest-might-have-spurred-u-va-gang-rape-debacle/?utm_term=.d0adf026d99d.
Shulevitz, Judith. 2015. In College and Hiding from Scary Ideas. *New York Times*, March 21. https://www.nytimes.com/2015/03/22/opinion/sunday/judith-shulevitz-hiding-from-scary-ideas.html?_r=0.
Sinozich, Sofi, and Lynne Langton. 2014. *Rape and Sexual Assault Victimization Among College-Age Females, 1995–2013*. Washington: U.S. Department of Justice.

Soave, Robby. 2013. EXCLUSIVE: Shocking Discovery in Hoax Bias Incident at Vassar College. *The Daily Caller*, November 27. http://dailycaller.com/2013/11/27/exclusive-shocking-discovery-in-hoax-bias-incident-at-vassar-college/.

Sokol, Chad. 2017. Gozaga Stops Selling 'Boys Will Be Boys' T-Shirt After Complaint That It Perpetuates Rape Culture. *The Spokesman-Review*, March 31. http://www.spokesman.com/stories/2017/mar/31/gonzaga-stops-selling-boys-will-be-boys-t-shirt-af/.

Sommers, Christina Hoff. 2014. Rape Culture Is a 'Panic Where Paranoia, Censorship, and False Allegations Flourish.' *Time*, May 15. http://time.com/100091/campus-sexual-assault-christina-hoff-sommers/.

Stoltzfoos, Rachel. 2016. Here Are All the Hate Crime Hoaxes That Have Plagued the Country Since Trump's Election. *The Daily Caller*, November 30. http://dailycaller.com/2016/11/30/here-are-all-the-hate-crime-hoaxes-that-have-plagued-the-country-since-trumps-election/.

Suhr, Jim, and John Hanna. 2017. Neighbor: Kansas Bar Shooting Suspect a 'Drunken Mess,' Not Political. *Chicago Tribune*, February 26. http://www.chicagotribune.com/news/nationworld/ct-kansas-bar-shooting-suspect-20170225-story.html.

Taylor, Stuart, Jr., and K.C. Johnson. 2008. *Until Proven Innocent: Political Correctness and the Shameful Injustices of the Duke Lacrosse Case*. New York: Thomas Dunne Books/St. Martin's Griffin.

Tjaden, Patricia Godeke, and Nancy Thoennes. 2006. *Extent, Nature, and Consequences of Rape Victimization: Findings from the National Violence Against Women Survey*. Washington, DC: National Institute of Justice.

Trocmé, Nico, and Nicholas Bala. 2005. False Allegations of Abuse and Neglect When Parents Separate. *Child Abuse and Neglect* 29: 1333–1345.

Valenti, Jessica. 2014. Who Is Jackie? Rolling Stone's Rape Story Is About a Person—And I Believe Her. *The Guardian*, December 8. https://www.theguardian.com/commentisfree/2014/dec/08/who-is-jackie-rolling-stone-rape-story.

Venema, Rachel. 2017. Denial Perpetuates Rape Culture. *The Banner*, May 5. https://thebanner.org/departments/2017/05/denial-perpetuates-rape-culture.

Victor, Jeffrey S. 1998. Moral Panics and the Social Construction of Deviant Behavior: A Theory and Application to the Case of Ritual Child Abuse. *Sociological Perspectives* 41 (3): 541–565.

"When a Hate Crime Isn't a Hate Crime: Racial Hoaxes on College Campuses." 1998–1999. *Journal of Blacks in Higher Education* 22: 52.

Weiss, Karen G. 2009. "Boys Will Be Boys" and Other Gendered Accounts: An Exploration of Victims' Excuses and Justifications for Unwanted Sexual Contact and Coercion. *Violence Against Women* 15 (7): 810–834.

———. 2013. *Party School: Crime, Campus, and Community*. Boston: Northeastern University Press.

Weiss, Karen G., and Corey Colyer. 2010. Roofies, Mickies and Cautionary Tales: Examining the Persistence of the "Date-Rape Drug" Crime Narrative. *Deviant Behavior* 31 (4): 348–379.

Wilcox, Laird. 1996. *Crying Wolf: Hate Crime Hoaxes in America*. Olathe: Editorial Research Service.

Yoffe, Emily. 2014. The College Rape Overcorrection. *Slate*, December 7. http://www.slate.com/articles/double_x/doublex/2014/12/college_rape_campus_sexual_assault_is_a_serious_problem_but_the_efforts.html.

———. 2015. *The Hunting Ground*: The Failures of a New Documentary About Rape on College Campuses. *Slate*, February 27. http://www.slate.com/articles/double_x/doublex/2015/02/the_hunting_ground_a_campus_rape_documentary_that_fails_to_provide_a_full.html.

Zamichow, Nora, and Stuart Silverstein. 2004. As Hate-Crime Concerns Rise, so Does the Threat of Hoaxes. *Los Angeles Times*, April 20. http://articles.latimes.com/2004/apr/20/local/me-hoax20.

CHAPTER 5

Opposition, Imitation, and the Spread of Victimhood

When we first wrote on the subject in 2014, there were still many in academia who had never heard of microaggressions, and hardly anyone outside of academia talked about them at all. Since then the term has become much more common and well known, as have the other victimhood concepts we described in the previous chapter. An internet search of the news on any given month will show numerous results for microaggressions, safe spaces, and the like, many from sources critical of the phenomena, and others from those defending them. And as we noted in the previous chapters, victimhood culture's concepts and practices have not only spread across university settings, but they are also increasingly adopted or endorsed by figures in the arts, media, and government.

How exactly does a moral culture spread? What is the pattern and process of moral change? In this chapter we focus on some of the mechanisms involved in the spread of moral cultures in general and of victimhood culture in particular. Specifically, we address how people are socialized into victimhood culture, and how even the backlash against the rise of victimhood can inadvertently assist in its growth.

As we consider these patterns it is important to keep in mind what we mean by moral culture. The concept is shorthand for a particular cluster of social behaviors—the kinds of grievances people tend to have, the ways they tend to handle them, and, in a broader sense, whatever language and practices tend to go along with all this. The distinction between honor, dignity, and victimhood is useful for talking about broad patterns of morality and moral change. But we should not think of these cultures as monolithic. The more we get down into the details, the more fine variation we see. For example, people do not necessarily adopt a new moral culture all at once, taking on all its practices and ideas as a package. They might adopt some elements of the new culture more readily than others, producing a transition period that blends elements of the old with those of the new. Thus, in much of Europe, the shift away from a code of honor began with the forced suppression of violence, with decreased sensitivity to slight and ideals about moral equality coming later. In some places the transition involved a phase when people increasingly turned to courts to litigate honor conflicts. This was the case in seventeenth-century Muscovy (now Russia), where the state punished offenses against honor with fines and possibly corporal punishment, depending on the social status of the offender and of the person they had insulted (Kollman 1999:55).[1] Many people maintained a strong emphasis on public reputation, a high sensitivity to slight, and an unwillingness to tolerate insult, but they tended to rely on law rather than dueling or other violence.[2] Litigation over insult and dishonor also briefly flourished during France's and England's transitions to modernity, indicating a phase of moral evolution where insult remained potent but violent retaliation was dying out (Kollman 1999:2).[3] When we

[1] Both men and women could be dishonored by insult, and thus insults to either could be litigated, though it was typically the responsibility of men to bring cases on behalf of a dishonored female relative. Men were particularly sensitive to insults against their mothers (Kollman 1999:81).

[2] Visitors from England and France during this period noticed that Muscovy was less violent than their own societies. Notably, one English visitor, rather than praise the peacefulness of Muscovite society, emphasized the oppression and servility of the people there (Kollman 1999:130). While this characterization shows the disdain that honorable individuals had for those who relied on law, it also captures the reality that the emerging Russian state combined strong central power (which dominated the aristocracy) with effective penetration of society through an extensive system of courts that made it easy even for peasants to have cases heard. Indeed, honor litigation among peasants was still common in the Imperial Russia of the early twentieth century (Burbank 1999).

[3] This transition period resembled victimhood culture in its combination of sensitivity to slight with complaints to authority. One difference, perhaps, is the degree to which people in these earlier and highly stratified societies accepted social inequality and were jealous of their rank and privileges. Rather than take offense because their social group had been demeaned, many Muscovites were offended when they were mistaken for members of a lower ranking social group. According to historian Nancy Shields Kollman, "No matter how low in the social hierarchy, Muscovites objected if their ranks were insulted. Boyars declared that their

study the interaction between different moral cultures, we should expect to see not only clashes between different moral systems, but also cases of one moral culture blending into another.

We should also keep in mind that the concept of moral culture refers to moral behavior—what people say and do rather than what they feel deep down inside. Here again when we look closely we may see variation in how people relate to the prevailing moral culture. Some will be zealous and passionately devoted, some will passively go along with majority opinion, and some will cynically exploit moral ideas and practices for their own ends. But whether the adoption of a moral culture is enthusiastic or grudging, genuine or dishonest, it is adoption all the same.

Finally we should keep in mind that any large society will have multiple subcultures. Though it often makes sense to speak of the prevailing moral culture of an entire nation, we should also expect to see that moral culture varies across regions, social classes, and so forth. And we should not be surprised that the spread of a new moral culture often follows the contours of these divisions.

WHY MORAL CULTURES SPREAD

In Chap. 2 we outlined our explanation of victimhood culture—and by way of comparison, touched on the explanation of honor and dignity as well. We drew from the work of social psychologists and historians who have discussed and explained the geographic and historical distribution of honor and dignity (e.g., Nisbett and Cohen 1996). But our own approach is rooted most firmly in sociologist Donald Black's theories of conflict and social control. Recall that these theories explain people's behavior with its social structure—the patterns of intimacy, inequality, and cultural diversity between all the people involved in a given interaction. These variables shape the kinds of grievances people are apt to have and the ways they are likely to handle them.

The kinds of conflict and social control we call victimhood culture thus arise under a particular set of structural conditions. We propose that victimhood culture is greatest where culturally diverse people interact in relative but imperfect equality, where the parties in a conflict have ready access

families had never served as provincial gentry, provincial gentrymen bridled at being called musketeers, musketeers rejected the label of taxpaying city person, and even slaves objected to being called field workers when they worked as their master's bailiffs!" (Kollman 1999:47).

to a status superior, socially equidistant from both, and where people are socially atomized and aggrieved individuals have access to many relatively distant third parties. Victimhood culture emerges where these conditions are all present.

The core reason that victimhood culture spreads is that the conditions that encourage it spread. Earlier in Western history dignity culture spread in the same way, as conditions that undermined violent self-help and encouraged tolerance—such as effective law enforcement and commercial interdependence—spread outward from the industrialized countries of Northern Europe. Honor violence declined first in these centers of modernization, with the decline of honor and rise of dignity only later extending to Southern Europe and the Slavic countries as they modernized in turn. It followed a similar gradient within countries, generally proceeding most quickly in the urbanized core and reaching more remote areas much later (Pinker 2011:87). In more recent times victimhood culture has developed most extensively in college and university settings, where young people from different cultural groups have easy access to a large bureaucracy and lots of weak ties to potential partisans. Victimhood culture has spread across educational institutions as they have come to share these conditions, and as these conditions proliferate elsewhere, so does victimhood culture.

Yet additional dynamics are visible in the spread of victimhood culture. Concepts like microaggression, trigger warning, and safe space are not just independently reinvented again and again in each place they are adopted. As with any other human innovation, they are passed on through observation, teaching, and learning—the kinds of processes sociologists call socialization.

MORAL CULTURE AND CHILD SOCIALIZATION

Socialization into a moral culture starts early in life. It occurs through explicit teaching, passive observation and imitation of adults, or trial and error as the young discover which behaviors are best for navigating their social environment. Most likely it involves all three of these mechanisms. In any case, from a young age youth and adolescents acquire ideas about right and wrong and gain experience with different forms of social control (Baumgartner 1992).

Consider honor. In the modern West, honor continues to thrive in some segments of society, such as many poor black communities in the

United States. Sociologist Elijah Anderson, who studied one such neighborhood in Philadelphia, describes how children there come to learn the "code of the street" that governs social life (Anderson 1999). From a young age, these children understand that making a name for oneself—having a reputation for toughness thus being able to command respect—is valuable for survival. They learn this partly from teaching:

> The street-oriented adults with whom children come into contact ... help shape and reinforce this understanding by verbalizing the messages these children are getting through public experience: "Watch your back." "Protect yourself." "Don't punk out." "Respect yourself." "If someone disses you, you got to straighten them out." Many parents actually impose sanctions if the child is not sufficiently aggressive. For example, if a child loses a fight and comes home upset, the parent might respond, "Don't you come here crying that somebody beat you up; you better get back out there and whup his ass. I didn't raise no punks! If you don't whup his ass, I'll whup you' ass when you come the home!" (Anderson 1999:70–71)[4]

They also learn from their own direct experience on the streets. Here children begin socializing without parental supervision at a young age. Those from the most "street-oriented" families have the most leeway, coming and going as they please (Anderson 1999:69). Children and youth face a competitive social environment that is dominated by the most aggressive personalities and where appeal to parents and other adults is rarely feasible. Under such conditions even those whose parents do not encourage violence may learn from experience that "toughness is a virtue" and "might makes right" (Anderson 1999:70).

Compare all this to the way a child might be socialized into dignity culture. In a dignity culture parents coach their children in nonviolence, punishing them for fighting rather than for failing to fight. Children are also taught to ignore insults with sayings such as the "sticks and stones" aphorism mentioned in Chap. 1. Children's social interactions with peers take place in an environment where parents and other authorities are more

---

[4] Based on his interviews with violent criminals, criminologist Lonnie Athens (1989; see also Rhodes 1999) concludes that they invariably had some significant figure in their life—often a parent—who explicitly encouraged them to use violence, describing it as necessary or even glorious and possibly punishing them for timidity. He posits that such "violent coaching" is a universal feature of the socialization process that produces the most extreme and habitually violent criminals.

likely to break up fights and learn of and punish violent aggression, though they are often unwilling to intervene in other matters. A child who complains of being teased at school might be told, "They're only doing it to provoke a reaction, just ignore them and they'll stop." A youth who complains to adults too often will be derided by peers as a tattletale or a rat, but would also likely be punished for responding to these insults with force. Under such conditions the young learn that high sensitivity and high aggression are both costly, and they have incentives and opportunities to practice alternatives like avoidance, negotiation, and tolerance.

Socialization into victimhood culture would involve practices that encourage both moral sensitivity and moral dependence. We have discussed how these conditions are present at modern colleges and universities, but there is reason to believe that they have also become increasingly common at earlier stages of the socialization process. That is, recent cohorts of college students not only enter a social environment that facilitates victimhood, but arrive having already been trained in its habits.

Learning Victimhood

Some socialization into victimhood culture takes place in primary and secondary school, which to varying degrees have experienced some of the same changes—such as increasing bureaucratic regulation—that have occurred at universities. Jonathan Haidt relates experiences with students at elite high schools who already live in fear of giving offense to recognized victim groups and being referred to what they call the "diversity police"—the school's multicultural center (Haidt 2015). Similarly, Frank Furedi argues that the emphasis on vulnerability and fragility found among college students is visible at earlier stages of the educational process, where it is an object of official concern. For example, the transition from primary school to secondary school has become a site of professional intervention, as "experts offer transitional counseling for what was regarded, for decades, as a routine aspect of young people's lives" (Furedi 2017:23).

Both Haidt and Furedi attribute the rapid spread of victimhood culture to generational differences in childhood, with those growing up in recent decades experiencing drastically higher degrees of adult supervision, regulation, and protection. This happens partly because of greater involvement in school and other adult-supervised activities. For instance, since 1980, the amount of time young US children spend in school increased while their amount of free time declined (Kim and Cole 2001; Juster et al.

2004). Some schools have reduced or eliminated recess periods, in which previous generations of children had time to engage in spontaneous inter-action with peers (Chougule 2017; Murray and Ramstetter 2013). Adult supervision also takes the form of highly protective *helicopter parenting*, so called because of parents who are always hovering nearby, ready to step in and help their child manage life's problems.

High levels of adult intervention can breed various kinds of depen-dence, including moral dependence. Furthermore, intervention is coupled with an increased protectiveness. The once popular game of dodge ball, in which children compete to avoid being struck by a large ball of inflated rubber, has been banned by a number of schools for being too violent. The US National Association for Sport and Physical Education issued a statement condemning the game arguing that "it is not appropriate to teach our children that you win by hurting others" (Pinker 2011:379). A failed proposal to ban dodge ball in Louisiana's school system likewise claimed that "target games (e.g. dodge ball) and drills that promote aggressive behaviors by attacking and overpowering other humans are not to be permitted" (Owens 2017).

There is also the problem that such competitive games produce winners and losers, a degree of social inequality that some parents and school administrators see as a source of unreasonable psychological distress—hence the efforts of some adults to blur the distinction between winning and losing by providing participation trophies to all competitors in youth sports and competitions, as opposed to only awarding a trophy to the win-ner (Alsop 2008; Bennet 2011).[5] Desire to avoid mental harm can lead to attempts to prevent all manner of losses and disappointments. The concern with protecting children from failure can contribute to grade inflation at schools: "One survey found that more than 45 percent of college fresh-man graduate high school with an A average. A dean of admissions at a selective liberal arts school speaks of seeing thirty or forty *valedictorians at a single school* because no one wants to make a distinction among the kids" (McArdle 2014:15). Even the act of taking school examinations might be seen as damaging. Furedi recounts the example of British parents who organized a boycott of their children's secondary school exams because of their concerns over "exam stress" (Furedi 2017:23).

---

[5] Notably, younger survey respondents are more likely than older ones to approve of this practice (Blake 2014).

Adult protectiveness is not only more intense; it also tends to extend into ages where earlier generations established more distance and independence. Furedi recalls the response in 1997 to his description of the new phenomenon of students arriving at his university for interviews accompanied by their parents: "At the time, the idea that parents would accompany their children to a university interview struck many adults as preposterous. The subeditor of the draft of my book was incredulous, and queried the veracity of my observation." The observation was met with skepticism because for Furedi's generation, college was a time to break away from parental involvement and establish independence. By comparison, "What may strike a subeditor as bizarre today [is] the fact that I even raised it as an issue" because contemporary universities "produce brochures for parents" and "the sight of adults accompanying their children on campuses has become a regular occurrence" (Furedi 2017:6). Recent decades have also seen the emergence and growth of college parent associations, advisory councils, and university offices for parent relations (Alsop 2008:57). There is a high continuity in moral dependence, with university students under the supervision of both helicopter parents and helicopter colleges (Friedersdorf 2017).

Moral Culture and Social Class

Different strata of society often have different moral cultures, and when a new moral culture arises and spreads it might arise first among one class and spread to others only gradually, or in some cases not at all.

For example, the historical decline of honor and rise of dignity came first and foremost to the middle classes. In England and France it was the yeoman farmers, artisans, and master craftsmen who enthusiastically turned to courts at a time when the nobles were still fighting duels with swords (Kollman 1999:2). The campaign against dueling was a movement of the middle class, led by ministers, academics, and newspaper editors (Careau 2013:14). Social elites eventually abandoned dueling and codes of honor, but honor culture persisted at the opposite end of the status scale, among the very poor, unconventional, or disreputable. As noted above, honor culture in the United States still thrives in many poor black communities, where conflicts over respect and cycles of retaliatory violence lead to high rates of homicide (Cooney 1998:Chapter 5; Jacobs and Wright 2006; Leovy 2015). Elements of honor are also strong among the Scots-Irish hillbillies of Appalachia (Vance 2016). In the words of author

J.D. Vance, whose family originated in the hills of eastern Kentucky, "We were taught to raise our fists if someone insulted our mother" (quoted in Dreher 2016). We might even think of the distribution of honor as something of a gradient: Though extremes of honor are found only in some communities, elements of honor culture—approval of moralistic violence, admiration of physical toughness, and so forth—generally increase as one moves downward in the status distribution.

There are structural reasons why dignity and honor have this status distribution, and why dignity eventually spread to social elites. Historically, conditions that encourage restraint and discourage self-help came first to the growing middle classes. Earlier in Western history, it is these classes that would have had the most access to authorities who settled their conflicts. Wealthier and more respected than peasants and laborers, they would have found the legal system responsive to their complaints. But also crucial was that they were not too elite. Sociologist Mark Cooney, building on Black's theories of law, argues that in older times elites were more violent because sociologically speaking they were literally above the law (Cooney 1998:Chapter 2). At a time when states were smaller and weaker, while nobles were still powerful, the former lacked authority over the latter. Aristocrats and gentry would not lower themselves by allowing mere public servants to handle their affairs, and the legal apparatus was not yet powerful enough to force them to do so. They were effectively lawless and relied on self-help rather than settlement.

Honor eventually declined among the elites because, with economic and social change, their status declined while the status of the state grew. As honor retreated, dignity culture spread upward in the status structure, eventually dominating the elites. It also spread downward, but at lower levels it ran into another structural obstacle: Being too inferior to the state and its agents also reduces reliance on law (Black 1976:Chapter 2, 1998:Chapter 2; Cooney 1998:Chapter 2). Cultural minorities, criminals, the poor, and the uneducated might experience high levels of law in the form of drug arrests, traffic stops, and other state-initiated complaints, but they often lack legal recourse for conflicts among themselves. Some of their disputes, such as those involving drugs or gambling, are about matters that are themselves illegal. Others, such as thefts of small amounts of money, are crimes that legal officials consider trivial. Even serious crimes such as homicides attract less attention when they have poor and minority victims (Cooney 2009:Chapter 3; Leovy 2015). These patterns breed distrust and hostility to the legal system, which further hampers legal effectiveness by reducing cooperation with investigations (Leovy 2015). The result is that self-help flourishes, and dignity fails to conquer honor.

Class and Victimhood

We can also observe class patterns in the distribution of victimhood culture. As we have seen, victimhood culture is most developed at institutions of higher learning. The students who attend colleges and universities come disproportionately from the upper end of the status distribution—from families that are relatively wealthy and, increasingly, from parents who were themselves highly educated. Because a college degree is highly predictive of financial success, the students at these institutions are likely to remain in the middle and upper classes after graduation. Even among institutions there seems to be some correlation between elite status and victimhood culture. Although we have seen some severe victimhood eruptions at large state schools such as the University of Missouri, victimhood culture appears most prominent at more expensive and highly selective institutions whose student populations tend to be from wealthier backgrounds. Private colleges like Oberlin and Brown were at the leading edge of the movement to document microaggressions, while California's Claremont colleges seem especially conducive to microaggression protests, safe space demands, and the banning of speakers. These institutions are expensive even by the standards of contemporary higher education. At Claremont McKenna, for example, tuition is over $50,000 per year, and the student body has a median family income of over $200,000 (*New York Times* 2017a). The student furor over Erika Christakis questioning the regulation of Halloween costumes occurred at Yale, a member of the prestigious Ivy League where tuition can run over $60,000 per year. And an analysis of 90 cases in which speakers were disinvited from campus found that disinvitation was more likely at colleges where students have wealthier parents: The median parental income at these institutions was $32,000 higher than for the student population as a whole (Reeves and Halikias 2017). The median family income of students at Middlebury College, where protesters shut down a talk by social scientist Charles Murray, is over $240,000—twice that of Saint Louis University, where Murray was allowed to speak, and nearly five times that of all US families (Reeves and Halikias 2017; *New York Times* 2017b).

The affinity between elite schools and victimhood culture is likely due to several factors. Upper-middle-class families are more likely to engage in what sociologist Annette Lareau calls "concerted cultivation," an intensive style of parenting that involves filling children's time with a busy schedule of adult-planned and supervised activities (Lareau 2003). Such intensive grooming, particularly when coupled with high levels of protectiveness, can facilitate moral dependence. It may also be that, just as law is more responsive to the complaints of higher status citizens, schools and other institutions are more responsive to the complaints of higher status students and parents, so elite schools tend to cater more closely to their elite student body.[6] And since wealthy students and alumni make wealthy schools, elite institutions are probably both more willing and more able to grow their administrations. Indeed, it seems that the growth in the power and scope of campus administrations is proportionately greater at institutions that combine larger endowments with smaller student bodies. For example, Pomona College, a member of California's Claremont Consortium of private colleges, has 1640 students, 186 regular faculty, and 271 administrators (Seery 2017). This works out to an administrator for every six students. Compare this ratio to the larger but still prestigious public institutions of the University of California system, which has one administrator for every 23 students. At the still less expensive and less selective California State University system, the ratio is one to 123 (*San Diego Union-Tribune* 2017).

The prominence of victimhood culture in higher education, especially at elite institutions, indicates that victimhood culture is concentrated among the relatively affluent and successful members of the upper middle class. We should expect the initial spread of victimhood culture to reflect its origins. Since the graduates of elite universities disproportionately occupy influential positions in law, government, business, and media, we should not be surprised to see the ideas and ideals of victimhood culture

[6] As we noted in Chap. 2, it is not necessarily the case that the activists most involved in advancing victimhood culture at these institutions are the ones with the highest social standing. They may tend to be from families that are less wealthy than their peers—though being below average at Claremont or Yale can still mean being in the top 20 percent of the wealth distribution for the nation as a whole. Many activists also belong to minority groups, including groups (such as American blacks) with much lower levels of wealth and education—though the presence of the activists at elite colleges means they are likely above the average for these groups as well. They may also be above the average for Americans in general. Jonathan Butler, the black University of Missouri student who went on a hunger strike to pressure the university's president to resign, is the son of railroad company vice president who earns over $8 million a year (Holleman 2015).

gaining increasing influence in modern society. Graduates of these institutions carry this moral culture with them as they pursue careers as teachers and administrators at various levels of the educational system, intensifying the socialization into victimhood that occurs through formal education. Some become journalists and writers for mainstream newspapers, magazines, and other outlets, and so help bring victimhood culture into the public eye. Some enter the corporate world, heading up new departments dedicated to diversity and inclusion. Many of them congregate in places such as New York City, Washington DC, and other cosmopolitan cities that tend to attract the young, educated, and affluent, and we should expect victimhood culture to grow among the credentialed classes in these locales. And we should expect the rise of victimhood to accelerate as younger generations, more comfortable in its norms, increasingly supplant older cohorts in the workplace and in society as a whole.

Victimhood as Cultural Capital

The adoption by social elites of victimhood culture, or any other moral culture, can add an additional dynamic to its spread. The ideas and fashions of higher status people are highly attractive to those just beneath them in the status structure (Black 2000).[7] Those seeking upward mobility are especially likely to emulate the culture of the stratum they wish to enter. Ambitious people who do not adopt elements of the higher status culture might find their mobility limited, as cultural clashes and prejudices hamper their relations with teachers, employers, and others. Knowledge of victimhood culture, including its moral jargon and its rules about what can and cannot be said, can thus act as what sociologists call *cultural capital* (Bourdieu 1984). In the words of one commentator, "Political correctness requires more than ordinary courtesy: It's a ritual, like knowing which fork to use, by which superior people recognize each other" (quoted in Bovy 2017:212). Ignorance of the language and norms of educated professionals marks one as immoral, unintelligent, or socially incompetent in their eyes, while knowledge of their culture facilitates upward mobility.

---

[7] In his theory of ideas, Black (2000) proposes that the success of an idea—that is, the degree to which it is treated as true and important—depends on the social status and social distance of the source relative to the audience. Ideas from social superiors are more successful than ideas from inferiors, and ideas from people who are socially close are more successful than ideas from people who are distant.

In the United States in recent decades the highly educated have grown more successful, while wages have stagnated or fallen for the less educated (Luhby 2016). The middle class is shrinking, while elites and non-elites are increasingly separated, financially, geographically, and culturally (Murray 2013; Pew 2015). Such trends could make it more difficult for those who wish to improve or maintain the social standing of themselves and their children, and this could place greater pressure on them to adopt the moral culture of prestigious universities and the settings dominated by their graduates. In earlier times dignity culture expanded partly because the dignified middle class of merchants and entrepreneurs grew, and the wealthiest among them eventually surpassed the declining landed elite. Should victimhood culture continue to spread throughout the modern upper class, the retreat of dignity might be a mirror image of this process. We may thus see victimhood culture spreading down the status distribution into a shrinking middle class, subsiding as it reaches the lowest elevations where it seems likely that honor will continue to thrive.

OPPOSITION AND BACKLASH

The spread of a new moral culture does not go unchallenged. Any social change will have its opponents, and with moral change this opposition is likely to be fierce. The contemporary rise of victimhood culture is no exception. As we noted in Chap. 1, various manifestations of victimhood culture attract criticism and condemnation. Critics come from across the political spectrum, and include moderates, liberals, libertarians, and socialists (e.g., Bailey 2015; Bovy 2017; Chait 2015; DeBoer 2017a, b; Etzioni 2014; Haidt 2015; Lukianoff 2014; Lukianoff and Haidt 2015; McArdle 2015; McWhorter 2014; Rauch 2014). We understand this opposition as a clash between dignity culture and victimhood culture. The distinction between these moral cultures is not synonymous with the conventional political distinction between left and right. Yet it is also true that victimhood culture is most advanced among some segments of the left. It is relatively more congenial to the leftist worldview and to liberals' moral focus on harm and fairness (Haidt 2012). And it is currently most entrenched on college campuses, where faculty and administrators are overwhelmingly liberal, and where it is most visibly advanced by student activists in the name of liberal and progressive causes. Conversely it is also true that opposition to victimhood culture is most frequent and strenuous on the right. Furthermore, in their attacks conservative critics frequently make no distinction between victimhood culture and liberalism as a whole, and they might use the most extreme examples of campus victimhood eruptions to condemn the political left. Thus, at least in the US context, the backlash against victimhood culture has played out along lines of political partisanship and has helped attract voters to conservative candidates.

The political backlash against victimhood culture is often described as a reaction to *political correctness*. The term first gained currency among conservatives in the 1990s as a way of referring to socially approved terminology and euphemisms. Common examples from the time were changes in the preferred nomenclature for minority groups—blacks were to be called *African–Americans*, American–Indians were to be called *Native Americans*, the disabled were to be called *differently abled*, and so forth. The new labels were politically correct; the old ones were politically incorrect.

The concept of political correctness is now used in a variety of ways, but most often it refers to the rules about what words and ideas are forbidden for being offensive, particularly if they are offensive to women and minorities. People might say that it is politically incorrect to state certain facts, such as observing that rates of homicide offending are higher among black Americans than among white Americans. Or they might worry about not knowing the most politically correct label for referring to a cultural minority—is it Hispanic, Latino, or Latinx? It is no surprise then that the concept is also applied to the words and actions that are classified as microaggressions, trauma triggers, or violations of safe spaces. The rise of victimhood culture means an increasing number of things are defined as bigoted, threatening, and otherwise offensive, leading to an expansion of terms and ideas that are politically incorrect.

In our prologue, we alluded to the importance of opposition to political correctness in the 2016 US presidential election. As Donald Trump's campaign gained momentum a number of commentators described support for the unapologetically offensive candidate as a backlash against political correctness. We mentioned examples such as the man who spoke of how it was a grind to deal with the elevated threat of giving offense, adding that "the sensitivity is over the top and counterproductive" (quoted in Friedersdorf 2015). Another Trump supporter wrote, "I have a very difficult time keeping up with all the various appropriate and inappropriate terms used to reference people and their causes. Trump makes brash and uncompromising statements about issues many people feel very passionate about" (quoted in Friedersdorf 2015). J.D. Vance argued that working class people resented the constrictions imposed by culturally alien speech norms:

> All the talk about "political correctness" isn't about any specific substantive point, as much as it is a way of expanding the scope of acceptable behavior. People don't want to believe they have to speak like Obama or Clinton to participate meaningfully in politics, because most of us don't speak like Obama or Clinton. (Quoted in Dreher 2016)

The idea is that Trump won support exactly because so many found him coarse and vulgar—and he did not seem to care, even when faced with accusations of racism. As one journalist notes, referring to the furor surrounding Trump's claim that illegal immigrants were mostly rapists and drug dealers, "More significant than Trump's words was the fact that he didn't apologize for them, which he could easily have done" (McConnell 2016). Trump himself directly attacked political correctness. He criticized his opponents for being reluctant to speak of "Islamic terrorism" or "radical Islam," arguing that "the current politically correct response cripples our ability to talk and to think and act clearly" (quoted in Nelson 2016).

Those who oppose what they see as unreasonable restrictions on speech may come to support and admire anyone who boldly flouts such rules. Trump supporter Milo Yiannopoulos, who called Trump "an icon of irreverent resistance to political correctness," capitalized on this in his speaking tour of US universities (Soave 2016). His talks were intentionally provocative, laced with profanity, slurs, and insults toward various groups and individuals. Even the name of his "Dangerous Faggot Tour" was clearly designed to cause outrage. He justified his behavior by styling himself a defender of free speech on campuses strangled by political correctness, and he argued he was standing up to liberal faculty on behalf of bullied conservative students (Yiannopoulos 2017).

Note that neither Trump nor Yiannopoulos are emissaries of dignity. Neither of them preaches or practices dignity ideals such as restraint, toleration, or trying to avoid giving unnecessary offense. Trump is notoriously sensitive to slight and quick to verbally attack his critics, while Yiannopoulos thrives on causing offense and controversy. Their success suggests the backlash against victimhood culture can itself undermine dignity culture. In their rebellion against victimhood culture's hypersensitivity, its opponents might countenance behaviors that would be considered extreme and inappropriate in dignity culture as well—perhaps even behaviors that these same opponents would, in the recent past, have condemned as undignified.[8]

Opposition to victimhood does not merely focus on heightened moral sensitivity. Many critics also object to the strong moralism directed at the privileged. As two psychologists of victimhood note, "Privileged group members now feel stigmatized due to their reversed moral standing" (Young and Sullivan 2016:32). Accusations of microaggression and privilege tend to target whites and males, and, as we discussed in the last chapter, offenses such as racism and sexism might even be defined such that whites and males are uniquely and inherently guilty. Many resent such developments. According to conservative columnist Scott McConnell, "Trump is probably quite sincere in his assertion that he himself is 'the least racist person' in politics, but there is little doubt his campaign has benefited from a white reaction to an emerging liberal cultural and educational discourse that depicts whites, especially white males, as more dangerous and immoral than any other people" (McConnell 2016).

Opposition to such vilification is particularly acute among lower status males and whites. Several commentators drew attention to Trump's support among less educated, working class whites. Writing in *The Atlantic*, Derek Thompson notes that "the single best predictor of Trump support in the GOP primary is the absence of a college degree" (Thompson 2016). Because victimhood culture focuses on intercollective grievances between genders and ethnic groups, it tends to apportion moral worth based on these groups' average levels of wealth and other advantages. This seemingly ignores that individuals within these categories might differ greatly from the average. A poor, uneducated, and unemployed white man might be infuriated at being morally condemned for leading a life of privilege—what must seem, from his point of view, a false accusation. The same goes for those with less extreme deprivation. In a letter to columnist Rod Dreher, a reader of *The American Conservative* makes a complaint of this nature:

> I am very lower middle class. I've never owned a new car, and do my own home repairs as much as I can to save money. I cut my own grass, wash my

---

[8] Trump's verbal belligerence and insistence on responding aggressively to any criticism (he calls himself a "counter puncher") is closer to the norms of honor culture than to dignity culture—something that might have added to his appeal among Appalachians, rural Southerners, and others on the honorable side of dignity (McConnell 2016).

own dishes, buy my clothes from Walmart. I have no clue how I will ever be able to retire. But oh, brother, to hear the media tell it, I am just drowning in unearned power and privilege, and America will be a much brighter, more loving, more peaceful nation when I finally just keel over and die. (Quoted in Dreher 2017)

Just as opposition to high moral sensitivity might incline people to be more favorable to provocateurs, the vilification of whites and males might lead to greater support for those who champion the superiority of these groups. As we discussed in our prologue, claims that the Trump campaign was openly racist or that most Republican voters are white supremacists are unrealistic. Even among the populist right, white nationalists and their ilk are but one small faction. But while it is true that racialist ideologues remain unconventional and disreputable, it is likely that the influence of white identity politics is beginning to grow and will continue to gain in popularity as victimhood culture expands.

The 2016 election brought attention to a far right movement known as the *alt-right*. It appeared to surge in popularity, but its boundaries were never clearly defined. Media sources tend to equate the movement with white nationalism, as does white nationalist Richard Spencer. Others who identified with the label during the election year disagreed, and sought to distance themselves from Spencer and his followers. It seems that the alt-right label quickly gained currency as a vague symbol of right-wing opposition to the status quo. According to one commentator, in 2016 the label was adopted by "pretty much everyone else who was sick of what had become of establishment conservatism. Then Richard Spencer came along, throwing up Nazi salutes.... He effectively made the term toxic and then claimed it for himself. We all abandoned using it in droves" (quoted in Marantz 2017b).[9] Some who originally embraced the label have now taken to calling themselves *alt-lite* to distinguish themselves from the white nationalists. White nationalism did gain greater prominence in

---

[9] Social movements can benefit from a bandwagon effect whereby appearing to be popular and rapidly growing can arouse more interest from potential converts, thus creating further popularity and growth. Spencer thus has incentives to strengthen the association between an increasingly popular political label and his own ideology, even if a substantial number of these new alt-rightists were not interested in his particular alternative to the mainstream. His interests certainly converged with those of left-wing critics who sought to associate Trump and the right in general with white supremacy, and he appears to have won the "branding war" over the meaning of alt-right (Marantz 2017b).

2016, and perhaps new converts as well. But the subsequent factioning of the alt-right, and the number of people who have since abandoned the label, suggests that most of the growth of the alt-right during the election was not due to growth in white nationalism or white supremacism. Still, the broader movement, including those who now reject the alt-right label, seems receptive to positions its members describe as prowhite, pro-male, and pro-Western. The alt-lite's Gavin McInnes, for instance, is the founder of a "pro-Western fraternal organization," known as Proud Boys, for men who "refuse to apologize for creating the modern world" (Marantz 2017a). The movement seems to have attracted many who, even if they personally reject white supremacy and white nationalism, are willing to tolerate racial ideologues as strategic allies, fellow travelers, or at least a lesser threat than the progressive left. It therefore seems likely that the influence of white identity politics is growing, and may continue to grow for some time.

Overt hostility toward white males is apt to increase the audience for those who style themselves as defenders of these groups.[10] And if whites and males increasingly face a moral world divided between those who vilify them and those who glorify them, we should not be surprised if many find the latter more appealing than the former. In the words of one conservative, who says he rejects such racialist movements but understands their appeal, "I recoil from the uglier stuff, but some of it—the 'hey, white guys are actually okay, you know! Be proud of yourself, white man!' stuff is really VERY seductive ... it's one of the only places I can go where people are not always telling me I'm the seed of all evil in the world" (quoted in Dreher 2017). Of course, some of these ideologues go beyond telling white males that they are not inferior and preach their superiority. Here again, the backlash against victimhood may not necessarily advance the ideals of dignity, such as the moral equality of all people. Victimhood culture deviates from this moral equality by producing a moral hierarchy with white males at the bottom; the reaction it provokes may be the resurgence of a moral hierarchy that places them at the top.

Of course opposition to victimhood culture need not involve racism, sexism, verbal belligerence, or right-wing populism. Prominent critics from across the political spectrum reject these things, and some even warn against victimhood culture specifically because they fear the backlash it

---

[10] Since defending whites and males is deviant in victimhood culture, even critics who deny they are doing this might be accused of it (see, e.g., Bovy 2017:72–73).

might create. Many who are skeptical of safe spaces, microaggression complaints, and trigger warnings call for the strengthening of dignity norms. Yet it is still sociologically significant that a backlash against victimhood culture could contribute to the erosion of dignity culture. In some cases, as counterintuitive as it might seem, opposition can even transform into imitation.

COMPETITIVE VICTIMHOOD

There is a proverb that states, "Choose your enemies carefully, for you will become like them." The dynamics of conflict can lead adversaries to become more similar to one another over time as they competitively adopt one another's tactics, strategies, and forms of social organization. For example, violence often begets violence, and organization on one side often begets organization on the other. According to criminologist William B. Sanders, this dynamic can cause the formation of new street gangs. For example, the original members of San Diego's Del Sol gang were a group of teenage boys from a new housing subdivision, Del Sol, which had been built in between two communities with established gangs. The Del Sol boys often faced challenges and attacks from members of these gangs, who considered them weaklings (or "punks"). Tiring of this harassment, several Del Sol boys decided to carry weapons to their next party, respond aggressively to verbal challenges by claiming membership in a Del Sol gang, and retaliate if attacked. They soon became a recognized part of the gang landscape, engaging in violent conflict with rival gangs (Sanders 1994:43–44). The area's Southeast Asian gangs were likely formed in a similar fashion, as the children of immigrants from Laos, Cambodia, and Vietnam banded together to protect themselves from existing black, Mexican-American, and mixed-ethnicity gangs (Sanders 1994:163).

We can see this sort of dynamic at work even in cases of clashing moral cultures, such as dignity and victimhood. Insofar as they share a social environment, the same conditions that lead aggrieved people to publicly complain of their victimization will encourage their adversaries to respond in kind. As clinical psychologist David J. Ley notes, the response of those labeled as oppressors is frequently to "assert that they are a victim as well." Thus, "men criticized as sexist for challenging radical feminism defend themselves as victims of reverse sexism, [and] people criticized as being unsympathetic proclaim their own history of victimization" (Ley 2014).

The result is *competitive victimhood*, in which both sides of a conflict vie to portray themselves as the truly victimized party. Like other manifestations of victimhood status, competitive victimhood is not limited to modern colleges and universities. Indeed, people everywhere make a moral distinction between victim and offender, wrongdoer and wronged. Since many conflicts involve both sides insisting that they are in the right and their adversary is in the wrong, competing claims of victimhood are common. Scholars have documented competitive victimhood in several long-running, violent political struggles, such as the Northern Irish Troubles or the Israeli–Palestinian conflict. In these cases, partisans on each side argue that it is their side that has suffered the most, and so is most justified in retribution or deserving of aid (Noor et al. 2012; Schori-Eyal et al. 2014; Sullivan et al. 2012).

Recall that emphasis on victimization is a matter of degree, and the highest degrees are found in victimhood culture. It is in victimhood culture that privilege is most shamed, marginality most celebrated, and the handling of grievances increasingly dependent on convincing others that one is the underdog. We should thus expect competitive victimhood to be a frequent occurrence in both individual and collective disputes. For example, those who have been accused of microaggressions might find that their best way of silencing a critic is by labeling the criticism as an act of microaggression itself. Journalist Megan McArdle relates an example from her own life:

> I ended up in a Twitter discussion with a guy who chided me for letting my privilege blind me to the ways that minorities (specifically women in tech, and more broadly on the Internet), experience microaggressions. You know how that conversation ended? When I pointed out that he had just committed a classic microaggression: mansplaining to me something that I had actually experienced, and he had not. As soon as I did, he apologized, though that hadn't really been my intent. My intent was to point out that microaggressions are often unintentional (this guy clearly considered himself a feminist ally). But I inadvertently demonstrated an even greater difficulty: Complaints about microaggressions can be used to stop complaints about microaggressions. There is no logical resting place for these disputes; it's microaggressions all the way down. (McArdle 2015)

People might also respond to accusations of being privileged by listing various disadvantages or hardships to disprove the accusation. When a Twitter user noted with apparent disapproval that he doubted CEO

Brandon Friedman had ever had to work a job while in college, Friedman responded, "I worked in a scrap yard cutting copper ends off AC cooler cores with a blowtorch in 100+ degree heat in Louisiana" (quoted in Bovy 2017:61). Likewise, in an essay in *The Princeton Tory*, conservative student Tal Fortgang responds to the phrase "check your privilege," which he says "floats around college campuses," by recounting his own family's many victimizations—a grandfather who did hard labor in Siberia, a grandmother who survived a death march through Poland, and others shot in an open grave (Fortgang 2014).

People accused of privilege might also counter that their accusers are really the privileged ones. As writer Phoebe Maltz Bovy notes, "critics of the recent student activism have flipped the 'privilege' script" by pointing out that the subjects of many student complaints are the kind of so-called "first-world problems" that only those who live in material comfort and safety tend to worry about (2017:94). Discussing the fracas at Yale surrounding guidelines for Halloween costumes, journalist Conor Friedersdorf observes that "these are young people who live in safe, heated buildings with two Steinway grand pianos, an indoor basketball court, a courtyard with hammocks and picnic tables, a computer lab, a dance studio, a gym, a movie theater, a film-editing lab, billiard tables, an art gallery, and four music practice rooms" (quoted in Bovy 2017:94). Conservative critics are particularly likely to highlight that leftist activists are part of the ideological majority on college campuses and enjoy the advantages that go along with that. In an article in *The College Fix*, Princeton's Tal Fortgang lists 38 forms of "left-wing privilege," arguing that "it might behoove left-wingers on college campuses to think about the various privileges from which they benefit simply by being members of the overwhelmingly dominant group in their academic communities" (Fortgang 2015). A piece in *The Federalist* makes a similar argument: "It is a privilege when your views conform with those of more than 90 percent of your professors" (quoted in Bovy 2017:209). As these examples suggest, conservative critics of political correctness and campus activism can also appeal to victimhood.

Conservative Victims

Conservative complaints of victimhood have occurred for some time. For decades there have been complaints that hiring and college admission policies that favor blacks and other minorities—known in the United States as *affirmative action*—are unfair and detrimental to non-minorities. As victimhood culture expands the number of victim groups that deserve special consideration, it may also increase the resentment of those who remain in categories that do not receive such concern. One student published an editorial in *The Wall Street Journal* in which she laments that she offers "about as much diversity as a saltine cracker" and suggests she would have gotten into her preferred school if her parents were lesbians (Weiss 2013). The importance of martyrdom in Christian tradition can also be congenial to narratives of religious persecution among religious conservatives. For example, in 2005 an event organized by the Family Research Council featured speakers who talked about the founding of the United States by "oppressed pilgrims" seeking religious freedom, and the threat posed to religious freedom by rise of "judicial tyranny" that enforced "the moral views of elites, universities, media, Hollywood, and so on" (quoted in Castelli 2007:158). And following the 2005 publication of John Gibson's book *The War on Christmas: How the Liberal Plot to Ban the Sacred Christian Holiday is Worse than You Thought*, the notion that the holiday is under threat by liberal and progressive forces has become a common trope among segments of the religious right (Stack 2016).[11]

But though not entirely new, victim narratives on the right seem to have become especially prominent during the 2016 presidential campaign. During this time a particular victim narrative gained currency on the left—one in which Trump's campaign was a movement of hateful bigotry that threatened to oppress or even kill various minorities. Such claims provoked responses from those who sympathized with Trump supporters, if not with their choice of candidate. Defenders of Trump supporters usually drew attention to the hardships and disadvantages many of them faced. For example, many drew attention to the declining employment and wages for less educated men. As one journalist argued, "Non-college men have been trampled by globalization, the dissolution of manufacturing employment, and other factors" (Thompson 2016). A conservative col-

---

[11] Fox New commentator Billy O'Reilly often promoted the idea. For example, in 2011 Rhode Island Governor Lincoln Chafee announced that the state Christmas tree would now be called a "holiday tree," a change meant to be "respectful of everyone" (McCalmont 2013). Responding to an interview in which the governor likened the change to the acceptance of immigration and gay marriage, O'Reilly claimed that, "The secular progressives want a new America and traditional Christmas isn't a part of it" (O'Reilly 2012). In another example, a 2016 headline at *Fox News Insider* read, "LOOK: Obamas' Holiday Card Doesn't Mention Christmas for 8th Year" (*Fox News Insider* 2016).

umnist similarly wrote that "an embittered red-state America has found itself left behind by elite-driven globalization" such that, in many counties, "rural life has become a mirror image of the inner city, ravaged by drug use, criminality, and hopelessness" (Hanson 2017). Another piece carried the headline "Even if You Don't like Donald Trump, You Should Understand the Pain of His Poor White Supporters" (Hunter 2016). Similarly, one story about Trump supporters took as emblematic the quote of an Arkansas man: "I'm just a poor white trash motherfucker. No one cares about me" (Irvin 2016). The piece's author laments that "instead of fighting for better education for the white underclass, we call them ignorant rednecks. Instead of fighting for them to have better health care, we laugh at their missing teeth. Instead of fighting for them to have better housing, we joke about tornados hitting trailer parks" (Irvin 2016).

Accusations of racism, sexism, and the like were themselves seen as an element of these people's victimization. As anthropologist Christine Walley notes, people interviewed in sociological studies of white conservatives "deny charges of racism, which they defined as personal hatred" (Walley 2017:233). To be falsely accused of an offense is itself offensive, and it lowers one's moral standing in the eyes of any who believe the accusation. Some sympathizers argued that the belief that poor, rural, Southern, or Appalachian whites are overwhelmingly bigots allows elites to justify their disdain for social inferiors as a fight against oppression. In a discussion of Trump's appeal to Appalachian voters, J.D. Vance recounts that his grandmother once told him that in modern America hillbillies "are the only group of people you don't have to be ashamed to look down upon" (quoted in Dreher 2016).

In their attempt to win partisans and sway authorities, even victimhood culture's strongest critics might adopt its moral framework. Those who respond to accusations of privilege with strenuous denial and counteraccusations are implicitly participating in the vilification of advantage and valorization of disadvantage. In making their case, they might increasingly come to focus on minor, verbal, and even unintentional slights. For example, a *New York Times* story describes the complaints of a sophomore at the University of Michigan who supported Trump and was offended by the university's reaction to his electoral victory, including the fact that her biology professor cancelled class on the assumption that students would be too distraught to focus on the course. When the president sent out a letter to the student body advising them of counseling resources and advertising a vigil to mourn the results, she circulated an online petition accusing the administration of favoring the liberal majority by suggesting the superiority of their ideology (Hartocollis 2016).

Note the similarity between this last case and the microaggression complaints we have discussed so far. The grievance revolves around a verbal offense that was in all likelihood completely unintentional. The aggrieved responded by using public complaint to recruit socially distant weak partisans—that is, those who offered a small amount of support to her cause by signing the petition—and subsequently presenting the collective complaint to authorities. The student does not call the offense a microaggression, but her way of handling it is otherwise nearly identical.[12]

Those exasperated by complaints of microaggression on campus might respond by pointing out similar slights against Christians, rural whites, military veterans, and others who are not the object of activists' concern.[13] Doing so will likely make them more prone to notice and dwell on such offenses. Some will no doubt compile lists to document these offenses, if only to bring them up in arguments with supporters of the current microaggression program. Even if these arguments amount to little more than charges of hypocrisy, they nonetheless involve treating unintentional verbal offenses as a serious matter.

Other kinds of imitation occur as well. Some on the right, in their criticism of political correctness, might make highly exaggerated or even false claims of victimization. During a television interview following the 2016 election, Trump's former campaign manager Corey Lewandowski said, "Merry Christmas, because Donald Trump is now the president, you can say it again, it's okay to say"—as if the previous administration had suppressed the phrase (*Fox News* 2016). In Chap. 4 we described hate crime hoaxes carried out by conservatives, such as the Republican partisan who

---

[12] If this student were to follow the naming conventions that victimhood culture uses for other offenses, she might say her professors committed the microaggression of *liberalnormativity*.

[13] For example, J.D. Vance relates the following story from one of his classes at Yale Law School: "I was the only veteran in the class, and when this came up somehow in conversation, a young woman looked at me and said, 'I can't believe you were in the Marines. You just seem so nice. I thought that people in the military had to act a certain way.' It was incredibly insulting, and it was my first real introduction to the idea that this institution that was so important among my neighbors was looked down upon in such a personal way. To this lady, to be in the military meant that you had to be some sort of barbarian. I bit my tongue, but it's one of those comments I'll never forget" (Dreher 2016). Vance attributes great significance to this unintentional insult, making his story very similar to a microaggression complaint.

claimed to have been attacked by an Obama supporter during the 2008 presidential campaign. Though hate crime hoaxes are currently most common among the campus left, we should not be surprised to see a growing number from the right. As people become aware that many hate crime reports are false, some may retaliate by crafting "hoax hoaxes," making up dubious evidence to "debunk" hate crime claims that are actually valid (Tait 2016). A social environment that is conducive to false accusations could thus lead to people being falsely accused of falsely accusing others.

There are already those on the right who adopt the moral language of the campus activists they oppose. For example, some adopt campus activists' tactic of disrupting speaking events and denouncing offensive speech as violence. In New York City in 2017 a production of the play *Julius Caesar* became controversial for its thinly veiled portrayal of the titular Roman dictator—who is stabbed to death by assassins—as President Donald Trump. Right-wing protesters disrupted one performance by charging the stage shouting, "This is violence against the right!" One of the protesters turned to the audience and told them "You are all Nazis" (Shapiro 2017).

When some on the right imitate the tactics and language of campus activists, they attract the same kinds of criticism from those who oppose victimhood culture as such. Conservative commentator Ben Shapiro denounced the disruption of *Julius Caesar* as "idiotic snowflake-ism" and argued it was no different from leftist activists trying to block his own speech at California State University, Los Angeles a year prior: "The minute you equate speech with violence and attempt to forcibly shut it down, you're a snowflake" (Shapiro 2017). The conflict between victimhood and dignity occurs within as well as across party lines and common ideological divides. Competitive victimhood likewise occurs not just between left and right, but even within circles of progressive activists at the heart of victimhood culture.

Purity Spirals

Any individual person can be classified in terms of multiple socially meaningful categories. A person might be black or white, male or female, gay or straight, Christian or Muslim, and so forth. This means that many people will have memberships in some more disadvantaged categories but also in some more advantaged ones. And those who combine many victim identities will claim and be accorded greater moral status than those with only a few. The result is that not even members of marginalized groups are safe from accusations of being privileged and insensitive to the suffering of the less fortunate. A gay man who critiques heteronormativity, homophobia, and straightsplaining may in turn be criticized for being a man (and thus more privileged than a woman, especially a lesbian) as well as for identifying with his biological sex (making him less oppressed than a transgender person). For example, in 2016 the UK's National Union of Students' LGBT Campaign passed a motion for campus LGBT groups to exclude gay men because they "don't face oppression" (Duffy 2016). The author of an essay in *Jezebel* begins with, "I am a white, cisgender gay guy ... the queer equivalent of 'The Man' ... parties become less diverse when I walk in" before asking, "Can a nontrans, white gay man ever truly leave the comforts of his own identity without having to make frequent and loud apologies for the crimes of his ilk?" (Rosen 2011, cited in Bovy 2017:35). In 2017 three Jewish participants in an annual Chicago LGBT event called the "Dyke March" were asked to leave because they carried a rainbow colored flag emblazoned with the Star of David, a symbol of Judaism. They were told the flag, a symbol of LGBT Jewish identity, "made people feel unsafe" because the Star of David is also on the Israeli flag, and the march was "pro-Palestinian" and "anti-Zionist" (Haaretz 2017). That same year, the black director of the Claremont colleges' LGBT center tweeted his preference to keep his distance from "white gays and well-meaning white women" (Dordick 2017).

Such infighting between activists and victim groups is sometimes referred to as a *purity spiral.* The idea is that members of ideological and religious movements might strive to outdo one another in displays of zealotry, condemning and expelling members of their own movement for smaller and smaller deviations from its core virtues. Perhaps only a minority of the most aggressive members take the lead in this, but because failing to condemn deviants opens one up to charges of being deviant oneself, others tend to either join in or passively acquiesce.[14] The result is an ever-increasing demand for moral purity, and ever-greater effort to meet the standards of the group.

---

[14] For this reason people may even condemn others for failing to adhere to norms they themselves privately reject (Willer et al. 2009). This dynamic—condemning in order to avoid being condemned—is similar to the moral panics we discussed in Chap. 4.

In a victimhood culture, purity spirals revolve around claims of victimhood, privilege, and oppression. They are led by those with the greatest victimhood status and those who have the greatest sensitivity to slight. And their primary targets are not those fully outside of the culture, and thus less sensitive to the opinions of its members. Instead it is ideological sympathizers and allies who most fear being shamed. Writing in *The National Post*, Jonathan Kay argues that aggressive leftist Twitter users act as a "crowdsourced ideological autocracy" whose shaming tactics primarily victimize "public figures who ... are creatures of the left ... since these are the same figures whose legitimacy as politicians, activists and writers depends" on appeasing those who shame them.[15] He notes that "elected politicians and established mainstream media figures" are especially likely to attract social media shaming because "the more actual power one is perceived as having in a society suffused with sexism, heteronormativity, white supremacism etc., the less moral capital is ascribed to you" (Kay 2017). But even rank and file activists may live in fear of being shunned. "There is an underlying current of fear in my activist communities," writes graduate student Frances Lee. "It is the fear of appearing impure. Social death follows when being labeled a 'bad' activist or simply 'problematic' enough times" (Lee 2017). Lee goes on to elaborate:

I self-police what I say in activist spaces. I stopped commenting on social media with questions or pushback on leftist opinions for fear of being called out. I am always ready to apologize for anything I do that a community member deems wrong, oppressive, or inappropriate—no questions asked. The amount of energy I spend demonstrating purity in order to stay in the good graces of a fast-moving activist community is enormous.... At times, I have found myself performing activism more than doing activism. I'm exhausted, and I'm not even doing the real work I am committed to do. (Lee 2017)

---

[15] He gives as an example the case of Canadian Member of Parliament Niki Ashton, who in 2017 tweeted, "Like Beyoncé says, to the left. Time for an unapologetic left turn for the #NDP, for social, racial, enviro and economic justice." In response, the Vancouver chapter of Black Lives Matter demanded she apologize for her "appropriation" of performer Beyoncé, whose lyric "to the left" she had quoted in her tweet. Ashton quickly offered an apology for the racial insensitivity of quoting a lyric from a popular song, co-written with two Norwegians, in a public statement advocating for racial justice.

Given the activists' goals, such attempts to vie for superior moral status and purify their own ranks are likely counterproductive. Social movements succeed by growing and expanding their numbers and by winning the support and patronage of the powerful and influential. Expelling those who are insufficiently righteous hampers the growth of any religious or ideological movement and may present a special challenge for a movement that condemns privilege. Writing in *The Guardian*, Zoe Williams argues, "If only the truly marginalised can speak as feminists, that depletes our numbers.... And if people 'with a platform' are disqualified for being part of the power structure, that leaves us without a platform" (Williams 2013, quoted in Bovy 2017:174). Thus, among those who have adopted victimhood culture, competitive victimhood can simultaneously lead to an intensification of their morality as well as sowing divisions that slow its spread.

*   *   *

There are many self-reinforcing processes in human society. We recognize them in sayings like "It takes money to make money" and "Nothing succeeds like success." We can also observe them in the spread of moral cultures. Changing social conditions encourages some forms of conflict and social control to increase and others to decline. These changes can penetrate the moral socialization of children and youth and result in younger generations who are trained in the ways of the new moral culture and are much quicker to engage in its defining behaviors. The more widespread these moral ideas and practices become, the more advantageous it becomes to adopt them. This is especially so when the moral culture becomes common among elites, rendering competing moral cultures a mark of low status. Even those who criticize the new moral culture and its adherents may find themselves adopting its logic and tactics, their opposition ironically contributing to its spread. All these processes are visible in the rise of victimhood culture, and all contribute to its growing visibility in modern society. Yet no social process accelerates indefinitely. Competitive victimhood can both encourage and limit the spread of victimhood culture. It may lead the clash between dignity and victimhood to transform into a clash between competing victimization narratives, or it may cause the victimhood revolution to devour its own, eventually burning itself out.

REFERENCES

Alsop, Ron. 2008. *The Trophy Kids Grow Up: How the Millennial Generation Is Shaking Up the Workplace*. San Francisco: John Wiley & Sons.

Anderson, Elijah. 1999. *Code of the Street: Decency, Violence, and the Moral Life of the Inner City*. New York: W. W. Norton.

Athens, Lonnie H. 1989. *The Creation of Dangerous Violent Criminals*. New York: Routledge.

Bailey, Ronald. 2015. Victimhood Culture in America: Beyond Honor and Dignity. *Reason*, September 11. https://reason.com/blog/2015/09/11/victimhood-culture-in-america-beyond-dig.

Baumgartner, M.P. 1992. War and Peace in Early Childhood. In *Virginia Review of Sociology, Volume 1: Law and Conflict Management*, ed. James Tucker, 1–38. Greenwich: JAI Press.

Bennet, James. 2011. The Trophy Generation. *The Atlantic*, July/August. https://www.theatlantic.com/magazine/archive/2011/07/the-trophy-generation/308542/.

Black, Donald. 1976. *The Behavior of Law*. San Diego: Academic Press.

———. 1998. The Social Structure of Right and Wrong. Rev ed. San Diego: Academic Press.

———. 2000. Dreams of Pure Sociology. *Sociological Theory* 18 (3): 343–367.

Blake, Aaron. 2014. The "Participation Trophy" Generation. *Washington Post*, August 20. https://www.washingtonpost.com/news/the-fix/wp/2014/08/20/meet-the-participation-trophy-generation/?utm_term=.384693d354fa.

Bourdieu, Pierre. 1984. *Distinction: A Social Critique of the Judgment of Taste*. Cambridge: Harvard University Press.

Bovy, Phoebe Maltz. 2017. *The Perils of 'Privilege': Why Injustice Can't Be Solved by Accusing Others of Advantage*. New York: St. Martin's Press.

Burbank, Jane. 1999. Insult and Punishment in Rural Courts: The Elaboration of Civility in Late Imperial Russia. *Études Rurales* 149 (1): 147–171.

Careau, Gabrièle. 2013. Duelling Gentlemen, Dual Rhetoric: Duelling and Anti-Duelling Rhetoric in Antebellum New York, 1804–1838. *Historical Discourses* 72: 86–202.

Castelli, Elizabeth A. 2007. Persecution Complexes: Identity Politics and the 'War on Christians'. *Differences: A Journal of Feminist Cultural Studies* 18 (3): 152–180.

Chait, Jonathan. 2015. Not a Very P.C. Thing to Say: How the Language Police Are Perverting Liberalism. *New York Magazine*, January 27. http://nymag.com/daily/intelligencer/2015/01/not-a-very-pc-thing-to-say.html.

Chougule, Pratik. 2017. Is American Childhood Creating an Authoritarian Society? *The American Conservative*, June 20. http://www.theamericanconservative.com/articles/will-american-childhood-create-an-authoritarian-society/.

Cooney, Mark. 1998. *Warriors and Peacemakers: How Third Parties Shape Violence*. New York: New York University Press.

———. 2009. *Is Killing Wrong? A Study in Pure Sociology*. Charlottesville: University of Virginia Press.

DeBoer, Fredrik. 2017a. Why Is This So Hard? *Medium*, April 8. https://medium.com/@freddiedeboer/why-is-this-so-hard-91ba11624d2f.

———. 2017b. Marginalized People Don't Need Politeness, They Need Power. *Medium*, June 8. https://medium.com/@freddiedeboer/marginalized-people-dont-need-politeness-they-need-power-dba5200b6072.

Dordick, Elliot. 2017. I'm 'Wary of "White Gays,' 'Women,' Says New LGBTQ Director. *The Claremont Independent*, July 8. http://claremontindependent.com/im-wary-white-gays-women-says-new-lgbtq-director/.

Dreher, Rod. 2016. Trump: Tribune of Poor White People. *The American Conservative*, July 22. http://www.theamericanconservative.com/dreher/trump-us-politics-poor-whites/.

———. 2017. Creating the White Tribe. *The American Conservative*, January 25. http://www.theamericanconservative.com/dreher/creating-the-white-tribe/.

Duffy, Nick. 2016. NUS Tells LGBT Societies to Abolish Gay Men's Reps Because 'They Don't Face Oppression.' *Pink News*, March 22. http://www.pinknews.co.uk/2016/03/22/nus-tells-lgbt-societies-to-abolish-gay-mens-reps-because-they-dont-face-oppression/.

Etzioni, Amitai. 2014. Don't Sweat the Microaggressions. *The Atlantic*, April 8. http://www.theatlantic.com/politics/archive/2014/04/dont-sweat-the-microaggressions/360278/.

Fortgang, Tal. 2014. Checking My Privilege: Character as the Basis of Privilege. *The Princeton Tory*, April 2. http://theprincetontory.com/main/checking-my-privilege-character-as-the-basis-of-privilege.

———. 2015. 38 Ways College Students Enjoy 'Left-Wing Privilege' on Campus. *The College Fix*, June 24. https://www.thecollegefix.com/post/23072/.

Fox News. 2016. Twitter Account, December 3. https://twitter.com/FoxNews/status/806337793597181956.

Fox News Insider. 2016. Look: Obamas' Holiday Card Doesn't Mention Christmas for 8th Year. December 14. http://insider.foxnews.com/2016/12/14/look-obamas-holiday-card-doesnt-mention-christmas-8th-year.

Friedersdorf, Conor. 2015. What Do Donald Trump Voters Actually Want? *The Atlantic*, August 2017. https://www.theatlantic.com/politics/archive/2015/08/donald-trump-voters/401408/.

———. 2017. The Problem with Helicopter Colleges. *The Atlantic*, July 14. https://www.theatlantic.com/politics/archive/2017/07/steven-pinkers-critique-of-helicopter-colleges/533667/.

Furedi, Frank. 2017. *What's Happened to the University?: A Sociological Exploration of Its Infantilization*. New York: Routledge.

Haaretz. 2017. Chicago 'Dyke March' Bans Jewish Pride Flags: 'They Made People Feel Unsafe'. June 26. http://www.haaretz.com/us-news/1.797650.

Haidt, Jonathan. 2012. *The Righteous Mind: Why Good People Are Divided by Politics and Religion.* New York: Pantheon Books.

———. 2015. Coddle U vs. Strengthen U: What a Great University Should Be. *Righteous Mind Blog,* October 6. http://righteousmind.com/coddle-u-vs-strengthen-u/.

Hanson, Victor David. 2017. Trump and the Great American Divide. *City Journal,* Winter. https://www.city-journal.org/html/trump-and-american-divide-14944.html.

Hartocollis, Anemona. 2016. On Campus, Trump Fans Say They Need 'Safe Spaces'. *The New York Times,* December 8. https://www.nytimes.com/2016/12/08/us/politics/political-divide-on-campuses-hardens-after-trumps-victory.html.

Holleman, Joe. 2015. Mizzou Hunger-Strike Figure from Omaha, Son of Top Railroad Exec. *St. Louis Post-Dispatch,* November 11. http://www.stltoday.com/lifestyles/columns/joe-holleman/mizzou-hunger-strike-figure-from-omaha-son-of-top-railroad/article_20630c03-2a68-5e63-9585-edde16fe05f3.html.

Hunter, Jack. 2016. Even if You Don't Like Donald Trump, You Should Understand the Pain of His Poor White Supporters. *Rare Politics,* July 24. http://rare.us/rare-politics/even-if-you-dont-like-donald-trump-you-should-understand-the-pain-of-his-poor-white-supporters/.

Irvin, Jonna. 2016. I Know Why Poor Whites Chant Trump, Trump, Trump. *Stir Journal,* April 1. http://www.stirjournal.com/2016/04/01/i-know-why-poor-whites-chant-trump-trump-trump/.

Jacobs, Bruce A., and Richard Wright. 2006. *Street Justice: Retaliation in the Criminal Underworld.* Cambridge: Cambridge University Press.

Juster, F. Thomas, Hiromi Ono, and Frank P. Stafford. 2004. Changing Times of American Youth: 1981–2003. University of Michigan Institute for Social Research. http://ns.umich.edu/Releases/2004/Nov04/teen_time_report.pdf.

Kay, Jonathan. 2017. Jonathan Kay on the Tyranny of Twitter: How Mob Censure Is Changing the Intellectual Landscape. *National Post,* June 22. http://nationalpost.com/news/world/jonathan-kay-on-the-tyranny-of-twitter-how-mob-censure-is-changing-the-intellectual-landscape/wcm/c94cb9be-3eef-4982-9e65-7f4e934c2afb.

Kim, Walter, and Wendy Cole. 2001. What Ever Happened to Play? *Time,* April 22. http://content.time.com/time/nation/article/0,8599,107264,00.html.

Kollman, Nancy Shields. 1999. *By Honor Bound: State and Society in Early Modern Russia.* Ithaca: Cornell University Press.

Lareau, Annette. 2003. *Unequal Childhoods: Class, Race, and Family Life.* Berkeley: University of California Press.

Lee, Frances. 2017. Kin Aesthetics // Excommunicate Me from the Church of Social Justice. *Catalyst Wedding Co.*, July 10. http://www.catalystwedco.com/blog/2017/7/10/kin-aesthetics-excommunicate-me-from-the-church-of-social-justice.

Leovy, Jill. 2015. *Ghettoside: A True Story of Murder in America*. New York: Spiegel & Grau.

Ley, David J. 2014. The Culture of Victimhood: Hoaxes, Trigger Warnings and Trauma-Informed Care. *Psychology Today*, June 18. Retrieved September 8, 2014. http://www.psychologytoday.com/blog/women-who-stray/201406/the-culture-victimhood.

Luhby, Tami. 2016. Working Class White Men Make Less Than They Did in 1996. *CNN Money*, October 5. http://money.cnn.com/2016/10/05/news/economy/working-class-men-income/index.html.

Lukianoff, Greg. 2014. *Unlearning Liberty: Campus Censorship and the End of American Debate*. New York: Encounter Books.

Lukianoff, Greg, and Jonathan Haidt. 2015. The Coddling of the American Mind. *The Atlantic*, September. http://www.theatlantic.com/magazine/archive/2015/09/the-coddling-of-the-american-mind/399356/.

Marantz, Andrew. 2017a. Trump Supporters at the DeploraBall. *The New Yorker*, February 6. http://www.newyorker.com/magazine/2017/02/06/trump-supporters-at-the-deploraball.

———. 2017b. The Alt-Right Branding War Has Torn the Movement in Two. *The New Yorker*, July 6. http://www.newyorker.com/news/news-desk/the-alt-right-branding-war-has-torn-the-movement-in-two.

McArdle, Megan. 2014. *The Up Side of Down: Why Failing Well Is the Key to Success*. New York: Penguin Books.

———. 2015. How Grown-Ups Deal with Microaggressions. *Bloomberg View*, September 11. http://www.bloombergview.com/articles/2015-09-11/how-grown-ups-deal-with-microaggressions-.

McCalmont, Lucy. 2013. Chafee Decks Christmas Title on Tree. *Politico*, December 2. http://www.politico.com/story/2013/12/lincoln-chafee-christmas-tree-100532.

McConnell, Scott. 2016. Why Trump Wins. *The American Conservative*, June 27. http://www.theamericanconservative.com/articles/why-trump-wins/.

McWhorter, John. 2014. "'Microaggression' Is the New Racism on Campus. *Time*, March 21. http://time.com/32618/microaggression-is-the-new-racism-on-campus/.

Murray, Charles. 2013. *Coming Apart: The State of White America, 1960–2010*. New York: Three Rivers Press.

Murray, Robert, and Catherine Ramstetter. 2013. The Crucial Role of Recess in School. American Academy of Pediatrics. http://pediatrics.aappublications.org/content/pediatrics/131/1/183.full.pdf.

Nelson, Louis. 2016. Trump: Clinton, Obama Protecting Terrorists to Be 'Politically Correct.' *Politico*, June 13. http://www.politico.com/story/2016/06/donald-trump-muslim-ban-224272.

New York Times. 2017a. Claremont McKenna College. https://www.nytimes.com/interactive/projects/college-mobility/claremont-mckenna-college.

———. 2017b. Middlebury College. https://www.nytimes.com/interactive/projects/college-mobility/middlebury-college.

Nisbett, Robert A., and Dov Cohen. 1996. *Culture of Honor: The Psychology of Violence in the South*. Boulder: Westview Press.

Noor, Masi, Nurit Shnabel, Samer Halabi, and Arie Nadler. 2012. When Suffering Begets Suffering: The Psychology of Competitive Victimhood Between Adversarial Groups in Violent Conflicts. *Personality and Social Psychology Review* 16 (4): 351–374.

O'Reilly, Bill. 2012. Bill O'Reilly: The War on Christmas: The Big Picture. *Fox News*, November 29. http://www.foxnews.com/transcript/2012/11/30/bill-oreilly-war-christmas-big-picture.html.

Owens, Eric. 2017. VICTORY: Politically Correct Wusses Fail to Ban Dodgeball in This State's Public Schools. *The Daily Caller*, April 24. http://dailycaller.com/2017/04/23/victory-politically-correct-wusses-fail-to-ban-dodgeball-in-this-states-public-schools/.

Pew Research Center. 2015. The American Middle Class Is Losing Ground. December 9. http://www.pewsocialtrends.org/2015/12/09/the-american-middle-class-is-losing-ground/.

Pinker, Steven. 2011. *The Better Angels of Our Nature: Why Violence Has Declined*. New York: Viking.

Rauch, Jonathan. 2014. *Kindly Inquisitors: The New Attacks on Free Thought*. Expanded ed. Chicago: University of Chicago Press.

Reeves, Ricard V., and Dimitrios Halikias. 2017. Illiberal Arts Colleges: Pay More, Get Less (Free Speech). *Real Clear Markets*, March 14. http://www.realclear-markets.com/articles/2017/03/14/illiberal_arts_colleges_pay_more_get_less_free_speech_102586.html.

Rhodes, Richard. 1999. *Why They Kill: The Discoveries of a Maverick Criminologist*. New York: Vintage Books.

Rosen, Zack. 2011. In Defense of the Gay White Male. *Jezebel*, January 25. http://jezebel.com/5745172/in-defense-of-the-gay-white-male.

San Diego Union-Tribune. 2017. UC Tuition Hikes? First Justify Your Administrative Bloat. January 6. http://www.sandiegouniontribune.com/opinion/editorials/sd-uc-tuition-hikes-administrative-bloat-20170105-story.html.

Sanders, William B. 1994. *Gangbangs and Drive-bys: Grounded Culture and Juvenile Gang Violence*. New York: Aldine de Gruyter.

Schori-Eyal, Noa, Eran Halperin, and Daniel Bar-Tal. 2014. Three Layers of Collective Victimhood: Effects of Multileveled Victimhood on Intergroup Conflicts in the Israeli-Arab Context. *Journal of Applied Social Psychology* 44: 778–794.

Seery, John E. 2017. Somewhere Between a Jeremiad and a Eulogy. *Modern Age: A Conservative Review* 59 (3): 61–71.

Shapiro, Ben. 2017. Watch: Pro-Trump Protesters Try to Shut Down Anti-Trump 'Julius Caesar' Production, Scream 'Nazis!' at the Audience. *The Daily Wire*, June 16. http://www.dailywire.com/news/17641/watch-pro-trump-protesters-try-shut-down-anti-ben-shapiro.

Soave, Robby. 2016. How Political Correctness Caused College Students to Cheer for Trump. *Reason*, February 23. http://reason.com/blog/2016/02/23/how-political-correctness-caused-college.

Stack, Liam. 2016. How the 'War on Christmas' Controversy Was Created. *The New York Times*, December 19. https://www.nytimes.com/2016/12/19/us/war-on-christmas-controversy.html.

Sullivan, Daniel, Mark J. Landau, Nyla R. Brandscombe, and Zachary K. Rothschild. 2012. Competitive Victimhood as a Response to Accusations of Ingroup Harm Doing. *Journal of Personality and Social Psychology* 102 (4): 778–795.

Tait, Amelia. 2016. Hate Crimes, Social Media, and the Rise of the 'Hoax Hoax.' *New Statesman*, November 17. http://www.newstatesman.com/science-tech/2016/11/hate-crimes-social-media-and-rise-hoax-hoax.

Thompson, Derek. 2016. Who Are Donald Trump's Supporters, Really? *The Atlantic*, March 1. https://www.theatlantic.com/politics/archive/2016/03/who-are-donald-trumps-supporters-really/471714/.

Vance, J.D. 2016. *Hillbilly Elegy: A Memoir of a Family and Culture in Crisis.* New York: Harper Collins.

Walley, Christine J. 2017. Trump's Election and the 'White Working Class': What We Missed. *American Ethnologist* 44 (2): 231–236.

Weiss, Suzy Lee. 2013. To (All) the Colleges That Rejected Me. *The Wall Street Journal*, March 29. https://www.wsj.com/articles/SB10001424127887324000704578390340064578654.

Willer, Rob, Kuwabara Ko, and Michael W. Macy. 2009. The False Enforcement of Unpopular Norms. *American Journal of Sociology* 115 (2): 451–490.

Williams, Zoe. 2013. Are You Too White, Rich, Able-Bodied and Straight to Be a Feminist? *The Guardian*, April 18. https://www.theguardian.com/commentisfree/2013/apr/18/are-you-too-white-rich-straight-to-be-feminist.

Yiannopoulos, Milo. 2017. Milo: Daniel Brewster Is a Warning; I'm Coming for Liberal Professors. Video clip. https://www.youtube.com/watch?v=MUUoH1b5HNo.

Young, Isaac F., and Daniel Sullivan. 2016. Competitive Victimhood: A Review of the Theoretical and Empirical Literature. *Current Opinion in Psychology* 11: 30–34.

CHAPTER 6

Sociology, Social Justice, and Victimhood

Victimhood culture makes it hard to avoid wrongdoing. If you have any kind of privilege, the social world is full of peril; you always risk giving offense. Engage in small talk and you might be guilty of a microaggression. Cook a new dish or adopt a new hairstyle and you might be guilty of cultural appropriation. Teach about something unpleasant and you might be guilty of triggering someone. Express your religious or political beliefs and you might be guilty of violence. Whatever you do, you must do it in a way that is supportive of victims and reproachful of their oppressors. Doing sociology is no exception.

According to sociologist Richard Felson, "avoid blaming the victim" amounts to "a procedural rule in sociology today" (1991:21, n. 11). "Today" was 1991, so a concern for victims has played a role in sociological explanation for decades now. To blame someone is to hold that person morally culpable, so holding someone who is raped culpable for the rape, or someone who is killed culpable for the homicide, is *victim blaming*. Even to say a victim is partly at fault might be victim blaming. Felson explains that this is because blame is often "treated as a fixed quantity." A "zero-sum treatment of blame" means that "if we say a crime victim has made a mistake (e.g., 'he shouldn't have jogged in that park that night'), it implies that we are assigning less blame to the offender." If you want to assign maximum blame to the offender, then, "you will prefer to deny any sort of blame to the victim" (Felson 1991:7).

© The Author(s) 2018
B. Campbell, J. Manning, *The Rise of Victimhood Culture*,
https://doi.org/10.1007/978-3-319-70329-9_6

Victim blaming, to whatever degree, can therefore be very offensive. *Logically* this should present no problem for sociologists. Describing and explaining human behavior is not the same as evaluating it. Causal responsibility is thus not the same as moral culpability, and so explaining an outcome with someone's actions is not the same as blaming them for that outcome. It may be true that a person would not have been mugged if they had not gone out at night, and their going out is thus relevant to explaining why a mugging took place when and where it did. But this explanation would not assign blame to the victim. An explanation of crime blames neither victim nor offender, in whole or in part.

But this is poorly understood, even by sociologists. So while *logically* the offensiveness of victim blaming should not present a problem, in practice it does. In ordinary life we usually do not blame people for behavior they have not caused. Thus, when we want to appear blameless for something, we claim that we were not the cause, or else de-emphasize our causal role. And when people want to avoid being blamed for their behavior they might explain their behavior as having resulted from external causes (forces outside of themselves, such as the economy or legal system) rather than internal causes (such as their own actions or beliefs). According to Felson, "the safest way to avoid blame … is to deny any internal causality" (Felson 1991:6). Many people then conflate cause and blame: To explain something with internal factors is to assign blame for what is bad or to give praise for what is good; to explain something with external factors is to make excuses for what is bad or to deny credit for what is good.

If people view certain kinds of explanation as blame, and if victim blaming is always morally wrong, then applying these explanations to people seen as victims will be morally wrong as well. So sociologists might avoid explanations in their own work that appear to blame victims, and they might condemn such explanations when they see them in the work of others.

Felson calls this approach to evaluating theory *blame analysis*, which he says inhibits scientific analysis by requiring different kinds of theories depending on whose characteristics we are explaining and whether we see those characteristics as good or bad. For example, in explaining differences in economic success, sociologists might point to more proximate cultural factors, explaining people's wealth or poverty with their values, beliefs, and habits. Or they might point to more distal structural factors, such as economic cycles or access to good schools. There is no reason in advance to suppose that either of these is the sole cause of wealth or poverty. But to say poverty results at all from the culture of the poor appears to blame the poor for their condition, so cultural explanations are less acceptable, particularly in explaining racial or ethnic differences.[1] Even pointing to culture as an intervening variable—one that is itself caused by external forces like racial discrimination—is suspect. On the other hand, it is more acceptable to use culture to explain the dominant group's discriminatory practices. Doing so might be preferable, even, as a kind of "offensive strategy" of blaming oppressors rather than a "defensive strategy" of avoiding blaming victims (Felson 1991:12).

Blame analysis also affects the explanation of crime. Sociologists often see criminals as victims, at least in part, led to crime by a lack of opportunities or other social factors. But when sociologists focus on crimes such as rape or spousal abuse, structural explanations that seem to mitigate blame are less popular. Since the targets of these crimes are normally women, the criminal deserves the blame. We have seen that explaining rape on college campuses by pointing to rape culture is not only acceptable but that it is taboo to do otherwise. As Felson points out, sociologists also respond to the notion of *victim precipitation* differently depending on the identities of the victims. Victim precipitation is the idea that the victim's initial violence toward the killer contributed to the occurrence of the crime, and while it might be fine to say that the killing of husbands by their wives were victim-precipitated killings—responses to spousal abuse, for example—it is more taboo to say this about the killing of wives by husbands (Felson 1991:16).

Blame analysis might be inadvertent, a result of bias, but as Felson points out, "many sociologists openly acknowledge that they are rejecting certain theories because they blame the victim" (1991:10). Felson also points out that blame analysis affects scholarship regardless of the author's motivation. Work that assigns a causal role to victim groups is less likely to make it through the review process, so scholars "understand that they had better take into account issues of blame if they want to see their work in print" (Felson 1991:10).

To the extent that blame analysis successfully shapes scholarship, sociology becomes less about understanding the workings of the social world and more about presenting a morality tale of oppressors and victims.

---

[1] Such explanations also imply that the wealthy achieve their status, at least in part, from their values, beliefs, and habits. This is seen as giving them credit for their success, and as morally justifying inequality.

Explanation becomes a tool for assigning moral responsibility, and it is easy to know who receives blame and who receives praise. The concern for victims extends beyond the analysis of theory, too, sometimes leading to the truncation of data that fail to fit the proper narrative of victimhood (Martin 2016:188–121). For example, sociologists have come to use the term *white privilege* to refer to all the day-to-day advantages that whites in the modern United States have over other groups. As sociologist Chris Martin points out, the fact that on average blacks have lower incomes than whites typically serves as an example of white privilege, but Asians actually have higher average incomes than whites. This is an "inconvenient fact" for the narrative of white privilege, but not the only one: "Blacks (and Asians) have better mental health than Whites," "Hispanics have better physical health and lower mortality," and "Asians have a higher average educational level" (Martin 2016:122). Those who discuss white privilege seldom give any caveats. The implication is that whites "have it better on *every* sociological dimension" relative to every other group (Martin 2016:121). They do not, but facts that would complicate things are simply ignored.

Examples abound of sociologists' moral concerns leading them to do bad social science or even to abandon social science altogether. Bad social science might result from systematic bias, but to embrace blame analysis as a way of evaluating theory or to transform sociology into advocacy for the oppressed is to do something else entirely. Many sociologists have done just that, abandoning science in pursuit of social justice. Often they have become propagandists of victimhood culture.

THE PROMISE OF SOCIOLOGY

Sociology began as something new: a science of social life. The Enlightenment had exalted reason over faith, progress over tradition, and the individual over community. Then came the violence of the revolution in France and the upheavals of industrialism in England, to which conservative intellectuals such as Edmund Burke, Louis de Bonald, and Joseph de Maistre reacted by articulating a defense of the old values and the old social order. For them societies could not just suddenly be made anew and designed according to reason. Nor are societies just collections of autonomous individuals. Rather, individuals belong to families and other communities that socialize individuals and mediate their experience with the larger world. Within those communities people receive and follow the traditions that have been passed down. They perform rites and worship gods together. And they obey authority. Tradition, authority, community, and the sacred are not forms of social oppression individuals need to be liberated from. They hold societies together and give meaning to people's lives, the conservatives said, and in abandoning or denigrating them, Enlightenment thought had led to alienation, disorder, and a host of other failures.

Sociology followed these political and economic tumults, and it arose amid the concern and debates over them. The approach was unusual, though, in that advocates of the new discipline drew heavily from both Enlightenment and counter-Enlightenment ideas (Hadden 1997:Chap. 1; Nisbet 1966:Chap. 1).

Sociology and the Enlightenment

Sociology was an Enlightenment project. The early sociologists embraced liberal epistemology, rejecting authority and revelation and instead relying on reason and observation to understand the social world. As a science, sociology was not to be simply a continuation of centuries of humanistic social thought. For Auguste Comte, who coined the term *sociology*, human society had already moved through two stages of development, the *theological* and the *metaphysical* stages, and was now entering the *positive* stage, where knowledge would come from science rather than religion or philosophy. In this stage sociology would be the "Queen of the Sciences." Sociologists would identify social regularities—the laws of social life—and their discoveries would aid in the design of a better society.

Where sociologists broke with Enlightenment thought was in rejecting its individualism. Like the conservatives, they believed liberalism had erred in ignoring the reality of social entities. Comte even looked to medieval society for a model of social order. But where conservatives might, for example, recognize the importance of the Church in medieval society and seek to return it to its position of authority, Comte wanted a new "religion of humanity," complete with feast days, sacraments, and a priesthood of sociologists. Other sociologists did not create new religions, but they too accepted some of the conservative critiques of Enlightenment thought and had an interest in the collective parts of society. Emile Durkheim rejected the Enlightenment conception of society as a contract between individuals, as if individuals had simply decided to form society. He argued that no contract is even possible except among people who already have pre-existing social ties that enable them to trust one another to honor the contract. Durkheim was interested in what produced these ties that held societies together—what produced social solidarity. Studying primitive societies led him to examine the sacred and to observe how a group's notions of sacredness, and the social rituals that mark the sacred, lead to collective feelings that bind people together.

Religion, the sacred, social solidarity—these were the concerns of the counter-Enlightenment thinkers. So were concepts like authority and status that Max Weber later explored. That early sociological thought had affinities with conservatism did not mean sociologists shared the same political goals as the conservatives—most did not—but it did mean they often agreed with the conservatives on what were the important components of society. Sociologist Robert Nisbet called this the "paradox of sociology": that despite the liberal "political and scientific values of its principal figures ... its essential concepts and its implicit perspectives place it much closer ... to philosophical conservatism" (1966:17). Or as sociologist Richard Hadden put it, "while sociology acquires much of its rationalist approach to society from liberal thought, it had to rely on the conservative tradition for its subject matter, including society, community, tradition, and authority, in short, collective matters" (1997:24).

As the science of social life, then, sociology had promise. If previously those who did science had no interest in social life, while those concerned with social life did not examine it scientifically, then the new discipline had the potential for discoveries that would challenge long-held beliefs and perhaps aid in the design of better societies. To some extent sociology had overpromised, though. Certainly Comte had. Sociologists were never going to become the High Priests of Humanity; the sciences were never going to replace religion and philosophy as sources of meaning.[2] Sociology can be of use to social reformers, but its use is limited.

---

[2] Comte's view of sociology is idiosyncratic, but it is not hard, even now, to find fairly grandiose claims about sociology's potential in helping to bring about a better society. Earl Babbie, for example, says that because of potential problems such as nuclear war and over-population, "there is a more pressing need for sociological insights today than at any time in history" (1994:1).

Value-Free Sociology

One reason sociology is of limited use to social reformers is that as a science sociology is value-free. Policymaking is controversial in part because people disagree about morality. They disagree about what is good for society and about how to balance competing goods. But as Max Weber (1958) and a number of other sociologists (e.g., Babbie 1994; Berger 1963; Black 2013) have made clear, sociology cannot adjudicate moral disputes. To understand why, consider how factual statements differ from value judgments. Factual statements (also called *empirical claims* or *"is" statements*) describe something. They are statements about an observable aspect of reality. Value judgments (also called *normative claims* or *"ought" statements*) evaluate something, whether by condemning or praising it. They are statements about what is right or wrong, good or bad, or in some way desirable or undesirable. These are different kinds of statements, so distinct, in fact, that factual statements cannot ever lead logically to value judgments. This is known as "Hume's law," or "Hume's guillotine," after eighteenth-century philosopher David Hume (2000:302), who showed that anyone claiming to have derived a value judgment from a fact was making an illogical leap.

It should be easy to see why Hume was right about facts and values, and why, accordingly, Weber was right about sociology. For example, to say, as Durkheim did, that low social integration leads to high rates of suicide is to make a factual statement. Durkheim's theory points to two observable aspects of reality, the level of social integration and the rate of suicide in a society, and it posits a relationship between the two. To say that suicide is immoral, though, that people should not commit suicide, is to make a value judgment. The first statement is a sociological statement; the second is not. The first can be tested; the second cannot be (Popper 1963, 2002). And the second statement cannot be derived from the first. Durkheim's theory of suicide tells us nothing on its own about the morality of suicide. Nor can any other theory or factual statement tell us anything about whether we should or should not do something.

Sociology involves describing and explaining the social world, not evaluating it. This is what it means to say sociology is value-free. It does not mean, as some critics of value-free sociology have supposed, that sociologists are not influenced by their values, that they do not use their values in determining what to study and how to study it, or that sociology has no human significance (Black 2013; Campbell 2014). It just means value judgments are not sociology. It means sociology cannot answer what Weber considered the most important question of all: "What shall we do and how shall we live?" (1958:143). Given this limitation, Weber asked, what is the value of sociology? Those who have been drawn to sociology out of their desire for social change might wonder whether a value-free sociology has any value at all, but Weber concludes that it does. The value of sociology is not in answering moral questions but in providing clarity in moral decision making (Weber 1958:151).

To see how this might be so, consider an exchange from the debates between US presidential candidates George W. Bush and Albert Gore in 2000. On being asked whether they believed the death penalty deters crime, Bush and Gore both said yes, and Bush went on to say, "I do, that's the only reason to be for it. I don't think you should support the death penalty to seek revenge.... I think the reason to support the death penalty is because it saves other people's lives" (quoted in Campbell 2014:445, n. 21). Whether or not the death penalty deters crime is a factual matter and a proper subject for sociological investigation and theorizing. And because it is a factual matter, the answer to that question does not in itself have any bearing on the question of whether the death penalty should be abolished. If a death penalty supporter believes in executing murderers simply as retribution for their crime, or if a death penalty opponent is against all killing of unarmed, unresisting people, the deterrent effect of the death penalty is irrelevant in any debate between them.[3] In his debate answer, though, Bush made clear that he believed the only reason to support the death penalty was to save lives. As long as this, or something like it, is one's moral position on the death penalty, then, it *is* relevant whether or not the death penalty is a deterrent. Presumably people holding this view would change their position if they came to believe that they had been wrong about the facts. In this case theories of deterrence and studies of the deterrent effects of punishment become germane to the moral debate and to the policy questions. Sociology does not have any moral significance on its own, but when someone's moral position is that a behavior is appropriate only under certain conditions, sociology can help to determine when those conditions are present.

---

[3] This is not simply hypothetical; support or opposition to the death penalty may have no connection to one's view of its deterrent effect. Economist Naci Mohan, for example, is personally opposed to the death penalty, but he believes his own research shows that each execution saves five lives (Liptak 2007).

Sociological Technology

Sociology can help to clarify moral debates because it can help to identify the likely consequences of certain policies. This is also what is involved in another of sociology's uses for social reformers: Just as knowledge of the physical world enables the development of technology that allows for all sorts of marvels, from cell phones to space flights, knowledge of the social world can enable the development of sociological technology. Would-be legal reformers, for example, could use Donald Black's theory of law to reduce what they see as injustices in the legal system. Among other things, Black's theory predicts that crimes against high-status victims will be punished more severely than crimes against low-status victims. Prosecutors are more likely to pursue cases against the killers of wealthy victims, juries are more likely to convict them, and judges are more likely to give them stiff sentences. But social information has to be present in order to be consequential—legal actors cannot treat people differently based on their status if they do not know what their status is. Those who see it as unjust to treat offenders differently based on the status of their victims, then, might look for ways to make sure decision makers at various stages of the legal process do not have access to certain kinds of social information (Black 1989; see also Phillips 2008).

This is just one example of how people might use sociology to achieve their moral aims, but any sociological technology has its limits. This is in part just because, again, the implementation of policy involves value judgments sociology cannot answer. In this case even if it is clear that a given policy would reduce status-based discrimination, and even if people agree that reducing such discrimination would be desirable, the policy would likely also have effects people see as undesirable. And how to make moral tradeoffs, to balance competing goods, is a matter for moral rather than sociological reasoning.

Another limitation is that the sociological knowledge we use to develop any policy is likely to be imperfect. To go back to our earlier example, it is a sociological question whether the death penalty deters murder. Leading criminologists overwhelmingly believe the evidence shows that it does not, but even so the evidence is somewhat mixed (Liptak 2007; Radelet and Lacock 2009; Tittle 2004:1641). Sociologist Charles Tittle points out that almost always in matters pertaining to public controversies, "there is conflicting evidence," which is "not surprising given that research is limited, and our data are always incomplete, error prone, and accepted as supporting an argument if it simply shows something 'better than chance'" (2004:1641). Any policy might thus fail to have the consequences we expect, but even if it does, it might also have other, unintended consequences, perhaps undesirable ones, which due to our imperfect knowledge we could not foresee (Merton 1936).

Too often sociologists have not properly accounted for sociology's inherent limitations. At present they commonly identify sociology with the pursuit of social justice, with little understanding of what this means. The failure to make clear the distinction between facts and values, between science and morality, between sociology and social justice, has marred the discipline's integrity. But the promise of sociology, properly understood, is as it always has been. A science of social life cannot answer every question we might ask, not even the most important ones, but better knowledge of societies can help us reform them. The pursuit of social justice is not sociology, but those pursuing social justice should find sociology indispensable in making progress toward their goals.

The Promise of Social Justice

If you have spent any time at all on a college campus lately, you have probably heard the term *social justice*. It is everywhere. The University of Oklahoma has a "Center for Social Justice." Case Western Reserve University has a "Social Justice Institute." The University of Wyoming has a "Social Justice Research Center." The University of Arizona and Northeastern University each have a "Social Justice Resource Center." The University of Tennessee has a "Center for the Study of Social Justice." Georgetown University has a "Center for Social Justice Research, Teaching, and Service." The University of Southern Indiana has a "Center for Social Justice Education." The University of Toronto has a "Department of Social Justice Education." Occidental University has a "Department of Critical Theory and Social Justice." Saint Louis University has a "College for Public Health and Social Justice."

A number of schools offer students undergraduate or even graduate degrees in social justice. Miami University has a major in "social justice studies." Ohio Wesleyan University has a major in "social justice." The University of San Francisco has a major in "performing arts and social justice." Delta State University has a major in "social justice and criminology." Northland College has a major in "sociology and social justice." Roosevelt University has a major in "social justice studies." Kean University has an MA in "sociology and social justice." Others, such as Coastal Carolina University, the University of Portland and the University of Colorado Denver have minors in "social justice," and Brandeis University has a minor in "social justice and social policy." Some sociology departments offer their majors various kinds of concentrations in social justice. Sociology students at the University of Montana and the University of South Florida, for example, have an option to concentrate in "inequality and social justice," and at California State University, Northridge they can concentrate in "social welfare and social justice."

Clearly social justice activism has institutional support in sociology departments and elsewhere, and the institutionalization of the concept keeps expanding. The University of California, Los Angeles has "social justice advocates" who hold workshops on social justice (Zhen 2017). Recently the University of Arizona announced plans to hire students as "social justice advocates," who would report "bias incidents" to the administration, though they put the idea on hold in response to claims they were creating speech police (Fischer 2017). And at Case Western University, faculty can apply for up to $10,000 for help with social justice related research, and up to $2500 for help in redesigning their courses so that they more effectively promote social justice. The grants come from the university's Social Justice Institute, which also has support available for students doing social justice research—up to $2500 for undergraduate students and $3500 for graduate students (Airaksinen 2017).

Social justice is important to the moral lives of sociologists and of university students, faculty, and administrators more broadly. In these communities social justice seems to be the premier virtue, perhaps the only virtue to receive any attention. But what does it mean? The term is no doubt unfamiliar to many outsiders. Though social justice is not a new concept, it is not an ancient one in the way that virtues such as honesty, bravery, and kindness are. And it is surprisingly hard to find out what people mean by it, and what exactly makes *social* justice different from ordinary justice. In the words of theologian David Hollenbach, "Social justice is a much used but rarely defined term" (2001:201). Few of the various university centers and departments of social justice make any attempt to define it.[4] Even books and treatises about social justice may fail

---

[4] Those that do define social justice (or purport to) just make things more confusing. The website for the University of Wyoming's Social Justice Research Center has a 169 word paragraph under the heading "What is social justice," but while this tells what social justice

to do so (Novak 2000). The economist Friedrich Hayek once said he had searched "to discover the meaning of what is called 'social justice' ... for more than 10 years" and that he had "failed in this endeavor." He concluded that the concept was "an empty formula, conventionally used to assert that a particular claim is justified without giving any reason" (Hayek 1979:3). He is correct that it is hard to see the value of a virtue when those seeking to impose it cannot clearly or consistently define it, or when they cannot define it at all. But we think some iterations of the concept can have value. Certainly some are clearer than others.

Though moral philosophers, sociologists, politicians, activists, and others have adopted the idea of social justice, its origins are in nineteenth-century Catholic social thought. One of the more succinct definitions comes from the Catechism of the Catholic Church: "Society ensures social justice when it provides the conditions that allow associations or individuals to obtain what is their due, according to their nature and vocation. Social justice is linked to the common good and to the exercise of authority" (Catholic Church 1994:521).[5] This leaves much unanswered. What is due to associations or individuals might not be obvious, and it is not part of the concept of social justice itself. But the idea is that laws, policies, and social institutions—not just individual behaviors—are part of the moral sphere. The organization of society might contribute to fairness and to human flourishing or it may not, for example, or do so in some ways and not others. Those pursuing social justice might evaluate societies accordingly and perhaps seek to improve them.

Social justice is not a comprehensive ethical system, much less a comprehensive political ideology. To evaluate institutions on how well they

---

grew out of ("the history of the Civil Rights Movement"), what it draws on ("decades of work in Anti-Racist, Black and Ethnic Studies, and Women's Studies"), what it utilizes ("a vocabulary and framework that considers the dominant or targeted social group identities of participants within an analysis of social hierarchies"), and so on, there is nothing about what it is (University of Wyoming 2017).

[5] The nineteenth-century English philosopher John Stuart Mill had a similar conception of social justice as having to do with organizing society so that, to the extent possible, people are given their due. "If it is a duty," he wrote, "to do to each according to his deserts, returning good for good, as well as repressing evil by evil, it necessarily follows that we should treat all equally well (when no higher duty forbids) who have deserved equally well of *us*, and that society should treat all equally well who have deserved equally well of *it*... This is the highest abstract standard of social and distributive justice, toward which all institutions and the efforts of all virtuous citizens should be made in the utmost possible degree to converge" (Mill 1957:76).

create conditions to give people their due, or to achieve the common good, requires more specific notions of fairness and goodness, as well as ideas about moral tradeoffs—how to balance competing moral goods. It also requires an understanding of how institutions do in fact work—knowledge of what results existing arrangements actually produce, and what the results of other arrangements would be. This is why sociology and other social sciences should be indispensable to those seeking social justice. Sociology cannot tell us what the moral aims of a society should be, but it can help us in figuring out what social arrangements will achieve them.

Sociologist Carl Bankston points out that social justice tends to be "viewed primarily as a matter of redistributing goods and services to improve the situations of the disadvantaged" (2010:165). One way social justice differs from other notions of justice is that those who see inequality as morally problematic may do so even it does not result from individual acts of injustice such as theft or fraud. Still, those who agree that the current system produces unjust levels of inequality that should be reduced through redistribution would have no way of knowing how to proceed without theory or data to compare economic systems or to gauge the effects of various redistributionist policies.

Police violence, too, is often considered to be a social justice issue. It makes sense to think of it this way even though people tend to conflate social injustice with ordinary injustice when discussing it. This conflation occurs when people examine and debate whether or not a particular case of a homicide by the police was justified, and assume that if it was not justified then it is evidence of systematic injustice, but if it was justified it has no moral relevance. But that is not really the logic of social justice. Even a just homicide—one where people agree the police officer acted appropriately at the moment of the shooting—might still be evidence of social injustice if it is part of an undesirable pattern of killing that would not occur under another set of possible social conditions.[6] Sociologist and former police officer Peter Moskos (2016) does this kind of analysis in pointing to the differences in the rates of killing by police in different parts of the United States. He says focusing so much on individual cases avoids

---

[6] Conversely, even an unjust homicide—where the police have committed a crime—might be only an act of individual injustice, rather than social injustice, if organizing society so that such events never happened were either impossible or would produce outcomes that would be seen as a greater injustice.

the question of what is "an acceptable level of police-involved shooting" and that to avoid that question, or to answer "zero," means "you're not a productive part of the solution." He points instead to patterns such as the fact that "people in Oklahoma City are *20 times* as likely as people in New York City to be shot and killed by police." In the state of Oklahoma they are 12 times more likely (Moskos 2016). Moskos says he assumes that most of the extra killings in Oklahoma are legally justifiable—in the sense that the officer responded reasonably to the situation—but that a large percent of them are not necessary, in the sense that better policing practices could prevent these situations from arising in the first place. Reducing Oklahoma's rate to the national average would mean 14 fewer people each year would be killed by the police, something Moskos says is doable and good: "It's good for the people not to get shot. And it's good for social and racial justice." Finding out why discrepancies such as these exist— Moskos thinks they have to do with differences in police training—could help to save lives, "yet nobody seems to notice or care" (Moskos 2016).

No one seems to notice or care because however promising the idea of social justice might be in providing a moral framework for evaluating societal institutions, in practice those who use the term tend to use it as a shorthand for leftwing politics, or increasingly, as a label for the agenda arising from the extreme version of victimhood culture found among campus activists. They seldom make the kinds of empirical comparisons or employ the kind of moral nuance Moskos does.

Social Justice and Victimhood Culture

Whatever else social justice might mean, it increasingly refers to the various manifestations of victimhood we have described here: condemnations of microaggressions and other new offenses, calls for trigger warnings and safe spaces, and attempts to silence or punish dissidents. Journalist Tanzina Vega, writing in *The New York Times*, calls microaggression the "social justice word du jour," and *Atlantic* writer Simba Runyowa says it is part of the "lexicon of social justice" (Vega 2014; Runyowa 2015). Accordingly, campus social justice efforts often involve promoting the microaggression program. At the University of Washington-Bothell, librarians undergo social justice training, which involves a class on microaggressions and a workshop on the concept of privilege (Cheong 2017). At the University of Central Florida, an emergency "Social Justice Week" held in response to Donald Trump's election to the US presidency featured workshops on microaggression (Mikelionis 2017). And California State University, Long Beach has a "Social Justice Workshop" series for faculty and students that includes classes examining microaggressions (Manly 2016).

The idea of safe spaces is another component of victimhood culture, and as we saw in Chap. 3, this sometimes leads to university policies enabling the residential segregation of official victim groups. This also goes by the name of social justice, as at the University of Colorado, where one dorm was transformed into a "Social Justice Living Environment." With the transformation, part of the dorm was to be set aside for "black-identified students and their allies" and another part for "LGBTQIA students and their allies" (Gockowski 2017). The social justice infrastructure not only props up victimhood culture, but it sometimes also displays intolerance of any disagreement about the meaning of social justice. So at the University of Minnesota, Justine Schwarz, a community adviser with the Housing and Residential Life department, was not rehired after receiving a performance review that found she had not "demonstrated a commitment to social justice and promotion to residents." Her error was apparently in playing "devil's advocate" when "discussions about diversity or social justice took place" (Foley 2017).

Given how central the concept of social justice is to the morality of those promoting victimhood culture, we initially considered calling it *social justice culture* instead. But *victimhood culture* works better in comparison with honor and dignity cultures, since victimhood is a kind of status like honor and dignity. And like other kinds of status, it varies considerably in its importance, allowing us to observe different degrees of it in a variety of contexts. Still, *social justice culture* works as an alternative, and though it fails to take into account conceptions of social justice that have little to do with victimhood, it does have the advantage of corresponding more closely with the way the culture's adherents describe themselves. It even corresponds with the way the culture's harshest critics describe them, since *Social Justice Warriors* (or *SJWs*) has become a pejorative term for campus activists and others who embrace the morality of victimhood (Ohlheiser 2015). The activists' vision of social justice is really just one of many, but with both sides in the clash of victimhood and dignity using the term to refer to that vision, social justice increasingly just means that and nothing else.

SOCIOLOGY AND SOCIAL JUSTICE

Sociology and social justice each have potential only when operating within their limits. The promise that a science of social life could aid social justice efforts was reasonable, but when social justice becomes an ideology unmoored from empirical reality, it needs no science.[7] And when sociology becomes nothing more than the pursuit of social justice, it is no longer science anyway; it no longer has any knowledge to provide reformers. The line between sociology and social justice has long been blurred, so as social justice has become identified with victimhood culture, so has sociology. Given the diversity of the field, the extent of this varies. Still, a concern for victims permeates the field, leading to blame analysis and other kinds of bias even among the more scientific sociologists. At the extreme, some sociology is nothing more than political ideology, perhaps indistinguishable from that of the most strident campus activists. A number of factors enable this: sociologists' shared moral understandings, the widespread rejection of the idea of value-free sociology, the prominence of Marxist and Marxist-inspired theories, and the recent enthusiasm for public sociology.

Sociology's "Sacred Project"

Sociologists as a group have long had a shared morality that sociologist Christian Smith (2014) calls a "sacred project." Smith uses *sacred* in the sense that Durkheim did, as identifying something that is set apart from the ordinary. The term has a religious connotation, since religious rituals, symbols, and relics are sacred, but sacredness need not involve any notion of the supernatural. The flag of a nation, the slogan of a political movement, the clothing of a dead celebrity, and many other things might be sacred. For most American sociologists, sociology has a purpose. Sociology is for them a kind of moral enterprise, one they imbue with sacredness. According to Smith they see the discipline as "at heart committed to the visionary project of *realizing the emancipation, equality, and moral affirmation of all human beings as autonomous, self-directing, individual agents*

---

[7] Campus activists and administrators seem uninterested in research showing that the assumptions of the microaggression program are baseless (Lilienfeld 2017), just as they seem uninterested in analyses of whether campus diversity programs achieve their stated goals (Haidt and Jussim 2016). They might even take offense at any empirical work that calls into question the activists' claims.

(who should be) out to live their lives as they personally so desire, by construct-ing their own favored identities, entering and exiting relationships as they choose, and equally enjoying the gratification of experiential, material, and bodily pleasures" (2014:7–8). Smith goes on to explain that sociology's sacred project is "about disrupting the status quo." It seeks dramatic change, change that is "systemic, institutional, and sometime radical.... So when the new world envisioned by this spiritual project is finally realized, it will be very different from the present world" (Smith 2014:12). This will be a world where people are "set free from everything external that oppresses, constrains, and dehumanizes them, whether that takes the form of ignorance, racism, poverty, patriarchy, heterosexism, or any other dis-crimination or obstruction, perhaps including the institutions of marriage and religion" (Smith 2014:13). And sociologists have to take the lead in pushing for this new world. Ordinary people and established institutions for the most part "do not 'get it'.... So those who *do* 'get it'—who have a 'sociological imagination'—must (somehow) compel the state to socially structure equality, freedom, and justice for all, especially those against whom mainstream society would discriminate" (Smith 2014:13).

This seems quite a task for a science of social life, but Smith says that if sociology's practitioners had not had this kind of shared morality, it might not have even survived as a discipline. Even now the sacred project pro-vides the impetus for most of the work sociologists do and provides a source of solidarity for an otherwise very divided field. Smith's analysis calls to mind Jonathan Haidt's dictum that "morality binds and blinds" (2012:191). Sociology's sacred project might be the only thing that binds its practitioners together, but it also keeps them from seeing clearly. Worse, it can turn them into something resembling the most zealous religious communities, quick to panic over minor or imaginary threats and to pun-ish the heretics and witches among them.

Smith tells of an "Author Meets Critics" session at the 2002 meeting of the American Sociological Association. The book under discussion drew from decades of research to make an argument for the benefits of mar-riage, and one of the critics, denouncing the author for her heresy, exclaimed, "You have betrayed us!" (quoted in Smith 2014:90). In another case, sociologist Mark Regnerus published an article in the jour-nal *Social Science Review* that presented a study's findings "that adult chil-dren of parents who had had one or more same-sex romantic relationships fared significantly worse as adults on many emotional and material mea-sures than their adult peers who were raised in intact, biological family"

(Smith 2014:102). The study had flaws, to be sure, as had previous studies that had found no such effects. But the attacks directed toward Regnerus's study, and toward Regnerus personally, seem mostly due to the fact that the critics disliked the study's findings. Using the kind of blame analysis we discussed earlier, these critics viewed the study as unsupportive of the cause of gay marriage. Smith describes what followed as "a genuine, modern-day academic Inquisition and political witch trial" (2014:107). The critics attacked the journal, which ended up investigating the publication of the article. They made allegations of scientific misconduct to Regnerus's university. Some, such as Darren Sherkat, Professor of Sociology at Southern Illinois University, insulted Regnerus and mocked his religious beliefs. In a blog post taking note of Regnerus's participation at a meeting of the Association of Christians Teaching Sociology, Sherkat complains that "sociology has been a closet full of Christians teaching sociology since before Karl Marx kicked the bucket," but at least most of them "taught at the Christianist Bible Colleges." Later "devious christianists decided to infiltrate higher education and destroy it from within," and "rich christianists … donated money to lure the best and the brightest christianist children to college and grandcollege." He speculates that Regnerus "will be telling his fans about his bullshit study, where he got nearly a million dollars from his boyfriend Bradley Wilcox's foundation to prove that gays and lesbians make their children homos by molesting them and cause all manner of negative outcomes, too" (Sherkat 2013).

These are not in line with ordinary reactions to flawed research. Regnerus in particular seems to have been the target of a kind of moral panic. Smith gives more examples, and it is not hard to think of others. Sociologist Randall Collins tells of a small-scale moral panic among sociologists that occurred in 2011 after right-wing television commentator Glenn Beck began criticizing Frances Fox Piven, an activist sociologist and former president of the American Sociological Association. Based on the idea that Beck's criticisms were leading to death threats and putting Piven in danger, sociologists sent messages through various email listservs to raise awareness of the conflict and to call for action. "The tone of the messages," according to Collins, "was one of desperate urgency for action…. . The action being demanded was that we should join in signing a petition supporting our poverty-activist sociologist and condemning her opponents, and that the ASA [the American Sociological Association] should take the lead" (2012:7). In response the officers of the ASA (including Randall Collins) quickly put out a statement condemning Beck, but Collins says there had never been any real likelihood of violence: Piven "had received these death threats sporadically over the past year, and there was no imminent danger. As a general pattern ... overt death threats are a disruptive tactic and are virtually never carried out; real assassination attempts do not announce themselves in advance" (Collins 2012:6).[8]

The sacred project can encourage distortions, double standards, and hysteria. Moral homogeneity leads sociologists to exaggerate threats from perceived common enemies and to unite to confront them. Whether it is Mark Regnerus from within or Glenn Beck from without, those who work against the sacred project are wrong, evil, and dangerous. The errors of those who work on behalf of the sacred project are less noticeable and more tolerable. So when sociologist Lenore Weitzman found that men's standard of living increased drastically after divorce, while women's standard of living declined even more drastically, she received praise, won awards, and influenced legislation. Though no one could replicate these findings, Smith says they "provided a grand-slam hit for sociology's spiritual project that was too wonderful to be doubted or criticized" (2014:100). Eventually an analysis of Weitzman's data—which she long tried to prevent—showed the reported findings to be completely wrong. Weitzman blamed it on an error by a graduate student who had helped with the project. Seemingly unaffected, Weitzman has had a successful career since then. And 15 years after the exposure of the error, a major introductory sociology textbook was still citing the original findings (Smith 2014:100).

---

[8] The ASA officers' statement on the matter takes a different view. Given Collins's involvement, we found this puzzling, even prior to Collins's later remarks, since the statement seemed at odds with the theory presented in Collins's (2008) book on violence. It seemed to endorse the very kind of view (that people are easily driven to violence by heated rhetoric and the like) that Collins opposes in the book. While the ASA statement does have some caveats (e.g., "It is true that death threats are generally only a form of extremist rhetoric"), the thrust of it is to blame Glenn Beck for the death threats and thus to blame him for putting Piven in danger. The ASA officers say that "an overheated emotional atmosphere" can lead "deranged individuals ... to real violence against those targeted by demoguery" (Collins et al. 2011). They even claim that the shooting of US Representative Gabrielle Giffords was an example of "how abundant, polarizing rhetoric by political leaders and commenters can spur mass murder" (Collins et al. 2011). In fact, though, Jared Loughner, who targeted Giffords as part of a mass shooting in which he killed six others, was angry with Giffords because she had failed several years earlier to adequately answer a question he put to her: "What is government if words have no meaning?" Loughner was mentally ill and believed the government was controlling grammar (Douthat 2017). He was not motivated by political rhetoric.

Smith imagines the reaction to Weitzman from fellow sociologists going something like this: "She meant well, it seems, and she helped to advance the sacred project" (2014:101). This is likely the attitude within the field to all sorts of misbehavior. Most sociologists are not radical activists, but they see their work as serving the same basic cause as those who are. Most do not use their work or their classes simply to promote their political views, but still they tolerate or even praise those who do, probably with the idea that the activists mean well and are advancing the project in their own way, even if they are perhaps a little too overt about it.

The Rejection of Value-Free Sociology

Another thing that opens the door to overtly ideological sociology is the fact that sociologists overwhelmingly tend to reject the idea of value-free sociology. As we discussed earlier, factual statements and value judgments are different kinds of statements, and sociology cannot answer value questions. This is an inherent limit of sociology—and all sciences—and to ignore it weakens sociology by pretending it is something it is not and directing it toward tasks it can never accomplish. For decades, though, many sociologists have rejected Weber's reasoning, often while displaying "almost inconceivable misunderstanding[s]" about what value-free sociology means (Weber 1949:11; see also Black 2013). Alvin Gouldner (1962) called value-free sociology a myth, nonexistent like the Minotaur. Howard Becker said we cannot do sociology without taking sides, and the only question is "Whose side are we on?" (1967:239). David Gray said value-free sociology was "a doctrine of hypocrisy and irresponsibility" (1968:176). More recently, in the journal *Society*, a number of contributors to a symposium on "Facts, Values, and Social Science" argued against value-free sociology. Philip Gorski (2013), in the symposium's lead article, calls the divide between facts and values "leaky," and he says sociologists can use Aristotelian ethics to advance human flourishing. Christian Smith (2013) was another contributor, and he likewise opposes value-free sociology. His problem with sociology is not that sociologists are seeking to implement a sacred project, but that they fail to allow room for alternative sacred projects such as his own.[9]

Smith is right that sociology would benefit from more moral diversity. If more sociologists adopted Gorski's Aristotelianism or Smith's critical

---

[9] For critical commentary on the symposium, see Campbell 2014 and Fein 2014.

realist personalism (see Smith 2014:199–204) instead of the moral project currently dominant, it would go some way toward solving the problems arising from moral homogeneity. But again, while we might use sociology to assess how well we are achieving certain values, sociology cannot determine which values we should adopt. The critics have it backward. It is evaluative sociology that is impossible; it is a sociological morality that is as mythical as the Minotaur (Black 2013; Campbell 2014). Value-free sociology is just sociology—the science of social life. Gorski suggests opening the door more widely to allow value judgments, but value judgments would still be value judgments, not descriptions or explanations of the social world. What is strange, though, is his implication that the door is currently closed. Far from being restrained in making value judgments, many sociologists do little else.

Conflict Theory and Victimhood Culture

Smith says sociologists' common morality—the sacred project—provides some unity to an otherwise fragmented discipline. The canon of sociological classics does, too, while also reflecting this fragmentation. Sociology is unusual among social sciences in the prominence it gives to the founders of the discipline. Both undergraduate and graduate students in sociology study classical sociological theory, which everywhere covers Emile Durkheim, Max Weber, and Karl Marx.[10] Sociologist Arthur Stinchcombe says the study of the classics serves as a ritual "to express the solidarity and common concerns of the discipline" (1982:2). But the classics can also serve as intellectual small change, or "intellectual badges." The first footnotes of a paper, for instance, generally allow the reader to know the author's perspective. By identifying with one of the classical theorists (and, in doing so, *not* identifying with the others), authors signal which sociological tradition they are working in (Stinchcombe 1982).

Durkheim, Weber, and Marx retroactively became sociology's founders as mid-twentieth century sociologists selected them from among the many names associated with sociology to represent the field's then-current intellectual strands. Talcott Parsons was a key figure in this canon-forming

---

[10] Theory textbooks and courses might also count Georg Simmel, George Herbert Mead, W.E.B. Du Bois, Harriet Martineau, and various others among the classical theorists, but Durkheim, Weber, and Marx predominate as a kind of sociological "triumvirate" or "holy trinity" (Bratton et al. 2009:3).

enterprise. Many people took his discussion in *The Structure of Social Action* of Durkheim and Weber, along with Alfred Marshall and Vilfredo Pareto, as a kind of origin story for sociology. Later another prominent sociologist, C. Wright Mills, listed Durkheim, Weber, and Marx, along with Herbert Spencer, Mannheim, and Thorstein Veblen, as classical social analysts. Others identified their own contenders, but soon the lists narrowed, at first with only Durkheim and Weber as undisputed parts of the canon. With Marx's inclusion in the 1960s, the canon took its present form (Connell 1997). This late addition resulted from the increasing popularity of leftist politics at the universities and among sociologists, and to the extent that the classical theorists serve as intellectual badges for present-day sociologists, Marx is the badge of the activists and radicals. Marx was interested in the workings of societies, but he did not consider himself a sociologist, and his conception of science was very different from that of either Durkheim or Weber. Those who argue for a more activist sociology are fond of quoting Marx's conclusion to his "Theses on Feuerbach": "The Philosophers have only interpreted the world, in various ways; the point is to change it" (quoted in Van den Berg 2014:68).

According to Marx class struggle has driven historical change, as the outcomes of these struggles have always previously led to new class systems. In capitalist societies, the owners of the means of production—the capitalists, or the bourgeoisie—dominate and exploit the non-owners—the workers, or the proletariat. The system of wage labor that defines their relationship is inherently exploitative since the capitalists profit from the workers' labor. Ultimately, Marx believed, as the proletariat became aware of their situation, they would join with one another and revolt against their rulers, putting an end to private ownership of the means of production and thus an end to class and class struggle.

Marx employed a new kind of analysis—conflict theory, which "explains human behavior as a struggle for domination" (Black 2001). Conflict theory can take various forms, but Donald Black (2001) says it usually has four assumptions: (1) that clashes of interest are inherent to social life, (2) that they have zero-sum outcomes, with one side gaining at the other's expense, (3) that over the long term elites gain at the expense of others, and (4) that only radical change can significantly reduce the domination of the elites. In Marxist theory, the clash of interests is between classes, the ruling class gains at the expense of others, and only a revolution that ends private ownership of the means of production can end class conflict. Following Marx's general framework subsequent conflict theories employed a similar kind of analysis, but with different oppressor and victim groups. For feminist theorists the groups were men and women, for critical race theorists they were whites and people of color, for queer theorists they were heterosexuals and homosexuals as well as the cisgendered and transgendered, and for world systems theorists they were core nations and periphery nations.

That certain groups dominate and exploit others is an assumption of these frameworks and the task is to analyze things in those terms. Marxist theorists do not try to determine *whether* capitalist relations are exploitative; they try to show *how* they are. Often this takes the form of showing how something that might not have seemed exploitative actually is. Marx had already done this by showing that wage labor, though often called free labor because it was voluntary, was simply the means by which the capitalists dominated the workers. Marxists later argued that aspects of liberal legal systems are also means of furthering capitalist rule. One feature of these systems is equality before the law, which would seem to benefit the disadvantaged. But Marxists say it is a way of disguising oppression by treating as equal those who are not equal. New kinds of conflict theories similarly conceptualize various features of society in terms of other kinds of oppression. Feminist law professor Catharine MacKinnon (1989), for example, argues that the equal treatment of men and women by the legal system reinforces patriarchal relations. In conflicts between men and women, the law and legal procedures, by treating men and women equally, make male dominance invisible. "No law guarantees that women will forever remain the social unequals of men," she says, but "this is not necessary, because the law guaranteeing sexual equality requires, in an unequal society, that before one can be equal legally, one must be equal socially" (MacKinnon 1989:239). Feminist theorists also sometimes make an argument about sex and rape that is similar in form to Marx's argument about wage labor. Marx said that as agreements between unequals, employment contracts are actually coercive and exploitative, and feminists might view relations between men and women similarly. Remember from Chap. 4 that Dianne Herman says it can be "very difficult in our society to differentiate rape from 'normal' heterosexual relations" (1984:45). Likewise feminist writer Andrea Dworkin said intercourse is "a means or the means of physiologically making a woman inferior, communicating to her cell by cell her own inferior status" (2007:174). MacKinnon says something similar: "Perhaps the wrong of rape has proved so difficult to define because the unquestionable starting point has been that rape is defined as distinct from intercourse, while for women it is difficult to distinguish the two under conditions of male dominance" (1989:174). Since the idea is that male dominance is pervasive, the implication is that all heterosexual behavior, voluntary or not, might be exploitative.[11]

Despite the stylistic and logical similarities, orthodox Marxism is incompatible with the other versions of conflict theory due to its historical materialism. For the Marxist it is class struggle that matters. All else, such as gender conflict or racial conflict, is a reflection of class relations. But most student activists and activist sociologists are not orthodox Marxists; nor do they adhere to any other unidimensional conflict theory. They have embraced what Patricia Hill Collins (1990) calls the "matrix of domination," where race, class, gender, and other identities all act as systems of oppression. More recently they have added the idea of *intersectionality*, meaning that sexism, racism, and other kinds of oppression cannot be studied independently (Crenshaw 1989). One has to examine oppression at the intersections—what is it like to be black and female, say, or gay and undocumented?

Most conflict theorists do not present their work as value-free or as scientific in any sense. Indeed much of it is not theory at all, if theory refers to a system of statements about the relationships between variables. What the twentieth-century sociologist George Homans (1967) said of Marxism is true of its imitators. At their best they provide orienting statements that tell us what to look for or how to look at it. An orienting statement can be important, "but it tells us little about the thing studied." It provides "an approach, not an arrival" (Homans 1967:18). The amalgam of conflict theories that constitutes the worldview of many contemporary sociologists does not explain anything; it provides an interpretation of social life. It enables people to see the world in terms of domination, to see all institutions and interactions in terms of the oppression or liberation of designated victim groups.

Those who embrace this worldview condemn the oppression they believe they have discovered and advocate an agenda to address it. The interpretive work is so closely connected to this agenda that in practice the framework acts almost exclusively as a comprehensive moral and political

---

[11] Key to such interpretations, too, is that the victims might not recognize their exploitation. Women or wage laborers might have a *false consciousness*, the idea goes, that might even lead them to believe they are benefiting from marriage or capitalist employment. One goal of activists, then, has been to raise the *awareness* or *consciousness* of some group of victims.

ideology rather than a sociological theory. It is the intellectual source behind all the moral features of victimhood culture we have discussed here. When students and other activists label awkwardness in conversation a microaggression, when they call their critics' speech violence and seek to censor it, when they call for censorship and violence against their critics' free speech, when they claim women cannot be sexist and blacks cannot be racist, outsiders to the culture might be confused by a morality they find unfamiliar and topsy-turvy. This is all the more true of expressions of extreme hostility toward whites, men, and others perceived to be privileged, as when a college professor says that an American college student killed by the North Korean government "got exactly what he deserved" because his behavior (he was accused of stealing a poster) was like that of the "young, white, rich, clueless males" she teaches (quoted in Spada 2017), or when another professor tweets, "All I Want for Christmas is White Genocide" (quoted in Mikelionis 2016), or when yet another professor posts the following on Facebook: "SERIOUSLY JUST BE QUIET. ONLY APPOINTED/APPROVED WHITES CAN SPEAK (AND ONLY WHEN SPOKEN TO)" (quoted in Zimmerman 2017).[12] However unfamiliar to outsiders, recent expressions of victimhood culture come from ideas that have been percolating in classrooms and in journals for decades, though they are sometimes crude versions of those ideas. And in sociology those ideas continue to increase in prominence.

Public Sociology and the Triumph of Victimhood Culture

Most sociologists are not conflict theorists and are not actively pushing the full-blown version of victimhood culture. But consider the position the more radical approaches have in sociology. The most recent president-elect of the American Sociological Association (ASA) is Eduardo Bonilla-Silva, a Duke professor and former member of the "Group of 88" Duke faculty who in April 2006 placed an ad thanking the protesters responding to what we now know to be false allegations of rape by Duke lacrosse players. Recall from Chap. 4 that the protesters were demanding the lacrosse players provide information about the alleged rape, and they held up signs

---

[12] One anonymous critic of our work (Friedersdorf 2015) says that what we call victimhood culture is really *empathy culture,* but as these statements indicate, a key feature of the new morality seems to be an extreme *lack* of empathy for those belonging to groups deemed privileged or oppressive.

saying things like "Castrate" and "You can't rape and run." Previously, when Bonilla-Silva was a professor at Texas A&M University, on his syllabus for his "Sociology of Minorities" class he referred to "The United States of Amerikkka" and said he would "remove the three K's from this word when the USA removes racial oppression from this country!" (quoted in Veres 2005). In his scholarly work he argues that what he calls *color-blind racism* is the dominant ideology in the United States and that it became dominant "as the mechanisms and practices for keeping blacks and other minorities 'at the bottom of the well' changed" (Bonilla-Silva 2010:2–3). He says "color-blind racism serves today as the ideological armor for a covert and institutionalized system in the post-Civil Rights era." "And the beauty of this new ideology," he says, "is that it aids in the maintenance of white privilege without fanfare." It allows whites to "enunciate positions that safeguard their racial interests without sounding 'racist'" (Bonilla-Silva 2010:3–4). Bonilla-Silva also describes the methodology of mainstream sociology as "White," and he says that when he was at the University of Michigan presenting preliminary findings of the data for his book *Racism without Racists*, he was asked "'White questions' hidden behind the cover of (White) methodology." The whiteness, he says, "seeped through the (racial) cracks in all the questions" (Bonilla-Silva and Zuberi 2008:13).

Recent ASA presidents have also included Marxist theorist Erik Olin Wright; Patricia Hill Collins, whose concept of the "matrix of domination" we mentioned earlier; Frances Fox Piven, who, as we also noted, became the subject of strident criticism from Glenn Beck and the target of death threats, presumably from some of Beck's viewers, after she made a statement that seemed to advocate leftist rioting in the United States; Joe Feagin, who co-authored a book called *Liberation Sociology* (Feagin and Vera 2001), and whose ASA presidential address, "Social Justice and Sociology: Agendas for the Twenty-First Century," called for "the discipline to fully recover and celebrate its historical roots in a sociology committed to social justice in ideals and practice" (Feagin 2001:10); and Michael Burawoy, who used his term to advocate a move in the discipline toward a "public sociology" intended "to transform the world" (Burawoy 2005:317–318). While, as sociologist Axel Van den Berg points out, "Burawoy advocates a number of quite different things under the label of public sociology," the attention given the idea had to do with his "call to constitute the discipline as a 'public that acts in the political arena' and to turn the ASA into 'a political venue unto itself'" (2014:54, 64). Some scientifically minded sociologists objected (e.g., Deflem 2005; Nielsen 2004; Tittle 2004; Turner 2005), but Burawoy's call mostly elicited "enormous enthusiasm ... from sociologists the world over" (Van den Berg 2014:68). More than two dozen journals featured symposia on public sociology, for example, and some universities began offering certificates or degrees in public sociology, while many more made it a focus of their sociology programs (Campbell 2014:448). Van den Berg suggests that public sociology's reception had to do in part with the growing impatience of "would-be world reformers" for whom "having to go through the hoops of learning rigorous quantitative and qualitative methods seems to be a useless distraction from the much more urgent business of getting on with changing the world." For them, "the call for liberation, from the president of the American Sociological Association no less, must have felt like a long awaited vindication" (Van den Berg 2014:68). Whatever the reason, as sociology abandons scientific work entirely and becomes just another moral project, it even loses any relevance it would have had for those trying to learn how to more effectively pursue social justice. Like Van den Berg, we think "it still makes sense to try to understand the world a little better before we rush off to change it" (2014:69).

BEYOND SOCIOLOGY

We have focused on our own discipline of sociology, but it is not the only discipline that cultivates victimhood culture, and even with the recent trend toward public sociology, sociology is fragmented enough that many sociologists still produce work that has little to do with the latest theoretical and activist fads. Victimhood culture on campuses is the culture of radical activists, so in general it has less of a place in less politicized disciplines. The natural sciences, mathematics, and engineering have little of it, while the social sciences and humanities have much more.[13] Within the

---

[13] The natural sciences, mathematics, and engineering are not completely immune, however. Engineering professor Donna Riley, for example, has received awards for "her work on implementing and assessing critical and feminist pedagogies in engineering classrooms" and for "her work on combining social justice work and pedagogy" (Vivian 2013). And at the University of Saskatchewan the academic governing body recently "agreed that all of the 17 colleges and schools, from dentistry to engineering, should include indigenous knowledge." One course developed in response is an "indigenous wellness" course for kinesiology students, which "includes sharing circles, oral storytelling and participation in ceremonies" (Porter 2017).

social sciences and humanities, economics has little of it, psychology much more, and sociology and anthropology more still, while many of the humanities and the various "studies" disciplines that combine social sciences and humanities are about little else.

Psychologists are among those developing the concepts of victimhood, as we have seen with Derald Wing Sue and his colleagues' work on microaggressions. This work is not in the mainstream, though, and the bigger issue in psychology is similar to what we saw with blame analysis in sociology. The tendency is to analyze things in a way that promotes a narrative of blameless victims, and this can distort research and theory. Psychology has of late had a replication crisis as it has turned out that people trying to replicate some of the most celebrated findings of recent years have been unable to do so. A number of factors led psychologists to produce and accept ideas that turned out to be false, but it seems that one of them has been a bias resulting from the acceptance of a victimhood narrative. Research on *implicit prejudice*, for example, was supposed to have shown that unconscious racism was widespread, hard to eradicate, and consequential. But psychologist Lee Jussim (2016) notes that none of the research has actually shown that any measures of implicit prejudice are associated with increased discriminatory practices. *Stereotype threat* research, previously interpreted as showing that the presence of stereotypes affects individuals' performance on tests and accounts for group differences, has also been discredited. That psychology is scientific enough to even have a replication crisis, though, distinguishes it from sociology and other more ideological fields where activist scholars are much less constrained by empirical reality.

Cultural critic Bruce Bawer tells of how what he calls the "victims' revolution" transformed the humanities so that they became "preoccupied with an evil triumvirate of isms—colonialism, imperialism, capitalism—and with a three-headed monster of victimhood: class, race, and gender oppression" (2012:12). Philosophers began "preaching that there was no such thing as objective truth," historians began "to reduce the rich drama of the human story to a series of dreary, repetitive lessons about groups, power, and oppression," and scholars of literature began to approach the works they studied as "simply fields on which to play language games and wage political battles that had little or no intrinsic connection to the works themselves" (Bawer 2012:8).

Bawer tells of a Cultural Studies Association Conference he attended in 2010, where one presenter chastised homeowners for their participation in global capitalism, another lamented that a young Vietnamese girl photographed running from a napalm attack in 1972 had grown up to lovingly embrace America and thus betray the anti-American message in the photograph. Another presenter, whose talk was called "Towards a Green Marxist Cultural Studies: Notes on Value and Human Domination over Nature," explained that she was "sort of reviving a Gramscian-style Marxism" and described global warming as "sort of, like, a crisis, in the human relationship to nature." According to Bawer these young scholars know little about any "traditional field of learning," but they have an "ideology and the jargon to go with it. And they have the arrogance of innocents who really have no clue how little they know" (2012:2).

What has also happened, as the humanities have changed their mission and embraced victimhood culture, is that new disciplines that overlap with various humanities and social sciences now specialize in one part of the victimhood framework. Women's studies, black studies, queer studies, and Chicano studies each concentrate on a victim group, as do additions and offshoots such as disability studies and fat studies, while more recent additions such as men's studies and whiteness studies concentrate on an oppressor group (Bawer 2012). The studies programs tend to be even more identified with victimhood culture than the traditional humanities and social sciences, where the new social justice agenda still has to compete with older conceptions of the disciplines. But even though not every discipline is on board, or on board fully, much of the university is now committed to a single vision of social justice, and alternative views are becoming sparse and sometimes forbidden.

*   *   *

Despite being so morally involved with the contemporary world, sociologists seem to know very little about it. This is true of related fields, too, but the practitioners of a science of social life ought to be well positioned to explain the world around them to others. But do sociologists have any expertise to share? Do sociology majors end their studies having better knowledge of the world than when they started? Sociologists seem to have understood no better than others what was happening amid the allegations of gang rape at Duke and UVA that we discussed in Chap. 4. If anything, they seem to be even more credulous than others in the face of media driven sensationalism, more prone to error and moral panic. Those who should be experts on human behavior very easily accept whole hog the wildest claims of victimhood, even in the absence of evidence, as long as those claims fall somewhere on the matrix of domination.[14] And events always seem to take them by surprise, whether it is the exposure of a false rape claim or something larger in scale like the 2016 US presidential election.

It is remarkable that Donald Trump won first the Republican nomination and then the general election despite opposition from much of the Republican party, from nearly all of its elites, from conservative publications like *National Review* and *The Weekly Standard*, from the major American newspapers, from all major news networks other than *Fox*, from the universities, and from Wall Street, Silicon Valley, and Hollywood. That Trump did so by winning over many working class voters who had previously voted for Democrats, thus winning states that he was expected to lose, and that all of this was a surprise, even a shock, to so many (including us) would seem to beg for sociological analysis. Sociologists study social movements, social media, moral conflict, culture, charisma, celebrity, and much else that should be relevant to understanding the election. Yet when the newsletter of the American Sociological Association published comments on the election from four sociologists, this was the extent of the analysis: A sociologist who teaches and researches about climate change and admits it is hard to do so "without it becoming personal and emotional" simply laments that climate change was discussed in the presidential debates for only six minutes (Beer 2016). Another discusses the "casual Islamophobia [that] was a recurring theme in Donald Trump's presidential campaign" (Kurzman 2016). Another tells about teaching her "Social Inequality" class the day after the election, when the expressions on students' faces looked like they had after the terrorist attacks of September 11, 2001. "Some students sat stoically, listening

---

[14] And their recurring blunders do not seem to alter their thinking. In late December of 2014, for example, even after news reports had already debunked the *Rolling Stone* rape story (e.g., Shapiro 2014), the University of Virginia's sociology department put out a statement, signed by most of the sociology faculty, that began, "We stand in solidarity with the survivors of sexual violence at the University of Virginia." The statement almost seemed to imply that the authors still believed the basics of the story, as it acknowledged only that *Rolling Stone* had released a statement "questioning the details of its published story" and said that "it did not change the reality that UVA and other college campuses have a problem with sexual assault" (Blumberg et al. 2014). The statement expressed no concern about the falsely accused fraternity members or about the protests, threats, and property destruction that had followed the story's publication. It provided references to articles and books about rape and about things like "hegemonic masculinity," but to none dealing with false accusations or moral panics.

and nodding," she says, "while others silently shed tears." Other students expressed concerns, such as one student who "shared that her grandfather had survived a concentration camp and wondered aloud whether or not something similar could happen again." This sociologist suggests that sociology "can counter racist and xenophobic scapegoating by providing counter-narratives around the pain marginalized communities will and are experiencing." "Now more than ever," she concludes, "our role as sociologists is to inform and participate in broader collective responses to the threats to marginalized communities and the ongoing progressive project" (Martinez 2016). And the fourth sociologist attributes the election's outcome to *masculinism*, an ideology that "justifies and naturalizes male domination," and which might have been "intensified by the gains made by marginalized groups over the past several decades" (Bridges 2016).

Faced with a world in upheaval, sociologists seem to have nothing to offer but the same old stories of victims and oppressors. Much of what passes for sociology is the proper wielding of a specialized lexicon used to classify people as one or the other and then to side with the victims. All the while activist sociologists keep telling themselves and others about how much the world needs them. If the world needs explaining, though, or even if it needs reforming, their work is mostly irrelevant.

References

Airaksinen, Toni. 2017. Case Western Reserve Offers Professors up to $10,000 to promote Social Justice. *The College Fix*, June 22. http://www.thecollegefix.com/post/33779/.

Babbie, Earl. 1994. *The Sociological Spirit*. 2nd ed. Belmont: Wadsworth Publishing Company.

Bankston, Carl L. 2010. Social Justice: Cultural Origins of a Perspective and a Theory. *The Independent Review* 15 (2): 165–178.

Bawer, Bruce. 2012. *The Victims' Revolution: The Rise of Identity Studies and the Closing of the Liberal Mind*. New York: Broadside Books.

Becker, Howard S. 1967. Whose Side Are We On? *Social Problems* 14 (3): 239–247.

Beer, Todd. 2016. Climate Change and the Election. *Footnotes* 44 (8). http://www.asanet.org/news-events/footnotes/dec-2016/features/sociologists-reflect-2016-presidential-election.

Berger, Peter L. 1963. *Invitation to Sociology: A Humanistic Perspective*. New York: Anchor Books.

Black, Donald. 1989. *Sociological Justice*. New York: Oxford University Press.

————. 2001. *Lectures in Contemporary Sociological Theory (SOC 506)*, University of Virginia.

————. 2013. On the Almost Inconceivable Misunderstandings Concerning the Subject of Value-Free Sociology. *The British Journal of Sociology* 64 (4): 763–780.

Blumberg, Rae, Sarah Corse, Elizabeth Gorman, Thomas M. Guterbock, Paul W. Kingston, Krishan Kumar, Ekaterina Makarova, Jeffrey Olick, Sabrina Pendergrass, Simone Polillo, Andrea Press, Allison Pugh, Rachel Rinaldo, Josipa Roksa, Adam Slez, Miranda Waggoner, and W. Bradford Wilcox. 2014. *Sociology Departmental Statement on Sexual Violence*. University of Virginia Department of Sociology website. http://web.archive.org/web/20141226232941/http://sociology.virginia.edu/news/statement_on_sexual_violence.

Bonilla-Silva, Eduardo. 2010. *Racism Without Racists: Colorblind Racism and Racial Inequality in Contemporary America*. 3rd ed. Lanham: Rowman and Littlefield.

Bonilla-Silva, Eduardo, and Tukufu Zuberi. 2008. Toward a Definition of White Logic and White Methods. In *White Logic, White Methods: Racism and Methodology*, ed. Tukufu Zuberi and Eduardo Bonilla-Silva, 3–30. Lanham: Rowman and Littlefield.

Bratton, John, David Denham, and Linda Deutschmann. 2009. *Capitalism and Classical Sociological Theory*. Toronto: University of Toronto Press.

Bridges, Tristan. 2016. Masculinity, Inequality, and the 2016 Presidential Election. *Footnotes* 44 (8). http://www.asanet.org/news-events/footnotes/dec-2016/features/sociologists-reflect-2016-presidential-election.

Burawoy, Michael. 2005. The Critical Turn to Public Sociology. *Critical Sociology* 31 (3): 313–326.

Campbell, Bradley. 2014. Anti-Minotaur: The Myth of a Sociological Morality. *Society* 51 (5): 443–451.

Cheong, Ian Miles. 2017. WA Colleges to Train Librarians in 'Social Justice' and 'Interrupting Microaggressions.' *Heat Street*, January 14. https://heatst.com/culture-wars/wa-colleges-to-train-librarians-in-social-justice-and-interrupting-microaggressions/.

Church, Catholic. 1994. *Catechism of the Catholic Church*. New York: Doubleday.

Collins, Patricia Hill. 1990. *Black Feminist Thought: Knowledge, Consciousness, and the Politics of Empowerment*. New York: HarperCollins.

Collins, Randall. 2008. *Violence: A Micro-sociological Theory*. Princeton: Princeton University Press.

————. 2012. C-Escalation and D-Escalation: A Theory of the Time-Dynamics of Conflict. *American Sociological Review* 77 (1): 1–20.

Collins, Randall, Erik Olin Wright, Evelyn Nakano Glenn, and Sally T. Hillsman. 2011. ASA Officers Respond to Attacks on Frances Fox Piven. *American*

Sociological Association website, January 24. http://www.asanet.org/news-events/asa-news/asa-officers-respond-attacks-frances-fox-piven.

Connell, R.W. 1997. Why Is Classical Theory Classical? *American Journal of Sociology* 102 (6): 1511–1557.

Crenshaw, Kimberle. 1989. Demarginalizing the Intersection of Race and Sex: A Black Feminist Critique of Antidiscrimination Doctrine, Feminist Theory, and Antiracist Politics. *University of Chicago Legal Forum* 140: 139–167.

Deflem, Matthieu. 2005. Public Sociology, Hot Dogs, Apple Pie, and Chevrolet. *The Journal of Public and Professional Sociology* 1 (1): Article 4. http://digitalcommons.kennesaw.edu/cgi/viewcontent.cgi?article=1001&context=jpps.

Douthat, Ross. 2017. Notes on a Political Shooting. *New York Times*, June 17. https://www.nytimes.com/2017/06/17/opinion/notes-on-a-political-shooting.html.

Dworkin, Andrea. 2007. *Intercourse*, twentieth anniversary edition. New York: Basic Books.

Feagin, Joe. 2001. Social Justice and Sociology: Agendas for the Twenty-First Century. *American Sociological Review* 66 (1): 1–20.

Feagin, Joe, and Hernan Vera. 2001. *Liberation Sociology*. Boulder: Westview Press.

Fein, Melvyn L. 2014. Social Science and Morality: An Empirical Analysis. *Society* 51 (5): 452–463.

Felson, Richard B. 1991. Blame Analysis: Accounting for the Behavior of Protected Groups. *The American Sociologist* 22 (1): 5–23.

Fischer, Howard. 2017. Social Justice Advocate Position at University of Arizona Questioned. *Arizona Daily Sun*, May 15. http://azdailysun.com/news/local/social-justice-advocate-position-at-university-of-arizona-questioned/article_2246246d-40cf-5b90-8f18-f3cf384920b4.html.

Foley, Kyle. 2017. U of Minnesota Student Loses Campus Job for Not Promoting Social Justice Agenda. *Heat Street*, February 8. https://heatst.com/culture-wars/university-of-minnesota-student-loses-campus-job-for-not-promoting-social-justice-agenda/.

Friedersdorf, Conor. 2015. Is 'Victimhood Culture' a Fair Description? *The Atlantic*, September 19. http://www.theatlantic.com/politics/archive/2015/09/the-problems-with-the-term-victimhood-culture/406057/.

Gockowski, Anthony. 2017. CU-Boulder to Offer 'Social Justice Living Environment.' *Campus Reform*, May 10. https://www.campusreform.org/?ID=9162.

Gorski, Philip S. 2013. Beyond the Fact/Value Distinction: Ethnical Naturalism and the Social Sciences. *Society* 50 (6): 543–553.

Gouldner, Alvin W. 1962. Anti-Minotaur: The Myth of a Value-Free Sociology. *Social Problems* 9 (3): 199–213.

Gray, David. 1968. Value-Free Sociology: A Doctrine of Hypocrisy and Irresponsibility. *The Sociological Quarterly* 9 (2): 176–185.

Hadden, Richard W. 1997. *Sociological Theory: An Introduction to the Classical Tradition*. Petersborough: Broadview Press.

Haidt, Jonathan. 2012. *The Righteous Mind: Why Good People Are Divided by Politics and Religion*. New York: Pantheon Books.

Haidt, Jonathan and Lee Jussim. 2016. Hard Truths about Race on Campus. *Wall Street Journal*, May 6. https://www.wsj.com/articles/hard-truths-about-race-on-campus-1462544543.

Hayek, F. A. 1979. Social Justice, Socialism, and Democracy: Three Australian Lectures. Centre for Independent Studies. http://www.cis.org.au/app/uploads/2015/07/op2.pdf?

Herman, Dianne F. 1984. The Rape Culture. In *Women: A Feminist Perspective*, ed. Jo Freeman, 45–53. Mountain View: Mayfield.

Hollenbach, David. 2001. *The Common Good and Christian Ethics*. Cambridge: Cambridge University Press.

Homans, George C. 1967. *The Nature of Social Science*. New York: Harcourt, Brace, and World.

Hume, David. 2000. *A Treatise of Human Nature*. New York: Oxford University Press.

Jussim, Lee. 2016. Are Most Published Social Psychology Findings False? *Psychology Today*, February 26. https://www.psychologytoday.com/blog/rabble-rouser/201602/are-most-published-social-psychology-findings-false.

Kurzman, Charles. 2016. Islamophobia and the Trump Campaign. *Footnotes* 44 (8). http://www.asanet.org/news-events/footnotes/dec-2016/features/sociologists-reflect-2016-presidential-election.

Lilienfeld, Scott O. 2017. Microaggressions: Strong Claims, Inadequate Evidence. *Perspectives on Psychological Science* 12 (1): 138–169.

Liptak, Adam. 2007. Does Death Penalty Save Lives?: A New Debate. *New York Times*, November 18. http://www.nytimes.com/2007/11/18/us/18deter.html.

MacKinnon, Catharine. 1989. *Toward a Feminist Theory of the State*. Cambridge: Harvard University Press.

Manly, Richard. 2016. Multicultural Affairs Offers Training. *Inside CSULB*, October 3. http://web.csulb.edu/misc/inside/2016/10/03/new-office-of-multicultural-affairs-offers-training/.

Martin, Chris C. 2016. How Ideology Has Hindered Sociological Insight. *The American Sociologist* 47: 115–130.

Martinez, Lisa M. 2016. How Sociology Helps to Process the 2016 Election. *Footnotes* 44 (8). http://www.asanet.org/news-events/footnotes/dec-2016/features/sociologists-reflect-2016-presidential-election.

Merton, Robert. 1936. The Unanticipated Consequences of Purposive Social Action. *American Sociological Review* 1 (6): 894–904.

Mikelionis, Lukas 2016. Drexel U Professor Calls for 'White Genocide', Dismantling of Police. *Heat Street*, December 26. https://heatst.com/culture-wars/drexel-professor-wishing-white-genocide-claims-reverse-racism-is-a-myth-wants-to-abolish-police/.

———. 2017. U of Central Florida Launches Emergency 'Social Justice Week' Featuring Ball Pit to Fight Oppression. *Heat Street*, January 23. https://heatst.com/culture-wars/central-florida-u-launches-emergency-social-justice-week-featuring-ball-pits-to-fight-oppression/.

Mill, John Stuart. 1957. *Utilitarianism*. New York: Liberal Arts Press.

Moskos, Peter. 2016. They're Just Sooner to Shoot in Oklahoma. *Cop in the Hood* (blog), September 22. http://www.copinthehood.com/2016/09/theyre-just-sooner-to-shoot-in-oklahoma.html.

Nielsen, Francois. 2004. The Vacant 'We': Remarks on Public Sociology. *Social Forces* 82 (4): 1619–1627.

Nisbet, Robert A. 1966. *The Sociological Tradition*. New York: Basic Books.

Novak, Michael. 2000. Defining Social Justice. *First Things*, December. https://www.firstthings.com/article/2000/12/defining-social-justice.

Ohlheiser, Abby. 2015. Why 'Social Justice Warrior,' a Gamergate Insult, Is Now a Dictionary Entry. *Washington Post*, October 7. https://www.washingtonpost.com/news/the-intersect/wp/2015/10/07/why-social-justice-warrior-a-gamergate-insult-is-now-a-dictionary-entry/?utm_term=.29b54a2f652d.

Phillips, Scott. 2008. Racial Disparities in Capital Punishment: Blind Justice Requires a Blindfold. American Constitution Society for Law and Policy Issue Briefs. http://www.acslaw.org/IssueBrief.

Popper, Karl R. 1963. *Conjectures and Refutations: The Growth of Scientific Knowledge*. New York: Routledge.

———. 2002. *The Logic of Scientific Discovery*. London: Routledge Classics.

Porter, Catherine. 2017. A College Built for Canadian Settlers Envisions an Indigenous Future. *New York Times*, June 19. https://www.nytimes.com/2017/06/19/world/canada/a-college-built-for-canadian-settlers-envisions-an-indigenous-future.html.

Radelet, Michael L., and Traci L. Lacock. 2009. Do Executions Lower Homicide Rates?: The Views of Leading Criminologists. *The Journal of Criminal Law and Criminology* 99 (2): 489–508.

Runyowa, Simba. 2015. Microaggressions Matter. *The Atlantic*, September 18. http://www.theatlantic.com/politics/archive/2015/09/microaggressions-matter/406090/.

Shapiro, T. Rees. 2014. U-Va. Students Challenge Rolling Stone Account of Alleged Sexual Assault. *Washington Post*, December 10. https://www.washingtonpost.com/local/education/u-va-students-challenge-rolling-stone-account-of-attack/2014/12/10/ef345e42-7fcb-11e4-81fd-8c4814dfa9d7_story. html?utm_term=.630ef6428c43.

Sherkat, Darren. 2013. "Let's All Laugh at the Christianist 'Sociologists' with an Actual Sociologist Who Is Not Dumb." *Wonkette*, May 31. http://wonkette. com/518227/lets-all-laugh-at-the-christianist-sociologists-with-an-actual-sociologist-who-is-not-dumb.

Smith, Christian. 2013. Comparing Ethical Naturalism and "Public Sociology". *Society* 50 (6): 598–601.

———. 2014. *The Sacred Project of American Sociology*. New York: Oxford University Press.

Spada, Shannon. 2017. Prof Says Otto Warmbier 'Got Exactly What He Deserved.' *Campus Reform*, June 22. http://www.campusreform.org/?ID=9350.

Stinchcombe, Arthur L. 1982. Should Sociologists Forget Their Fathers and Mothers? *The American Sociologist* 17 (1): 2–11.

Tittle, Charles. 2004. The Arrogance of Public Sociology. *Social Forces* 82 (4): 1639–1643.

Turner, Jonathan H. 2005. Is Public Sociology Such a Good Idea? *The American Sociologist* 36 (3–4): 27–45.

University of Wyoming Social Justice Resource Center. 2017. "What Is Social Justice?" https://www.uwyo.edu/sjrc/whatissocialjustice/.

Van den Berg, Axel. 2014. Public Sociology, Professional Society, and Democracy In *The Public Sociology Debate: Ethics and Engagement*, edited by Ariane Hannemaayer and Christopher J. Schneider, 53-73. Vancouver: UBC Press.

Vega, Tanzina. 2014. Students See Many Slights as Racial 'Microaggressions.' *New York Times*, March 21. https://www.nytimes.com/2014/03/22/us/as-diversity-increases-slights-get-subtler-but-still-sting.html?mcubz=0.

Veres, Steve. 2005. "Students, Profs Question Class Climate." *The Chronicle*, July 20. http://www.dukechronicle.com/article/2005/07/students-profs-question-class-climate.

Vivian. 2013. Queered Science Interview: Dr. Donna Riley and Engineering Social Justice. *Autostraddle*, October 18. https://www.autostraddle.com/queered-science-interview-dr-donna-riley-and-engineering-social-justice-200233/.

Weber, Max. 1949. *The Methodology of the Social Sciences*. Glencoe: The Free Press.

———. 1958. Science as a Vocation. In *From Max Weber: Essays in Sociology*, ed. H.H. Gerth and C. Wright Mills, 129–156. New York: Oxford University Press.

Zhen, Sharon (Yu Chun). 2017. Social Justice Advocates Program Persists Despite Facing Criticism. *Daily Bruin*, June 4. http://dailybruin.com/2017/06/04/social-justice-advocates-program-persists-despite-facing-criticism/.

Zimmerman, Michael. 2017. The Evergreen State College Implosion: Are There Lessons to Be Learned. *Huffington Post*, July 2. http://www.huffingtonpost. com/entry/the-evergreen-state-college-implosion-are-there-lessons_us_5959 507ee4b0f078efd98b0e.

CHAPTER 7

Victimhood, Academic Freedom, and Free Speech

Speech that transgresses a culture's norms can be dangerous. Cultures that value religious orthodoxy might punish heresy or blasphemy; cultures that value political orthodoxy might punish sedition. Sixteenth-century Protestants in Geneva executed Michael Servetus for heresies such as denying the Trinity, sixteenth-century Catholics in Rome executed Giordano Bruno for similar heresies, and twentieth-century Soviets sentenced Aleksandr Solzhenitsyn to forced labor for criticizing Soviet leader Joseph Stalin. Even when it violates no law and goes unpunished by the state, speech might attract severe sanctions. In the white supremacist culture of the early twentieth-century American South, blacks were addressed by first names only, and one black clergyman was forced to flee north with his family after his daughter "imprudently insisted that a local telephone operator address her as 'Miss'" (McMillen 1990:24). More recently Islamic terrorists killed 12 persons at the offices of the satirical newspaper *Charlie Hebdo* in Paris because the newspaper had published cartoons that many Muslims viewed as blasphemous.

Different moral cultures target different kinds of speech. In honor cultures, where people are quick to perceive slights and to respond to them violently, talking frankly about people can be risky. In the antebellum American South this meant newspaper editors had to deal with angry gentlemen wanting to fight them. Because one did not duel with someone of lower status, and the status of newspaper editors was ambiguous, sometimes

© The Author(s) 2018
B. Campbell, J. Manning, *The Rise of Victimhood Culture*,
https://doi.org/10.1007/978-3-319-70329-9_7

the aggrieved parties would simply cane or whip editors (Williams 1980:29). Often they would duel, though, and some editors fought multiple duels over things published in their papers. *Richmond Enquirer* editor O.J. Wise fought at least eight duels, and Dr. James Hagan of the Vicksburg, Mississippi *Sentinel* "had several so-called desperate encounters, including some duels," before "he himself was gunned down in 1843 by the son of a judge about whom he had written unkind remarks" (Williams 1980:31–32). The lives of subsequent *Sentinel* editors were also violent: T.E. Robins was shot in a duel, and his replacement, Walter Hickey, killed a man in a duel. *Sentinel* editor James Ryan was killed by the publisher of a rival newspaper (Williams 1980:32–33). Newspaper writers could also offend people. Emile Hirairt, a drama critic for the *Daily Delta* in New Orleans, "offended several gentlemen admirers of a singer with his caustic comments concerning her performance" (Williams 1980:34). He fought two duels over the matter, the first a pistol duel where both parties remained unharmed, and the second a shotgun duel that left Hirairt injured and his adversary dead. Certainly some in the newspaper business wholeheartedly accepted the ideals of honor culture and were willing to write what they wanted and bravely face the consequences, but generally the threat of violence was "real enough that it dampened the ardor of much of the press" and "many chose instead elaborate politeness in their references to local citizens" (Williams 1980:30).

Honor could also disrupt university life, leading to duels and other forms of violence. In 1833 two South Carolina college students handled a dining hall dispute by fighting a duel that left one of them dead and the other injured for life. In 1852 a student at the Virginia Military Institute sought a duel with Professor Thomas Jackson (who later became the Confederate general known as "Stonewall Jackson") because he believed Jackson had insulted him during class. At the University of Georgia in 1853, a student challenged a professor who had accused him of dishonesty, and the professor accepted, but the would-be duel was averted (Williams 1980:28). And according to Rex Bowman and Carlos Santos, the University of Virginia from its very beginning "crashed headlong into the culture of honor" (2013:Introduction). They describe the student culture of the early 1800s:

> These students of the first two decades, often the spoiled, self-indulgent scions of southern plantation owners, sometimes the sons of prosperous merchants, led a life of dissipation. With a sense of honor easily bruised, they were reflexively violent. The wrong word, the wrong look could easily

lead to a scuffle, if not a duel. Calling a young man a 'puppy' [meaning a dandy] ... could get one shot. Cursing in the presence of a lady could lead to a whipping. The students brandished guns freely, sometimes shooting in the air, sometimes at each other. They secreted dirks and daggers and, with little to no thought and even less hesitation, stabbed each other. They pummeled, kicked, bit, and gouged each other. They brawled with town merchants, they scuffled with the local wagoners.... They cursed each other, townsfolk, and professors. They vandalized property ... and mutilated cows. They drank and drank and drank. And rioted. (Bowman and Santos 2013:Introduction)

Prudent students would have been careful of what they said to peers. The same goes for faculty addressing students, especially those who reprimanded them for their wild conduct. For example, in 1839, when students William Binford and Thomas Russell were suspended for rule violations, Professor Gessner Harrison ordered them to leave and said they had disgraced themselves. Binford and Russel believed Harrison had dishonored them, and the next month they came back to the university grounds and confronted him. When Harrison declined to retract his statement and also declined to fight them, Binford called him a coward and held him down while Russell began horsewhipping him. Bystanders intervened to stop it, but when Harrison again told Binford and Russell they had disgraced themselves, they horsewhipped him again. After they fled, the university offered an award for their arrest. Eventually Russell was injured and Binford was put in jail, but a crowd of University of Virginia students, who now saw Binford and Russell as victims, gathered at the jail to demand Binford's release. Under pressure from local gentlemen, the university soon dropped the legal charges (Bowman and Santos 2013:Chapter 1).

"Neither of them pretended I had done him any injury," Harrison wrote of the students who had horsewhipped him (Bowman and Santos 2013:Chapter 1). He meant he had not assaulted them or treated them unfairly. He had done them no wrong, certainly not anything warranting violence. But the students' view differed. The injury, of course, was that Harrison's rebuke challenged their honor.[1] Professors today who suddenly

---

[1] In defense of dueling, eighteenth-century English author Samuel Johnson similarly compared honor offenses to physical invasion: "A man may shoot the man who invades his character, as he may shoot him who attempts to break into his house" (quoted in Pinker 2011:22).

become the targets of students' wrath must be as befuddled as Harrison was. Nicholas and Erika Christakis at Yale could likewise say that the activists hounding them did not even pretend the professors had injured them in any way. But again, the students of both periods have a higher sensitivity to slight and different conceptions of injury. Only now it is the culture of victimhood rather than the culture of honor that is causing tumult on campuses and leading to the intimidation of faculty and students as they speak their minds or simply go about their work.

Across societies and across history, few moral cultures have valued free speech much. Even societies that do value it still restrict some kinds of speech. And voluntary associations of all kinds tend to restrict speech formally or informally. For several reasons, though, victimhood culture is particularly hostile to free speech. It shares with honor culture a tendency to perceive and to react to slights and a tendency to blur the distinction between speech and violence. And even more so than honor culture its strictures are potentially all encompassing. Small talk and course lectures, jokes and hobbies, books and tweets, artistic expressions, and scientific theories—just about anything might cause offense, with offended parties demanding offenders be silenced, fired, assaulted, banished, or reeducated. Ultimately this is irreconcilable with the academy's commitment to free speech and academic freedom, and one ideology will have to give way to the other. Let us consider each ideology in turn.

THE IDEA OF FREE SPEECH

Surely not all speech is of equal value. Why should we tolerate speech that is boring, impertinent, hateful, or wrong? If ideas have consequences, why should we allow people to spread ideas that will corrupt minds and disrupt the social order? What if someone comes along preaching heresy, leading souls astray? What if a charlatan contradicts scientific ideas that we all know are settled? What if a political reformer's rebellious rhetoric is undermining social order? What if a reactionary's deceitful words are stymieing our reform efforts? Are we really supposed to tolerate error? Free speech advocates say yes. Nineteenth-century English philosopher John Stuart Mill put it this way: "If all mankind minus one were of an opinion, mankind would be no more justified in silencing that one person than he, if he had the power, would be justified in silencing mankind" (2005:42). In this view other people, no matter how numerous or powerful, simply have no right to prevent you from thinking freely and expressing your thoughts.

Mill went further. Silencing speech is an offense against those who are prevented from speaking, but also against those prevented from hearing them. On this point nineteenth-century abolitionist and former slave Frederick Douglas was in agreement. "To suppress free speech is a double wrong," said Douglas. "It violates the rights of the hearer as well as those of the speaker. It is just as criminal to rob a man of his right to hear and speak as it would be to rob him of his money" (quoted in Smith 2017). Mill likened speech suppression to robbery as well: "The peculiar evil of silencing an expression of opinion," he said, "is that it is robbing the human race, posterity as well as the existing generation—those who dissent from the opinion, still more than those who hold it. If the opinion is right, they are deprived of the opportunity of exchanging error for truth; if wrong, they lose, what is almost as great a benefit, the clearer perception and livelier impression of truth produced by its collision with error" (Mill 2005:42). In other words, whatever speech we would wish to silence might be correct, or partly correct. And calling "any proposition certain, while there is anyone who would deny its certainty if permitted, but who is not permitted, is to assume that we ourselves, and those who agree with us, are the judges of certainty, and judges without hearing the other side" (Mill 2005:47–48). But suppose we do know for certain an idea is wrong. Even so, it benefits us to be exposed to wrong ideas. Otherwise we become unable to defend and ultimately unable to understand the correct ideas we hold. We come to hold them "in the manner of a prejudice," and their meaning is "in danger of becoming lost, or enfeebled" (Mill 2005:83). "He who knows only his own side of the case," Mill said, "knows little of that" (2005:64).

One thing to note about this kind of robust defense of free speech is that it is not just about government censorship. Government censorship is especially pernicious in this view, but any violent suppression of speech would violate the rights of the speakers and hearers, even if carried out by nongovernmental actors like lynch mobs, rioters, terrorists, or duelists. A legal system that effectively protects people from violence is necessary to secure people's speech rights. A culture that values free speech is important, too, even in the absence of violence. Freedom of association means that people will form all kinds of voluntary associations that restrict their members' speech in various ways. Where the culture is generally hospitable to free speech, those restrictions tend to be narrow. Most groups do not expect conformity on all matters, and in any case there is plenty of interaction with outsiders and exposure to other views. But if tolerance for diverse ideas is not the norm, and if informal speech restrictions become so extreme and commonplace that people are reluctant to express themselves and rarely come into contact with unconventional ideas, then the dominant beliefs will go untested. A society where expressing unpopular ideas means you will be fired from any job, exposed in the media, and shunned by the community is not the kind of free speech society Mill described, even if you will not be burned at the stake. Still, government repression—burning heretics, sending dissidents to the Gulag—has historically been a major obstacle to free speech, and drawing from Enlightenment ideals, liberal democracies have typically allowed government regulation of speech only within strict limits. This has been especially true of the United States.

Free Speech and the First Amendment

The First Amendment to the US Constitution prevents Congress from establishing a state church, from prohibiting the free exercise of religion, and from abridging the freedom of speech, the freedom of the press, the right to peaceful assembly, and the right to petition the government. Originally this restricted only the federal government, but it is now understood to apply to the state governments as well.[2] The First Amendment, and the body of jurisprudence that now interprets it, protects speech much more than is typical even of other modern liberal democracies.

Still, the US Supreme Court has allowed for a number of exceptions—that is, expression the government may restrict. Generally, what are known as *content-neutral* "time, place, and manner" restrictions on expression are more acceptable than *content-based* restrictions. Banning loudspeakers in a neighborhood after 10:00 p.m. would be content neutral, while banning speech about abortion would be content based (Weinstein 2009:82). Acceptable content-based restrictions fall into a number of specific categories—for example, obscenity, child pornography, indecency, defamation, harassment, fighting words, true threats, incitement, copyright and trademark violations, speech that endangers national security, and the disclosure of certain kinds of personal information (Melkonian 2012:8; Silvergate et al. 2012; Weinstein 2009:82). Governments can regulate some of these and other exceptions only minimally, while they

---

[2] This is due to what is known as the *incorporation doctrine*, which means that much of the Bill of Rights (the Constitution's first 10 amendments) now applies to the states based on the general guarantee of due process found in the 14th Amendment.

can ban others completely, but they can almost never regulate expression based on the opinion that it conveys. This is known as *viewpoint discrimination*, which the twentieth-century Supreme Court Justice William Brennan once called "censorship in its purest form" (quoted in Silvergate et al. 2012:83). Thus, unlike in many liberal democracies, there is no exception for what is sometimes called *hate speech*. A number of other liberal democracies do have hate speech bans, but as James Weinstein points out, this is an example of a "speech regulation that would be summarily invalidated under contemporary American free speech jurisprudence" (2009:84). In general, whereas other countries "tend to employ soft, flexible standards that balance the free speech interest at issue in a particular case against the government's interest in suppressing the speech, American doctrine is determined by hard-edged, determinative rules" (Weinstein 2009:90). This is deliberate. The idea is that clear rules should protect free speech by constraining the discretion of governments, and they should enable people to know "with adequate certainty what they can safely say" (Weinstein 2009:91).

The Court has defined each free speech exception very narrowly so that governments cannot simply prohibit unpopular speech by labeling it obscenity, incitement, harassment, defamation, or whatever. Consider defamation. Legal scholar Harry Melkonian describes "the right to reputation protected by privacy and defamation laws" as "one of the countervailing values to freedom of expression" (2012:xxvii). In honor cultures reputation is sacrosanct, and we have seen that offended parties simply mete out their own justice against those who insult them. As honor gave way to dignity, the state began handling some offenses that might otherwise lead to honor violence—as when it punishes violence and prevents people from handling it on their own—but remember that dignity culture enjoins people to ignore insults. Sociologist Peter Berger pointed out that in American law "insult itself is not actionable," and the fact that it is not, he said, is an indicator of "the obsolescence of the concept of honor" (1970:339). Defamation is not mere insult; it usually must involve material damage or at least psychic harm, "a far cry from a notion of offence against honor" (Berger 1970:339). It also must be false, so true statements or opinions cannot be defamation no matter how much they harm someone's reputation. Defamation law means free speech is not absolute, but its narrowness points to the weight that dignity cultures give to free speech over other ideals, particularly in the United States, where "the preference for freedom of speech found in modern U.S. Supreme Court interpretations of the First Amendment" contrasts sharply with, say, "the extremely strict common law libel regime in Australia" (Melkonian 2012:xxviii).

Berger pointed to defamation law to illustrate the obsolescence of honor because even though defamation law deals with something important to those in honor cultures—reputation—it does so using a completely different moral logic. In light of that, another free speech exception—the exception for so-called *fighting words*—seems like an anomaly. Mere insults, matters of opinion, are protected speech and have nothing to do with defamation, but fighting words are a kind of insult. And laws criminalizing fighting words were an attempt to limit honor violence in a culture where the norms of honor were still prevalent. In that context words could provoke fights. Insults such as "coward, liar, rascal, scoundrel, and puppy all demanded an immediate challenge." "Any man who uttered them in a dispute," historian Joanne Freeman says, "was declaring his intention to engage in an affair of honor" (quoted in Rosen 2002). Following this logic, anti-dueling laws of the nineteenth century often outlawed not just the dueling but also the provocation for it. A law passed in Virginia in 1810, for example, banned "all words from which their usual construction and common acceptation are considered as insults, and lead to violence and breach of the peace" (quoted in Rosen 2002). A number of other states had similar laws, but it was not until 1942 that the Supreme Court officially recognized fighting words as a category of unprotected speech.

In that case Walter Chaplinsky, a Jehovah's Witness, had been on a public sidewalk passing out pamphlets. When city marshal James Bowering told him to stop because it was angering the crowd, Chaplinsky called him a "God damned racketeer" and a "damned Fascist." The Court upheld Chaplinsky's arrest and conviction under a New Hampshire statute that prevented the use of "any offensive, derisive, or annoying word" to people gathered in a public place. The Court said that fighting words such as Chaplinsky had used "by their very utterance inflict injury or tend to incite an immediate breach of the peace" and that the prevention and punishment of such speech "has never been thought to raise any Constitutional problem" (quoted in Friedersdorf 2017).

The idea of fighting words was already antiquated when the Supreme Court upheld the New Hampshire law. Legal scholar Jeffrey Rosen says that "it was hardly obvious even in the middle of World War II that being called a 'damned Fascist' would have provoked an average man to a fistfight" (2002). Later rulings under courts generally more reluctant to allow free speech restrictions have not upheld any convictions for fighting words, and it is hard to imagine any application of such laws that would pass muster today. Certainly the offense in the Chaplinsky case—insulting a police officer—would now be protected speech (Silvergate et al. 2012:33–38). Fighting words laws are vestiges of the era of transition from honor to dignity. The rationale for them makes little sense in a dignity culture where the right way to handle insults is to ignore them. As we shall see, though, as dignity wanes some of those now clamoring for the censorship of offensive speech want to revive and repurpose the fighting words exception.

Free Speech and the University

The First Amendment protects free speech at the many public universities in the United States. Such universities can have content-neutral restrictions that prevent disruptions of normal activities, but they cannot engage in viewpoint discrimination (Lukianoff 2014:Chapter 1). This is the law, but many people see free speech as integral to the mission of the university regardless of what the law is. Universities tend to agree, at least in their brochures and catalogs, where both public and private universities typically extoll the idea of free speech and promise to guard the free speech rights of their faculty and students. For example, California State University, Los Angeles says that "exposure to the widest possible range of ideas, viewpoints, opinions, and creative expression is an integral and indispensable part of a university education for life in a diverse global society" (California State University, Los Angeles 2009). The University of California, Los Angeles "is committed to assuring that all persons may exercise the constitutionally protected rights of free expression, speech, assembly, and worship" (University of California, Los Angeles 2010). Claremont McKenna says that "guaranteeing the rights of free speech and peaceable assembly is a basic requirement for any academic community" (Claremont McKenna College 2015). Harvard says few other communities "place such a high priority on freedom of speech" (quoted in Petri 2012). Oberlin "is devoted to free and open inquiry" (Oberlin College General Faculty 1986). Yale echoes John Stuart Mill and Frederick Douglas when it says that "whoever deprives another of the right to state unpopular views necessarily also deprives others of the right to listen to those views" (quoted in Gallagher 2015). And Evergreen State College says that "only if minority and unpopular points of view are listened to and are given opportunities for expression will Evergreen provide bona fide opportunities for significant learning" (Evergreen State College 2017).

The idea that teaching and learning best take place in an environment of free expression means that colleges and universities should be *more* free than the surrounding society, that students and professors should be able to speak their mind more freely than people can in other professional environments. As campus free speech advocate Greg Lukianoff puts it, "the function of higher education is nothing less than to serve as the engine of intellectual, artistic, and scientific innovation." Free speech limits thus "endanger the entire academic endeavor" (Lukianoff 2014:Chapter 1). Lukianoff notes that the US Supreme Court has even said that imposing "any strait jacket upon the intellectual leaders in our colleges and universities would imperil the future of our Nation" (quoted in Lukianoff 2014:Chapter 1). In this view universities should be what Thomas Jefferson hoped the University of Virginia would be: places that protect "the illimitable freedom of the human mind," places where people "are not afraid to follow truth wherever it may lead, nor to tolerate any error so long as reason is left free to combat it" (Jefferson 2011:196).

Free Speech and Academic Freedom

The notion that universities contribute to the larger society in part by serving as a forum for the clash of ideas is closely connected with the idea of academic freedom. Academic freedom can mean a number of different things, but it usually means at least that professors should have leeway beyond what many other workers do to speak and write freely. Law professor Stanley Fish (2014) identifies several "schools of academic freedom" based on how broad or narrow they view the rights of professors. These range from the narrow "It's just a job school," which Fish himself embraces, to the broad "Academic freedom as revolution school." Under the narrowest conception professors "are not free in any special sense to do anything but their jobs," though doing their jobs does mean they need the ability to research, write, and teach freely within their areas of expertise (Fish 2014:10). The broadest view is that of those who view themselves as social revolutionaries whose task is to pursue social justice or some revolutionary agenda. Fish describes physicist Denis Rancourt as the "poster boy" for this school. While on the faculty at the University Ottawa, Rancourt would practice *academic squatting*, which means "turning a course with an advertised subject matter and syllabus into a workshop for revolution" (Fish 2014:14).

Usually academic freedom means something in between these extremes. That is, it does not mean that professors can abandon their responsibility to teach the subject matter of their courses, but it does mean that professors have the right to comment freely on matters of broader concern. Thus, according to the American Association of University Professors, academic freedom means "full freedom in research and in the publication of results," "freedom in the classroom in discussing their subject," and the freedom to "speak or write as citizens ... free from institutional censorship or discipline" (American Association of University Professors 1940).

Academic freedom is one component of the vision of a university as a place of free inquiry and hardy debate. According to education scholar Joanna Williams, "academic freedom simply asserts the importance of free speech, as a foundational right of everyone in society, to scholars in particular" (2016:7). She says it lies "at the heart of the university" and is "integral to the collective enterprise to critique and advance knowledge" (Williams 2016:20). If the aim of the university is the pursuit of truth, free speech becomes its core value. But what if the aim of the university is something else?

THE IDEA OF CENSORSHIP

When people talk about universities pursuing truth, what they usually have in mind, Williams notes, is "not a search for an ultimate truth for all time, but a contestable truth ... [to] be countered and superseded when new and better knowledge" comes along (2016:15). Campus activists, though, may believe they possess the full truth already. Unlike others they are aware, conscious, or in the know—or to use a more recent term, *woke* (Hess 2016). Or they may see all truth claims as exercises of power. In any case, for them the university's mission is social justice rather than truth. The university is not to be a place where people hash out ideas and where even error is tolerated because others are free to contest it. It is to be set apart from the larger society not as a haven of free expression, but instead as a safe space where students are protected from oppression. As they see it, those defending the permissibility of speech that causes harm are defending oppression. Some activists even mock free speech advocates as defenders of what they call *freeze peach* (Lee 2013).[3]

Obviously censorship is not new, but the rationale for it now tends to arise from the ideals of victimhood culture. Political scientist April Kelly-Woessner (2015) finds that today's young people are actually less politically

---

[3] One user of the term explains that "the social justice community" uses this as "a punny homophonic description" of a kind of "whiny, entitled behavior" (Lee 2013).

tolerant than the previous generation, a reversal of a 60-year-old trend. And among the younger generation (those under 40), those who are most concerned about social justice are the most intolerant. That this is not the case for those who are older suggests that the idea of a conflict between social justice and free speech is new. One likely source of this idea, Kelly-Woessner says, is the New Left theorist Herbert Marcuse, who argued that a "liberating tolerance ... would mean intolerance against movements from the Right and toleration of movements from the Left" (quoted in Kelly-Woessner 2015). Whatever the source, though, campus activists have come to believe they may "limit the rights of their political opponents, so long as they frame their intolerance in terms of protecting others from hate" (Kelly-Woessner 2015).

Speech and Status

The offensiveness of speech is often less about what people say than about who says it and to whom or about whom they say it. This is why gentlemen in the honor culture of the antebellum South responded differently to insults depending on who insulted them. An insult from someone of low status might be safely ignored, or it might be handled brutally, such as by whipping the offender. An insult from another gentlemen, though, could not be ignored and might lead to a duel governed by elaborate rules. A speaker's social position matters in other kinds of status systems, too, such as in the Jim Crow South, where blacks could not say certain things to or about whites. Free speech thrives more easily in a culture of dignity because the egalitarian idea of everyone's equal worth leads to the idea that whatever one person may say anyone else may say too.

Victimhood culture again makes social identity central to the moral analysis of speech. The speech of the oppressed is different from that of the oppressors and the privileged. This is why some people are told to check their privilege when speaking about certain topics (e.g., Dang 2017). This is why, as we saw in Chap. 1, Derald Wing Sue says a white male elementary school teacher cannot be the victim of microaggressions (Hampson 2016). It is why, as we also saw previously, some activists argue that censorship on behalf of the oppressed should not even be called censorship ("The oppressed by definition cannot censor their oppressor") (Dean-Johnson et al. 2015). It is why, according to journalism professor Jelani Cobb, "the arguments about the freedom of speech become most tone deaf" when they fail to take into account that "the freedom to offend the powerful is not equivalent to the freedom to bully the relatively disempowered" (2015). And it is why Ulrich Baer, Vice Provost for Faculty, Arts, Humanity, and Diversity at New York University, says, "Some topics, such as claims that some human beings are by definition inferior to others, or illegal or unworthy of legal standing, are not open to debate because such people cannot debate them on their own terms." An "absolute notion of free speech" thus places "under severe attack" the legal and cultural rights "of minorities to participate in public discourse" (Baer 2017).

Speech as Violence

If people experience speech differently based on their victimhood status, censorship of the speech of the powerful might be needed to protect the powerless. Some campus activists have even begun to argue that speech that harms the powerless is actually violence, or something akin to it, and that if administrators and other authorities will not protect students from this violence, the students have the right to protect themselves. For example, after rioters at UC Berkeley forced the cancellation of an event featuring right-wing provocateur Milo Yiannopoulos, the student run newspaper *The Daily Californian* published "Violence as Self Defense," a collection of articles defending "the use of violence in protests" (Senju 2017). The contributors view Yiannopoulos's presence as an act of violence against the campus community, which means the protesters were only defending themselves when they used violence to prevent him from speaking. In this view the defenders of free speech who wanted the talk to go on were as complicit in the "violence" as Yiannopoulos and the student group that was hosting him. According to Berkeley alumna Nisa Dang, "asking people to maintain peaceful dialogue with those who literally do not think their lives matter is a violent act." And to Yiannopoulos she has this to say: "Here's a big fuck you from the descendants of people who survived genocides by killing Nazis and people just like them" (Dang 2017). Berkeley student Juan Prieto chides the university for not being "bold enough to stand against hate and cancel the speech," and he praises those who used violence to do so: "A peaceful protest was not going to cancel that event, just like numerous letters from staff, faculty, Free Speech Movement veterans and even donors did not cancel the event. Only the destruction of glass and shooting of fireworks did that.... Everything else was an act of passive acceptance to the hate speech that was about to take place on our campus" (Prieto 2017). Neil Lawrence, himself one of the masked protesters, has a similar argument for those who think the tactics were too extreme: "I understand.... But when you consider everything that activists already tried—when mass call-ins, faculty and student objections, letter writing campaigns, numerous op-eds (including mine), union grievances and peaceful demonstrations don't work, when the nonviolent tactics have been exhausted—what is left?" He says the acts of violence were actually "acts of self defense" and ends with a warning to Yiannopoulos and those who invited him: "Our shields are raised against you. No one will protect us? We will protect ourselves" (Lawrence 2017). Another protester, Desmond Meagley, writes, "I put my safety and freedom on the line because letting Yiannopoulos speak was more terrifying to me than potential injury or arrest." To anyone who condemns "the actions that shut down Yiannopoulos' literal hate speech," he says, "you condone his presence, his actions and his ideas; you care more about broken windows than broken bodies" (Meagley 2017).

The idea of speech as violence might seem like a fringe view, but sociologist Laura Beth Nielsen (2017), writing in the *Los Angeles Times* in favor of hate speech restrictions, makes a similar argument. She says that if we think of speech restrictions as efforts to avoid hurt feelings, we will rightly prefer to have free speech. But the idea that we are only talking about hurt feelings, she says, "demonstrates a profound misunderstanding of how hate speech affects its targets." Racist hate speech is much more like violence in the harm it does, given that research has linked it to "cigarette smoking, high blood pressure, anxiety, depression and post-traumatic stress disorder." Nielsen does not call such speech violence, exactly, but she says it is not "just speech" because it results in "tangible harms that are serious in and of themselves and that collectively amount to the harm of subordination" (Nielsen 2017).

Psychologist Lisa Feldman Barrett (2017) is another prominent proponent of this view. She writes in the *New York Times* that speech can have powerful and negative physical effects, including illness and aging. It can do so by causing stress, but merely *offensive* speech that causes only short bouts of stress is not harmful and can even be beneficial. *Abusive* speech, however, causes "long stretches of simmering stress." Barrett says this distinction can guide us deciding whether or not to ban speakers from campus. In her view students at Middlebury College were wrong to try to prevent political scientist Charles Murray from speaking there. She says that Murray's arguments about racial differences in IQ scores—the impetus behind the desire to ban him—might be offensive but are not abusive. She says Milo Yiannopoulos should be banned from campuses, though, because he engages in abusive speech. Speech like Yiannopoulos's "bullies and torments" people, and "from the perspective of our brain cells ... is literally a form of violence" (Barrett 2017).

Censorship, Academic Freedom, and the First Amendment

The moral logic of victimhood culture requires speech restrictions, but university academic freedom protections and First Amendment jurisprudence forbid many of the restrictions campus activists demand. Some activists simply ignore this problem, but others contend head on with current laws and policies.

Academic freedom tends to be celebrated by professors, even those most sympathetic to campus activists. This is no surprise since academic freedom protects the rights of activist professors to speak out about public matters both inside and outside of class. Free speech advocates Harry Silvergate, David French, and Greg Lukianoff say that the idea of academic freedom still has emotional resonance in university communities—much more than the First Amendment does. Their campus free speech organization, the Foundation for Individual Rights in Education (FIRE), has "on more than one occasion ... persuaded administrators to lift speech restrictions or end oppressive practices by arguing that those policies or behaviors impair academic freedom." "Even the most totalitarian professors and administrators," they say, "will often pay lip service to academic freedom, and they can be called to task and, indeed, shamed when their actions do not match their words" (Silvergate et al. 2012).

As victimhood culture advances, though, the problem is that academic freedom also protects faculty whose research or teaching deviates from or challenges the activists' worldview. Former Harvard student Sandra Korn thus rejects academic freedom altogether. Writing in the *Harvard Crimson*, she argues that "the liberal obsession with 'academic freedom' seems misplaced," and that academic freedom should be replaced by what she calls *academic justice*. This would allow the community to ensure that research that promotes or justifies oppression would be silenced. "Why," she asks, "should we put up with research that counters our goals simply in the name of 'academic freedom'?" (Korn 2014).

This would still leave in place First Amendment protections at public universities and many other places. Some activists hope to avoid First

228 B. CAMPBELL AND J. MANNING

Amendment problems by adding hate speech as a category of unprotected speech along with obscenity, incitement, true threats, and the others. Laura Beth Nielsen says that courts and legislatures need to think about allowing "the restriction of hate speech as do all of the other economically advanced democracies of the world" (2017). Others just talk as if hate speech were already a First Amendment exception. For example, when Ted Wheeler, the mayor of Portland, Oregon, was trying to prevent two rallies from taking place in his city because, in his view, the organizers "were coming to peddle a message of hate and bigotry," he said, "They have a First Amendment right to speak, but my pushback on that is that hate speech is not protected by the First Amendment" (quoted in Andone and Simon 2017). Likewise, after planned talks by Milo Yiannopoulos and Ann Coulter were canceled at UC Berkeley, former Vermont governor Howard Dean tweeted, "Hate speech is not protected by the first amendment" (quoted in Volokh 2017). And after Islamic terrorists attacked an exhibit in Garland, Texas, that featured images of Mohammed, CNN journalist Chris Cuomo, who found the exhibit offensive, tweeted, "Hate speech is excluded from [First Amendment] protection. Don't just say you love the Constitution. Read it" (quoted in Adams 2015).

Cuomo was roundly mocked for this, especially because he kept defending his tweet long after he had been corrected. Asked where the hate speech exception was in the Constitution or the case law, he referred to the Chaplinsky case. Remember that this case had to do with fighting words rather than hate speech, and it was the only time the Court has upheld a speech restriction based on the fighting words exception. Remember too that laws against fighting words were originally intended to stop dueling and other honor violence in a culture where certain kinds of face-to-face insults inevitably led to a fight. And remember that in the Chaplinsky case itself the Court upheld Chaplinsky's conviction for insulting a policeman. The fighting words doctrine is narrow, but also fairly reactionary, and it is thus interesting to see it conjured up as a justification for the new progressive cause of speech regulation.

Cuomo is not the only one who has done this. The Chaplinsky decision at one point described fighting words as words that "by their very utterance inflict injury or tend to incite an immediate breach of the peace" (quoted in Friedersdorf 2017). Elsewhere the decision makes clear that the Court defines fighting words more narrowly than this—the words have to be likely to immediately provoke a fight—but in the 1980s and 1990s, critical race theorists argued that some forms of racist speech should be banned on the basis that they inflict injury (Friedersdorf 2017). Universities with speech codes sometimes defend them using similar logic. For example, in the case of *UWM Post v. Board of Regents of the University of Wisconsin*, the University of Wisconsin argued that the fighting words doctrine allowed the university to ban racist speech because it is "understandable to expect a violent response to discriminatory harassment" (quoted in Silvergate et al. 2012). The university lost the case, and the courts so far have rejected any contemporary application of the fighting words doctrine, much less an expansion far beyond the original ruling. But if victimhood culture ever triumphs outside of the university, expect this to change. Hate speech will become a new category of unprotected speech, possibly by classifying it as fighting words.

Honor culture and victimhood culture are similar in encouraging sensitivity to insult and in blurring the distinction between speech and violence. They differ in their preferred method of dealing with offense, though. Honor culture says deal with it yourself, perhaps violently, and victimhood culture says appeal to authorities to prevent and punish it. When the state suppresses violence, people who still have some notion of honor might reluctantly eschew violence if the state steps in to prevent insults—as with fighting words laws. Similarly, the activists who embrace the new victimhood culture may turn to violence as a second option when administrators refuse to prevent offensive speakers from coming to campus. The preference is still for authorities to act, though, and a hate speech exception or a new use of the fighting words doctrine would allow them to do so.

Censorship on Campus

Threats to free speech on campus do not all come from victimhood culture. Sometimes administrators simply want to prevent people from criticizing them, as when Ronald Zaccari, president of Valdosta State University, expelled a student who had protested Zaccari's plans to build a $30 million parking garage (Lukianoff 2014:Introduction). Threats to free speech are not new, either. One that has been around for decades is the establishment of special *free speech zones* that make up only a small part of the campus. Lukianoff says these started in the 1960s and 1970s as "an additional area on campus where one could always engage in free speech," but soon they transmogrified into "a method of restricting free speech to as small a space as possible" (2014:Chapter 3). Another decades-old threat is the speech codes on many campuses that prevent students from using racial epithets and other kinds of slurs.

For as long as these speech restrictions have been around, they have been subject to criticism, legal challenges, and mockery. As we noted in Chap. 5, critics in the 1980s and 1990s began describing efforts to reform and police language as *political correctness*. Examples include efforts to classify as offensive previously unoffensive words like "fireman" (to be replaced with "firefighter") or "wife" (to be replaced with "partner"). Political correctness might also refer to efforts to classify as racial slurs words that had never had any racial connotation. One notorious case of this occurred in 1993 when the University of Pennsylvania charged a Jewish student with racial harassment for yelling, "Shut up, you water buffalo!" out of his window when his study was disturbed by noise from members of a black sorority. The idea behind the charge was that *water buffalo* was an anti-black slur no one had heard before. It was in fact a translation of a Hebrew colloquialism applied to rowdy or thoughtless people, and the negative media attention eventually led the university to drop its case against the student (Lukianoff 2014:Chapter 2). In another case, this one from the late 1990s, a supporter of the University of Wisconsin's speech code attempted to provide an example of why it was needed by reporting to the Faculty Senate that a professor had used the word *niggardly* while teaching about Chaucer (who used the word in his work). *Niggardly* means *miserly*, and it has no relation to the racial epithet *nigger*, but the student described herself as "in tears, shaking" even after the professor explained it. "It's not up to the rest of the class to decide whether my feelings are valid," she said (quoted in Kors 1999). This complaint ended up turning opinion against the speech code—the opposite of what the complainant intended. An editorial in the *Wisconsin State Journal* even thanked the complainant "for clarifying precisely why the UW-Madison does not need an academic speech code" (quoted in Kors 1999).

Then as now, most speech restrictions were attempts to protect members of historically disadvantaged groups. Still, despite excesses like these, speech restrictions were supposed to be about intentional racial and ethnic slurs and the like. More recently, though, with the ascendance of a full-blown campus victimhood culture, activists and administrators have dropped the pretense that they only want to interfere with the most offensive speech. The entire microaggression program is rooted in the notion that when members of victim groups interact with outgroups they are constantly wounded by inadvertent slights. This is not just a matter of activists trying to raise awareness about microaggressions, either. We have seen that universities themselves address microaggressions in documents and training programs, with the University of California and universities throughout the country encouraging faculty to avoid microaggressions like "Why are you so quiet?" and "America is a melting pot." Remember too that the lists of microaggressions are not exhaustive; anything could be a microaggression, including, presumably, saying water buffalo or niggardly, since the microaggressor's intentions do not matter. The Wisconsin student's insistence that it was not up to others to decide whether her feelings were valid is now in line with many universities' official policies. Universities trying to involve themselves in preventing or punishing microaggressions are claiming jurisdiction over every word spoken on campus, over every glance or expression. Under any conception of free speech the exceptions are rare while most speech is protected, but this is far from that. The logic of victimhood culture means no speech is clearly protected.

Riots, Censorship, and Visiting Speakers

In Chap. 1 we discussed the many efforts (sometimes successful) to prevent Milo Yiannopoulos and Ben Shapiro from speaking on campuses whenever a university student group invites one of them. DePaul University has banned them both, and at public universities, which are not free to engage in viewpoint discrimination, activist students and faculty mobilize against their presence. At Berkeley university officials cancelled a Yiannopoulos event out of safety concerns after a riot by students and others opposed to the event resulted in $100,000 worth of damage to the university. Ann Coulter is another conservative speaker who attracts controversy, and not long after the anti-Yiannopoulos riots, two student groups who were sponsoring a talk Coulter was to give at Berkeley cancelled it due to threats of violence (Peters and Fuller 2017).

Yiannopoulos is a young, gay, British Trump supporter and former editor at *Breitbart News*. As we discussed in Chap. 5, he is a provocateur whose talks seem designed to offend the campus left as much as possible and generally cause a scene. The talks involved mixtures of political commentary, stand-up comedy, and flamboyant theatrics, such as appearing at one talk in drag and announcing his drag queen name was Ivana Wall (a reference to presidential candidate Trump's promise to build a wall on the Mexican border). Elsewhere "he has paraded into hissing crowds of students accompanied by a mariachi band and wearing a poncho while shaking maracas," and once he "ascended to the stage on a throne hoisted above the shoulders of a dozen young white men in *Make America Great Again* hats to chants of 'USA! USA!'" (Moore 2016). Yiannopoulos combines the merely outlandish, including much that not too long ago would have mainly offended conservatives, with extreme right-wing rhetoric and attacks on the left. He says feminism is cancer (Yiannopoulos 2016). He says Islam is cancer (Oppenheim 2017). He calls Black Lives Matter a terrorist organization (Asimov 2017). Those in favor of censoring him, though, often say it is not because of these statements but because of his tendency to single people out for ridicule. He was banned from Twitter after repeatedly insulting actress Leslie Jones, for example, and at the University of Wisconsin–Milwaukee he projected an image of a transgender student who was in the audience and said the student had "forced his way into the women's locker rooms this year" (quoted in Frechette et al. 2016). No doubt this is part of what drives the efforts to ban Yiannopoulos, but preventing personal attacks cannot be the whole reason behind moves to ban him or other speakers. Speakers such as Ann Coulter and Ben Shapiro might say things that are offensive, but no one has accused them of outing transgender students. Yet they face similar levels of opposition.

Ann Coulter is also a Trump supporter, and she is known for some inflammatory statements of her own. Shortly after the terrorist attacks of September 11, 2001, for example, she wrote that the United States should invade Islamic countries, "kill their leaders and convert them to Christianity" (Coulter 2001). And she has written of wishing that Oklahoma City bomber Timothy McVeigh had gone to the *New York Times* building (Volokh 2017). Ben Shapiro, on the other hand, is a mainstream conservative who has been outspoken in his opposition to Donald Trump—and in his opposition to Milo Yiannopoulos, whom he views as "a clown who is simply trying to get attention by stoking and excusing the very same extremism that is hollowing out American conservatism" (Singal 2016). But Shapiro, the author of a book called *Brainwashed: How Universities Indoctrinate America's Youth*, is a strident critic of campus victimhood culture, and this is what he seems to have in common with Coulter and Yiannopoulos.

At this point it might seem that campus activists only want to censor a few conservative firebrands. True, Yiannopoulos is not their only target, but one could argue that Coulter and Shapiro are also provocateurs who are not on campus to present scholarly arguments. Yet campus censorship does not stop there. Charles Murray is a libertarian political scientist with the American Enterprise Institute, a conservative think tank, and the author of a number of widely discussed books. One of these, *Coming Apart*, analyzes the increasing divergence in the behavior and values of the upper and lower classes in the United States. In early 2017 Murray was to give a talk based on this book at Middlebury College, but some students wanted to prevent this based in part on their belief that Murray was a white supremacist. The Southern Poverty Law Center had characterized him as such because of his 1994 book *The Bell Curve*, coauthored with Richard Herrnstein, which examined the connection between intelligence and stratification. The book's most controversial chapter dealt with ethnic differences in IQ scores, and the authors suggested these differences might have genetic as well as environmental causes (though they ultimately concluded that there was not enough evidence to decide the matter). This has been controversial since its publication, but as Cornell human development professors Wendy Williams and Stephen Ceci point out, the book as a whole, including this small portion of it, "has generated an enormous literature of scholarly response and rebuttal," and even its strongest academic critics have treated it as "a data-based argument with which they must engage in order to disagree" (2017). But Murray's talk, which was not even about *The Bell Curve*, was by normal standards fairly noncontroversial and not even particularly conservative. Williams and Ceci sent out transcripts of the speech to 70 professors without telling them who the author was and to another 70 who knew the author was Murray. They also divided up and sent the portions out to samples of US adults. Overall, each group rated the speech as fairly centrist—not particularly liberal or conservative (Williams and Ceci 2017).[4]

---

[4] Though the students who opposed Murray's presence at Middlebury did so mainly on the basis of *The Bell Curve*, or what they had heard about it, some even condemned *Coming Apart*, the book he was there to talk about. A group called White Students for Racial Justice, for example, called Murray "classist" and said the book "uses largely anecdotal evidence to blame poor people in America for being poor, attempting to explain economic inequality through a perceived gap in virtue" (quoted in Beinart 2017). Beinart is right when he says that what is "considered morally legitimate at Middlebury differs dramatically from what's considered morally legitimate in large swaths of America" (2017). But Williams and Ceci (2017) show that what Middlebury activists consider morally legitimate differs even from what is considered morally legitimate in large swaths of the university.

Yet when it came time for Murray to speak at Middlebury, dozens of students stood up and turned their backs to him while chanting things like "Racist, sexist, anti-gay, Charles Murray go away!" (quoted in Seelye 2017).[5] As this went on, Middlebury professor Allison Stanger, a liberal who had been invited to debate Murray after his talk, implored, "Can you just listen for one minute," noting that she had spent time preparing difficult questions. "No," the students replied (quoted in Beinart 2017). With Murray unable to give the talk, the organizers moved the participants to a secret location where it would be broadcast for those who wanted to hear it. The protesters discovered the location, though, and when the talk was finished surrounded the participants as they tried to leave. They assaulted Stanger, who later went to the hospital and received a neck brace, and when Murray, Stanger, and others got into a car, the protesters jumped on the hood and made the car rock back and forth. Once Murray and Stanger got away, they ended up leaving town after learning the students also planned to disrupt their planned dinner at a local restaurant (Beinart 2017; Seelye 2017).

Similar treatment awaited another conservative scholar when she came to speak at Claremont McKenna College. Heather Mac Donald, who is affiliated with the Manhattan Institute think tank, is a critic of the Black Lives Matter movement and generally a defender of the police, and she was there to talk about her recent book, *The War on Cops: How the New Attack on Law and Order Makes Everyone Less Safe*. Mac Donald's analyses are controversial, but they are certainly part of the mainstream debate about policing. The economist Glenn Loury of Brown University, for example, is quoted on the back cover of *The War on Cops* saying that while he often disagrees with Mac Donald's work, he is "invariably edified" by reading it, and he says, "All serious students of urban America today should read this book and reckon with its arguments" (quoted in Mac Donald 2016).

A number of students at Claremont McKenna and the other nearby Claremont colleges, though, did not believe Mac Donald's arguments were worth reckoning with. They characterized her views as denying that blacks have a right to exist, and they called her a "fascist, a white supremacist, a warhawk, a transphobe, a queerphobe, [and] a classist ... [who is] ignorant of interlocking systems of domination" (quoted in Friedersdorf

---

[5] While the charge of racism is connected to perceptions of *The Bell Curve*, it is not clear that the accusations of being sexist and anti-gay have any connection to Murray's work at all.

2017).[6] When it came time for her talk, 250 protesters blocked the entrance of the building where she was supposed to speak. Out of safety concerns she then spoke in a secret location to small number of people while the talk was live-streamed to a larger audience. Protesters found the new location and were waiting outside, but as Mac Donald explains, "An escape plan through the kitchen into an unmarked police van was devised. I was surrounded by about four cops. Protesters were sitting on the stoop outside the door … but we had taken them by surprise and we got through them" (quoted in Blume 2017).

Riots, Censorship, and Professors

At this point it might still be tempting to think this kind of thing only affects certain kinds of speech or certain kinds of people. If it is not just right-wing provocateurs, maybe it is just conservatives, or just invited speakers, who are the targets. But remember from previous chapters that Yale students vilified Erika and Nicholas Christakis over an email Erika sent about Halloween costume policies. The Christakises were neither outsiders nor conservatives. Neither was Evergreen State College biology professor Bret Weinstein. Since the 1970s Evergreen had observed a tradition called the "Day of Absence," where nonwhite faculty and students would leave the campus and meet elsewhere as a symbolic act to show how valuable nonwhites are in the life of the college. In 2017, though, the organizers reversed this and asked white faculty and students to leave instead. Weinstein objected. "There is a huge difference," he wrote, "between a group or coalition deciding to voluntarily absent themselves from a shared space to highlight their vital and under-appreciated roles and a group or coalition encouraging another group to go away." The latter, he said, "is an act of oppression in and of itself" (quoted in Weiss 2017). About 50 student protesters confronted him and demanded he "stop supporting white supremacy" (quoted in Weiss 2017), that he "stop telling people of color they're fucking useless," and that he "get the fuck out of here" (quoted in Dreher 2017b). When students asked Weinstein

[6]As with the allegations of bigotry against Charles Murray, most of these labels applied to Mac Donald have no obvious connection to her work. The logic of campus activists seems to be that if a person is guilty of one kind of bigotry, they must be guilty of all kinds, and perhaps of other bad things as well. A similar logic might lie behind the accusations that presidential candidate Donald Trump employed homophobic rhetoric on the campaign trail (discussed in the Prologue).

for an explanation of his remarks, he asked, "May I answer that question," only to receive an emphatic "No!" from the crowd (quoted in Dreher 2017b). Weinstein left campus and held class elsewhere when police told him they could not ensure his safety, and the activists then put "Fire Bret" graffiti around campus and put the names and pictures of his students online (Weiss 2017). Shortly after all of that, Evergreen's president, George Bridges, held a town hall meeting where he said he was "grateful to the courageous students who expressed their concerns" and for "this catalyst to expedite the work to which we are jointly committed" (quoted in Haller 2017; Weiss 2017).[7]

Note that what seems most dangerous is criticism of any of the manifestations of victimhood culture or challenges to its core ideology. This is perhaps the only thing Milo Yiannopoulos, Brett Weinstein, and the others we have talked about have in common with each other. It is also what they have in common with theologian Paul Griffiths of Duke Divinity School. When Professor Anathea Portier-Young sent out an email on behalf of the Faculty Diversity and Inclusion Standing Committee encouraging faculty to attend the Racial Equity Institute Phase I Training, which she described as a first step in ensuring that Duke Divinity School becomes "an institution that is both equitable and anti-racist in its practices and culture," Griffiths responded, describing the training as "a waste" and encouraging others not to attend: "It'll be, I predict with confidence, intellectually flaccid: there'll be bromides, clichés, and amen corner rah-rahs in plenty. When (if) it gets beyond that, its illiberal roots and totalitarian tendencies will show." Griffiths encouraged faculty to focus instead on their mission as faculty of the Divinity School: "to think, read, write, and teach about the triune Lord of Christian confession" (quoted in Dreher 2017a).

Elaine Heath, Dean of the Duke Divinity School, responded with a mass email chastising Griffiths for making "disparaging statements—including arguments ad hominem—in order to humiliate or undermine individual colleagues or groups of colleagues" he disagreed with. "The use of mass emails," she added, "to express racism, sexism, or other forms of

---

[7] Bridges eventually reversed his position and said he was "immensely disappointed" in the students he had previously called courageous. Writing at the libertarian magazine *Reason*, Ben Haller says Bridges's reversal "almost certainly stems from the massive backlash the school received over its handling of the protests." The Board of Trustees condemned the protests, a state lawmaker proposed defunding the college, enrollment is down by 35 percent, and Weinstein is suing the college for $3.8 million (Haller 2017).

bigotry is offensive and unacceptable, especially in a Christian institution." Another professor responded to defend Griffiths, noting that Griffiths was only saying publicly what others were saying privately and disputing Heath's claim that Griffiths had expressed "racism, sexism, or other forms of bigotry." "To suggest anything of the sort," he said, "strikes me as either gravely imperceptive or as intellectually dishonest" (quoted in Dreher 2017a). Heath did not retract her claims, though, and instead summoned Griffiths to a meeting so that she could talk with him about professional conduct. When they were unable to agree on the terms of the meeting, Heath banned Griffiths from faculty meetings and from access to travel funds (Dreher 2017a). Meanwhile Portier-Young, the professor who had sent out the email about the training session, filed a complaint against Griffiths with the university's Office of Institutional Equity on the basis that he had engaged in racist and sexist speech that created a hostile work environment. Soon afterward Griffiths resigned from his position with Duke (Beyer 2017).

Though speech that challenges the ideals and practices of victimhood culture provokes activists the most, they may punish professors for other kinds of speech as well. Even those who identify with the activists are not immune. Certainly Mary Spellman, Dean of Students at Claremont McKenna, had no idea she would cause offense when she wrote to thank a student for sharing her article. The student, Lissette Espinosa, had written an op-ed about her struggles as a working-class Mexican–American student. When Espinosa emailed the op-ed to Spellman, Spellman responded by asking if Espinosa would like to meet with her some time. "We have a lot to do as a college and a community," Spellman wrote, adding that the issues the student raised were important to her and to her staff, and that they were "working on how we can better serve students, especially those who do not fit our CMC [Claremont McKenna College] mold" (quoted in Shire 2015). That she was agreeing with Espinosa was clear, but student activists treated the part about fitting the mold not as clumsy phrasing but as if Spellman were declaring Espinosa did not belong at the college. Soon there were protests and hunger strikes, and Dean Spellman eventually resigned.

At the University of Kansas, communications professor Andrea Quenette likely also had no idea she was saying anything offensive when in a discussion on race in her graduate class, she responded to questions from students about how to approach sensitive issues in their teaching. At one point, according to the students, she said, "As a white woman I have just never seen the racism … it's not like I see 'nigger' spraypainted on the walls" (quoted in Gockowski 2016). Quenette explains that this was in the context of talking about racial incidents at other universities. She also seems to have been trying to acknowledge her privilege, something campus activists normally encourage, but some of her students notified the administration and demanded she be fired, both for saying the word *nigger* and for what they interpreted as her claim that "because she has not experienced or witnessed discrimination, it is not happening [on campus]" (quoted in Flaherty 2016). Quenette was suspended from teaching while the university conducted an investigation of the charges, but when the investigation eventually cleared her, she was dismissed anyway, ostensibly for other reasons (Flaherty 2016; Gockowski 2016).[8]

Title IX, Bias Response Teams, Censorship, and Students

Of course it is not just invited speakers and professors whose speech campus activists deem oppressive. The speech codes and free speech zones have mainly been about restricting student speech, and students are still subject to discipline through these and other mechanisms. The Title IX tribunals that we discussed in Chap. 4 in the context of sexual assault accusations are also used to investigate and punish allegations of offensive speech. Laura Kipnis tells of a student investigated by his university's Equal Opportunity Office for laughing at a sexual joke someone made during a card game. And a graduate student, whom Kipnis calls Darren, was investigated for joking with friends at a bar that all the new graduate teaching assistants should have an orgy. When one of the friends told Darren's ex-girlfriend what he had said, she initially reported it, but when she then decided not to file an official complaint, the Title IX investigator became the complainant. While the investigation was going on Darren was banned from campus, and when he complained about that he was threatened with arrest. After he threatened to sue he received notice that he had been found not guilty (Kipnis 2017:164–165).[9]

---

[8] She had asked for a one-year extension for her three-year review, given that she had been on suspension for a substantial part of the time, and though her department and tenure review committee recommended that she get the extension, the dean denied the request (Flaherty 2016; Gockowski 2016).

[9] Faculty might also be subject to these kinds of investigations. Sociologist Nicholas Wolfinger, a professor at the University of Utah, faced a Title IX investigation over an off-campus conversation more than 10 years earlier in which he told female colleagues about his

In one of the more bizarre attempts at censorship, residential advisors at the University of Massachusetts Amherst warned students they could be in violation of Title IX if they continued making jokes about Harambe, a gorilla who had been shot at a Cincinnati zoo to protect a child who had entered his enclosure. The jokes borrowed from Internet memes that treated Harambe as a kind of folk hero or religious figure. Thus one can purchase shot glasses that say "Take a shot for Harambe; he took one for you" or shirts that say "Dicks out for Harambe." Some students had begun writing the latter phrase on each other's white boards, and the residential advisors warned, "Any negative remarks regarding 'Harambe' will be seen as a direct attack to our campus's African American community." They went on to say that phrases or hashtags that "encourage the exposition of body parts runs the risk of being reported as a Title IX incident" (quoted in Soave 2016). One reason for their concern was that *Harambe*, a Swahili word, was also the name of the university's African and African–American residential community, but Harambe jokes also worried administrators at Clemson University, where this was not a factor. There an administrator sent a message to resident advisors saying, "Due to an incident that happened earlier this week, we are no longer allowing any reference to Harambe … to be displayed on doors, halls, billboards, or windows." Later, Graduate Community Director Brooks Artis, in an email to a student who had asked about the ban, wrote, "There have been reports that [Harambe] and the incident surrounding his death have been used to add to the rape culture as well as being a form of racism" (quoted in Ecarma 2016). The student had asked if the university was banning students from saying the name *Harambe*, and Artis said it was not, but he added, "My hopes are that you are being inclusive in your words, whichever you choose to say, so that you are not reported to OCES or Title IX" (quoted in Ecarma 2016). If the student was trying to find out what Clemson students could safely say, Artis's warning that the university could still punish students for using a word it had not officially banned actually provided a clear answer: Nothing.

That nothing is ever safe does not mean that everything results in punishment. It should be clear by now that a defining characteristic of campus censorship is its arbitrariness. Professors question university policies all the time, and some even criticize the left or articulate conservative ideas, but

marriage proposal in a strip club. The university eventually dropped the case, but only after Wolfinger had spent $14,000 in attorney fees to defend himself (Wolfinger 2017).

suddenly a moral panic ensues over a Christakis or a Weinstein. Rarely is any student punished even for unquestionably racist or sexist jokes or slurs, vulgarities, and the like, which would normally not even come to the attention of administrators, but suddenly just laughing at a sexual joke in a private setting or saying the name of a deceased gorilla might get a student in serious trouble with the university. And universities are making it easier for students to report not just their professors, but also their fellow students whenever they say anything that offends them. In addition to the Title IX bureaucracy, which as we discussed in Chap. 4, is partly a response to guidance from the US government, universities have begun setting up various kinds of bias response teams. More than 200 colleges and universities now have them, and usually they allow anyone on campus to make a report about anyone else (FIRE 2017). At the University of California, Santa Cruz, for example, a single poster advertising a "mafia" game was removed after a student filed a bias incident claim. The student said the poster was offensive to her as an Italian American and "could result in the harassment of Italian American students on campus." At the University of Michigan, someone reported a "phallic snow object" (quoted in Snyder and Khalid 2016). At Colby College the bias response team investigated a complaint about someone having a luau, and another about someone who used the phrase "on the other hand," which the complainant characterized as "ableist" (Owens 2017). At the University of Oregon the bias response team received complaints about a newspaper not giving enough coverage to ethnic minorities and transgender students, about students "expressing anger about oppression," about a faculty member giving "relationship advice that was sexist and heterosexist," about a professor belittling a student's request for trigger warnings, and about an email marketing "a program by praising Columbus and Lewis & Clark as role models" (quoted in Steinbaugh 2016). And at the University of Wisconsin-Platteville someone reported three students for dressing up as the Three Blind Mice, since people might have thought the costumes were mocking people with disabilities (FIRE 2017).

Right-Wing Censorship

Most of the bias incidents are the usual fare: complaints about words and behaviors seen by the complainant as offensive in some way to one or more victim groups. These arise from the victimhood culture embraced by campus radicals, but some complaints come from the right. These are complaints that the campus activists are the ones who are offensive. At Cornell University someone reported a professor for comparing police to terrorists, and someone else reported the student government for its attempts to make Cornell a sanctuary campus. At Appalachian State University someone reported a student activist for, among other offenses, hating white men and for expressing disregard for the lives of police officers. And at John Carroll University someone reported the African American Alliance because their protest made white students uncomfortable (FIRE 2017).

The more serious threats from the right, though, come from outside the university. Jonathan Haidt describes the basic pattern. First, a "left-wing professor says something provocative (and sometimes truly inflammatory)," then "right-wing media sites … pick up the story and report it in a way designed to cause maximum outrage," then many readers and viewers "demand the university fire the professor," with some of them writing "racist and sexist social media posts" or even "rape threats and death threats," and then the university's administration, "paralyzed by the public relations crisis," condemns the professor, and if the professor is not tenured, puts "him or her 'on leave' in order to begin the termination process" (Haidt 2017). Thus, when Katherine Dettwyler, an anthropology lecturer at the University of Delaware, gained attention after writing that American college student Otto Warmbier, who had recently died from his imprisonment and abuse by the North Korean government, "got exactly what he deserved," the university put out a statement saying her opinions did not reflect their values and that she would not be teaching there in the future (Quintana 2017; Spada 2017). And when Johnny Eric Williams, a sociology professor at Trinity College, shared an article called "Let Them Fucking Die," which argued that the white congressmen injured by a shooter in June 2017 should have been left to die, and followed it up with Facebook posts saying things such as, "The time is now to confront these inhuman assholes and end this now," Trinity's president quickly announced that Williams would be put on leave (Gockowski 2017; Quintana 2017). Here the statements drawing public ire and university censorship are statements that campus activists would certainly call hate speech if they were directed toward members of victim groups. Campus victimhood culture accepts such speech when directed at oppressors, and sometimes praises it, but it tends to cause scandal when exposed to a wider audience.

*   *   *

In the spring of 2016 the appearance of messages in chalk on the sidewalks of Emory University caused alarm. Emory's president met with a group of concerned students and emailed the university community about it afterward. He assured the students he would review security footage to determine the identity of the chalkers, and "if they're students," he said, "they will go through the conduct violation process." He also said that because of the chalkings the university would refine its "bias incident and response process." And what were the chalked messages that led to all of this? "Trump" and "Trump 2016" (Snyder and Khalid 2016). The attention the Emory incident received then led conservative students throughout the country to put pro-Trump messages in chalk on their campuses. They called it *The Chalkening* (LaChance 2016). The response was as expected. The Hate Response Team at the University of Wisconsin–La Crosse, for example, called the messages "discriminatory" and "hostile" (quoted in Owens 2017).

Those who make arguments for restricting speech on campus have never before said they had in mind preventing expressions of support for a major party candidate in a US presidential election. But as we have argued here, victimhood culture is inherently hostile to free speech, even the speech normally thought to be most in need of protection. Dignity culture is compatible with free speech, and we do see clashes between dignity culture and victimhood culture over free speech on college campuses. But free speech has seldom been an ideal historically. Most people have wanted to ban speech that offends them and allow speech that does not. This is what the adherents of victimhood culture want, and increasingly, it may be what many of their opponents want too. The attacks on speech emanating from campus victimhood culture might increasingly be met with counterattacks from ideological enemies rather than defenders of free speech. Here again, opposition leads to imitation. We have seen that conservative students make reports of their own to the bias response teams and that members of the public often demand the firing of left-wing professors over offensive comments. Conservative students who invite Milo Yiannopolous to speak likewise are not embracing a culture of dignity, which abhors personal insults as well as sensitivity. Outside of the university we have seen Trump supporters behaving much like the anti-Yiannapolous rioters in storming the stage during a performance of the Shakespeare play *Julius Caesar* that depicted a Trump-like Caesar being assassinated (Jenkins 2017). The clash between dignity culture and victimhood culture, though still ongoing, may prove to be short-lived.

Victimhood culture may triumph at colleges and universities while dignity culture withers away everywhere. The only opponents of victimhood in the larger society may end up being right-wingers who eschew dignity and are just as thin skinned and intolerant as the campus left.

References

Adams, Becket. 2015. Cuomo Clarifies His 'Clumsy' Claim About First Amendment. *Washington Examiner*, May 7. http://www.washingtonexaminer.com/cnns-cuomo-clarifies-his-clumsy-claim-about-first-amendment/article/2564175.

American Association of University Professors. 1940. *1940 Statement of Principles on Academic Freedom and Tenure.* https://www.aaup.org/report/1940-statement-principles-academic-freedom-and-tenure.

Andone, Dakin, and Darran Simon. 2017. Portland Mayor Asks Feds to Stop 'Alt-Right' Rallies. *CNN*, May 30. http://www.cnn.com/2017/05/29/us/portland-scheduled-demonstrations/index.html.

Asimov, Nanette. 2017. Provocateur Milo Yiannopoulos to Have His Say at UC Berkeley. *San Francisco Chronicle*, January 29. http://www.sfchronicle.com/education/article/Provocateur-Milo-Yiannopoulos-to-have-his-say-at-10892849.php.

Baer, Ulrich. 2017. What 'Snowflakes' Get Right About Free Speech. *New York Times*, April 24. https://www.nytimes.com/2017/04/24/opinion/what-liberal-snowflakes-get-right-about-free-speech.html.

Barrett, Lisa Feldman. 2017. When Is Speech Violence? *The New York Times*, July 14. https://www.nytimes.com/2017/07/14/opinion/sunday/when-is-speech-violence.html.

Beinart, Peter. 2017. A Violent Attack on Free Speech at Middlebury. *The Atlantic*, March 6. https://www.theatlantic.com/politics/archive/2017/03/middlebury-free-speech-violence/518667/.

Berger, Peter L. 1970. On the Obsolescence of the Concept of Honor. *European Journal of Sociology* 11: 339–347.

Beyer, Adam. 2017. Divinity School Professor Resigns After Dispute with Colleagues About Diversity Training, Calling It a 'Waste.' *The Chronicle*, May 9. http://www.dukechronicle.com/article/2017/05/divinity-school-professor-resigns-after-dispute-with-colleagues-about-diversity-training-calling-it-a-waste.

Blume, Howard. 2017. Protesters Disrupt Talk by Pro-Police Author, Sparking Free-Speech Debate at Claremont McKenna. *Los Angeles Times*, April 9. http://www.latimes.com/local/lanow/la-me-ln-macdonald-claremont-speech-disrupted-20170408-story.html.

Bowman, Rex, and Carlos Santos. 2013. *Rot, Riot, and Rebellion: Mr. Jefferson's Struggle to Save the University That Saved America*. Charlottesville: University of Virginia Press.

California State University, Los Angeles. 2009. *Faculty Handbook*. http://www.calstatela.edu/academicsenate/handbook/ch3a.

Claremont McKenna College. 2015. *CMC Demonstrations and Response Policy*. https://d28htnjz2elwuj.cloudfront.net/wp-content/uploads/2013/10/28031540/CMC-Demonstrations-and-Response-Policy-Claremont-McKenna-College-Acalog-ACMS™.pdf.

Cobb, Jelani. 2015. Race and the Free-Speech Diversion. *The New Yorker*, November 10. http://www.newyorker.com/news/news-desk/race-and-the-free-speech-diversion.

Coulter, Ann. 2001. This Is War. *Townhall*, September 14. https://townhall.com/columnists/anncoulter/2001/09/14/this-is-war-n865496.

Dang, Nisa. 2017. Check Your Privilege When Speaking of Protests. *The Daily Californian*, February 7. http://www.dailycal.org/2017/02/07/check-privilege-speaking-protests/.

Dean-Johnson, Liam, Aidan Dunbar, Anastasiya Gorodilova, Nico Sedivy, and Madison Shiver. 2015. Dean-Jonson '16, Dunbar '16, Gorodilova '16, Sedivy '17, Shiver '17: On Whiteness, Free Speech and Missing the Point. *The Brown Daily Herald*, October 19. http://www.browndailyherald.com/2015/10/19/dean-johnson-16-dunbar-16-gorodilova-16-sedivy-17-shiver-17-on-whiteness-free-speech-and-missing-the-point/.

Dreher, Rod. 2017a. Duke Divinity Crisis: The Documents Are Out. *The American Conservative*, May 7. http://www.theamericanconservative.com/dreher/duke-divinity-crisis-griffiths-documents/.

———. 2017b. The Hunting of Bret Weinstein. *The American Conservative*, May 25. http://www.theamericanconservative.com/dreher/hunting-of-bret-weinstein-evergreen-state/.

Ecarma, Caleb. 2016. Clemson Bans Harambe Memes for Promoting 'Rape Culture,' Racism. *Campus Reform*, September 26. http://www.campusreform.org/?ID=8173.

Evergreen State College. 2017. *Evergreen's Social Contract*. Evergreen State College website. http://www.evergreen.edu/about/social.

FIRE. 2017. *Bias Response Team Report*. Foundation for Individual Rights in Education (FIRE). https://www.thefire.org/first-amendment-library/special-collections/fire-guides/report-on-bias-reporting-systems-2017/.

Fish, Stanley. 2014. *Versions of Academic Freedom: From Professionalism to Revolution*. Chicago: University of Chicago Press.

Flaherty, Colleen. 2016. Professor Cleared and Still Out of a Job. *Inside Higher Ed*, May 18. https://www.insidehighered.com/news/2016/05/18/professor-says-she-was-fired-over-well-intentioned-ill-received-class-discussion.

Frechette, Nicole, Luis de Leon, Keaton Walkowski, Jenna Daroszewski, and Kaliice Walker. 2016. Transgender Student Tells UW-Milwaukee Chancellor to 'F' Off After Yiannopoulos Speech. *Media Milwaukee*, December 14. http://mediamilwaukee.com/top-stories/milo-yiannopoulos-milwaukee-tour-twitter-uw-uwm-transgender-lockerroom-policy-breitbart-alt-right.

Friedersdorf, Conor. 2017. Words Which by Their Very Utterance Inflict Injury. *The Atlantic*, April 19. https://www.theatlantic.com/politics/archive/2017/04/words-which-by-their-very-utterance-inflict-injury/523344/.

Gallagher, Maggie. 2015. Yale Wasn't Made for People Like Me Either. *National Review*, November 13. http://www.nationalreview.com/article/427041/yale-wasnt-made-people-me-either-maggie-gallagher.

Gockowski, Anthony. 2016. KU Prof Loses Job Despite Being Cleared by Investigation. *Campus Reform*, May 26.

———. 2017. Prof Calls Whites 'Inhuman Assholes,' Says 'Let Them Die.' *Campus Reform*, June 20. http://www.campusreform.org/?ID=9334.

Haidt, Jonathan. 2017. Professors Must Now Fear Intimidation from Both Sides. *Heterodox Academy*, June 28. https://heterodoxacademy.org/2017/06/28/professors-must-now-fear-intimidation-from-both-sides/.

Haller, Ben. 2017. Professor Bret Weinstein Files $3.8 Million Claim Against Evergreen State College. *Reason*, August 2. http://reason.com/blog/2017/08/02/professor-bret-weinstein-files-38-millio.

Hampson, Sarah. 2016. Derald Wing Sue on Microaggression, the Implicit Racism Minorities Endure. *The Globe and Mail*, July 8. http://www.theglobeandmail.com/life/relationships/derald-wing-sue-on-microaggressions-racism/article30821500/.

Hess, Amanda. 2016. Earning the 'Woke' Badge. *New York Times Magazine*, April 19. https://www.nytimes.com/2016/04/24/magazine/earning-the-woke-badge.html.

Jefferson, Thomas. 2011. *The Writings of Thomas Jefferson: Volume 7*, ed. H.A. Washington. New York: Cambridge University Press.

Jenkins, Aric. 2017. Pro-Trump Protesters Interrupt 'Shakespeare in the Park' Performance of 'Julius Caesar.' *Time*, June 17. http://time.com/4822840/shakespeare-in-the-park-donald-trump-protests/.

Kelly-Woessner, April. 2015. How Marcuse Made Today's Students Less Tolerant Than Their Parents. *Heterodox Academy*, September 23. https://heterodoxacademy.org/2015/09/23/how-marcuse-made-todays-students-less-tolerant-than-their-parents/.

Kipnis, Laura. 2017. *Unwanted Advances: Sexual Paranoia Comes to Campus*. New York: HarperCollins.

Korn, Sandra Y.L. 2014. The Doctrine of Academic Freedom. *The Harvard Crimson*, February 18. http://www.thecrimson.com/column/the-red-line/article/2014/2/18/academic-freedom-justice/?page=single#.

Kors, Alan Charles. 1999. Cracking the Speech Code. *Reason*, July 1. http://reason.com/archives/1999/07/01/cracking-the-speech-code/print.

LaChance, Mike. 2016. #TheChalkening—Students for Trump Troll Campuses. *Legal Insurrection* (Blog), April 2. http://legalinsurrection.com/2016/04/thechalkening-students-for-trump-troll-campuses/.

Lawrence, Neil. 2017. Black Bloc Did What Campus Should Have. *The Daily Californian*, February 7. http://www.dailycal.org/2017/02/07/black-bloc-campus/.

Lee, Adam. 2013. Free Speech Vs. Freeze Peach. *Daylight Atheism* (Blog), May 31. http://www.patheos.com/blogs/daylightatheism/2013/05/free-speech-vs-freeze-peach/.

Lukianoff, Greg. 2014. *Unlearning Liberty: Campus Censorship and the End of American Debate*. New York: Encounter Books.

Mac Donald, Heather. 2016. *The War on Cops: How the New Attack on Law and Order Makes Everyone Less Safe*. New York: Encounter Books.

McMillen, Neil R. 1990. *Dark Journey: Black Mississippians in the Age of Jim Crow*. Urbana: University of Illinois Press.

Meagley, Desmond. 2017. Condemning Protesters Same as Condoning Hate Speech. *The Daily Californian*, February 7. http://www.dailycal.org/2017/02/07/condemning-protesters-condoning-hate-speech/.

Melkonian, Harry. 2012. *Freedom of Speech and Society: A Social Approach to Freedom of Expression*. Amherst: Cambria Press.

Mill, John Stuart. 2005. *On Liberty*. Lanham: Rowman and Littlefield.

Moore, Chadwick. 2016. Send in the Clown: Internet Supervillain Milo Doesn't Care That You Hate Him. *Out*, September 21. https://www.out.com/out-exclusives/2016/9/21/send-clown-internet-supervillain-milo-doesnt-care-you-hate-him.

Nielsen, Laura Beth. 2017. The Case for Restricting Hate Speech. *Los Angeles Times*, June 21. http://www.latimes.com/opinion/op-ed/la-oe-nielsen-free-speech-hate-20170621-story.html.

Oberlin College General Faculty. 1986. Faculty Statement on Freedom of Speech and Expression. *Oberlin College Website*. https://new.oberlin.edu/students/policies/oberlin-college-policies-and-procedures-for-protests-and-demonstration.

Oppenheim, Maya. 2017. Milo Yiannopoulos Sparks Outrage After Calling for Muslim Group Ban at Glasgow University. *Independent*, March 16. http://www.independent.co.uk/news/uk/home-news/milo-yiannopoulos-rector-glasgow-university-muslim-uni-group-ban-a7633936.html.

Owens, Eric. 2017. *The Daily Caller* Presents: The 12 Dumbest Ever 'Bias Incidents' on America's College Campuses. *The Daily Caller*, February 25. http://dailycaller.com/2017/02/25/the-daily-caller-presents-the-12-dumbest-ever-bias-incidents-on-americas-college-campuses/.

Peters, Jeremy W., and Thomas Fuller. 2017. Ann Coulter Says She Will Pull Out of Speech at Berkeley. *New York Times*, April 26. https://www.nytimes.com/2017/04/26/us/ann-coulter-berkeley-speech.html.

Petri, Alexandra. 2012. Harvard's Free Speech Problem—In Defense of the Bad Joke. *Washington Post*, December 5. https://www.washingtonpost.com/blogs/compost/wp/2012/12/05/harvards-free-speech-problem-in-defense-of-the-bad-joke/?utm_term=.db3b3c161e34.

Pinker, Steven. 2011. *The Better Angels of Our Nature: Why Violence Has Declined*. New York: Viking.

Prieto, Juan. 2017. Violence Helped Ensure Safety of Students. *The Daily Californian*, February 7. http://www.dailycal.org/2017/02/07/violence-helped-ensure-safety-students/.

Quintana, Chris. 2017. Under Fire, These Professors Were Criticized by Their Colleges. *The Chronicle of Higher Education*, June 28. http://www.chronicle.com/article/Under-Fire-These-Professors/240457.

Rosen, Jeffrey. 2002. Fighting Words. *Legal Affairs*, May/June. http://www.legalaffairs.org/issues/May-June-2002/scene_rosen_mayjun2002.html.

Seelye, Katharine Q. 2017. Protesters Disrupt Speech by 'Bell Curve' Author at Vermont College. *New York Times*, March 3. https://www.nytimes.com/2017/03/03/us/middlebury-college-charles-murray-bell-curve-protest.html?_r=2.

Senju, Haruka. 2017. Violence as Self Defense. *The Daily Californian*, February 7. http://www.dailycal.org/2017/02/07/violence-self-defense/comment-page-5/.

Shire, Emily. 2015. P.C. Police Tearing Apart California's Claremont McKenna College. *The Daily Beast*, November 13. http://www.thedailybeast.com/pc-police-tearing-apart-californias-claremont-mckenna-college.

Silvergate, Harvey A., David French, and Greg Lukianoff. 2012. *FIRE's Guide to Free Speech on Campus*. 2nd ed. Philadelphia: Foundation for Individual Rights in Education (FIRE). https://www.thefire.org/wp-content/uploads/2014/02/FIRE-Guide-to-Free-Speech-on-Campus-2nd-ed.pdf.

Singal, Jesse. 2016. Explaining Ben Shapiro's Messy, Ethnic-Slur-Laden Breakup with Breitbart. *New York Magazine*, May 26. http://nymag.com/daily/intelligencer/2016/05/ben-shapiros-messy-breakup-with-breitbart.html.

Smith, Isaac. 2017. *Say It Again for the People in the Back: Freedom to Speak Includes the Freedom to Hear*. Foundation for Individual Rights in Education (FIRE), July 19. https://www.thefire.org/say-it-again-for-the-people-in-the-back-freedom-to-speak-includes-the-freedom-to-hear/.

Snyder, Jeffrey Aaron, and Amna Khalid. 2016. The Rise of 'Bias Response Teams' on Campus. *The New Republic*, March 30. https://newrepublic.com/article/132195/rise-bias-response-teams-campus.

Soave, Robby. 2016. UMass-Amherst: Harambe Jokes Are Racist Microaggressions, Violate Title IX. *Reason*, September 6. http://reason.com/blog/2016/09/06/umass-amherst-harambe-jokes-are-racist-m.

Spada, Shannon. 2017. Prof Says Otto Warmbier 'Got Exactly What He Deserved.' *Campus Reform*, June 22. http://www.campusreform.org/?ID=9350.

Steinbaugh, Adam. 2016. *University of Oregon on 'Bias Response Team': Nothing to See Here*. Foundation for Individual Rights in Education (FIRE), May 27. https://www.thefire.org/university-of-oregon-on-bias-response-team-nothing-to-see-here/.

University of California, Los Angeles. 2010. *UCLA Regulations on Activities, Registered Campus Organizations, and Use of Properties*. https://equity.ucla.edu/wp-content/uploads/2017/05/UCLA-TPM-Regulations.pdf.

Volokh, Eugene. 2017. No, Gov. Dean, There Is No 'Hate Speech' Exception to the First Amendment. *Washington Post*, April 21. https://www.washington-post.com/news/volokh-conspiracy/wp/2017/04/21/no-gov-dean-there-is-no-hate-speech-exception-to-the-first-amendment/?tid=a_inl&utm_term=.be82be9664b3.

Weinstein, James. 2009. An Overview of American Free Speech Doctrine and Its Application to Free Speech. In *Extreme Speech and Democracy*, ed. Ivan Hare and James Weinstein, 81–91. New York: Oxford University Press.

Weiss, Bari. 2017. When the Left Turns on Its Own. *New York Times*, June 1. https://www.nytimes.com/2017/06/01/opinion/when-the-left-turns-on-its-own.html.

Williams, Jack K. 1980. *Dueling in the Old South: Vignettes of Social History*. College Station: Texas A&M University Press.

Williams, Joanna. 2016. *Academic Freedom in an Age of Conformity: Confronting the Fear of Knowledge*. New York: Palgrave Macmillan.

Williams, Wendy M., and Stephen J. Cici. 2017. Charles Murray's 'Provocative' Talk. *New York Times*, April 15. https://www.nytimes.com/2017/04/15/opinion/sunday/charles-murrays-provocative-talk.html.

Wolfinger, Nicholas. 2017. How I Survived the Title IX Star Chamber. *Quillette*, August 24. http://quillette.com/2017/08/24/survived-title-ix-star-chamber/.

Yiannopoulos, Milo. 2016. Full Text: Milo on How Feminism Hurts Men and Women. *Breitbart News*, October 7. http://www.breitbart.com/milo/2016/10/07/full-text-milo-feminism-auburn/.

CHAPTER 8

Conclusion

The Marquis de la Donze, a seventeenth-century French aristocrat, killed his brother-in-law in a duel. He was arrested, tried, and condemned to death. A priest visited him prior to the execution and asked if he wanted to pray for forgiveness for his crime. The condemned man exclaimed, "Do you call one of the cleverest thrusts in Gascony a crime?" (Baldick 1965:62, cited in Black 1989:33).

To the end this duelist did not accept the state's judgment of his conduct—he had defended his honor, as any man of good standing would. If anything, people should admire the swordsmanship that granted him victory. Many others arrested and condemned for dueling must have been similarly bewildered to see their actions punished rather than praised. What was wrong with people? Did honor mean nothing these days?

Contemporary people might feel some sympathy with these baffled duelists, even if they feel none for their code of honor. The clash of different moral frameworks is often bewildering, and the clashes of our own time are no different. For some the shock is to see innocuous statements and innocent questions result in such uproar. Protests, public shaming, firings, investigations, expulsions—all over things that are rude at worst and often not even that. For others it can be almost inconceivable that anyone would not share their outrage. Racism, sexism, homophobia—oppression saturates our society, and many people are too blinded by privilege to see the damage it causes. And there are still those who are unaware that any moral clash is taking place, tending their own lives in blissful ignorance of the distant storm—until it heads their way.

THE PUZZLE OF MORAL CULTURES

The culture we share with others has a kind of invisibility. We tend to take the customs of our own culture for granted. They seem natural and inevitable, simply the way the world works. This is true of shared morality as well. Right and wrong seem to be self-evident, matters of objective fact. It is only when faced with deep differences, with cultural miscommunication and moral conflict, that we become aware that our way of seeing the world is not universally shared.

Even then it can be difficult to comprehend that others view things so differently. Our usual tendency is to see those who violate our moral norms as simply lacking morality altogether. In a context where a single moral framework dominates, this may even have some truth (Leung and Cohen 2011).[1] But oftentimes the reality is that others have their own ideas about right and wrong—ideals that might run counter to ours but that they nonetheless take quite seriously. It can sometimes strain the moral imagination to see that this is true, but it is true nonetheless. A first-century Roman aristocrat would be genuinely mystified by the argument that slavery was evil and not the natural order of things. A slave who had recently purchased his freedom and harbored ambitions of one day owning slaves of his own might not understand either. How would you convince them that such a taken-for-granted aspect of their world was fundamentally wrong? What shared moral principle might you appeal to? And how would you respond if either of them criticized you for your failure to adhere to their virtues, such as dutiful sacrifice to the gods or obedience to the authority of a paterfamilias?

People from the same nation and time period are rarely so different. The moral cultures of the modern West overlap in various ways, and they present more opportunities for persuasion through appeal to common

---

[1] In a series of innovative experiments, Angela Leung and Dov Cohen (2011) found that people from more honorable cultures (such as the US South) who endorsed honor violence were more likely to be honest and helpful than those who did not. In contrast, people from dignity cultures (such as the US North) who endorsed honor violence were less likely to be honest and helpful than those who did not. Their explanation for this is that people who fail to adhere to one aspect of the prevailing moral code are more likely to fail to adhere to other aspects as well. The honor and dignity cultures represented in the study both value honesty and helpfulness in similar ways, but have opposing values regarding violence. Therefore endorsement of violence is an indicator of less integrity in one culture and greater integrity in the other.

ideals. Yet the differences that exist can still be stark—and quite confusing when we first encounter them.

In our work we have striven to make sense of these differences. We have done this by making a distinction between three moral systems: cultures of honor, dignity, and victimhood. The first two concepts have a long history in the social sciences; the last is our innovation.[2] It may be that readers see problems with these concepts. Perhaps you dislike our terminology and would prefer different labels for these things. Perhaps you would prefer to classify things differently—dividing, merging, or completely replacing our categories. In any case, the moral variation we point to is a fact—or rather, a set of facts. And we believe our classification helps us order these facts and contributes to our ability to explain them.

We explain moral variation with social structure. Drawing from the work of a pioneering sociologist of conflict, Donald Black, we sought relationships between each aspect of victimhood culture and a social condition that encourages people to behave in that way. A combination of diversity and equality makes ethnic slurs and other intergroup offenses extremely deviant. The presence and power of social superiors makes reliance on third parties increasingly attractive. Combined with a shortage of strong ties and a surfeit of weak ones, it makes public complaint increasingly likely. The combination of all three conditions leads to complaints of oppression and condemnation of privilege. Once initiated, the ideals and practices of victimhood culture themselves alter social conditions, setting in play dynamics that are likely to cause this moral system to intensify and spread.

Our analysis is necessarily limited: We can tackle only so many problems at once. We have only briefly touched on some topics related to moral culture and changing social conditions and have addressed others not at all. The reader may think of other ways of characterizing modern society and contemporary social change, many of which also speak of the transformation from one kind of culture to another. The odds are that none of these various descriptions are mutually exclusive, but are merely drawing attention to different, if related, things. After all, at any given time there are many social trends. We have barely touched on the growth of class divisions or the effects of declining social capital. We have not focused on the ability of social media to create ideological echo chambers or on the

---

[2] The term *victimhood culture* has been used before, but we have seen no one else define it as we have and classify it as a moral culture distinct from honor and dignity cultures.

roots and consequences of increasing political polarization. These trends and others surely interact with the kind of moral variation we discuss, but addressing these interactions is simply beyond the scope of this book.

We have also neglected some aspects of the moral cultures we describe. Some scholars will no doubt see our failure to discuss gender differences as a major flaw. It is true that men and women often relate to prevailing moral cultures in different ways, and those cultures might proscribe different behaviors to each. Honor, for example, tends to be highly gendered, with male and female honor meaning quite different things. Given the central role of violence, it also tends to emphasize masculinity and to occur in patriarchal societies where men thoroughly dominate public life. Victimhood culture, which asks men to confess their privilege but is sensitive to slights against women, appears to do much the opposite. This issue and others are worth investigating further. Our analysis is not exhaustive, and it invites extension. No theory is ever perfect or final, and ours will almost certainly require revision as systematic studies provide more evidence. But as a first approximation we believe it is both correct and useful.

Others agree. Indeed, we wrote this book in part because our first article on this topic received a great deal of attention, much of it positive, in the form of news articles, editorials, and blog posts. Our academic readers, at least, will understand how unusual it is for anyone outside our specialties to pay attention to what we write. In hindsight, though, we understand why so many were interested. Victimhood culture's rapid rise to prominence has been both startling and confusing. Indeed, for many, especially those outside of the academy, the more extreme manifestations of victimhood culture must seem like the manners and customs of some foreign land. The conflicts that arise as campus activists encounter opposition and detractors are also interesting, perhaps bewildering.

Those seeking to understand this new culture or contextualize campus debates have little else available to help them. The academic articles by proponents are little more than propaganda, while the polemics of opponents tend to offer condemnation without insight. Many are hungry for a better understanding of what is going on, and our work offers to place the debate in a larger context. Those who have strong moral reactions to the focus on minor slights can now see this as an alternative morality, one with its own logic, which in this respect resembles the honor cultures of the past. Hopefully they can better understand their own views, too, as emanating from the ideals of dignity. Those who object that microaggressions and similar offenses are not minor, and who have strong moral reactions to those who say otherwise, might gain a similar understanding.

Yet there will be others who see our analysis quite differently. These critics will not just point out whatever empirical shortcomings or scientific imperfections they see in our work. Rather, they will find moral imperfections and judge our work to be an act of deviance itself.

Sociology as Deviance

Sociology at its best is still an imprecise science. Unlike physicists we express our theories in ordinary words instead of mathematical equations. We rarely use controlled experiments and often rely instead on observations of behavior in natural, uncontrolled settings. Even when we do use experiments—or rely on the experiments of our colleagues in social psychology—we face the problem that the study of human beings simply cannot involve the same rigorous degree of control found in the study of objects.

Still, what makes a science *science* is that it involves considering observations and generating ideas that can be tested against evidence. A scientific theory proposes relationships between aspects of the world—gravity and mass, or social distance and partisanship—that can be used to derive hypotheses about what sort of patterns we should expect to see. These hypotheses can then be compared to our observations and accepted, discarded, or revised as necessary. Our theory of victimhood culture is a scientific theory in this sense. Throughout this book we have proposed and suggested empirical relationships. The ideas in our analysis are about matters of fact and can be tested against observations.

Yet it seems inevitable that some will view our work as a polemic and our claims as moral ones rather than empirical ones. They will view our work as moral opposition. As we noted in Chap. 1, some of this is because of the cultural contradictions involved in championing victims and denouncing the privileged. To the extent that people embrace this moral framework, it will be difficult for them to view victimhood as a source of moral status that can provide social advantages. When one's worldview is focused on dividing people into victims and oppressors, the marginalized and the privileged, it might seem completely wrongheaded to observe that the privileged can in anyway be disadvantaged and the disadvantaged can be in any way privileged. As Donald Black writes, referring to political criticisms of his own theories of law and social control, "If I disturb your universe I may be worthy of contempt. I may appear to be your favorite political enemy, a conservative if you are radical, a radical if you are conservative" (1995:867).

There is also the fact that few people try to explain beliefs and behaviors that they view as obviously correct. We believe in something because it is true, and it is only the errors of those we disagree with that need explaining (Bloor 1976). This is all the more so for morality. Right and wrong can seem so natural and obvious that it never occurs to us that our reactions require an explanation. Any attempt to scientifically explain one's own closely held beliefs and strong moral reactions might thus seem not only bizarre but almost sacrilegious. Our morality is sacred, and subjecting it to sociology can be an act of serious deviance.

This is why our work is most successful with those whose own views clash with victimhood culture and who find its rise fascinating and confusing. It is also why victimhood culture's strongest adherents find our work morally offensive and interpret it as a criticism of their beliefs. That we try to explain victimhood culture marks us as outsiders rather than believers.

And to some degree they are right: We *are* outsiders. When we describe dignity culture in terms of proverbs parents teach their children, such as the "sticks and stones" saying, we are relating statements we heard from adults when we were children. We find microaggression complaints and related behaviors fascinating in large part because they diverge so much from our prior experience and from our own moral ideals. In much the same way, earlier scholars looking back at the duels of a bygone age were fascinated by how different this morality was from that of their own time. The concept of honor culture came not from the honorable themselves, but from twentieth-century scholars who stood outside of its norms. True, they labeled this culture with a term—honor—that its adherents saw as positive. But the honorable would likely bridle at many other descriptions of themselves and their culture—that they were thin-skinned, sensitive to slight, belligerent, and so forth. They might also take umbrage at being contrasted with a culture of dignity, which might seem like an accusation that they were undignified. It seems inevitable that moral codes are described by outsiders in contrast to their own, and that these descriptions are likely to provoke offense to insiders.

Yet we reiterate that our analysis neither condemns nor praises anything. It makes no moral claims at all. It is true that, as with anyone else who studies anything at all, our values, interests, and preconceptions shape what we give attention to and how we go about understanding it.[3] Clearly we have focused on some subjects, such as the state of sociology and threats to academic freedom, that are relevant to our own lives and livelihoods. Perhaps we have given more attention to the consequences of victimhood culture that we and other readers find undesirable and less to those that our readers would find beneficial. But the objectivity of our work, and of science in general, does not lie in the minds and motives of individuals. It arises from making testable claims that are open to argument and debate in light of evidence. And even if our claims are exactly accurate, they have no moral implications of their own. Our analysis might imply more or less effective ways of pursuing moral goals, but it can never tell you what these goals ought to be. You bring those to the table yourself.

CLARIFYING THE CAMPUS CULTURE WARS

As we discussed in Chap. 6, value judgments are not sociology, and sociology, as such, does not make value judgments. But sociology and other social sciences are certainly relevant to debates over policy, even if these are fundamentally driven by moral concerns. The relevance of social science is to provide empirical clarity about what the consequences of a policy are likely to be, so that decision makers can weigh its costs and benefits in light of competing moral values.

One place where empirical clarity might be relevant to the current campus culture wars is in measuring the extent to which certain types of verbal slight cause harm. As we discussed in Chap. 3, *harm* can be defined in many ways. But to the extent that people can roughly agree on how to define and measure it, they might be able to at least agree on the extent of the problem. This would not necessarily end the debate, as protecting students from verbal slights and trauma triggers necessarily requires curtailing

---

[3] That this is so can lead to the charge that because we have not addressed some topic in detail, we do not find it morally or practically significant. That we have focused more on hate crime hoaxes than actual hate crimes, more on the far left than on the far right, more on moral panics over rape than on the problem of rape itself, can lead readers to jump to the conclusion we are not at all concerned with hate crimes, rape, or right-wing extremism. This is simply not so. We focus here on a phenomenon that we find sociologically interesting because of its newness and because of its contrast with the moral cultures we have been writing and teaching about for years. Our interest does not imply anything about the relative moral importance of any widely recognized problems in the modern world.

freedom of speech, and even two people who value both might assign different weights to each value when making their moral calculus. But among those who are similar in their values, this information would be important.

Note that any such research would need to look at empirically defined offenses—such as a particular statement or use of a particular slur. Otherwise the researcher could not distinguish the harm inflicted by an offense from the harm of defining something as offensive. And as we discussed in Chaps. 1 and 3, this is an important distinction to make. The current microaggression program advances no behavioral definition of microaggression—a microaggression is whatever individuals from victim groups define as such. This makes it impossible to tell whether or not a correlation between experiencing microaggression and some outcome is due simply to viewing things as microaggressions. This undermines Lisa Feldman Barrett's (2017) proposal that we distinguish harmful speech by its physiological effects, such as the impact of elevated stress hormones. As experimental work by psychologist Dov Cohen et al. (1996) has shown, moral culture shapes how people react to slights, including how their bodies react. People raised in cultures with stronger notions of honor, such as the US South as compared to the US North, actually experience greater physiological stress when insulted than do those from more dignified cultures (Cohen et al. 1996). Lukianoff and Haidt (2015) have similarly proposed that the stress and mental health issues associated with microaggressions and trauma triggers may be due less to the actual content of these offenses than to the way people are taught to view them. Thus if we are to argue about the costs and benefits of speech codes in terms of the harms they might prevent, we must have research that can measure harm in an appropriate way. Until we do there is little way to adjudicate the dispute between those who say trigger warnings, safe spaces, and microaggression training are beneficial and those who say they are counterproductive.

Lukianoff and Haidt's (2015) argument points to a possibility not often considered in campus debates, which tend to focus on balancing the interests of those who might be harmed by microaggressions with the interests of those whose freedoms would be curtailed by anti-microaggression policies. Now we must question whether such policies would benefit anyone at all, and whether they would in fact harm those they are intended to help. Regardless of one's moral stance, this is an important point, exactly because it is a point that proponents of these policies—or, for that matter, just about any policy at all—are unlikely to consider.

Sociological analysis raises a similar question. Those who campaign against microaggression on campus often have the stated goal of minimizing intercollective conflicts. Ethicist Regina Rini (2015), for example, says the goal of microaggression policies is "a culture in which no one is denied full moral recognition." Since the idea is that even perceived slights deny people full moral recognition, what she is hoping for is a world without offense, a world without conflict. Sociologists might immediately think of Emile Durkheim, whose work we quoted in Chap. 1. Durkheim held that social groups by their nature find and police deviance, such that in a society of saints, without crimes as we know them, the least saintly would still be branded criminals (Durkheim 1982:100). This indeed seems to be the logic of the purity spirals we discussed in Chap. 5, in which activists police their ranks and shame their own allies and sympathizers for being insufficiently devoted or overly privileged. It also appears to be the case when we look at the highly tolerant, diverse, and egalitarian environments of college campuses, where words and images that are considered completely normal in the broader society are a source of great outrage and pain.

Donald Black's (2011) theory of conflict helps us explain why this would be so, and it implies a way to mitigate it. Social changes, both small and large, cause conflict—beginning or ending a relationship, rising or falling in status, accepting or rejecting an aspect of culture. In this view conflict inheres in social life and will exist as long as social life exists. Conflict is inevitable, but it is also variable. To reduce conflict, reduce its causes. One cause of conflict is conflict itself, as ways of expressing and handling grievances provoke new grievances in turn: "Punishment might cause more crime by a criminal, for instance, or it might cause someone else to retaliate against those who inflicted the punishment. Conflict causes more conflict, possibly continuing far into the future" (Black 2011:9).

One way to reduce conflict is to attempt to avoid giving offense—to follow norms of restraint and politeness. This is consistent with the norms of dignity culture, and to some degree with the contemporary microaggression program—which may help call attention to some of the ways we can accidentally give offense, and thus allow us to be more polite. But another way to reduce conflict is to avoid taking offense—to be tolerant of others and restrained in one's response to minor slights. This too is consistent with dignity culture, particularly its admonitions to ignore insults and eschew violence. But it is not at all consistent with the microaggression program and with victimhood culture in general. Victimhood culture encourages less tolerance of slight; indeed, it promotes constant vigilance and outrage. In this respect, it is similar to honor cultures, which are also intolerant of slights and demand a severe response. Honor cultures maximize conflict, allowing a single insult to escalate into a chain of retaliatory violence. Though victimhood culture does not encourage violence in the same way that honor cultures do, it too maximizes conflict and encourages chains of unending recrimination. Microaggression complaints encourage less tolerance for slight, and they invite backlash and counterclaims of victimhood. The likely result of microaggression complaints is not the kind of culture Rini and others envision; it is instead a culture rife with animosities, with ethnic conflict even more pronounced.

Again this is not a moral argument, and even if we are correct it does not resolve the moral debate. Conflict is not always undesirable compared to other options, or tolerance desirable. Recall that dignity culture encourages the toleration of verbal offenses, but not of violence. The idea is that some offenses are too serious to tolerate. Many victimhood adherents likely believe something similar about microaggressions. In Chap. 1 we quoted law professor Catharine Wells, who rejected the "stick and stones" saying because "these words are hurtful" (2013:337). Others who see the emotional hurt of microaggressions as morally equivalent to violence may find it appropriate to police them even at high cost.

Sociology cannot tell us whether victimhood culture is right to blur the line between violence and speech or whether dignity culture is right to see them as ethically distinct. Sociology's potential benefits are considerable, but they are connected to its limitations. Sociology can provide clarity in moral disputes, but it cannot solve them. To claim that it does so is to confuse things and thus fail to benefit from any clarity it might have provided. Our analysis of victimhood culture, if it is true, can add to our understanding of debates about microaggression and other phenomena, but whether it is true or false does not depend on how people decide to evaluate those phenomena. Nor does an acceptance of our analysis require a particular evaluation. It could coexist with several different responses to victimhood culture: condemnation, partial acceptance, full acceptance, or praise.

Still, as we have acknowledged, the greatest interest in our work is likely to come from those who are to some degree, like us, outsiders to victimhood culture and perhaps skeptical or critical of its more extreme manifestations. Thus we end this book by illustrating how our work could be applied by those who embrace the ideals of dignity culture and want to see victimhood culture recede.

Moral Technology

We discussed in Chap. 6 how the theories and findings of sociology can be used to create sociological technology. Just as knowledge of the physical world can improve our ability to shape it, so too can knowledge of the social world. Altering moral culture requires altering social structure, and those whose goal is to halt victimhood culture might begin by identifying the aspects of its social structure that would be the easiest or most desirable to change.

We have identified equality and diversity as two conditions that facilitate victimhood culture. Reducing these would thus reduce victimhood culture, but adherents of dignity culture value these things as well. At the fringes of political life are some who wish to see a return to strict and stable ethnic hierarchies, or even to have the United States and other Western nations partitioned into racially homogeneous ethnostates, but these alt-right or white nationalist opponents of the leftist victimhood culture are also opponents of the egalitarian ideals of dignity culture. The vast majority of those who oppose victimhood culture would abhor these strategies, and they might be comforted to realize they are not particularly feasible anyway.

It is also unlikely, even if you oppose victimhood culture, that you would want to eliminate the modern communications technologies that allow people access to potential supporters and that allow the social media mob to act as an authority in its own right. We have all become heavily reliant on these technologies for various purposes, and few of us would want to lose the benefits they provide along with their costs. And again this solution is not particularly feasible.

Growth in the scope and accessibility of authority also encourages victimhood, and this seems more promising as an avenue for intervention. The degree to which the state should control or regulate various behaviors is already a topic of mainstream political debate, as is the growth in the size and scope of university administrations. If you want to limit the moral dependency that arises when authorities are highly involved in their subordinates' lives, you can seek ways to limit authority.

This can be done on several levels and to varying degrees, and it is conceivably compatible with both mainstream liberalism and conservatism. For example, you could start by trying to undermine the helicopter parenting that socializes people into moral dependency at a young age and leads them to arrive at college fearful of independence and primed to expect intervention and protection. If it is the case that moral self-sufficiency begins at home, you might even support the "free-range parenting" movement (Skenazy 2009). In concrete terms this might mean not only advocating the social acceptability of allowing children higher levels of independence and autonomy, but perhaps also organizing and contributing to legal funds for the defense of parents who have been charged with neglect for giving their children leeway that would have been perfectly normal a generation prior. You might explore other possible ways to promote independence, too, such as the Japanese practices of "caring by waiting" and "standing guard," in which a teacher, though present, does not intervene in preschoolers' conflicts until it seems absolutely necessary (Hayashi and Tobin 2011; see also Jacobs 2015).

More importantly, reducing victimhood culture would involve altering the structures of the universities. In his discussion of *legal overdependency*—overreliance on law—Black (1989) points out that we often deal with drug dependency in one of two ways: by providing a substitute, like methadone for heroin addicts, or by simply cutting off access to the drug, the cold turkey approach. Likewise where people are dependent on law, one strategy is to provide them with alternative forms of dispute resolution, and another is to simply restrict their access to law—for example, by repealing laws or restricting the behavior of legal officials (Black 1989:Chapter 5). We might deal similarly with students who begin their higher education accustomed to dependence on authority. The analog of a methadone plan would prepare students gradually for a world full of offense and disagreement. This might involve some kind of intervention by authorities in dealing with perceived microaggressions and other minor conflicts, but it would have to be temporary. Perhaps certain kinds of counseling or mediation services could be available for new students only, with the expectation that more experienced students could deal on their own with political disagreements or inadvertent slights. Reformers would need to decide whether to provide such alternatives or to expect incoming students to go cold turkey and abandon right away the notion that the university should protect them from emotional discomfort. Either way they would need to stop and even reverse the expansion of authority.

In the United States, constitutional free speech protections limit the reach of administrators at state universities to some extent. But as we discussed in Chap. 7, even there many restrictions remain in place, such as free speech zones that relegate controversial speech to small parts of the campus (Lukianoff 2014:Chapter 3). More expansive speech protections and other policies limiting administrators' involvement in certain aspects of students' lives would remove the incentive to appeal for their help. Another way of reducing administrators' power would be to reduce their numbers. Over the past 40 years, faculty and student enrollment increased by about 50 percent, while the number of administrators increased by 85 percent and their staff by 240 percent (Ginsberg 2011:25). The expansion of administrative authority is a condition conducive to the growth of moral dependency among students. Moreover, many of the new positions were created specifically to deal with the concerns of campus activists and others who share their perspective, and those who fill these positions tend to be carriers of victimhood culture. Even amid a recession and state budget cuts, for example, the diversity-related administration of the University of California expanded. In 2010, UC San Francisco hired a vice chancellor of diversity and outreach. In 2011, UCLA hired a dean for campus climate. In 2012, UC San Diego hired a vice chancellor for equity, diversity, and inclusion. Each of these was a newly created position (Mac Donald 2013). And the tendency is for such positions to proliferate. At UC Davis, there is "a Diversity Trainers Institute under an administrator of diversity education, who presumably coordinates with the Cross-Cultural Center. [UC Davis] also has: a Lesbian, Gay, Bisexual, Transgender Resource Center; a Sexual Harassment Education Program; a diversity program coordinator; an early resolution discrimination coordinator; a Diversity Education Series that awards Understanding Diversity Certificates in 'Unpacking Oppression'; and Cross-Cultural Competency Certificates in 'Understanding Diversity and Social Justice'" (Will 2012).

As we saw in Chap. 6, many of the social sciences and humanities also act as carriers of victimhood culture. Much scholarship is nothing more than political activism, and much teaching nothing more than indoctrination. This is currently so entrenched that it might be a hard problem to address, but if you are teaching you can at least make sure you expose your students to a range of social scientific thought, not just to conflict theory narratives of oppressors and victims. When discussing morality and policy you can avoid presenting your own moral or policy conclusions as facts and make sure your students learn about ideas different from your own. And you can try to promote more viewpoint diversity among university faculty—so that students become acquainted with alternative ideas, but also so that universities become more tolerant. Recall from Chap. 2 that only 12 percent of academics identify as conservatives. That tends to be much lower in the social sciences and humanities. In US sociology departments, for example, more than four times as many professors identify as Marxists (about 25 percent) than as Republicans (three to six percent) (Shields and Dunn 2016:69, 137). We noted in Chap. 2 that campus victimhood culture arises where ethnic diversity combines with this kind of cultural homogeneity. Ordinary conservatives, and even libertarians, moderates, and centrist liberals whose views diverge from those of the campus activists and other faculty might be treated as heretics who threaten ideological purity. Thus, victimhood culture leads not only to extreme vigilance in protecting those considered victims but also, in the name of tolerance, to vigilance in punishing any dissent. If you are a professor or a Ph.D student who objects to this, you can join Heterodox Academy, as we have. This organization of more than a thousand academics seeks to increase viewpoint diversity at colleges and universities, primarily because viewpoint homogeneity leads to problems with scholarship, but viewpoint diversity would also undermine victimhood culture.

None of this will be easy, though, as current trends are in the opposite direction. Viewpoint diversity has been decreasing among faculty, with the number of leftists and liberals increasing and moderates and conservatives decreasing (Haidt et al. n.d.). And the increasing intolerance this leads to will only make things more lopsided. For example, political scientists Jon Shields and Joshua Dunn (2016) report the findings of surveys showing bias against hiring conservatives. One study found that 30 percent of sociologists say they would be less likely to support a job candidate who was a Republican. Being an evangelical or a National Rifle Association member was even worse (Yancey 2011, cited in Shields and Dunn 2016:69). In this environment, professors are likely to ignore the concerns of Heterodox Academy. Paul Krugman, the *New York Times* columnist and economics professor, refers dismissively to Heterodox Academy members as outraged conservatives, despite the organization's political diversity and measured rhetoric (Krugman 2014; Haidt 2016).

University administrations continue to expand, too, and student protests and campus unrests commonly just lead administrators to institute even more diversity initiatives, more speech codes, more microaggression training programs, more segregated safe spaces, and more required victim studies courses. Victimhood culture keeps advancing, and we see no sign of it stopping any time soon. For now, at the behest of many of the students, the university continues to make itself into a normative outlier, and not because its members "follow truth wherever it may lead," in Thomas Jefferson's words. It becomes an environment not of robust debate but of atypical sensitivity, a censorious environment intended to protect against certain kinds of offense to a degree seldom seen among adults. Right now this continues despite opposition, but these trends are not necessarily unstoppable. Alter the way we socialize children, reverse the expansion of administration in higher education, find ways to limit the numbers and the authority of administrators, and increase viewpoint diversity in the academy, and the extreme form of victimhood culture will wither away.

* * *

Will victimhood culture subside and wither away? Or will it replace dignity culture as dignity once replaced honor? Will the "sticks and stones" aphorism come to be seen as a relic of a cruel past? Will people come to see the notion of having thick skin when slighted or insulted as morally foreign, perhaps crazy, the way we now view duelists and others in honor cultures who so readily faced physical danger? Or will the conflict instead continue for a long time, with small but influential groups of victimhood adherents controlling the universities while dignity mostly prevails elsewhere? What of the right-wing backlash against victimhood culture? Will the voters of more conservative states demand the defunding of public universities that censor conservative expression while tolerating and even promoting the most extreme rhetoric of the left? Will the rhetoric of white male victimhood gain more converts for extremist groups on the right? Will we see a devolution of society into competing tribes, their violent hostility suppressed by an increasingly authoritative police state?

Making confident forecasts about the future of a complex system is pure folly. The conditions in which victimhood culture flourishes—atomization, diversity, ethnic and gender equality, strong and stable authority, and access to modern communication technologies—seem to be spreading, so we suspect that in the near term victimhood culture is here to stay. But we have no crystal ball. Knowing the conditions that give rise to victimhood can help us imagine a likely trajectory, but the future is not certain enough or the theory precise enough to say exactly how far victimhood culture will develop or how long it will last. We do not know how exactly conditions will change in the years to come or how various other social trends will interact with those we focus on here. We only know that moral change inheres in social change, and we know that social change will continue for as long as humanity exists. All we can say for certain is that the present is not like the past, and the future will not be like the present.

REFERENCES

Baldick, Robert. 1965. *The Duel: A History of Dueling*. New York: Clarkson N. Potter.

Barrett, Lisa Feldman. 2017. When Is Speech Violence? *New York Times*, July 14. https://www.nytimes.com/2017/07/14/opinion/sunday/when-is-speech-violence.html.

Black, Donald. 1989. *Sociological Justice*. New York: Oxford University Press.

———. 1995. The Epistemology of Pure Sociology. *Law and Social Inquiry* 20 (3): 829–370.

———. 2011. *Moral Time*. New York: Oxford University Press.

Bloor, David. 1976. *Knowledge and Social Imagery*. Boston: Routledge and Kegan Paul.

Cohen, Dov, Richard E. Nisbett, Brian F. Bowdle, and Norbert Schwarz. 1996. Insult, Aggression, and the Southern Culture of Honor: An 'Experimental Ethnography'. *Journal of Personality and Social Psychology* 70 (5): 945–996.

Durkheim, Emile. 1982. *The Rules of the Sociological Method and Selected Texts on Sociology and Its Method*. New York: Free Press.

Ginsberg, Benjamin. 2011. *The Fall of the Faculty: The Rise of the All-Administrative University and Why It Matters*. New York: Oxford University Press.

Haidt, Jonathan. 2016. Krugman Is Wrong—We Are Neither Conservative Nor Outraged. *Heterodox Academy*, February 24. https://heterodoxacademy.org/2016/02/24/krugman-is-wrong-we-are-not-conservative/.

Haidt, Jonathan, Jussim Lee, and Chris Martin. n.d. The Problem. *Heterodox Academy*. http://heterodoxacademy.org/problems/.

Hayashi, Akiko, and Joseph Tobin. 2011. The Japanese Preschool's Pedagogy of Peripheral Participation. *Ethos* 39 (2): 139–164.

Jacobs, Alan. 2015. On Microaggressions and Administrative Power. *The New Atlantis*, September 11. http://text-patterns.thenewatlantis.com/2015/09/on-micro-aggressions-and-administrative.html.

Krugman, Paul. 2014. Academics and Politics. *New York Times*, January 4. https://krugman.blogs.nytimes.com/2016/01/04/academics-and-politics/.

Leung, Angela K.Y., and Dov Cohen. 2011. Within- and Between-Culture Variation: Individual Differences and the Cultural Logics of Honor, Face, and Dignity Cultures. *Journal of Personality and Social Psychology* 100 (3): 507–526.

Lukianoff, Greg. 2014. *Unlearning Liberty: Campus Censorship and the End of American Debate*. New York: Encounter Books.

Lukianoff, Greg, and Jonathan Haidt. 2015. The Coddling of the American Mind. *The Atlantic*, September. http://www.theatlantic.com/magazine/archive/2015/09/the-coddling-of-the-american-mind/399356/.

Mac Donald, Heather. 2013. Multiculti U. *City Journal*, Spring. http://www.city-journal.org/2013/23_2_multiculti-university.html.

Rini, Regina. 2015. Microaggression, Macro Harm. *Los Angeles Times*, October 12. http://www.latimes.com/opinion/op-ed/la-oe-1012-rini-microaggression-solidarity-20151012-story.html.

Shields, Jon A., and Joshua M. Dunn. 2016. *Passing on the Right: Conservative Professors in the Progressive University.* New York: Oxford University Press.

Skenazy, Lenore. 2009. *Free-Range Kids: Giving Our Children the Freedom We Had Without Going Nuts with Worry.* San Francisco: Jossey-Bass.

Wells, Catharine. 2013. Microaggressions in the Context of Academic Communities. *Seattle Journal for Social Justice* 12 (2): 319–348.

Will, George. 2012. Subprime College Educations. *Washington Post*, June 8. https://www.washingtonpost.com/opinions/george-will-subprime-college-educations/2012/06/08/gJQA4fGiOV_story.html.

Yancey, George. 2011. *Compromising Scholarship: Religious and Political Bias in American Higher Education.* Waco: Baylor University Press.

INDEX[1]

[1]Note: Page numbers followed by "n" refer to notes.

© The Author(s) 2018
B. Campbell, J. Manning, *The Rise of Victimhood Culture*,
https://doi.org/10.1007/978-3-319-70329-9

Made in the USA
Las Vegas, NV
26 February 2021